PARLIAMENT AND POLITICS IN THE AGE OF ASQUITH AND LLOYD GEORGE

THE DIARIES OF CECIL HARMSWORTH, MP, 1909–1922

PARLIAMENT AND POLITICS IN THE AGE OF ASQUITH AND LLOYD GEORGE

THE DIARIES OF CECIL HARMSWORTH, MP, 1909–1922

edited by
ANDREW THORPE and RICHARD TOYE

CAMDEN FIFTH SERIES
Volume 50

UNIVERSITY PRESS

FOR THE ROYAL HISTORICAL SOCIETY
University College London, Gower Street, London WC1 6BT
2016

Published by the Press Syndicate of the University of Cambridge
University Printing House, Shaftesbury Road, Cambridge CB2 8BS, United Kingdom
32 Avenue of the Americas, New York, NY 10013-2473, USA
477 Williamstown Road, Port Melbourne, VIC 3207, Australia
C/Orense, 4, Planta 13, 28020 Madrid, Spain
Lower Ground Floor, Nautica Building, The Water Club,
Beach Road, Granger Bay, 8005 Cape Town, South Africa

© Royal Historical Society 2016

First published 2016

A catalogue record for this book is available from the British Library

ISBN 9781107162457 hardback

SUBSCRIPTIONS. The serial publications of the Royal Historical Society, *Royal Historical Society Transactions* (ISSN 0080-4401) and Camden Fifth Series (ISSN 0960-1163) volumes, may be purchased together on annual subscription. The 2016 subscription price, which includes print and electronic access (but not VAT), is £176 (US $294 in the USA, Canada, and Mexico) and includes Camden Fifth Series, volumes 49, 50 and 51 as well as Transactions Sixth Series, volume 26 (published in December). The electronic-only price available to institutional subscribers is £148 (US $247 in the USA, Canada, and Mexico). Japanese prices are available from Kinokuniya Company Ltd, P.O. Box 55, Chitose, Tokyo 156, Japan. EU subscribers (outside the UK) who are not registered for VAT should add VAT at their country's rate. VAT registered subscribers should provide their VAT registration number. Prices include delivery by air.

Subscription orders, which must be accompanied by payment, may be sent to a bookseller, subscription agent, or direct to the publisher: Cambridge University Press, University Printing House, Shaftesbury Road, Cambridge CB2 8BS, UK; or in the USA, Canada, and Mexico: Cambridge University Press, Journals Fulfillment Department, 100 Brook Hill Drive, West Nyack, New York, 10994-2133, USA.

SINGLE VOLUMES AND BACK VOLUMES. A list of Royal Historical Society volumes available from Cambridge University Press may be obtained from the Humanities Marketing Department at the address above.

Printed in the UK by Bell & Bain Ltd.

CONTENTS

ACKNOWLEDGEMENTS	vii
INTRODUCTION	1
THE DIARIES	27
1909	29
1910	51
1911	73
1912	105
1913	139
1914	155
1915	177
1916	209
1917	239
1918	263
1919	289
1920	309
1921	319
1922	329
INDEX	343

ACKNOWLEDGEMENTS

This book has been a long time in the making. The papers of Cecil Bisshopp Harmsworth, First Baron Harmsworth, came up at auction in 2008. Harmsworth had corresponded with a wide range of well-known individuals and letters he had received from luminaries such as Winston Churchill and W.B. Yeats were naturally attractive to bidders. Therefore, the collection did not remain wholly intact. Happily, however, the University of Exeter's bid for Harmsworth's extensive diaries was successful. Subsequently, the University acquired further tranches of documents that had remained unpurchased at the original sale. It may be said that although incomplete, the Harmsworth Papers that have now been deposited in the University Library's Special Collections are both substantial in volume and valuable in terms of the light that they cast on twentieth-century British politics and society. We understand that Harmsworth's wife Emelie also kept a diary: it may still exist but sadly we failed to track it down. It would probably provide a very interesting complement to Cecil's.

It was our intention from the start to produce a published edition. This has been made possible by the agreement and support of the Harmsworth family, specifically Daniel Harmsworth (formerly McCulloch) and Kevin McCulloch as copyright holders. For this we are very grateful. We would also like to thank our colleagues at the Royal Historical Society (in particular Professor Arthur Burns and Professor Emma Griffin) for their support and encouragement, as well as Daniel Pearce and the production team at Cambridge University Press. Additionally, we would like to thank Simon Luterbacher and his colleagues at Dreweatts & Bloomsbury Auctions and Christine Faunch, head of the University of Exeter Special Collections. We profited greatly from the constructive comments of the RHS's anonymous readers of the original proposal, and were greatly encouraged by the interest shown in the project by Professor Larry L. Witherell of Minnesota State University. We are also grateful to Dr Richard Batten for compiling the index, to Miranda Bethell for the copy-editing, and to Dr David Thackeray for his assistance with locating sources.

The task of transcription and selection was undertaken chiefly by Richard Toye. The work of annotation and the writing of the introduction were carried out by both editors jointly. We have, as always, greatly enjoyed working together, and we would like to dedicate this volume to our colleagues in the Department of History and the College of Humanities at the University of Exeter.

INTRODUCTION

Cecil Bisshop Harmsworth (1869–1948) was the third brother of a large, famous and influential family. His elder siblings were Alfred Charles William Harmsworth and Harold Sidney Harmsworth. These two self-made men – Lords Northcliffe and Rothermere, as they became – were amongst the most powerful and notorious press proprietors of their age. Both of them, Alfred especially, were brilliant and energetic, but they were not exactly well liked. By contrast, Cecil was an able person who had, by normal standards, a successful career as a Liberal MP and junior minister, and yet never acquired – and indeed never aspired to attain – the high profile of his brothers. If he was overshadowed, though, he had an important gift that they lacked: 'a genius for friendship'.[1] It is related that, before he was elected to Parliament, Cecil was invited to the terrace of the House of Commons and made a very good impression on those he met. Supposedly, Northcliffe, when informed of this by one of his journalists, replied sardonically: 'Oh, I understand. They were delighted to meet a human Harmsworth.'[2]

To the degree that Cecil Harmsworth is remembered today, it is as a walk-on player in his brothers' lives. This does him scant justice, although it is true that a sense of promise unfulfilled hangs over his career. As the former MP J.M. Kenworthy (later Lord Strabolgi) recalled in 1933, he had been 'an able administrator and politician, very popular with all parties, and [he] should have gone far in the public life of this country. His retirement from Parliament has been a great loss'.[3] Elected to the Commons for the first time in 1906 Harmsworth developed a reputation as a capable but unflashy speaker: 'a shrewd hand in a debate, level-headed in his opinions, who never spoke without a real knowledge of the subject under discussion'.[4] Having secured minor office early in the Great War, he became a member of David Lloyd George's personal secretariat after the latter displaced H.H. Asquith as Prime Minister in 1916. The following year,

---

[1] 'Death of Lord Harmsworth', *Daily Mail*, 14 Aug. 1948.
[2] 'Pleasure and Problem in South Africa', *Otago Witness*, 4 Nov. 1908.
[3] J.M. Kenworthy, *Sailors, Statesmen and Others: An Autobiography* (London: Rich Cowan, 1933), 184.
[4] 'Obituary: Lord Harmsworth', *Manchester Guardian*, 14 Aug. 1948.

Lloyd George offered him the post of Coalition Liberal Chief Whip. He declined because he knew that the position involved the sale of honours to raise party funds, which caused him disquiet. After the war he became Under-Secretary of State for Foreign Affairs in the post-war Coalition government, an office of considerable importance during the period (after 1919) when the Foreign Secretary, Lord Curzon, was in the Upper House and thus not available to deal with government business in the Commons. He retired voluntarily as an MP in 1922, although it is quite possible that had he chosen to fight the general election of that year he would have lost his seat. Although created first Lord Harmsworth in 1939, he failed to make much of an impression in the House of Lords. Nevertheless, in the later part of his life he played a role as a public benefactor. His successful efforts to preserve Dr Johnson's house in Gough Square, London, for the nation form his enduring memorial.

Harmsworth's significance also lies in his role as a diarist. He was well connected, within both British and Irish society. Like all MPs, moreover, he sat at the nexus of high and low politics, simultaneously involved in the world of elite political manoeuvre and the retail zone of workaday constituency life. Harmsworth was an obsessive angler and the diary began as a record of his fishing. However, as the constitutional crisis developed in 1909 the entries became increasingly political. The diary forms a highly readable record of the politics of the period, detailing late-night Commons sittings and the rough-and-tumble of the campaign trail as well as giving skilful pen-portraits of the major figures of the day. Above all, it illuminates social and political culture in the age of Asquith and Lloyd George, being as valuable for its detail on the minutiae of campaigning as for the new light it casts on well-known episodes and individuals. He may have lacked the ambition to make it to the front rank of politics, but in his diary Harmsworth bequeathed to posterity both a valuable historical source and a fascinating document.

Cecil was the third son and fourth child of Alfred Harmsworth (1838–1889) and Geraldine Mary Maffett (1838–1925). Alfred was a barrister, Geraldine, the daughter of a County Down land agent. They started married life in Dublin but moved to London in 1867. They had eight boys and three girls who survived into adulthood (three further children died in infancy). Consequently, the family was usually short of money. Alfred and Geraldine's eldest son, also named Alfred (1865–1922), established the family firm in magazines and newspapers, founded the *Daily Mail* in 1896, received a peerage as Lord Northcliffe in 1905, and took over *The Times* in 1908. The second son, Harold (1868–1940), a key figure in the creation of the family media empire, was created Lord Rothermere in 1914 and took over the *Mail* after

Northcliffe's death. Next came Cecil, followed by Leicester (1870–1937), who was also important in the development of the family firm and sat as a Liberal MP. Together, these four brothers were the weighty figures of the family: Paul Ferris refers to them, rather disparagingly, as 'the "heavies" ': 'They were solid, dignified men with polished motor cars, their waists growing thicker and their vehicles getting bigger with the years.'[5]

By contrast, the fifth son, Hildebrand (1872–1929), was a louche figure, notorious for playing billiards in office hours and enjoying a somewhat hedonistic lifestyle. The three remaining sons, none of whom played a part in the business, were Charles (1874–1942), who lived as a reclusive invalid in Sussex, well supported by his brothers' finances;[6] the sporty St John (1876–1933) who, among other things, had an affair with Rothermere's wife;[7] and Vyvyan (1881–1957), who lived his life as a gentleman farmer in Sussex.[8] The daughters were the second child, the younger Geraldine (1866–1945) whose son, Cecil King (named after his eponymous uncle) would go on to be a major media figure in his own right; Violet (1873–1961); and Christabel (1880–1967). Geraldine Harmsworth, who bore fourteen children in twenty years, was a true matriarch, who held the family together, particularly after the death of her husband in 1889. The size of the family can be illustrated by the fact that by 1939 there would be five living Lady Harmsworths (the widows of Leicester and Hildebrand, as well as the wives of Cecil, Sir Alfred (son of Leicester) and Sir Hildebrand junior.[9] The Maffett family was also large, Geraldine being one of eight children. Overall, the extended family was huge (Geraldine had no fewer than forty-one grandchildren), but they were also close, with the elder Geraldine and the younger Alfred (Northcliffe), in their different ways, asserting considerable claims to primacy, which were, to a large extent, accepted by the rest.

Cecil Harmsworth was born in Hampstead, London, in 1869. He attended a prep school run by 'the Miss Budds' and subsequently the Philological School in Marylebone Road, London (later called the St Marylebone Grammar School), together with his brother Harold. Of

---

[5] Paul Ferris, *The House of Northcliffe: The Harmsworths of Fleet Street* (London: Weidenfeld & Nicolson, 1971), 90.

[6] Reginald Pound and Geoffrey Harmsworth, *Northcliffe*, (London: Cassell, 1959), 229, 773; Ferris, *House of Northcliffe*, 22, describes him as 'mentally subnormal'.

[7] D.G. Boyce, 'Harmsworth, Harold Sidney, first Viscount Rothermere (1868–1940)', *ODNB*, http://www.oxforddnb.com/view/article/33718/33718?back=,33717,33718,33717 (accessed 18 Feb. 2014). This information is not included in Cecil, Baron Harmsworth, *St John Harmsworth: A Brave Life, 1876–1932* (Tonbridge: privately printed, 1949).

[8] Pound and Harmsworth, *Northcliffe*, 229.

[9] Ferris, *House of Northcliffe*, 303.

one or two masters he had kindly memories, but principally he recalled with resentment 'the odious practice of summoning from class, in the loud voice of the school porter, the embarrassed urchins (myself sometimes among them) whose fees were in arrears'. He entered Trinity College, Dublin (TCD) in 1887, where his studies were to be sponsored by a long-standing friend of his father, George Robinson, and where his uncle-by-marriage Albert Maximilian Selss, Professor of German, allowed him free use of his rooms.[10] It was only after his father died in 1889 that the Harmsworth press empire really took off; from that point onwards Cecil never had any financial worries. For two years he studied theology, with a view to training for the Church. Two TCD figures who had a particular influence on him were the Revd Dr John Gwynn, the Regius Professor of Divinity, and Dr John Bernard, who would later become Archbishop of Dublin during a crucial phase of the Irish struggle for independence. Harmsworth, however, abandoned his plan of a religious career after experiencing a spiritual-intellectual crisis. As he recalled in some autobiographical reflections written during the First World War, he was unable to accept the Thirty-Nine Articles. 'I awoke suddenly to the disturbing realisation that I had all sorts of speculative views about them and about other things too that however permissible in the case of laymen were scarcely compatible with taking Holy Orders', he wrote. 'This was a dark and troubled time and I will not dwell on it.' He did, nonetheless, retain a 'nebulous' religious faith which was clearly important to him, although he felt little compulsion to discuss it with others. 'In a sort of way that I cannot define I have always been a clergyman at heart and my best and dearest friends have been and are still clergymen', he avowed.[11]

Harmsworth's TCD years were a formative experience and his existing family connections with Ireland were reinforced by his marriage in 1897 to Emilie Maffett (1873–1942). 'Em', as she was known, was Cecil's first cousin. She was the daughter of his mother's brother, the barrister William Hamilton Maffett of Finglas, County Dublin. The moderate Protestant circles in which he moved were far distant from die-hard Unionism. He was sympathetic to Irish national aspirations and understood the resentment caused by 'the blockheads of Dublin Castle', the seat of British administration in Ireland.[12] His connections with Bernard, and with the agricultural reformer Horace Plunkett and other liberal-minded Unionists, were to prove useful

---

[10] Cecil Bishopp Harmsworth (henceforward CBH), 'Lord N. and other Harmsworth memorials', unpublished MS, mid 1930s. Unless otherwise stated, all documents cited are part of the Cecil Harmsworth Papers, University of Exeter Special Collections.
[11] CBH, autobiographical notes, 1917, in diary volume for 1900.
[12] CBH, note of Oct. 1936 attached to diary of 19 Sept. 1911.

to him when he was involved in the British government's efforts to secure a political settlement in the aftermath of the 1916 Rising. Although a peaceful solution remained elusive, the existence of this non-doctrinaire elite Protestant milieu is illustrative of the complexities of Irish society in the revolutionary era. Harmsworth's own role in these networks also casts significant light on the Anglo-Irish political world.

After leaving Dublin, Harmsworth went into the burgeoning family business, under Alfred's tutelage. He recalled these as 'days of happy memories, days of youth and dawning success'.[13] He appears to have been roped in to help with anything, including dealing with the mass of entries generated by a competition in *Answers* in 1889.[14] The 1891 census lists him as living with his widowed mother and seven of his siblings (including Harold, but not Alfred) in Maida Vale, London. His occupation was given as 'Journalist/Author'. In 1895 he passed a Bar exam but seems to have taken the Law no further.[15] Harmsworth Brothers Ltd. was incorporated in 1896, bringing together the existing Harmsworth publishing interests; each brother was allocated a shareholding according to family seniority, giving Cecil the third largest stake. He was described as the firm's 'literary editor'.[16] He insisted later that in spite of the Northcliffe legend, 'others of the brothers contributed largely if not essentially to the success of the firm'. He acknowledged, however, that he himself lacked 'the instinctive sense for news or the sleepless interest in the passing events of the day that are essential elements in the make-up of the true journalist'.[17] He edited *Answers* and, notionally, all the firm's other publications too. In 1898 he became the first editor of the monthly *Harmsworth Magazine*, which published middlebrow popular fiction.[18] 'Its production should greatly increase the prestige of our business,' Alfred advised him.[19] It was a tremendous commercial success, the first issue selling around 800,000 copies. Cecil retained the role until circa 1902, although he probably delegated much of the work as his political interests grew.[20] Afterwards, he maintained a

---

[13] CBH, 'Lord N. and other Harmsworth memorials'.
[14] J. Lee Thompson, *Northcliffe: Press Baron in Politics 1865–1922* (London: John Murray, 2000), 13.
[15] 'Council of Legal Education', *The Times*, 24 Apr. 1895.
[16] 'Harmsworth Brothers, Limited', *The Times*, 19 Oct. 1896; 'The Harmsworths and their publications', *The Bookman*, Dec. 1897.
[17] CBH, 'Lord N. and other Harmsworth memorials'.
[18] Sue Thomas, *Indexes to Fiction in the Harmsworth Magazine, later, The London Magazine (1898–1915)*, Victorian Fiction Research Guides X (Brisbane: University of Queensland, 1984), 9.
[19] Pound and Harmsworth, *Northcliffe*, 236.
[20] Thomas, *Indexes to Fiction*, 9.

degree of involvement in the family business – notably as Chairman of Associated Newspapers Ltd., founded in 1905 – although it is hard to discern exactly how active he was.

In September 1899, Harmsworth was adopted as Liberal candidate for Mid-Worcestershire.[21] The next month, the second Boer War started. The conflict created major divisions within the Liberal Party, which was already struggling to find an ideological direction in the post-Gladstone era and which was confronted by a dominant Conservative/Unionist government under Lord Salisbury. Harmsworth associated himself with the Liberal Imperialists, led by former Prime Minister Lord Rosebery, who supported the war. He feared that unless the Liberal Party adopted 'an unmistakeably patriotic tone' it would face electoral annihilation.[22] In response to accusations of factionalism, he denied that the Liberal Imperialists constituted a 'group' or 'section'. Rather: 'They desire merely to bring the other members of the Liberal Party into the mainstream of political thought as it affects imperial concerns.'[23] At the general election of 1900, his opponent was the sitting Liberal Unionist MP R. Biddulph Martin, who had strong backing from the Colonial Secretary, Joseph Chamberlain, and his Birmingham political machine. While supporting the war in principle, Harmsworth criticised the government's conduct of it, which he argued had led to 'a great deal of avoidable suffering'.[24] He was forced to deny claims that he was a pro-Boer, but could at least rely on the *Daily Mail* to pour scorn on such charges.[25] (He later recalled that whenever he stood for election Northcliffe always sent a fleet of cars to help 'and awaited the result with anxious interest'.[26]) An adept baby-kisser and a prolific speaker, he proved a very popular candidate, but, in the face of a pro-government landslide, he was defeated by 268 votes.

The following year, Harmsworth fought a by-election in North-East Lanarkshire, which occurred due to the death of the sitting Liberal MP. He urged a speedy and honourable end to the war, and advocated a range of policies that included a Catholic university in Ireland, an eight-hour day for miners and better houses for the poor.[27] According to the anti-war *Manchester Guardian*, his selection was a disappointment to local Liberals, who found his opinions too

---

[21] *Daily Mail*, 9 Sept. 1899.
[22] Diary for 1 Mar. 1900.
[23] CBH to the editor of the *Daily Mail*, published 5 Sept. 1900.
[24] 'Mr. Cecil B. Harmsworth at Wollescote', *Birmingham Daily Post*, 27 Sept. 1900.
[25] 'Election items', *Daily Mail*, 9 Oct. 1900; 'Meeting at Hanbury', *Worcestershire Chronicle*, 13 Oct. 1900.
[26] CBH, 'Lord N. and other Harmsworth memorials'.
[27] 'Lanark campaign opened', *Daily Mail*, 5 Sept. 1901.

mild and indeed scarcely distinguishable from those of Sir William Rattigan, his Liberal Unionist opponent.[28] He was also damaged in the eyes of some by his association with the *Daily Mail*, which was seen as the epitome of distorted anti-Liberal journalism.[29] His chances were further prejudiced by the candidature of the trade unionist and socialist Robert Smillie. The United Irish League of Great Britain urged Irish nationalist voters in the constituency to vote for the latter rather than Harmsworth, who opposed Home Rule on the Gladstonian model, although he did strongly favour a more moderate measure of self-rule.[30] Rattigan polled 5,673 votes, Harmsworth 4,769 and Smillie 2,900. In an uncharacteristically bitter letter to *The Times*, Harmsworth blamed his defeat partly on the 'treachery' of Liberal MPs who had supported Smillie in opposition to his own official candidacy.[31] The setback was minor: he was quickly invited to stand again for Mid-Worcestershire, the seat that he would fight successfully at the next election.[32]

In the same year that he fought North-East Lanarkshire, Harmsworth founded the *New Liberal Review*, which he edited together with Hildebrand Harmsworth, the fifth of the brothers. In one of his rare entries before he started to keep a diary systematically Cecil recorded a visit to the Liberal elder statesman Sir Charles Dilke to discuss an article on the war, which in due course appeared in the first issue.[33] The *Review*'s aim was to 'clearly and faithfully reflect the best Liberal thought of the day', and it presented itself as pragmatic and non-sectarian.[34] However, the reception of the first number was mixed. 'It is put forth as an attempt to produce a 2s. 6d. review for 1s', observed the *Review of Reviews* caustically. 'It would be more accurate to describe it as an attempt to sell a sixpenny magazine for 1s. by eliminating the illustrations.'[35] *The Academy* was more generous, seeing it as 'a capital shilling's worth of opinion and criticism'.[36] Although the *Review* did have a Liberal Imperialist tinge, it attracted an impressive and eclectic range of contributors from well beyond the ranks of that group, including Lloyd George, Keir Hardie and the Irish nationalist leader John Redmond. Nevertheless, it survived only until 1904, presumably because it had failed to secure sufficient circulation.

---

[28] 'Our London correspondence', *Manchester Guardian*, 2 Sept 1901.
[29] 'The Lanarkshire election', *The Speaker*, 14 Sept. 1901.
[30] 'Lanark election', *Daily Mail*, 6 Sept. 1901.
[31] CBH to the editor of *The Times*, published 3 Oct. 1901.
[32] *Daily Mail*, 18 Nov. 1901.
[33] Diary for 29 Aug. 1900.
[34] 'Introduction', *The New Liberal Review*, 1, 1 (Feb. 1901).
[35] 'The New Liberal Review', *Review of Reviews*, Jan. 1901.
[36] 'The literary week', *The Academy*, 9 Feb. 1901.

Em and Cecil's first child, also called Cecil, was born in March 1898, but he died in February 1899. A daughter, Stella, followed in August 1899, but she lived for only two months. Three further children survived infancy: Daphne Cecil Rosemary (1901–1993), Cecil Desmond Bernard (1903–1990) and Eric Beauchamp Northcliffe (1905–1988). Em struggled for acceptance but appears to have been roundly disliked by both Geraldines: Cecil King's much later account of his family would repeat suggestions that the deaths of the first two children were in some way Em's fault.[37] It does seem likely that the tenderness that Cecil Harmsworth felt for his last three children was intensified by the loss of the first two. A notable feature of his diary, which cannot be fully reflected in an edition which focuses on politics, is his description of family life. He was no stern and forbidding paterfamilias but rather a doting father who was actively involved with the upbringing of his offspring. Although the pace of political life was much slower in the Edwardian period than today, it is clear that Harmsworth found it exhausting and was glad, whenever he could, to relax in the bosom of his family. He had a strong sense of public duty but no great relish for politics as an activity. Nevertheless, it was the life to which he committed himself when he entered Parliament on the back of the sweeping Liberal victory of 1906.

As noted above, Harmsworth's failure to win North-East Lanarkshire had been followed by his re-adoption as prospective Liberal candidate for the Mid-Worcestershire, or Droitwich, constituency. Proximity to the Chamberlainite stronghold of Birmingham had hit Worcestershire Liberalism hard, and Droitwich had been a Liberal Unionist seat since the schism of 1886; successive Liberal challengers had failed to wrest it from the MPs John Corbett and Richard Martin, and in 1895 Martin had even been re-elected unopposed. The only Liberal success in the county's seven constituencies between 1886 and 1905 came in the Northern division, in Gladstone's last victory of 1892. However, this should not mask the varied nature of the county. In particular, the Northern and Mid-Worcestershire constituencies contained significant amounts of industry, and were in effect a kind of outer ring of the Black Country.[38] In Mid-Worcestershire, heavy industry in Stourbridge and carpet weaving at Stourport were particularly important, and gave the constituency a substantial body of working-class voters, although

---

[37] Cecil H. King, *Strictly Personal* (London: Weidenfeld and Nicholson, 1969), 80–81.

[38] Henry Pelling, *Social Geography of British Elections, 1885–1910* (London: Macmillan, 1967), 197; Richard H. Trainor, *Black Country Elites: The Exercise of Authority in an Industrialized Area, 1830–1900* (Oxford: Clarendon Press, 1993), 1–4.

middle-class and agricultural voters were also important.[39] It was not a hopeless seat for the Liberals, and Harmsworth had done well in 1900 to cut Martin's majority to only 3.4% of the votes cast. The circumstances of 1906 were more favourable to the Liberals locally and nationally. Martin retired ahead of the election, and squabbles on the Unionist side led to a Conservative, E.A. Knight, rather than a Liberal Unionist, opposing Harmsworth. There seems little doubt that this cost the Unionists votes they could ill afford to lose. Harmsworth fought a campaign that drew heavily on the issues that would carry the Liberals to a sweeping victory nationally: there was little that was obviously 'New Liberal' about his stance. In his election address, free trade took pride of place, and was followed by a pledge to support national economy, in the belief that 'The best guarantee for flourishing industry and full employment [was] a careful and economical Government.' He called for the bringing of 'the culprits in [Boer] war scandals to justice'. He also denounced Chinese indentured labour in South Africa, and called for educational reform and a series of other changes, including the rating of land values, the reversal of the Taff Vale decision, and housing and temperance reform. On Ireland, though, his earlier enthusiasm for Chamberlain was combined with a canny reassurance to potential local Unionist defectors: he pledged that he would not see a Liberal victory as a mandate for the introduction of Home Rule, and that the introduction of same would need 'a special appeal to the country' — that is, a further general election.[40] Harmsworth won the seat, taking 5,165 votes (52.8%) to his opponent's 4,611 (47.2%), a majority of 554 votes (5.6%). Nationally, the Liberals won a landslide, with 399 seats to the Conservative and Liberal Unionists' 156. The Liberal government of Sir Henry Campbell-Bannerman was now in an exceptionally strong parliamentary position, especially because the 82 Irish nationalist and 29 Labour MPs could normally be expected to support it too.

In the autumn of 1907, Harmsworth took advantage of the fact that there was no autumn session of Parliament — which was itself indicative of the more relaxed pace of political life in those days — to travel to South Africa. The trip resulted in the publication of a travelogue, *Pleasure and Problem in South Africa* (1908), which also contained some political observations. Harmsworth was insistent that politicians and officials in London should leave the 'native problem' to their white fellow-subjects on the ground. 'The native in the town constitutes one of the gravest social problems in South Africa to-day', Harmsworth opined. 'Certainly it is the close contact between the two races in

---

[39] Pelling, *Social Geography of British Elections*, 196.
[40] Cecil Harmsworth, election address, 4 Jan. 1906.

the towns that is accountable for the largest part of dangerous racial prejudice.'[41] It may seem bizarre that he argued for separation of the races in the same breath as he deplored racial prejudice. However, his views were perfectly conventional for the time. The *Times Literary Supplement*'s reviewer scathingly commented that there was little in his account of South African problems that could not have been derived from a study of government Blue Books. At the same time, 'though we think that on most of these questions he gives a fair statement of the points at issue, we have not discovered a single suggestion which has not appeared in several of our English newspapers'.[42]

On the whole, at this time, Harmsworth was more focused on domestic affairs than foreign and imperial ones. The Liberal government of 1906 was, in many ways, a successful reforming administration. But the winter of 1908–1909 saw high levels of unemployment in industrial areas, while the government's dilemmas over public expenditure and how to balance demands for rearmament with those for greater social expenditure created real difficulties. When Asquith replaced Campbell-Bannerman on the latter's retirement in 1908, he was in turn replaced as Chancellor of the Exchequer by Lloyd George. Lloyd George's 1909 budget contained provisions, such as a land valuation ahead of a likely land tax, that were seen as particularly objectionable by many Unionists. The result was the unprecedented rejection of the budget by a House of Lords which had already obstructed significant parts of the government's programme; this, in turn, led to an intensification of radical demands for a reduction in the Lords' powers. This demand figured large in the Liberal and Labour campaigns at the general election that followed in January 1910. However, the Unionists recovered well from their 1906 disaster, helped by economic difficulties and some disillusionment with the failure of the Liberal government to fulfil its pledges in a number of areas, such as education. The Liberals fell back to 274 seats, as against 272 for the Unionists; the 82 Irish and 40 Labour MPs would keep the Liberals in power, but a third of the Liberal MPs had lost their seats. The election was taken as a mandate to pass the budget, but the failure of attempts at compromise meant that a further election had to be held in December 1910 to get a mandate for House of Lords reform; the Liberals came back with 272 seats, the Unionists with 271, the Irish with 84 and Labour with 42.

One of those defeated in January 1910 was Harmsworth. He had been a conscientious constituency MP, by the standards of the time, and had been an assiduous parliamentary performer. However,

---

[41] Cecil Harmsworth, *Pleasure and Problem in South Africa* (London: J. Lane, 1908), 143.
[42] Review of *Pleasure and Problem in South Africa*, in *Times Literary Supplement*, 28 May 1908.

his margin of victory in 1906 had not been great. The Unionists improved their prospects by agreeing on a candidate, the Hon. John Lyttelton, who stood as a Liberal Unionist on a tariff reform platform, which united the various wings of his support. Tariffs appealed to many workers who had suffered unemployment under the free trade Liberal government. The fact that Lyttelton was also the son of a local aristocrat, Viscount Cobham, whose seat was at Hagley Hall near Stourbridge, also helped to rally votes, not least in agricultural areas.[43] His youth (he was only 28) might also have assisted him. Harmsworth based his appeal around 'Liberalism, free trade, and the Rights of the House of Commons'. He praised the work of the Liberal government, and denounced the 'unpatriotic' actions of the House of Lords. He declared his support for Lloyd George's budget and for national insurance, and his opposition to tariffs. He also, finally, pledged to support 'the maintenance of Our Naval Forces on such a scale as to forbid danger or rivalry from any quarter or quarters whatsoever'.[44] But his energetic campaign was in vain: he took 4,973 votes (49.5%) to his opponent's 5,078 (50.5%), a majority of 105 votes (1.0%). His defeat brought rumours of rioting in Droitwich: electoral violence, or the threat of it, was not atypical in this period.[45]

Harmsworth had begun to make his way in parliament. Given the scale of Liberal losses, he might have expected preferment had he just been able to retain his seat. There seemed every chance that he might regain it at a subsequent election. However, after returning from a three-week holiday in France in February 1910, he became ill with what he later described as 'a specially complicated kind of influenza', which affected him acutely for three months and then to a lesser extent for a while thereafter. In November 1910 he stated definitively that he would not contest the seat again because continuing fatigue had left him unable to contest a geographically scattered constituency. This may have been true, but in reality he had been working with the Liberal Chief Whip, the Master of Elibank, to find a safer seat as early as June 1910. The relatively safe Scottish constituency of Dunbartonshire was offered to him, but he turned it down, not least because of its distance from London. However, he continued to take a keen interest in politics, as his diary shows, and spoke for a number of candidates in December 1910, including Dr C.H. Brookes, his successor in Droitwich. In the

---

[43] Pelling, *Social Geography of British Elections*, 196.
[44] Cecil Harmsworth, election address, Jan. 1910.
[45] See Jon Lawrence, *Electing our Masters: The Hustings in British Politics from Hogarth to Blair* (Oxford: Oxford University Press, 2009), 87–92.

event his efforts were in vain: Lyttelton just managed to hold on with a tiny majority of 72 votes (0.8%).

Harmsworth was a likeable and quite gregarious individual. His fellow Liberal MP, Alexander MacCallum Scott, noted in 1913 that he was 'a pleasant fellow, pleasant to look at, pleasant manners, & a pleasant talker' with 'an invaluable gift of curiosity'.[46] While he was also prone to melancholy at times, Harmsworth's diaries do not really bear out the view of him portrayed by Ferris (among others) as being a political dilettante unsuited for the rough and tumble of politics and irresolute about his political career.[47] As he was to tell his fellow Liberal, Walter Runciman, in May 1918, 'I am not a Liberal by birth or training, religion or convention, but simply because I believed in Liberalism & still believe in it as a political force.'[48] The events of 1910 had hit him hard, but he soon resumed his career in earnest. In June 1911, the Liberal MP Thomas Gair Ashton was ennobled, creating a vacancy in the constituency of South Bedfordshire, or Luton. This had been a Liberal seat without a break since 1885; Ashton had even held it in the 'khaki election' of 1900, albeit by only 103 votes in almost 11,000; his December 1910 majority was 978 (6.8% of the votes cast). South Bedfordshire was a mixed constituency, with significant stretches of agricultural land, but by 1901 half its inhabitants lived in Luton, and this process was continuing. Luton itself was an increasingly industrial town, with a particular specialisation in the manufacture of straw hats. This industry was mostly small scale and unions were not prominent, which made it unlikely territory for any kind of Labour incursion, although, as the diary shows, there was increasing diversification by the time Harmsworth became involved in the town's affairs: Vauxhall Iron Works moved there in 1905, changing its name to Vauxhall Motors two years later.[49] There were Conservative enclaves, such as the town of Leighton Buzzard, but overall, 'this was a safe Liberal seat'.[50] Helped by Elibank, Harmsworth was adopted on 21 June. In his election address he emphasised that he would continue to support 'the Liberal and Progressive Party in its noble efforts to improve the conditions of life of the masses of the people' through measures such

---

[46] University of Glasgow Special Collections, MacCallum Scott papers, MS Gen 1465/4, diary 11 June 1913.

[47] Ferris, *House of Northcliffe*, 180, where he suggests Cecil went into politics because of 'the corporate pride of the Harmsworths' and 'to please Northcliffe'.

[48] Cecil Harmsworth to Walter Runciman, 10 May 1918, Runciman papers WR 169, quoted in John Turner, *British Politics and the Great War: Coalition and Conflict, 1915–1918* (New Haven, CT: Yale University Press, 1992), 302.

[49] Katie Carmichael, David McOmish and David Grech, *The Hat Industry of Luton and its Buildings* (Swindon: English Heritage, 2013).

[50] Pelling, *Social Geography of British Elections*, 114.

as national insurance.⁵¹ On 21 July he was elected, with 7,619 votes (52.1%) against 7,006 votes (47.9%) for his Conservative rival, J.D. Hickman, a majority of 613 (4.2%).

Harmsworth's diary for this period gives fascinating insights into the life of a conscientious constituency MP. Luton was closer to London than Droitwich, which made it easier to juggle alongside parliament, his commercial and other interests, and his young family. One feature of his commitment to the constituency was a regular column in the *Luton News*, the first of which appeared on 27 July 1911, less than a week after his election. These reports kept his name firmly in the public eye and covered a wide range of topical issues from a loyal Liberal perspective. Much of his activity otherwise consisted of openings: allotment shows, sales of work by supporters, a new Liberal Hall at Shillington, new corporation baths in Luton. The diaries also offer insights into the life of the Edwardian backbencher. All-night sittings were not uncommon and MPs faced grisly meals at unmentionable times, while trying to work out at what time to stop drinking alcohol to sustain them and start drinking tea. The diaries show Harmsworth to be a defender of the rights of parliament: he voted against the guillotine on Home Rule in 1912, for example, and reflected many years later that 'In the arena of the H[ouse] of C[ommons] the fate of Empires is decided and not in outside activities however interesting and important.'⁵² The diary also shows that it was possible for backbenchers to make an impact on legislation, as with Harmsworth's 1911 amendment to the National Insurance Bill, which McKenna accepted on behalf of the government: this protected the position of medical institutes established by friendly societies.⁵³ Outside parliament, backbenchers were also part of the hidden wiring of the Edwardian Liberal party, as when Harmsworth and a number of his colleagues dined with Liberal lawyers and businessmen in 1911.

Harmsworth soon left the life of the backbencher behind. In November 1911 he was appointed parliamentary private secretary (PPS) to Runciman, President of the Board of Agriculture and Fisheries and one of the party's rising stars. That Harmsworth only accepted 'after serious hours of hard thinking' hardly suggested that he was eager for office at all costs.⁵⁴ But he soon found that he worked well with the president, and his new job gave him the chance to influence policy in a number of areas. First, in November 1912 Runciman appointed him to chair a committee of inquiry into the application

---

⁵¹Cecil Harmsworth, election address, June 1911.
⁵²Supplement, 23 June 1934, to diary, 8 Apr. 1914.
⁵³Hansard, 1 Aug. 1911.
⁵⁴15 Nov. 1911.

of Devon and Cornwall local fisheries committees for government grants to allow fishermen to install motor power in their boats. This was a question of considerable importance to an industry which had fallen on hard times, and Harmsworth threw himself into it with the assistance of his fellow committee members, the Indian civil servant S.H. Fremantle, and the author and social thinker Stephen Reynolds. They travelled widely in the area, and in April 1913 their detailed report, written in large part by Reynolds, pointed out that the position varied between the two counties, with the situation in Cornwall being rather worse, and also within them. It argued that the best form of state aid would be by means of loans to co-operative groups of fishermen, so it recommended that state grants should be made to establish such groups. Although only applying to one industry in one part of the country, this was in some ways a significant extension of the role of the state.[55]

Even while the committee was still deliberating in January 1913, Runciman appointed a larger body under Sir Stafford Howard to conduct a much wider investigation into the inshore fisheries of England and Wales. It was testament to their progress on Devon and Cornwall that the committee included both Harmsworth and Reynolds. Its report in 1914 recommended, among other things, raising the status of fisheries within the Board, relieving local authorities of any financial responsibility for fisheries administration and making it solely a charge on the national finances, and the creation of a Fisheries Organisation Society (FOS) to spread co-operative credit and other good practices among fishermen.[56] Harmsworth and Reynolds – who appear to have got on extremely well together – went on to play a major role in the creation of the FOS, which was to last until the 1990s. Harmsworth also helped to make policy in respect of the decrepit horse trade, after conducting a thorough investigation into the export of horses to France and Belgium. His investigation had been expected to come up with a simple denunciation of foreign cruelty to animals, but he found that the horses were often treated badly in Britain en route to the continent, too. This led him to make a timely intervention in the debate on the Exportation of Horses Bill in April

[55] Report of the committee appointed to consider applications of the Devon and Cornwall local fisheries committees for grants from the Development Fund for assisting fishermen to instal motor power in their boats, and for other purposes (Cd. 6752, 1913), esp. 3–17; *The Times*, 22 Apr. 1913.

[56] Report of the departmental committee on inshore fisheries appointed by the President of the Board of Agriculture and Fisheries to inquire into the present condition of the inshore fisheries, and to advise the Board as to the steps which could with advantage be taken for their preservation and development (Cd. 7373, 1914), esp. xxxv–xxxviii; *The Times*, 10 June, 11 Dec. 1914.

1914, arguing for much stronger powers to prevent the embarkation of horses that were clearly unfit to travel.[57] However, Harmsworth's hopes that he would soon move on from his subordinate PPS status were dashed in April 1912 when a plan to make him a junior whip had to be abandoned following fears that he might lose his seat at the by-election that such a promotion required. Asquith's consoling comment that preferment would not be long in coming did not bear fruit.

The years down to August 1914 had been characterised by periodic international crises, but it was not easy at the time to discern a particular pattern: reactions to events in Sarajevo in June 1914 appear to have met with an initially muted response. There is no sense in Harmsworth's diary of a crisis before late July. However, as is well known, the declaration of war on Serbia by Austria–Hungary triggered such an escalation of international tension that by 4 August Britain was at war with both Austria–Hungary and Germany. The Liberal Party went into the war largely united. When John Burns, the President of the Board of Trade, resigned in protest at British intervention, he was replaced by Runciman, who took his PPS with him. The Board of Trade was of major importance to the war effort, and Harmsworth was soon very busy indeed.

Harmsworth finally rose from the lowest rank in February 1915, becoming Parliamentary Under-Secretary at the Home Office. This did not involve him having to fight a by-election, and he was soon working well with the Home Secretary, Reginald McKenna. Harmsworth clearly revelled in the role, but he could never quite escape the shadow of Northcliffe, and when the latter launched a stinging attack on the Secretary of State for War, Lord Kitchener, in May 1915, Harmsworth felt compelled to offer McKenna his resignation. The matter then became subsumed in the creation of the Asquith Coalition government, the upshot of which was McKenna's translation to the Treasury and his post being taken up by Sir John Simon, who wasted no time in telling Harmsworth that he was one of the Liberals who would have to make way for a Coalition partner nominee – in his case the Labour MP, William Brace.

It said something about Harmsworth's abilities that that both his former chiefs immediately sought his services as their PPS; it may have said something about his ambitions at the time that he chose to follow McKenna to the Treasury rather than retrace his steps to Runciman at the Board of Trade. But what followed was not to be a happy period for Harmsworth. He had enjoyed working on discrete projects that might seem mundane but in which he was able to make

---

[57] Hansard, 3 Apr. 1914, Vol. 60 cols 1540–1543.

a difference. Now, he spent considerable amounts of time chairing various committees, and felt that he was unable to make a real mark: after the war he would look back on it as a period when he would have been better off on the back benches. Things were not helped by the fact that he struggled with the subject matter – after one discussion with ministers, bankers and officials he confided to his diary that 'Most of the discussion is metaphysics to me.'[58] Worse still, perhaps, his relationship with Northcliffe made his position difficult: first, because he tended to be used as a bridge to his more powerful older brother, but also, secondly, because Northcliffe's attacks on the government became stronger and stronger as the war effort continued to stutter.

The failure of the major offensive on the Somme in July–November 1916 was a significant factor damaging the image of the Asquith government, and in December 1916, aware that his position was weakening, the Prime Minister resigned in an attempt to show that he was, in the words of his Labour colleague Arthur Henderson, 'the indispensable man'. However, he was not: Lloyd George was able to form a Coalition which included Henderson and other Labour members as well as the Conservatives. The change of government put McKenna – a firm Asquithian – into opposition. There was little question other than that Harmsworth would follow Lloyd George. He felt some unease at breaking with his closest political friends – as he wrote to Runciman, he and Leicester did not attend the Asquithians' Reform Club meeting because it was 'excruciatingly uncomfortable for us to take part in proceedings in connection with the Party of so intimate and domestic a character which arise largely from the action of a member of our family'.[59] Lloyd George, recognising that around two thirds of his fellow Liberal MPs had gone into opposition, and keen to appease Northcliffe, saw the merits of promoting Harmsworth. In April 1917, therefore, he was offered the position of Coalition Liberal Chief Whip in succession to Neil Primrose, who was keen to return to his regiment.[60] But Harmsworth rejected the offer, and all Lloyd George's charm could not change his mind. Harmsworth was flattered to hear that he was popular among Liberal MPs, but he disliked the business of dispensing honours that came with the role; he was probably aware, too, that the 'trade' in honours was not likely to get any cleaner under Lloyd George. In some ways the decision was proof of the wisdom of Lord Birkenhead's aphorism, 'never refuse'. Had he taken office at this point, he would have placed himself on a

---

[58] 14 June 1915.
[59] John Turner, *Lloyd George's Secretariat* (Cambridge: Cambridge University Press, 1980), 25.
[60] Ibid. 20.

path that might have led him into the cabinet at some future point. It would certainly have given him the opportunity to show whether he was capable of such a role. Harmsworth himself seems to have realised this at the time: 'It is a pity and a disappointment and I am a fool – but there it is'.[61]

Lloyd George worked quickly to establish a small war cabinet, set up new ministries to offer closer intervention on the home front, and bring in businessmen and other 'outsiders' to offer a new urgency to government. He also established his own secretariat to offer advice in a number of policy areas, housed in temporary buildings in the garden of 10 Downing Street and hence known as the 'Garden Suburb'. Having turned down higher preferment, it was here that Harmsworth ended up working. The position suited Harmsworth well. He was one of five secretaries whose responsibility was to keep Lloyd George abreast of particular issues, and where possible to help resolve administrative crises as they arose. In Harmsworth's case, this involved working mainly on labour questions (where he sympathised considerably with working-class fears of profiteering and offered a broadly favourable view of labour in its relations with capital);[62] manpower (where he played a part in resolving the disputes between the Ministries of Munitions and Labour, the War Office, and the Director-General of National Service, Neville Chamberlain, which ended with Harmsworth helping to ensure Chamberlain's exit in 1917));[63] shipping and shipbuilding (where he played a major part in streamlining administration, with positive results);[64] and in the development of insurance against air raid damage.[65] The diary offers some useful detail on life in the Garden Suburb, and suggests that it did indeed play an important part in the war effort. It was happy and successful period of his career, and Turner's positive verdict on the enterprise as a whole – that 'It reflected confidence and sincerity in the pursuit of "progressive" measures at home and abroad' – was one that Harmsworth himself would have shared.[66]

It was logical that, after the 1918 Armistice, Lloyd George should waste no time in seeking the election of a new parliament to make the peace, but it did not take the most hardened cynic to believe that he was also keen to cash in on his reputation as 'the man who won the war' while party boundaries remained relatively fluid. On 23

---

[61] 26 Apr. 1917.
[62] Turner, *Lloyd George's Secretariat*, 39.
[63] Ibid. 29–30, 40–42.
[64] Ibid. 30–38.
[65] Ibid. 42–43.
[66] Turner, *Lloyd George's Secretariat*, 195.

November, Harmsworth was adopted as 'Liberal-Coalition' candidate for the revised constituency of Bedfordshire Luton. His possession of the 'Coupon' helped ensure that he did not face Conservative opposition, and his only opponent was a Labour candidate, Willet Ball. Harmsworth won a stunning victory, with 13,501 votes (69.4%) to Ball's 5,964 (30.6%), a majority of 7,537 (38.8%).

Immediately after the election, Rothermere raised his younger brother's hopes of a major position in government. But this was not a very likely outcome. Harmsworth had proved himself a reasonably safe pair of hands, but there could only be a limited number of Liberals in the leading roles, and Harmsworth's claims were weaker than they might have been if he had taken on the role of chief whip in 1917. All the same, he was offered and accepted a significant role as Under-Secretary of State for Foreign Affairs in January 1919. He also acted as Minister of Blockade, which reflected his wartime experience. When the formal cabinet was reinstated in October 1919, it contained only eight Liberals, including the Prime Minister; thus Harmsworth was certainly in the top dozen or so ministerial Liberals at the time. The diaries offer some insights into the part that Harmsworth played in the Paris peace talks, and, later, in the development of Anglo-Soviet relations. Lord Curzon's appointment as Foreign Secretary in November 1919 might have been a great opportunity for Harmsworth, since it left him as the leading Foreign Office minister in the Commons. But in reality Lloyd George conducted much of his own foreign policy, Curzon was not keen to delegate, and Harmsworth scarcely pushed himself forward at this point.

There was a sense, indeed, that Harmsworth was beginning to lose his appetite for politics. As early as April 1919, the spectre of Northcliffe again loomed over his career when he considered resigning after Lloyd George launched a ferocious attack on Northcliffe in the House of Commons, referring to his 'diseased vanity', implying mental illness, and saying that he would 'as soon rely on a grasshopper' for information.[67] In the event Northcliffe himself advised Harmsworth against resignation. But by early 1921 the latter was clearly losing his way, as when he went absent without leave from Commons questions on foreign affairs to go fishing on the River Wye. When parliament broke up in the summer of 1921, he bade farewell to 'The most wearisome and thankless parliamentary year in my experience!' A trip to the League of Nations in Geneva provided a temporary fillip, but it seems that he was, at best, marking time politically.

Moreover, as the economy turned downwards in 1920, and problems mounted at home, in Ireland and abroad, so doubts about the

---

[67] Hansard, 5 series, Vol. 114 cols 2952–2953, 16 Apr. 1919.

Coalition began to grow. The failure of attempts at 'fusion' between the Lloyd George Liberals and the Conservatives in March 1920 can be seen, in retrospect, as a turning point in the Coalition's long-term prospects.[68] By July 1922, Harmsworth had served as MP for Luton for 11 years and had been in ministerial or quasi-ministerial roles for most of that time. He was 53 and close to the height of his powers. Yet within four months he would be out of parliament. This was his own decision: he did not defend Luton at the general election that was held in November 1922. A number of reasons contributed to his decision to leave front-rank politics. In part, it came down to frustration. Harmsworth was far from being an unbridled office-seeker, but he had been a junior minister for many years and must have reflected that, if he was still not seen a serious contender for cabinet rank, then his chance had probably gone. Once this was the case, the prospects of continuing parliamentary life were probably a good deal less appealing, especially against the demands and attractions of family life. His doubts were not assuaged by the increasingly uncertain political future: there was doubt as to whether the Coalition would fight another election under Lloyd George or break up into its constituent parts. With no immediate prospect of Liberal reunion whether the Coalition survived or not, Harmsworth was making a rational calculation in deciding to give up his seat.

However, what really knocked Harmsworth off an even keel in the summer of 1922 was the death of Northcliffe, on 14 August, after eight weeks of 'dreadful illness'. Cecil had been devoted to him, despite their differences of temperament. (Northcliffe once described Cecil as having 'no judgement or brains' and probably felt frustration at his lack of ambition.)[69] Cecil and their brother Vyvyan were with Northcliffe when he died. Cecil became rather aimless and depressed, fishing when he could do so and working on Foreign Office affairs when he could not. Duff Cooper, at this time Harmsworth's Foreign Office private secretary, recalled: 'He told me he thought it [Northcliffe's death] was a warning that men of his family should not work too hard after a certain age. I was gently amused, for I doubted whether excessive devotion to hard work had ever been Cecil Harmsworth's failing, and a man less like his dynamic brother could hardly be imagined.'[70]

---

[68] K.O. Morgan, *Consensus and Disunity: The Lloyd George Coalition Government 1918–1922* (Oxford: Oxford University Press, 1979), 188–190.

[69] J.M. McEwen (ed.), *The Riddell Diaries 1908–1923* (London: Athlone Press, 1986), 125 (entry for 2 July 1915).

[70] Duff Cooper, *Old Men Forget* (London: Rupert Hart-Davis, 1954), 115.

On 5 October Harmsworth wrote to his constituency chairman to say that he did not intend to contest the next election. That event came sooner than perhaps he had expected, because the Coalition collapsed later that month. At the general election the Conservatives, led by Bonar Law, won a sound overall majority. In Luton, Sir John Prescott Hewett won for the Conservatives. Although Labour had come third, it had arguably split the 'progressive vote' and allowed the Conservatives to win; and in many ways the real story of the election was the advance of the Labour Party to become the second party in the state. Although many Liberals believed that this position need not be permanent, and would work hard for many years to overturn it, Cecil Harmsworth would not play a significant part in their struggle.

Harmsworth now entered a life of semi-retirement. He continued some public and philanthropic duties, which he mixed with low-key business activities, socialising, angling and some minor literary work. He and his brother St John edited for publication Northcliffe's diary of his round-the-world trip of 1921–1922; he wrote a little book of sketches about fishing; and he published a volume of eyewitness descriptions of famous historical and literary figures.[71] The diary for these years recounts some interesting encounters with, amongst others, Winston Churchill, W.B. Yeats and the painter Sir William Orpen (who painted Harmsworth's portrait). However, Harmsworth's engagement with politics was now limited. Years later, he would tell Collin Brooks that he had 'always missed being in the Commons' and that 'Had 1922 not been a bad year for him, owing to Northcliffe's illness, he would have stayed there.'[72]

Rothermere had become the proprietor of the *Daily Mail* on Northcliffe's death. In the early 1930s, notoriously, he used the paper to promote Sir Oswald Mosley's British Union of Fascists. It is interesting to consider Cecil's attitude to this. It has been alleged, on the basis of the memories of those who knew him, that he was 'extremely anti-Semitic'.[73] The diary certainly does contain some distasteful observations, yet to a certain extent he could see beyond

---

[71] Alfred, Viscount Northcliffe, *My Journey Round the World, 16 July 1921–26 Feb. 1922*, ed. Cecil and St. John Harmsworth (London: John Lane, 1923); Cecil Harmsworth, *A Little Fishing Book* (Dublin: Cuala Press, 1930); Cecil Harmsworth (ed.), *Immortals at First Hand: Famous People as Seen by their Contemporaries* (London: Desmond Harmsworth, 1933). CBH and his son Desmond had earlier published *Holiday Verses and Others* (Dublin: Cuala Press, 1922).

[72] N.J. Crowson (ed.), *Fleet Street, Press Barons and Politics: The Journals of Collin Brooks, 1932–1940*, Camden Fifth Series, Vol. 11 (Cambridge: Cambridge University Press for the Royal Historical Society, 1998), 226 (entry for 14 Oct. 1938).

[73] Richard Bourne, *Lords of Fleet Street: The Harmsworth Dynasty* (London: Unwin Hyman, 1990), 86–87.

his prejudices. Thus, in 1916 he described the Liberal politician Sir Alfred Mond as 'an "Hebrew Jew"' but thought him 'with all his thick utterance and swarthy appearance well-nigh as able a man as there is in the House'.[74] And although he did not treat Mosley himself as a social pariah and considered him to have 'great and courageous powers of leadership', he was nonetheless privately critical of Rothermere's political support of him. At the same time, he agreed with his brother's campaign for greater British rearmament.[75] He simultaneously supported the appeasement of the Nazis, but he did note in the aftermath of *Kristallnacht* in 1938 that 'The savage persecution of the Jews in Germany has angered people very greatly.'[76]

Harmsworth still considered himself a Liberal. In 1939, he was elevated to the House of Lords, which appears to have 'entirely rejuvenated' him. He had to be dissuaded by his family from becoming taking the title Lord Northcliffe that had become extinct on his brother's death. Instead, he became first Baron Harmsworth of Egham (where he now resided when not in London). What he did not know was that Harold had bought the peerage for him. Collin Brooks, one of Rothermere's intimates, recorded that 'the secret price of Cecil's peerage' was a £25,000 donation to Conservative Party funds.[77] Given his own manifest hostility to the sale of honours, Cecil would have been mortified had he discovered this. Having earlier praised Chamberlain's actions during the Munich Crisis, he used his maiden speech to further urge 'appeasement and conciliation', and suggested that there were some grounds for hope in one of Hitler's recent speeches.[78] During the Phoney War, the Conservative Earl of Crawford rated him as one of a 'little pacifist group' surrounding the German-sympathising Lord Brocket.[79] However, there is no sign that Harmsworth actively pursued the idea of a compromise peace. From this point onwards his few contributions in the Lords, the last of which he made in June 1945, focused on agricultural, town planning and post-war reconstruction matters.

---

[74] Diary entry for 9 May 1916.
[75] Diary entries for 2 Dec. 1937 and 12 June 1939; CBH, 'Lord N. and other Harmsworth memorials'.
[76] Diary entry for 27 Nov. 1938.
[77] Crowson, *Journals of Collin Brooks, 1932–1940*, 246 (entry for 20 Feb. 1939)
[78] CBH, 'The Wide Horizon', *Christian Science Monitor*, 29 Oct. 1938; Parliamentary Debates, Fifth series, House of Lords, Vol. 112, 2 May 1939, cols. 843–847.
[79] John Vincent (ed.), *The Crawford Papers: The Journals of David Lindsay, Twenty-Seventh Earl of Crawford and Tenth Earl of Balcarres 1871–1940, during the years 1892 to 1940* (Manchester: Manchester University Press 1984), 607 (entry for 15 Nov. 1939).

The death of Emilie in 1942 brought to an end a notably happy marriage. In his final years, Harmsworth maintained his connection with Dr Johnson's house in Gough Square, London. Built about 1700, the house had been Johnson's home from 1748 to 1759 and he had compiled his famous dictionary there. Though it was almost derelict when Harmsworth bought it in 1911, he paid for its renovation and presented it to the nation.[80] Unfortunately, the house was damaged by bombing during the Second World War. One of Harmsworth's final public acts, in May 1948, was to re-open it to the public. He died on 13 August that year.

What of the diary itself? Cecil Harmsworth first kept a systematic journal on a trip to Newfoundland in 1903, but it was only in 1905 that he started to keep one on a regular basis. At first, it lacked significant political comment. This changed, however, in the summer of 1909, as the budget controversy escalated, and it is at that point that the selection presented here opens. The diaries shed significant light on Liberalism and the Liberal Party in the period, but it would not do to overstate this: Harmsworth was not intimate with leading Liberals, although Lloyd George would occasionally flatter him otherwise for reasons that probably had as much to do with Northcliffe as with Harmsworth himself. If anything, the reader notices most the star-struck nature of some of Harmsworth's comments about ministers. For him, Asquith was always a remote figure, respected but not loved. For Lloyd George, on the other hand, he had a fascination, in part because he struggled to reconcile the small and rather unimpressive private man with the inspiring public leader.

But if the diary does not contain many new high-political revelations, it is nonetheless valuable for other reasons. For example, it sheds light on events in Ireland. Harmsworth rubbed shoulders with the leading Irish politicians of the day, particularly John Redmond and John Dillon. He paid regular visits to Ireland, combining holidays with fact finding, and almost always visiting Trinity. The 1916 Easter Rising took him completely by surprise, but the diary contains a valuable account of its aftermath, when Harmsworth travelled to Dublin and discussed matters with a range of leading figures including businessmen and the (Anglican) Archbishop of Dublin, feeding back information to Lloyd George at the latter's request. For the Great War itself, the diary is mainly useful in three ways. First, it gives a sense of how key events were received by an informed and articulate member

---

[80]Cecil Harmsworth, *Dr Johnson: A Great Englishman* (London: Jones, 1923); Cecil, Lord Harmsworth, *Dr Johnson's House, Gough Square, London* (London: Trustees of Dr Johnson's House 1947).

of the political and media elite. Secondly, it demonstrates aspects of the home front, such as air raids, Belgian refugees and recruiting. And, finally, it shows the effects of the war on the Harmsworth and Maffett families. Larry Maffett, Em's favourite brother, was killed in action in October 1914; Lucas King, Harmsworth's nephew, the following May. Two of Harold's sons, Vere and Vyvyan, were killed in November 1916 and February 1918 respectively. In the light of these losses, Harmsworth was understandably proud when Esmond, Harold's surviving son, was elected as the youngest MP in 1919.

The diary also sheds light on Harmsworth's many enthusiasms. It is perhaps fitting that this edition opens with the 1909 Henley Regatta, which was a pretty well unmissable event for him and his immediate family. Fishing was another great enthusiasm: indeed, he was to write a book about it,[81] and the diary shows him often having recourse to fishing for recreational purposes, sometimes with Northcliffe. It was a point of comment for him in 1915 that he did not manage a day's fishing until May, and then could not enjoy it because he could not get the Flanders battlefields off his mind. Golf was another pastime which he enjoyed, although perhaps not quite so much as Northcliffe. He was also a great enthusiast of aviation. These were pioneering years and Harmsworth's sense of excitement is palpable in the pages of the diary. He knew most of the leading aviators of the time; but he also saw the danger involved. In July 1910, he revelled in the sight of three planes in the air at once at an air show, before alluding to the death the previous day of Charles Rolls, the first Briton to be killed in an aviation accident. Perhaps more substantive than any of these, though, was his support for the Garden Cities movement and his wider interest in town planning. The first mention of the subject in the diary comes in 1911, when Harmsworth visited Letchworth. Impressed by what he saw, he agreed to become a director, and by 1912 he was closely involved in its work. Later that year, he combined this with his work in government, as a member of a departmental committee on buildings for smallholdings. He conducted the opening ceremony at Knebworth Garden Village in April 1912, and used his position as an MP to help raise funds for a town-planning tour of Australasia in 1914.

Harmsworth was not a compulsive diarist like, say, Cuthbert Headlam, who felt compelled to fill a page every day. Nor was he a deeply reflective diarist on the lines of Beatrice Webb. His entries were more matter of fact, briefer and to the point, sometimes frustratingly so for the historian. But nor were they the terse notes kept by Gladstone.

[81] Harmsworth, *A Little Fishing Book*.

Harmsworth wrote when he felt he had something to write about. In terms of the period, perhaps the closest parallels are with the diaries of the Richard Durning Holt, Liberal MP for Hexham 1907–1918, and the letters of Arnold Rowntree to his wife.[82] Harmsworth realised that he was part of an important family and came to understand that he had lived through politically important times. It is clear that he hoped to publish the diaries at some stage. By the early 1930s, there had been a number of diaries published from the era by the likes of Lord Riddell of the *News of the World* and the former Coalition Liberal minister Christopher Addison. Harmsworth was careful to keep the diaries in good condition; indeed, he had transcriptions made to help the process. He also periodically went through the diaries and added comments, most of which we have reproduced here alongside the entries to which they referred. Examples come from 1927, 1933, 1934, 1935, 1936 and 1937. Those later notes enhance understanding of the original entries but also provide insights into Harmsworth's own later reflections on his earlier actions. We have placed them in square brackets. Our editorial comments are in italic with occasional use of italicised square brackets when occurring mid-text. All ellipses without square brackets are original; editorial omissions are in (non-italic) square brackets.

In editing the diaries, we have been very conscious of the need to allow a full reflection of all aspects of Harmsworth's political life, as well as some insights into the more personal side. We agreed at an early stage that we should cover only the period from 1909 to his departure from parliament in 1922; although the later diaries (available in the University of Exeter Special Collections) are interesting, they are essentially reflections from the political sidelines, where they discuss politics at all. This concentration has allowed us to include the great majority of the content from that period in this edited volume. Overall, the significance of Cecil Harmsworth's diary lies chiefly in the light it casts on the activity of other, better known politicians, and in its illumination of the day-to-day life of a middle-ranking MP. As Ian Packer has noted, 'the world of the backbencher remains relatively obscure [...] This is largely because few of these men left any detailed records.'[83] Well-connected but unambitious, Harmsworth was able to provide a middle-ranker's inside account

---

[82] David J. Dutton (ed.), *Odyssey of an Edwardian Liberal: The Political Diary of Richard Durning Holt*, The Record Society of Lancashire and Cheshire, Vol. CXXIX (Gloucester, 1989); Ian Packer (ed.), *The Letters of Arnold Stephenson Rowntree to Mary Katherine Rowntree, 1910–1918*, Camden Fifth Series, Vol. 20 (Cambridge: Cambridge University Press for the Royal Historical Society, 2002).

[83] Packer, *Letters of Arnold Stephenson Rowntree*, 1.

of the workings of government and parliament. The diary above all illustrates the *texture* of politics – the ways in which it was connected to social life and civil society – as well, of course, as giving significant insight into the most powerful press dynasties of the age. If Cecil was a 'human Harmsworth', he also left behind him a very human record.

THE DIARIES

1909

8 July
Henley Regatta.

Changeable day growing gloriously fine in the afternoon. Crowds of visitors on the lawn. Most successful party. To town in the afternoon to attend Stationers' Hall Banquet with H.S.H.[1] Proposed toast of 'The New Livery'. Struck more than ever by the great beauty of the Hall and of the Court or drawing-room.

10 July

C.B.H.,[2] E.A.H.,[3] Gertrude Spencer[4] and Milla Deane[5] to Henley. [...]

---

[1] Harold Sidney Harmsworth (1868–1940): the second of the Harmsworth brothers; with his elder brother, Alfred, later Viscount Northcliffe launched *Daily Mail* 1896 and *Daily Mirror* 1903; created (cr.) baronet 1910, Baron Rothermere 1914, Viscount 1919; Director General of Royal Army Clothing Dept 1916–1917; Air Minister 1917–1918.

[2] The diarist, Cecil Bisshopp Harmsworth (1869–1948); editor of *Answers* and the *Harmsworth Magazine*; from 1905 Chairman of Associated Newspapers Ltd.; Liberal candidate for Mid-Worcestershire 1899–1900, Liberal candidate for North-East Lanarkshire 1901; MP Mid-Worcestershire 1906–1910, MP Luton 1911–1922; Parliamentary Private Secretary (PPS) to Runciman, President of the Board of Agriculture and Fisheries 1911, chairman of inquiry into Devon and Cornwall fisheries 1912–1913, member of inquiry into all inshore fisheries of England and Wales 1913–1914, investigated export of horses 1914; PPS to Runciman, President of the Board of Trade 1914–1915; Parliamentary Under-Secretary at the Home Office 1915; PPS to McKenna at the Treasury 1915–1916; member of Lloyd George's prime ministerial secretariat 1917–1918; Under-Secretary of State for Foreign Affairs 1919–1922; editor and author; cr. Baron 1939; married Emilie Alberta Maffett. He habitually resided in Henley when not in London.

[3] Emilie Alberta Harmsworth, née Maffett (1873–1942): the youngest of thirteen children, cousin of Cecil Harmsworth; they married in 1897.

[4] Gertrude Mary Spencer, née Maffett (b. 1859): the fourth of the Maffett children; m. Edward Spencer 1878.

[5] Marcella Amelia Deane, née Maffett (1862–1946): the seventh of the Maffett children; m. Alexander Sharpe Deane 1889.

To town to preside at the Annual Dinner of the Amalgamated Press, Holborn Restaurant. About 600 present. By midnight train back to Henley.

Another dreary day of a most unfortunate Summer. Frequent showers of rain and leaden skies.

12 July
House of Commons.

Budget in Committee still – the increment in land values duty under discussion for the 3rd or 4th week! To bed at 4 a.m.

13 July

Budget. Latish night again.

14 July

Budget! Real 'all-night' sitting this time. Supper of devilled bones about 2.30 a.m. Breakfast of ham and eggs and lager beer about 5.15. Lager beer and ham and eggs don't agree. One Member heard to observe that the worst of all-night sittings was he never knew when to leave off drinking whiskies and sodas and to begin drinking tea. To bed at 9.30 a.m.!

19 July

Budget. Reversion duty debate – exceedingly tedious. All-night sitting. Devilled bones at 1.30 or so – bread and milk and tea at 5.30. Home and to bed at 6.30. Lovely sunrise observed from the Terrace. Two submarines anchored opposite the House – the last up-River details of the great Naval Review.

20 July

Budget – still the Reversion duty. I spend most of the night on the Terrace with Herbert Craig[6] and S.O. Buckmaster[7] [afterwards Lord Chancellor]. Supper of bread and milk and tea and breakfast of poached eggs and tea. Innumerable divisions. A dull morning. To bed at 9. a.m.

28 July

Dinner party H. of Commons – Solicitor General and Lady Evans,[8] Solicitor General for Scotland and Mrs. Dewar,[9] Sir D. and Lady Brynmor Jones,[10] Lucas[11] and Geraldine,[12] Mr. and Mrs. Hemmerde,[13] H.J. Craig, Gertrude Spencer. Delightful evening on the Terrace – one of the few possible evenings this year for sitting out after dinner.

31 July

Em and I to the great Naval Review at Spithead – with the Lords and Commons on the White Star Liner 'Adriatic'. Grand Spectacle. Lovely day.

[6] Herbert James Craig (1869–1934): Lib. MP Tynemouth 1906–1918.
[7] Stanley Owen Buckmaster (1861–1934): Lib. MP Cambridge 1906–1910, Keighley 1911–1915; Solicitor General 1913–1915; Lord Chancellor 1915–1916; cr. Baron Buckmaster of Cheddington 1915; Viscount Buckmaster 1933.
[8] Samuel Thomas Evans (1859–1918): lawyer and judge; Lib. MP Mid-Glamorgan 1890–1910; Solicitor General 1908–1910; President of the Probate, Admiralty and Divorce Division of the High Court 1910; cr. GCB 1917. In 1905 he married his second wife, Blanche De Pinto (d. 1932).
[9] Arthur Dewar (1860–1917): Lib. MP Edinburgh South, 1899–1900, 1906–1910; Solicitor General for Scotland 1909–1910; Senator of the College of Justice 1910; cr. Lord Dewar 1910; married Letitia Dalrymple, the daughter of Robert Bell of Clifton Hall, Midlothian, 1892.
[10] David Brynmor Jones (d. 1921 at age 69): called to the Bar 1876, QC 1893; Lib. MP Stroud 1892–1895, Swansea 1895–1914; knighted 1906; m. 1892 Florence de Mocatta, née Cohen (d. 1920), a widow.
[11] Lucas White King (1856–1925): served in the Indian Civil Service 1878–1905; Professor of Oriental Languages at Trinity College, Dublin (TCD) 1905–1922; knighted 1919.
[12] Geraldine Adelaide Hamilton King (Dot), née Harmsworth (1866–1945): CBH's sister; m. Lucas White King 1897.
[13] Edward George Hemmerde (1871–1948): Lib. MP East Denbigh 1906–1910, North-West Norfolk 1912–1918; Lab. MP Crewe 1922–1924; KC 1908; Recorder of Liverpool 1909–1948; m. Lucy Elinor Colley 1906; the couple divorced in 1922.

2 August

To town. Speech in H. of Commons on Airships and Aeroplanes.

3 August

Alfred (Northcliffe)[14] and C.B.H. long talk with Mr. Lloyd-George[15] in his private room H. of Commons. Lloyd-G. exercising all his arts of persuasion to induce A. to support his schemes of Development, invalidity insurance, etc., etc.

[Later: I might well have given at the time and in its place a fuller account of an incident that is still very fresh in my memory. Lloyd-George's Budget was under interminable discussion and was meeting with the violent opposition that culminated in its rejection by the Lords. He had few newspaper friends, and none, think, outside the Liberal Press. Lord Rosebery[16] had gone into Opposition.

On the afternoon of the 3rd I spied N. in the Peers' Gallery. I went up to talk to him and, after listening to the debate for some time, he asked if Peers were admitted to the Members' tea room of the H. of C. I thought so, and I remember the interest he excited among Members there.

We were noted by Dalziel[17] who came up, had some chat with N., and then disappeared. In a few moments he returned saying that Ll.-G, would be much pleased if N. would go to see him in his room

---

[14]Alfred Charles William Harmsworth (1865–1922): eldest brother of CBH; press proprietor; launched *Answers to Correspondents* 1888, *Comic Cuts* 1890, *Daily Mail* 1896, *Daily Mirror* 1903; bought *The Times* 1908; cr. baronet 1904, Baron Northcliffe 1905, Viscount 1918; led British War Mission to United States 1917; Director of Propaganda in Enemy Countries 1918.

[15]David Lloyd George (1863–1945): Lib. MP for Caernarvon Boroughs 1890–1945; President of the Board of Trade 1906–1908; Chancellor of the Exchequer 1908–1915; Minister of Munitions 1915–1916; Secretary of State for War 1916; Prime Minister 1916–1922; leader of Liberal party 1926–1931; cr. Earl Lloyd-George of Dwyfor 1945.

[16]Archibald Philip Primrose (1847–1929): wealthy Scottish landowner and Liberal politician; Under-Secretary at the Home Office 1881–1883; Lord Privy Seal 1885; Foreign Secretary 1886, 1892–1894; Prime Minister 1894–1895; Liberal Imperialist; increasingly critical of Campbell-Bannerman and Asquith governments; succeeded (succ.) as 5th Earl of Rosebery 1868.

[17]Davison Alexander Dalziel (1852–1928): press proprietor and entrepreneur; Con. MP Brixton 1910–1923, 1924–1927; cr. Baron Dalziel 1927.

behind the Speaker's Chair. (He and N. had never met, I think.) So off-we went, and for an hour and more Ll.-G. exercised all his arts to win N. to the Budget. It was a tour de force – the most remarkable I have witnessed of the little Welshman's wizardry. N. was visibly impressed, not indeed by Ll.-G.'s main Budget proposals but by Ll.-G. himself.

Failing in one direction, Ll.-G. took up the question of Development and Road Improvement. Here he was on sure ground with N. who expressed himself as in full agreement with this part of the Budget. To explain it Ll.-G. quoted from the Statement about it that he was to make in the House the following day. He went much further. He handed the document to N. and said he might make any use of it he liked! N. was astonished and incredulous. Did he mean in the *Daily Mail* going to press that evening? Ll.-G. said Certainly yes. Before the House heard it? and exclusively in the *D.M.*? That would the House say? That would the other newspapers say? The Liberal newspapers?

Ll.-G. was after big game and sticking at nothing to win it. He did win N. as far as his Development and Road Improvement plans were concerned. And N. was a frank admirer of Ll.-G.'s working heartily with him on some problems of policy (notably in respect of an Irish Settlement, after the Rebellion of 1916) until their savage estrangement over Versailles.

So, the next morning the *Daily Mail* came out with its exclusive and premature disclosure and there were wigs on the green for the Chancellor in the House and in the Press.

C.H. (13.vi.1936)]

5 August

Both to Highcliffe to stay with Harold [Rothermere] and Lil.[18]

9 August
House of Commons.

Back to town – very reluctantly. Budget again in Committee. All night sitting. To bed at 7 a.m.

A regular dog day.

---

[18] Mary Lilian Harmsworth, née Share (d. 1937): m. Harold Harmsworth 1893.

10 August
House of Commons.

Another dog day. Budget in Committee. Clause 10 – undeveloped land duty. Successful speech – many congratulations. Harold and Vere[19] dine with me. House rises mercifully about 11.45.

11 August
House of Commons.

Doggier day than ever. Budget in Committee. Another sweltering all-nighter. To bed at 8 o'clock.

13 August
House of Commons.

Hot as ever. Still the Budget in Committee. Mr. Lloyd-George came up to me as I was sitting on the Terrace and said that my Speech on Tuesday was a 'topping fine speech' and thanked me for it. Long talk with John Burns[20] about everything under the sun. He wants the Government to stay in two more years – but then John's seat is not very safe.

---

[19] Vere Sidney Tudor Harmsworth (1895–1916): killed at the Battle of Ancre, 3 Nov. 1916. His father founded the Vere Harmsworth Chair of Naval History at Cambridge University in his memory.

[20] John Burns (1858–1943): leading member of Social Democratic Federation in 1880s; elected to London County Council (L.C.C.), 1889; Lib.-Lab. MP for Battersea 1892–1918; first working man to attain cabinet rank; President of the Local Government Board 1905–1914; President of the Board of Trade 1914; resigned in protest at British intervention in the First World War.

He is all for Asquith[21] and frankly hostile to the aggressive pretensions of Lloyd-George and Winston[22] whom he calls the 'Bounding Brothers'.

15 August

Another very hot day. By Mail Train (with Canfield and Kate [two of the maids]) to Ireland.

23 August
Costello Lodge[23]

I finish my article on 'A Plea for a Limitation of Speeches' for the *National Review*[24] and spend a few pleasant hours afterwards on the river – with one or two sea-trout rises.

15 September
Costello Lodge

I motored in to Galway with E. and caught the afternoon train for Dublin and so to Holyhead and Chester. Stayed night at Queen's Hotel, Chester.

---

[21] Herbert Henry Asquith (1852–1928): Lib. MP for East Fife 1886–1918, Paisley 1920–1924; Home Secretary 1892–1895; Chancellor of the Exchequer 1905–1908; Prime Minister 1908–1916; Secretary of State for War 1915; leader of the Liberal party 1908–1926; cr. Earl of Oxford and Asquith 1926.
[22] Winston Leonard Spencer Churchill (1874–1965): Con. MP Oldham 1900–1904; Lib. MP for Oldham 1904–1906, Manchester North-West 1906–1908, Dundee 1908–1922 (Co. Lib. 1916–1922); Con. MP for Epping 1924–1945, Woodford 1945–1964; Under-Secretary for the Colonies 1905–1908; President of the Board of Trade 1908–1910; Home Secretary 1910–1911; First Lord of the Admiralty 1911–1915, 1939–1940; Chancellor of the Duchy of Lancaster 1915; Minister of Munitions 1917–1918; Secretary of State for War and Air 1918–1921; Secretary of State for the Colonies 1921–1922; Chancellor of the Exchequer 1924–1929; Prime Minister and Minister of Defence 1940–1945; Prime Minister 1951–1955; leader of Conservative party 1940–1955; Knight of the Garter 1953.
[23] A fishing lodge in Galway.
[24] This article was published in October 1909.

16 September

Came on from Chester to Stourport. Met C.N. Nicholson[25] at Stourbridge Junction. Excellent meeting with him in Town Hall – Tontine Hotel.

17 September

In the evening to support Mr. Asquith at the great Bingley Hall Budget meeting. To Droitwich by late train (Raven Hotel).

18 September
Droitwich.

Good meeting. Chas. N. Nicholson, M.P., and John Morgan[26] speaking for me.
E.A. Goulding, M.P.,[27] Worcester lunches with C.N.N. and me.

20 September
Hyde Park Hotel & Montagu Square.

Budget in Committee (50th Day), Discussion on Income Tax and Super Tax. To bed at Hyde Park Hotel at 3.30. All sorts of rumours in the air. It is said that Mr. Balfour[28] and Lord Lansdowne[29] do

---

[25] Charles Norris Nicholson (1857–1918): Lib. MP Doncaster 1906–1918; cr. baronet 1912.

[26] John Morgan: Lib. parliamentary candidate for East Worcestershire 1906 (against Austen Chamberlain) and for Worcester in the first general election of 1910.

[27] Edward Alfred Goulding (1862–1936): Con. MP Devizes 1895–1906; Unionist MP Worcester 1908–1922; cr. Baron Wargrave 1922.

[28] Arthur James Balfour (1848–1930): Con. MP for Hertford 1874–1885, Manchester East 1885–1906, City of London 1906–1922; cr. Earl of Balfour 1922; President of the Local Government Board 1885–1886; Secretary of State for Scotland 1886–1887; Chief Secretary for Ireland 1887–1891; First Lord of the Treasury and Leader of the House of Commons 1891–1892, 1895–1902; Prime Minister 1902–1905; First Lord of the Admiralty 1915–1916; Foreign Secretary 1916–1919; Lord President of the Council 1919–1922, 1925–1929; leader of Conservative Party 1902–1911.

[29] Henry Charles Keith Petty-Fitzmaurice (1845–1927): (as Lib.) Under-Secretary for War 1872–1874, Under-Secretary for India 1880–1881; (as Lib. Unionist): Governor-General of Canada 1883–1888; Viceroy of India 1888–1894; Secretary of State for War 1895–1900; Foreign Secretary 1900–1905; leader of Unionist peers 1903–1916; succ. as 5th Marquess of Lansdowne 1866.

not wish the Lords to reject the Budget but that the wild Lords from the country are determined to do so. Rumour has it further that the Brewers are threatening to abandon the Tory Party and to withdraw their subscriptions to party funds unless the Budget is rejected.

Meeting of Executive Committee of Liberal League to consider Lord Rosebery's resignation of the presidency. Lord R. in the Chair – voice choked with emotion and so forth. After his Glasgow Speech denouncing the Budget as revolutionary and Socialistic, nothing for the League to do but to accept his resignation. Matter referred for final decision to a meeting of the Council to be summoned later.

23 September
House of Commons

Budget Committee (33rd day) Whiskey chiefly, and the Irish mustered in fair strength on behalf of one of the few remaining Irish industries. Late at night our majorities ran dangerously low – down to 13 in one instance. So many of our lads holiday-making or slipping off to bed at midnight without due notice to the Whips. To bed Hyde Park Hotel 6 o'clock.

27 September
House of Commons

Budget Committee (35th day). To bed at 1 o'clock, it having been agreed between the high contracting parties on both front benches that we are to have no more all night sittings on the Committee Stage.

I bet Sam Evans [afterwards President of the Admiralty and Divorce Division. Sam didn't pay me], the Solicitor-General, five pounds to one that the Lords would reject the Budget.

28 September
House of Commons

Budget Committee (36th day). Dank and dismal day. My fortieth birthday – Eheu fugaces anni labuntur![30]

---

[30] 'Alas! our fleeting years pass away.' A reference to Horace, *Odes* II 14.

A witty saying. I asked Clarendon Hyde (M.P. for Wednesbury):[31] 'When does a politician cease to be a politician and become a Statesman?'
'When he receives a salary' said C.H.

29 September
House of Commons

Budget Committee (37th Day)
To dinner with St. J.[32] at the Cavendish Hotel, Jermyn Street. Found him in conversation with Lord Ribblesdale,[33] the most picturesque man of our time. He is commonly called 'The Ancestor' and his lifelike portrait by Sargent[34] was a few years ago the sensation of the Academy. He seemed to know no more than we did what is to be the fate of the Budget in the Lords. Lord Ribblesdale is weak in his 'w's. He (almost not quite) says 'v' for 'w' a fact that imparts a distinctive flavour to his delightful and only too rare speeches in the Lords. There is a further embellishment of quaint analogies from the hunting field both in his public and private talk.

30 September
House of Commons

Mother to dine with me at the House. With us Herbert Craig, M.P. and John Burns. J.B. in excellent form, taking to Mother instinctively. He told us of an amusing conversation with the Kaiser,[35] during which he developed very frank views about the German Army and the social conditions of Berlin. Burns is, I think, of all remarkable men I have met the most highly endowed with natural force of character, as he is

---

[31] Clarendon Hyde (1858–1934): Lib. MP Wednesbury 1906–1910; knighted 1910.

[32] William Albert St John Harmsworth (1876–1933); known as St John; younger brother of Cecil Harmsworth, with whom he edited Lord Northcliffe's *My Journey Around the World*.

[33] Thomas Lister (1854–1925): Liberal politician; Lord-in-Waiting, 1880–1885; Master of the Buckhounds 1892–1895; trustee of the National Gallery 1909–1925; succ. as. 4th Baron Ribblesdale 1876.

[34] John Singer Sargent (1856–1925): American artist who lived mostly first in Paris and then, from 1886, London.

[35] Wilhelm II of Germany (1859–1941): abdicated 1918.

in conversation the most original. His glowing deep-set eyes and huge fists emphasising his vigorous arguments – to say nothing of his big voice and powerful chest – all combine to produce an impression of great physical and mental strength.
We had E.A.H.'s 2lb 6oz sea-trout from Costello for dinner.
Burns told us that he was the 16th of 18 children all by the same mother.
Budget Committee (38th day).

4 October
House of Commons

Budget Committee 40th Day. The Irish on the rampage in defence of their old allies the publicans.
[...]
I had some conversation with Mr. John Redmond[36] in the Smoking-room today. He does not believe that the sporting possibilities of Ireland will suffer under Land Purchase if the question is rightly taken in hand by sportsmen. He instanced a mountain in Wicklow belonging to a number of small farmers and used for grazing sheep. They let it to Mr. Redmond on condition that he leaves to them the business of safeguarding the game from poachers, and does not allow his keeper on the ground. He says that the grouse have increased 2- or three-fold since this arrangement was made.

7 October
House of Commons

Report Development Bill. Short speech.

8 October
House of Commons

Report Development Bill. Another short speech. By mail train in evening to Ireland.

---

[36]John Edward Redmond (1856–1918): Irish Nat. MP for New Ross 1881–1885, North Wexford 1885–1891, Waterford city 1891–1918; supported Charles Stuart Parnell on split of the Irish Parliamentary Party; took over leadership of Irish National League after Parnell's death, 1891; leader of reunited IPP 1900–1918.

15 October
Chester and Stourbridge

Morning spent reviewing once more the sights of Chester including the Roman Bath behind a stationer's shop. Then leisurely to Stourbridge (Talbot Hotel) by way of Wolverhampton. Grand pro-Budget meeting with Hon. E.S. Montagu, M.P.,[37] in Town Hall.

19 October
House of Commons

Finance Bill Report (1st Day), Lucas and Dot in from Totteridge to dine with me. Also with us J.D. Rees, M.P.,[38] and Cecil Beck, M.P.[39]

27 October
House of Commons

Mr. Birrell,[40] the Chief Secretary, tells me an amusing story illustrating the methods of the Lords in conducting their business. The Irish Land Bill (1909) was before their Lordships. Lord Atkinson[41] had an amendment on the paper but losing faith in it on second thoughts he moved a manuscript amendment of almost exactly opposite intention. This second amendment Lord A. moved with a cogent

---

[37] Edwin Samuel Montagu (1879–1924): Lib. MP West Cambridgeshire 1906–1918, Cambridgeshire, 1918–1922; Under-Secretary of State for India 1910–1914; Financial Secretary to the Treasury 1914–1915, 1915–1916; Chancellor of the Duchy of Lancaster 1915; Minister of Munitions 1916; Minister without Portfolio in charge of reconstruction 1917; Secretary of State for India 1917–1922.

[38] John David Rees (1854–1922): a member of the Indian Civil Service 1875–1901; Lib. MP Montgomery District of Boroughs 1906–1910; Unionist candidate Kilmarnock Burghs 1911; Unionist MP for Nottingham East 1912–1922; knighted 1910; cr. baronet year 1919; m. Mary Katherine Dormer 1891. Died after falling out of a moving train, and left a bizarre anti-Catholic will.

[39] Arthur Cecil Tyrrell Beck (1876–1932): Lib. MP Wisbech 1906–1910; Saffron Walden 1910–1918; Junior Lord of the Treasury 1915; Vice-Chamberlain of the Royal Household 1915–1917; Parliamentary Secretary to the Ministry of National Service 1917–1919; knighted 1920.

[40] Augustine Birrell (1850–1933): Lib. MP West Fife 1889–1900, Bristol North 1906–1918; President of the Board of Education 1905–1907; Chief Secretary for Ireland 1907–1916.

[41] John Atkinson (1844–1932): Con. MP Londonderry North 1895–1905; Lord of Appeal 1905–1928; cr. Baron Atkinson of Glenwilliam, County Limerick 1905.

and convincing speech of five minutes' length and it was intimated from the Government front bench that the Government was prepared to accept it. The Lord Chancellor put the original, abandoned amendment which their sapient Lordships carried! Note, that the original amendment had not even been moved!

2 November
House of Commons

Finance Bill – Third Reading.
Mr. Spencer Leigh Hughes,[42] the defeated Liberal Candidate for Bermondsey, is a man of much wit. He was speaking at a Liberal meeting during the notorious Peckham bye-election when the brewers flooded the constituency ankle-deep in beer. 'Ladies and gentlemen,' said Mr. Hughes, 'this is a stout and bitter contest!'

3 November
House of Commons

Finance Bill – Third Reading. Wonderful speech of Mr. Ure,[43] Lord Advocate, defending himself against Mr. Balfour's charge that he had been guilty of a 'frigid and calculated lie' in respect of the Tories' ability to pay for Old Age Pensions by the tariff. Mr. Asquith said it was the finest Parliamentary Speech for twenty years. It had been arranged that F.E. Smith,[44] the brilliant young K.C., was to follow Ure, but, half-way through the Lord Advocate's Speech, it became clear that Balfour would have to reply himself. I have never seen him so agitated nor the House in so dangerous a mood. Everybody's blood was up.

---

[42] Spencer Leigh Hughes (1858–1920): journalist; Lib. (then Coalition Lib) MP Stockport 1910–1920.
[43] Alexander Ure (1853–1928): Lib. MP Linlithgowshire 1895–1913; Solicitor General for Scotland 1905–1909; Lord Advocate 1909–1913; Lord Justice-General for Scotland and Lord President of the Court of Session 1913–1920; cr. Baron Strathclyde of Sandyford, County Lanark 1914.
[44] Frederick Edwin Smith (1872–1930): Con. MP Liverpool Walton 1906–1918, Liverpool West Derby 1918–1919; Solicitor General for England and Wales 1915; Attorney General for England and Wales 1915–1919; Lord Chancellor 1919–1922; Secretary of State for India 1924–1928; cr. Baron Birkenhead 1919, Viscount 1921, Earl of Birkenhead 1922.

4 November
House of Commons

Finance Bill Third Reading carried by Liberal and Labour majority of 230 – the Irish Nationalists abstaining on the plea that they do not support any measures increasing taxes in Ireland.

Luncheon at the House of Commons to Sir Benjamin Stone,[45] the amiable old Member for one of the Birmingham seats and 'photographer to the H. of C.'

5 November

To Sandown Park, Esher, to see M. Paulhan fly in his biplane.[46] A wonderful sight very pleasantly described in the *Daily Mail* of Saturday, Nov. 6th. The emotion of the voyager who first gazed 'silent on a peak in Darien' must have been trifling in comparison with mine when I saw Paulhan fly!

15 November
28 Montagu Square

C.B.H. takes chair at New Vagabonds dinner at Hotel Cecil. Dinner in honour of successful aviators – of whom only Mr J.T.C. Moore-Brabazon[47] present. Mr. M-B. has recently won *Daily Mail* £1000 prize for first circular mile flight on an all-British aeroplane. Also present Hon. Rodolphe Lemieux,[48] Postmaster General of Canada, Mr. Henniker Heaton, M.P.,[49] Dr. Glazebrook F.R.S.,[50] of the National

---

[45] John Benjamin Stone (1838–1914): Con. MP East Birmingham 1895–1910; knighted 1892; a prolific photographer, he was known as the 'Knight of the Camera'.

[46] Louis Paulhan (1883–1963): French aviator.

[47] John Theodore Cuthbert Moore-Brabazon (1884–1964): international racing driver and aviator; first person to pilot a powered aircraft in England 1909; first member of the Royal Aero Club 1910; served in the Royal Flying Corps (RFC) in Great War; Con. MP Rochester Chatham 1918–1929, Wallasey 1931–1942; cr. Baron Brabazon of Tara 1942; Parliamentary Secretary to the Ministry of Transport 1923–1924, 1924–1927; Minister of Transport, 1940–1942.

[48] Rodolphe Lemieux (1866–1937): held a range of offices in Canadian politics including Speaker of the House of Commons 1922–1930.

[49] John Henniker Heaton (1848–1914): Con. MP Canterbury 1885–1910; cr. baronet 1912.

[50] Richard Tetley Glazebrook (1854–1935): Director of the National Physical Laboratory 1899–1919; knighted 1917.

Physical Laboratory, Teddington and about 200 others. E.A.H. receives the company.

16 November
Worcestershire.

Meeting Wribbenhall Parish Room.

18 November
Chaddesley Corbett.

Meeting. Ernest Turner[51] and C.B.H. walk from over Kinver Edge to Kinver. Tea at the Harbour Inn. Then through the Wyre Forest to Bewdley. Dinner Lion Hotel, Kidderminster.

19 November
Stoke Works.

Social meeting (tea and cake) and concert.

21 November
28 Montagu Square.

By train to town. With Daff,[52] Bud[53] and Gol[54] to the Zoo in the afternoon.

22 November

Walk from Finchley Road Station to the Hampstead Garden Suburb and back over Hampstead Heath. Cold sunny day. Theatre, 'Our Miss Gibbs' at the Gaiety.[55]

[51] Ernest Turner (d. 1917): CBH's agent in Mid-Worcestershire; killed in action during the First World War.
[52] Daphne Cecil Rosemary Harmsworth (1901–1993): daughter of Cecil Harmsworth.
[53] Cecil Desmond Bernard Harmsworth (1903–1990): son of Cecil Harmsworth.
[54] Eric Beauchamp Northcliffe Harmsworth (1905–1988): son of Cecil Harmsworth.
[55] By 'Cryptos' and James T. Tanner.

The House of Lords begin their momentous debate on Lord Lansdowne's Budget motion: – 'That the House is not justified in giving its consent to this Bill until it has been submitted to the judgment of the country'.

23 November

House of Lords Debate. Gilded Chamber packed full and every gallery well occupied.

24 November

House of Lords Debate. Marquis of Salisbury[56] opens proceedings in a speech of unusual emphasis for the H. of Lords. Archbishop of Canterbury[57] follows in a brief statement to the effect that the Bishops as a body will not interfere. Then comes Lord Rosebery for whom everybody had been waiting. Lord R. in his later, melodramatic manner and at his best in this style. He has all the gifts of great oratory – a fine presence, beautiful voice, action, passion, language. The H. of Lords usually as cold as a place of tombs seems to spring into life under the influence of this man's speech. The revival of the year after winter-time – the strains of an organ waking the echoes in an empty Cathedral – the breathing of a spirit in a dead body – while Lord R. is speaking the H. of Lords seems equal even to its overweening pretensions of these days. Today he hits out right and left. The Budget is the most abominable thing ever devised by the malice of man – but their Lordships ought not to reject it. Such is the burden of the Speech.

---

[56]James Edward Hubert Gascoyne-Cecil (1861–1947), son of the third Marquess (who was Prime Minister 1885–1886, 1886–1892, 1895–1902): Con. MP (as Viscount Cranborne) Darwen 1885–1892, Rochester 1893–1903; Under-Secretary to the Foreign Office 1900–1903; Lord Privy Seal 1903–1905, also President of the Board of Trade 1905; Chancellor of the Duchy of Lancaster 1922–1923; Lord President of the Council 1922–1924; Lord Privy Seal 1924–1929; Leader of House of Lords 1925–1929; Conservative leader in House of Lords 1925–1931; succ. as 4th Marquess of Salisbury 1903.

[57]Randall Thomas Davidson (1848–1930): ordained as Anglican priest 1875; Bishop of Rochester 1891–1895; Bishop of Winchester 1895–1903; Archbishop of Canterbury 1903–1928.

25 November

House of Lords Debate on Budget. In the H. of Commons Lords' amendments to Development Bill considered. I make small speech on the clauses relating to Commons & Open Spaces. Very thin attendance in our House. Everybody thinking only of the action of the Lords.
[...] House rises until next Wednesday when the Prime Minister gives formal notice of Commons resolutions affirming privileges.

27 November

dine with Carr-Gomms,[58] Ashley Gardens. Afterwards to 'The Great Mrs. Alloway' – a dreary problem play.[59]

30 November
West House, Brighton.

With St. John[60] in the motor-car to the Devil's Dyke. Back by road – St. J. in his wheeled chair. Beautiful bright day.
Lords reject BUDGET by 350 to 75.

1 December
House of Commons

Mr. Asquith tables Commons remonstrance amidst much enthusiasm on our side.
...
Em and the babes came to the House this morning. We spent some time in the Lords who were sitting at an unwontedly early hour. They saw too the H. of Commons and Bud and Gol sat in the Prime

---

[58] Hubert William Culling Carr-Gomm (1877–1939): Lib. MP Rotherhithe 1906–1918; assistant private secretary to Sir Henry Campbell-Bannerman 1906–1908. In 1906 he married Kathleen Rome, divorcing her in 1913 after she had an affair with his fellow Liberal MP Eliot Crawshay-Williams.

[59] By Douglas Murray, which may have been a pseudonym.

[60] Albert St. John Harmsworth (1876–1933): the sixth Harmsworth brother; the first person to realise the commercial possibilities of Perrier water; a keen motorist, he was crippled in an accident in 1906.

Minister's seat. In Westminster Hall we met John Burns who shook hands with the babes and kissed his hand to them on parting.

2 December
House of Commons

I have never seen so many Members at Prayers as were present today. After Prayers the House rapidly filled up in every corner – the Strangers' Galleries, Peers' Gallery and the others too. There were a few notices of Motions for Returns and about 35 questions. The Prime Minister had a great reception when he came in – every Liberal Member rising to his feet and cheering wildly. His speech was superb – he is by far the greatest Parliamentary figure today. His fine deep voice as ever lent tone and colour to a splendid oration.

With his fresh massive clean shaven face and fine white hair Asquith suggests to me at times a Pilgrim Father. Then again I think of him as Oliver Cromwell whom he grows to resemble more and more every year – without the warts. The highest office and responsibility have 'made' Asquith. Until recently he was strangely undervalued even by his own side in politics. His grand Budget speeches, his noble oration on Sir H.C.-B,[61] and his speech and conduct since he became Prime Minister have raised him to what is easily the first place in the H. of Commons. Balfour, who had risen from a bed of sickness and was obviously unwell, made a wretched display. With all his brilliance B. always fails on great occasions. Today the circumstances were for him exceptionally difficult. It is an open secret that he wished the Budget to pass and as a 'H. of Commons man' of longer standing than almost any other Member he must deplore the action of the Lords – or rather the overwhelming pressure that has compelled him to acquiesce in that course.

3 December
House of Commons

The last day of a great Parliament. Almost immediately after Prayers Black Rod summoned us to the Lords where the Five

---

[61] Henry Campbell-Bannerman (1836–1908): Lib. MP for Stirling Burghs, 1868–1908; Secretary of State for War, 1892–1895; Prime Minister, 1905–1908; leader of Liberal party, 1898–1908; knighted 1895.

Commissioners – Lords McDonnell,[62] Althorp,[63] Loreburn,[64] Haversham[65] and Pentland[66] – were sitting all in a row. The Royal Assent was announced to several Bills and then the Lord Chancellor read the King's Speech. We then trooped back to the Commons where the Speaker read the Speech from the Chairman's seat. The passage specially addressed to the Gentlemen of the H. of Commons was greeted with a little fierce cheer from our side.

...

We all shook hands with Mr. Lowther[67] – the greatest Speaker by all admissions within living memory – as we filed out.

7 December
Evesham.

Open Congregational Bazaar, Stourbridge. Meeting in the evening at Evesham with Mr. Albert Stanley, M.P. (N.W. Staffs).[68]

[62] Anthony Patrick MacDonnell (1844–1925): Indian civil servant 1865–1901; Permanent Under-Secretary to the Lord Lieutenant of Ireland 1902–1908; cr. Baron MacDonnell 1908; Chairman of Royal Commission on Civil Service 1912–1914.
[63] Charles Robert Spencer (1857–1922): Lib. MP for North Northamptonshire 1880–1885, Mid-Northamptonshire 1885–1895, 1900–1905; cr. Viscount Althorp 1905; Lord Chamberlain 1905–1912; succ. as 7th Earl Spencer 1910.
[64] Robert Reid (1846–1923): Lib. MP for Hereford 1880–1885, Dumfries Burghs 1886–1905; Solicitor general 1894; Attorney General 1894–1895; Lord Chancellor 1905–1912; knighted 1894; cr. Baron Loreburn 1905; Earl Loreburn 1911.
[65] Arthur Divett Hayter (1835–1917): Lib. MP for Wells 1865–1868, Bath 1873–1885, Walsall 1893–1895; junior whip 1880–1882; Financial Secretary to the Treasury 1882–1885; chairman, Public Accounts Committee, 1901–1905; succ. as 2nd baronet 1878; cr. Baron Haversham 1906.
[66] John Sinclair (1860–1925): Lib. MP for Dunbartonshire 1892–1895 Forfar 1897–1909; Secretary of State for Scotland 1905–1912; Governor of Madras 1912–1919; cr. Baron Pentland 1909.
[67] James Lowther (1855–1949): Con. MP for Rutland 1883–1885, Penrith 1886–1918, Penrith and Cockermouth 1918–1921; Speaker of the House of Commons 1905–1921; cr. Viscount Ullswater 1921.
[68] Albert Stanley (1863–1915): MP North-West Staffordshire 1907–1915; first elected as a 'Lib-Lab', joined Labour Party 1910.

10 December
Droitwich

Big meeting Salters Hall with Lord Beauchamp.[69] Lord B. dined with us previously at the Raven Hotel and with us were Mr. and Mrs. Hobson[70] [...] and Mr. and Mrs. E. Turner.

Lord B. tells us that the King is very angry with the Lords for rejecting the Budget and that he has promised Asquith to do everything he can to help him if he achieves a majority. Lord B. as Lord Steward is in a position to know things.

16 December
Stourport.

Excellent meeting with Mr. Frank Wright[71] of Birmingham at Stourport.

17 December
Cookley & Lower Hagley.

Good meetings.

25 December
[28 Montagu Square]

We began our day with hymns sung by the babes outside our bedroom door 'Then Shepherds watched their flocks' and the first verse of 'Hark, the herald angels sing'. Then they brought in their stockings.

We took Daff and Bud to Church (St. Mary's, Bryanston Sq.). After that our first Christmas Dinner – turkey pudding and mince pies. A little Christmas tree in the centre of the table and lots of crackers. After dinner the opening of the too many and too generous gifts of Aunts and Uncles and Cousins.

---

[69] William Lygon (1872–1938): Governor of New South Wales 1899–1901; Lord Steward 1907–1910; Lord President of the Council 1910, 1914–1915; First Commissioner of Works 1910–1914; Liberal leader in the House of Lords 1924–1931; succ. as 7th Earl Beauchamp 1891.

[70] George Whitworth Hobson (d. 1940): active in Midlands Liberalism until the 1930s, serving as an Alderman.

[71] Frank Wright (1853–1922): Liberal politician and manufacturer in Birmingham.

I walked some of the way out to Poynters. E.A.H., babes and self arrive in time for tea. Mother's Christmas Dinner party[...]

30 December

Virtual opening of General Election campaign. Large Committee meeting at the Liberal Club, Lye.

1910

1 January

Adopted with much enthusiasm by the Liberal '300' at Droitwich. In the evening to a packed and rollicking meeting at Kidderminster. Sir Edward Fraser,[1] Liberal candidate for the Borough and Mr. Brooks,[2] our working-man humourist and orator of Stourbridge, also addressed meeting.

2 January
Stourbridge. Talbot Hotel.

Delightfully quiet morning reading Shakespeare's Henry IV. In the afternoon walk with E. Turner to Clent and tea with Mr. Higgs. Meeting of the A.S.R.S.[3] men at the Chequers Inn at night. Plenty of heckling from Socialist members but all in good temper.

3 January
Webheath.

Excellent meeting at the Rose & Crown. Mr. Baylis of Birchfield Road in the Chair, Afterwards in to Mr. Baylis's for supper.

4 January
Clent.

Admirable meeting in the new Parish Hall with Mr. Grosvenor Lee[4] in the Chair.

---

[1] Edward Fraser (1851–1921): Lib. candidate East Nottingham 1900 and for Kidderminster in the first general election of 1910; four times mayor of Nottingham; knighted 1908.
[2] Unidentified.
[3] Amalgamated Society of Railway Servants.
[4] Thomas Grosvenor Lee (c.1846–1916): solicitor; Lib. candidate Birmingham Central 1906; formerly a Liberal Unionist.

6 January
Stourbridge.

E.A.H. arrives in the Constituency. Magnificent meeting of 1200 people in the Town Hall. Great enthusiasm, Mr. Frank Taylor in the Chair and among the speakers Mr. Coysh the candidate for Kingswinford[5] and Mr. Henry Whitehead, an old age pensioner aged 88. Mr. Whitehead was the success of the meeting and it was delightful to hear him referring easily to Cobden, Palmerston and Lord J. Russell. He said that he had often bought 4 lb. loaves for his mother at 1/1 apiece.

7 January
Wychbold and Stoke Heath.

Some mistake about the meeting at Wychbold which was in consequence the only poorly-attended one of the series. Leaving Mr. G.W. Hobson to continue the meeting and to bring back E.A.H. I went on to the 'Ewe & Lamb' Stoke Heath. Admirable gathering.

8 January
Droitwich.

Off day. E.A.H. and I show ourselves in the High Street and after lunch I go with Cyril Hobson to a local foot-ball match.
...
I discover to my dismay today that I did not vote on the 3rd Reading of the Old Age Pensions Bill on July 9th 1908. Earle[6] and I examine anxiously the official Division List and sure enough my name is not there. What can be the reason that I, who was never absent from a vital Division during my 4 years of Parliamentary life, should have been absent on this most important occasion? It is truly an awkward circumstance. But there must have been a good reason.

We send up to Montagu Square for Hansards and old diaries of 1908.

There is another Old Age Pension complication. Under the Bill of 1908 it was found impossible to include otherwise eligible persons

---

[5] F. Coysh: Secretary of the United Kingdom Commercial Travellers' Association. He was defeated at the election.

[6] Arthur Earle (b. c.1879): private secretary to CBH.

who had received indoor or outdoor Relief. The reasons were (1) lack of adequate funds and (2) the fact that to do so would have disorganised the whole Poor Law system. It was agreed, however, that these persons should come on the list on Jan. 1st 1911. The artful Tories, however, moved an amendment to bring in these people at once. The Government was of course, obliged to defeat this amendment – and I voted with the Government. We shall hear more of this.

10 January
Chaddesley Corbett and Belbroughton.

Crowded meetings in the Schools in both villages. We return in the evening to the Raven Hotel, Droitwich. Another day of purgatory passed! It is the hideous unending length of a county contest that takes the starch out of a man. The two or three meetings a night are fatiguing enough and there is the gradual creeping up over the whole countryside of the miasma of suspicion and falsification. We hear today that a prominent Droitwich Primrose League dame in addressing a Mothers' Meeting (!) assured the poor women that before the Election of 1906 I promised to establish a *paper factory* in Droitwich and that having deceived Droitwich once I was not to be trusted again! These fantastic lies are amusing enough in retrospect but they gall and irritate at the time. This Primrose Dame must be twin sister to that other Sapphira who in 1906 went about Droitwich saying that we employed Germans in our London printing works.

Joy! Diaries etc. arrive from Montagu Square. On July 9th 1908 I attended the Annual Meeting of the Worcestershire Liberal Association at Caesar's Camp, Malvern. Well do I recall that dreary, damp occasion. J.W. Wilson (M.P. N. Worcs.)[7] was there, too. We were doing our duty by the W.L.A. – very reluctantly – but we were doing it and now our virtuous conduct is likely to cause us some embarrassment. Still, who could foresee that the Tories would be so mad as to divide against Old Age Pensions?

---

[7] John William Wilson (1828–1932): MP Worcestershire North 1895–1918, Stourbridge 1918–1922; first elected as a Lib. Unionist, re-elected as a Lib. in 1906; Privy Councillor 1911.

11 January
Bradley Green (Red Lion) and Himbleton.

A rather heavy snow-storm this evening. Poor little meeting at Bradley Green. Good meeting at the Recreation Room, Himbleton. With me Mr. G.W. Hobson and Mr. Thomas both of Droitwich, the Rev. Mr. Brockbank (Droitwich),[8] and the Rev. D.R. Fotheringham,[9] London.

Latest rumours. Tory canvassers in Droitwich saying that in 2 months' time the salt works in Droitwich will be closed.

12 January
Fairfield and Upper Hagley.

Splendid meeting in old Mr. Griffin's malt-house at Fairfield. Two rumours at Fairfield (1) that in order to prevent our meeting in the school-house this evening the Tory and Church-party had hastily improvised a Bible class in the school and (2) that Mr. Lyttelton's[10] meeting here yesterday having been broken up by our too zealous small-holders we were to look for like treatment. Nothing sensational happens however and all goes merry as a marriage bell. It is otherwise at the Prince of Wales Upper Hagley. On arriving I find the meeting in some disorder. A group of Tory youths flushed with strong drink and liberally decorated with red favours make things lively but give me a fairish hearing on the whole.

Telegram from Lloyd-George. 'Remind me at Criccieth next Wednesday when I shall do best to arrange day in following week if physically capable. Lloyd-George.' This is right good of the little Chancellor. I had written to him not daring to ask for a meeting and suggesting that he should send me a nice letter.

13 January
Wribbenhall & Stourport.

Finest meeting I have ever seen at Wribbenhall. Mr. E. Smith in the Chair. At Stourport a packed and glorious meeting in the Town

---

[8] J.W.K Brockbank: appointed to the pastorate of Droitwich in 1907; later Superintendent Chaplain to the Mariners' Friend Society.

[9] David Ross Fotheringham (d. 1939 at age 66): secretary of the Church of England Liberal and Progressive Union 1904–1912.

[10] John Cavendish Lyttelton (1881–1949). Con. MP Droitwich 1910–1916; Parliamentary Under-Secretary of State for War 1939–1940; succ. as 9th Viscount Cobham 1922.

Hall, with as many people in the street outside. Mr. Wm. Adam of Kidderminster in the Chair.[11] Speakers Sir E. Fraser, Mr. Maximilian Hope of the Midland Liberal Federation[12] and young Mr. Beakbane of Stourport.[13]

14 January
Wollescote and Wollaston.

Suffocating meeting in the Schools, Wollescote. Wonderful enthusiasm. Also packed and cheerful meeting in Edkin's repository at Wollaston.

Mild open weather since the snow went.

15 January

I attend meeting National Schools Amblecote for Mr. Coysh, Liberal candidate for Kingswinford. Fine gathering. [. . .]

First results – Birmingham, Manchester Salford, some London seats and a good many little Boroughs. Loud cheering of Tory youths outside the Raven. Gloomy report that Dudley has fallen.

16 January
Raven Hotel, Droitwich.

Peaceful day. Over to Stourbridge in the evening to meet the Locomotive Railway men at the Woolpack Inn. Back to Droitwich – walking as usual part of the way home.

17 January
Cutnall Green & Droitwich.

Canvassing the tradesmen in the morning with Mrs. Hobson. Meetings – Cutnall Green and Droitwich. Great meeting in the

---

[11] William Adam of Lyndholm, Kidderminster.
[12] Maximilian Hope (? c.1868–1922), of Birmingham, a collier's son and a National Liberal Federation speaker.
[13] Henry Beakbane (b. c.1879–1953), tanner.

Salter's Hall – Mr. Hobson, Mr. Brooks (our working-man orator of Stourbridge) and myself as speakers.

18 January
Lower Hagley and Oldswinford

Round the Oldswinford tradesmen with Mr. Frank Evers who is 83. Excellent meeting Free Church Hall Lower Hagley and a 'rouser' at the 'Bird in Hand' Oldswinford.

19 January
Finstall & Stoke Works.

Visiting the Stourbridge tradesmen with Mrs. Waugh. In the evening to Finstall (Mr. Brooks in the Chair) and afterwards to Stoke Works. Our old Stoke friends in fine fettle. Choir of little boys (all with blue rosettes) to sing the Land song.

Delightful walk back to Droitwich in the moonlight with A. Earle.

20 January
Droitwich.

Nomination Day. I attend at the Town Hall with Ernest Turner and hand the nomination papers (21) and £350 in notes to the Sheriff.

Meetings at Wolverley and Bewdley (with Mr. Brooks candidate for the West Division).

21 January
Stourbridge.

Round the High Street, Stourbridge, with Mr. Waugh.
Meetings:
Hoobrook
Foley Park and
Blakedown.

Blakedown is supposed to be the hottest little Tory corner of all and rumours had gone about as to a warm reception that was to be prepared for us. I am supposed to have alleged during the last Election that the young men of B. had 'more hair than brains'. I don't remember saying it. Anyhow we were to look out for squalls. The plot – if plot there was – completely failed. A posse of iron-workers from Belbroughton and a second force from faithful Wollescote came to Blakedown to safeguard us. They positively swamped the Blakedowners who melted away into the public-houses and masked their confusion behind pint-pots.

22 January
Wollescote.

Great open-air meeting at Wollescote at 3 in the afternoon, Afterwards in triumphal procession to Lye Cross to attend a similar meeting of J.W. Wilson's. Evening meetings:
   Wychbold and Stoke Prior.

24 January
Droitwich.

Round the High Street Stourport with Mr. Griffin. Meetings in the evening: Hanbury and Droitwich.
   Lloyd-George meeting in the Skating Rink with an overflow in the Town Hall.
   In the afternoon the Chief Constable and Mr. Willis Bund[14] Chairman of the C.C. and of Quarter Sessions, discovered in earnest colloquy in the Coffee Room at the Talbot. Would it be safe for Ll.-G. to journey from the Skating Rink to the Town Hall? Dreadful rumours as to special train-loads of roughs from Birmingham and contingents from Dudley. 150 police in Stourbridge. Decided that should the crowd in the streets in the evening seem to be of a dangerous character Ll.-G. to be whisked off to Droitwich directly after making his speech at the Skating Rink – A wonderful demonstration – between 4 & 5 thousand men. I take the Chair. Lloyd-G. in one of his more urbane moods. Message is brought to me in the middle of his Speech that he is not to go to the Town Hall. He leaves the rink with E.A.H. and Kathleen

---

[14]John William Willis Bund (1843–1928): Con. candidate North Worcestershire 1885; Chairman of Worcestershire County Council 1892–1923.

Carr-Gomm for Droitwich. After a brief speech I repair by back ways to the Town Hall. Another splendid meeting. Intense disappointment when I tell them Ll.-G. cannot come. General opinion that the police have been fussy and officious.

I stay the night at the Talbot, Stourbridge, and am serenaded by vast crowds of people, and afterwards outside the door of my sitting room by a number of the young Tory bloods of the Talbot bar.

26 January

C.B.H. and A. Earle over to Droitwich in the morning. Find Ll.-G. enjoying a very hearty breakfast and full of go. Quite a little ovation at the Station when he leaves for London.

Meetings: Belbroughton, Chaddesley and Aston Fields.

[Later: I well remember how angry Ll.-G. was at the interference of the authorities with his movements in Stourbridge. Their apprehensions he regarded as all silly nonsense. C.H. 13.9.33]

27 January
Wribbenhall & Stourport.

Fine meetings at Wribbenhall and at the Bark Shed at the Tannery, Stourport. Said to be the biggest meeting ever held at Stourport.

28 January

The Polling day.

E. and I set forth in Harold's covered car about 11 o'clock and visit every Polling Station. Lunch at the Talbot, Stourbridge, and tea provided by the Wribbenhall ladies in the Schoolroom.

29 January

The Count.

Poor E. so confident of our success that she comes into the counting-room – for the first time and the last.

Result:

    Hon. J.C. Lyttelton   5078
    C. Harmsworth   <u>4973</u>
    Majority   105

Our people at Droitwich utterly cast down. Rumours of rioting to take place in the evening.

E. and I and the Babes go over to Stourbridge and Wollescote and have tremendous ovations in both places. Our friends' disappointment is intense and numbers of them cry when I address them out of an upper window at the Committee Room. Torchlight procession at Wollescote improvised apparently at a moment's notice.

E., I and the Babes afterwards to the Foley Arms Hotel, Malvern.

30 January
Malvern. Foley Arms Hotel.

Dreary, dreary day.

31 January

Em and I to Droitwich. Mr. and Mrs. Hobson and Cyril H. to lunch at the Raven, E. and I run out to see our friends at Stoke Works. Men and women crying like babies.

We leave for town by the 2 something train. Affecting scene at the Station. Bouquets for E. and Daff. Everybody crying.

1 February
28 Montagu Square.

To Peter Pan with Daff, Bud and Gol.

2 February

Dinner with the Carr-Gomms and afterwards to theatre.

Harmsworth spent the period from 5 to 25 February on a winter sports holiday in St Moritz, after a brief stop-over in Paris. In Paris on 6 February he dined with 'Mr Lane ("Norman Angell", editor Paris Daily Mail').[15]

25 February

Arrive home from St. Moritz.

27 February

First symptom of influenza.
[...]
[This was the first day of my mysterious illness that lasted, with deceptive intervals, right into the Autumn. I don't think that the doctors, not even Dr. Dawson[16] [Afterwards, Lord Dawson of Penn], ever knew exactly what it was. A specially complicated kind of influenza, perhaps, is the likeliest explanation.
C.H. 28 X 1924]
Harmsworth was ill with 'influenza' for some considerable time, and most of the entries for the period to mid May 1910 are short ones relating to his continuing illness.

16 May

Influenza. My first real outing. Drive with E. and Bud to Hampstead to sit for half an hour or so in Hildebrand's lovely garden.[17] Heath swarming with Bank Holiday people. Perfect summer day.

[15]Ralph Norman Angell Lane, usually known as Norman Angell (1872–1967): journalist in USA and Paris; Paris editor of the *Daily Mail* 1905–1912; Lab. MP Bradford North 1929–1931; awarded Nobel Peace Prize 1933.
[16]Bertrand Edward Dawson (1864–1945): Physician Extraordinary to King Edward VII 1907–1910; Physician-in-Ordinary to King George V 1910–1936; cr. 1st Viscount Dawson of Penn 1936.
[17]Hildebrand Aubrey Harmsworth (1872–1929): the fifth of the Harmsworth brothers; Liberal Imperialist candidate for Gravesend 1900; Unionist candidate for Shropshire (Wellington Division) 1906; cr. baronet 1922; co-editor, with CBH, of the short-lived *New Liberal Review*.

20 May

Funeral of King Edward.[18] Perfectly lovely day. We had a splendid view of the Procession from a window (taken by Harold) opposite Brooks's Club. Daff and Bud with us. I suppose that no greater spectacle has ever before been seen in London or ever will be seen again.

26 May
Boulogne. Hotel Christol & Bristol.

St. J. and I leave Charing Cross for Boulogne. Meet Mother[19] and Alfred [Northcliffe] at the oddly-named Hotel at Boulogne. Alfred apparently a good deal better after his long rest at St. Raphael. With him Dr. Price[20] and Pyne[21] with the 115 H.P. Mercedes car.

It was at this Hotel that Alfred concluded negotiations for the purchase of *The Times*.[22]

Harmsworth spent the next three and a half weeks in and around Paris, returning to London on 21 June. On 18 June he dined again with Lane/Angell.

23 June
28 Montagu Square

In the morning to the Treasury, 12 Downing Street, to see the Master of Elibank,[23] Chief Liberal Whip, about a seat. He and I walk through St. James's Park, the Green Park and Hyde Park discussing the matter. He practically offers me Dumbartonshire from which Dundas White is retiring.[24] He tells me that Harold [Rothermere] is down in tomorrow's Honours List for a baronetcy.

---

[18] King Edward VII (1841–1910): reigned 1901–1910.
[19] Geraldine Mary Harmsworth, née Maffet (1838–1925).
[20] Probably Henry Gilbert Price (d. 1958 at age 78): principal private secretary to Northcliffe from 1909; OBE 1918. He was not, however, a doctor.
[21] Probably Northcliffe's chauffeur, and perhaps a misspelling; a man named Payne had previously raced a Northcliffe-owned Mercedes at Brooklands.
[22] In 1908.
[23] Alexander William Charles Oliphant Murray (1870–1920): styled The Master of Elibank 1871–1912; Lib. MP Midlothian 1900–1906, 1910–1912, Peebles and Selkirk 1906–1910; Comptroller of the Household 1905–1909; Under-Secretary of State for India 1909–1910; Parliamentary Secretary to the Treasury (Chief Whip) 1910–1912; resigned due to Marconi Scandal 1912; cr. Baron Murray of Elibank 1912.
[24] James Dundas White (1866–1951): Lib. MP Dunbartonshire 1906–1910, Glasgow Tradeston 1911–1918.

(In the afternoon I go out to Poynters[25] to see Mother.)
Dinner with Cecil Beck at the Reform. Also present:
Sir West Ridgeway,[26] Sir E. Tennant,[27] Hon. E.S. Montagu, MP, C.P.
Trevelyan, MP,[28] Col. Seely, MP,[29] H.H. Raphael, MP,[30] etc., etc.

28 June
Montagu Square

I see Dr. May[31] and Dr. Bertrand Dawson in the morning. Both a little surprised that I should still have symptoms of rheumatic stiffness, etc. They say it will be long before I am fully restored.
I write to Elibank definitely declining Dumbartonshire.
A dull sad day with rain.

29 June
28 Montagu Square.

With us to dine this evening J.H. Bernard, Dean of St. Patrick's.[32] He was my Tutor at Trinity College, Dublin, until he became Archbishop's King's Lecturer in Divinity. Afterwards Dean of St. Patrick's. Would be Archbishop of Armagh or Dublin at the next vacancy if he were a Low Churchman. One of the very best. We discussed the representation of

[25] Poynters Hall, Totteridge, Hertfordshire, the residence of Geraldine Harmsworth; Cecil Harmsworth commissioned some etchings of it by S.M. Litten in 1926.
[26] Colonel Sir Joseph West Ridgeway (1844–1930): civil servant and colonial governor; Governor of Ceylon 1896–1903; unsuccessful Lib. parliamentary candidate 1906, 1910; became President of North Borneo Company, 1910.
[27] Edward Priaul Tennant (1859–1920): Lib. MP Salisbury 1906–1910; succ. as 2nd baronet 1906; cr. Baron Glenconner 1911.
[28] Charles Philips Trevelyan (1870–1958): Lib. MP Elland 1899–1918; Lab. MP Newcastle Central 1922–1931; Parliamentary Secretary to Board of Education 1908–1914; President of Board of Education 1924, 1929–1931; succ. as 3rd baronet 1928.
[29] John Edward Bernard Seely (1868–1947): Con. MP Isle of Wight 1900–1904; Lib. MP Isle of Wight 1904–1906, Liverpool Abercromby 1906–1910, Ilkeston 1910–1922, Isle of Wight 1923–1924; Secretary of State for War 1912–1914; cr. Baron Mottistone 1933.
[30] Herbert Henry Raphael (1859–1924): Lib. MP South Derbyshire 1906–1918; cr. baronet 1911. He shared Harmsworth's interest in town planning.
[31] Gould May (1863–1944), MRCP: consulting gynaecologist to the Grosvenor Hospital for Women; knighted 1923. Together with Thomas Horder, he signed the bulletin announcing the death of Andrew Bonar Law in 1923.
[32] John Henry Bernard (1860–1927): Archbishop King's Lecturer in Divinity at TCD 1889–1911; Dean of St Patrick's Cathedral, Dublin 1902–1911; Bishop of Ossory, Ferns and Leighlin 1911–1915; Church of Ireland Archbishop of Dublin 1915–1919; m. Maude Nannie Bernard (d. 1940) 1885.

T.C.D. in Parliament – sagely agreeing that, as an obdurate Liberal, I should have no chance of election if I presented myself.

9 June
Henley.

I go up to town to take the Chair at the 16th Annual Dinner of the Amalgamated Press, Holborn Restaurant. Most enthusiastic gathering. I return by the 12.15 A.M. train to Henley.

13 July
Highcliffe Castle

I leave for Highcliffe in the morning. Lovely day. House-party including Sir Walter Lawrence,[33] Sir Francis Trippel,[34] Mr. Arnold White,[35] the eminent authority on naval and Imperial affairs, Mr. Grahame-White,[36] the aeroplanist, Mr. Dudgeon,[37] Capt. Cole,[38] Mr. and Mrs. Bartholomew[39] and Hugh Spottiswoode.[40]

Bournemouth is holding high revel with its centenary fetes the leading feature of which is the aeroplane meeting. Bunting everywhere, great crowds in the streets and on the sands and Sir Thomas Lipton's[41] steam yacht 'Erin' anchored off the pier. We visit Sir T.L. on board after lunch. He shows us all his splendid racing trophies and souvenirs from crowned heads, and expatiates in his usual genial way on the illustrious visitors he has entertained from time to time on the 'Erin'.

---

[33] Walter Roper Lawrence (1857–1940): Indian civil servant 1879–1903; cr. 1st baronet 1906.

[34] Major Henry Francis Trippel (d. 1930 at age 64): promoter of the Union Jack Club, a London institution for servicemen; knighted 1909.

[35] Arnold Henry White (1848–1925): journalist and publicist, author of *Efficiency and Empire* (London: Methuen, 1901); served on executive of Navy League; a controversial figure of the Edwardian radical right.

[36] Claude Grahame-White (1879–1959): pioneering aviator, first to fly at night (during *Daily Mail*-sponsored London–Manchester air race); established flying school and Grahame-White Aviation Group 1911.

[37] Unidentified.

[38] Unidentified.

[39] Unidentified.

[40] William Hugh Spottiswoode (1864–1915): director and manager of the printers and publishers Eyre & Spottiswoode.

[41] Thomas Johnstone Lipton (1848–1931): tea merchant; enthusiastic sailor, competed in America's Cup five times 1899–1930.

A most luxurious yacht with bedrooms, boudoirs and saloons of the greatest comfort. We arrive at the aerodrome in time to see Morane on his Bleriot monoplane soaring upwards in competition for the 'greatest altitude' prize. A superb flight. Grahame-White comes out in the evening in his biplane and takes single passengers. He had taken Mr. Arnold White in the morning and Capt. Cole flies two laps with him in the evening. At one time three flying-machines are in the air together. – All the aviators, I think, a little oppressed by the death of the Hon. C.S. Rolls[42] on the same ground the previous day. I had met him once or twice – a fine, eager, bright young fellow.

14 July

A lovely warm morning followed in the afternoon by a creeping sea-mist. After lunch we go to the Aerodrome at Bournemouth. Some splendid flights. The day closes gloomily with a bad accident to Rawlinson[43] at the far end of the ground. Suddenly there is a great cloud of dust and many mounted policemen hurrying in that direction. Rawlinson reported diversely to be slightly and very seriously hurt. We saw nothing of the accident but the dust.

15 July

Splendid flight of Morane[44] and Drexel[45] from the Aerodrome at Boscombe round the Needles and back. We witnessed it – or as much of it as the sea-mist will permit – from the cliff at Highcliffe. Sir T. Lipton's 'Erin' and other boats patrolling the line of flight across the sea.

Grahame-White tells us that he has received two communications from clairvoyants urging him to fly no more this week. Young Alan Boyle,[46] son of Lord Glasgow, and one of the aviators, lunches at

---

[42] Charles Stewart Rolls (1877–1910): motoring and aviation pioneer; co-founder of Rolls-Royce car company; first Briton to be killed in a flying accident, July 1910.

[43] Alfred Rawlinson (1867–1934): soldier; motoring and aviation pioneer; succ. as 3rd baronet 1925.

[44] Léon Morane (1885–1918): French aviation pioneer.

[45] John Armstrong Drexel (1891–1958): American aviation pioneer; co-founder of East Boldre Flying Club (2nd in Britain and 5th in world); set new world altitude record of 6,750 feet, 12 August 1910.

[46] Alan Reginald Boyle (1886–1958): youngest son of 7th Earl of Glasgow; founder of Scottish Aeroplane Syndicate 1909; producer of first British-built monoplane, the Avis.

Highcliffe today. He seems a little oppressed by the accidents to Rolls and Rawlinson and says that if he had witnessed the latter catastrophe he would give up aviation at once. By the way, Rawlinson reported today to be not very seriously injured.

**4 August
Montagu Square**

Swedish massage at 10 o'clock as usual. At 11.30 with Dr Gould May to see Dr. Bertrand Dawson in Wimpole Street to get what will prove, I hope, to be his final opinion on my case. He thinks me much better and prescribes very tolerable course for me – 3 weeks at Cromer, 3 weeks at Harrogate, and October fishing in Scotland.

In the afternoon we go with Con Baker[47] to Mr. Kinderman's old curiosity shop at 26 Golden Square. A most interesting Collection and we buy a few small things.

**27 August
Droitwich.**

Our last public appearance in Mid-Worcestershire, – a day long anticipated with anxiety and genuine regret. E. and I, Daff, Bud and Gol and Mrs. Parkes (nurse)[48] by the midday train to Droitwich. After lunch to Westwood House (lent by Mr. Partington)[49] to await the arrival of Lord and Lady Beauchamp. Streams of our good political friends and waggonettes full of them making for Westwood Park. Mr. Ward, Mr. Partington's son-in-law,[50] receives us in the beautiful Jacobean drawing-room which with its finely carved panelling and ceiling with stuccoed fruit and flowers is the most perfect apartment, I think, I know of. Mr. Ward though a strong Tory is always very friendly. Lord and Lady B. arrive in good time – his lordship a few

---

[47] Constance Mary Baker (c.1875–?1935): family friend.
[48] Elizabeth Parkes (b. c.1844).
[49] Oswald Partington (1872–1935): Lib. MP High Peak 1900–1910, Shipley 1915–1918; Progressive LCC Alderman 1913–1920; succ. as 2nd Baron Doverdale 1925. Westwood (just outside Droitwich) was his country seat.
[50] Robert Bruce Ward (c.1869–1943) married Lillie Partington (c.1867–1951), Oswald's sister, and so was in fact his brother-in-law.

more inches round the waist than when last saw him, Lady B. sweet and gracious as ever. We walk across the park to the place where marquees and a band-stand have been erected. Splendid and touching welcome from our friends. Fifteen hundred only were expected but nearly 3000, it is said, are present. Lord B. makes the presentation to me of the handsome silver tea-tray (with inscription) and tea and coffee service, and Lady B. presents the Worcester china tea and coffee service to E. and the gold watches to Daff, Bud and Gol. There is also a most tasteful illuminated address in book form for me. Speeches by Mr. G.W. Hobson of Droitwich, Lord B., Sir Thomas Barclay (President Midland Liberal Federation),[51] John Morgan, E., Daff and, of course, myself. E. almost petrified with emotion and nervousness. Many sympathetic tears from the women.

I find it more difficult to say what I have to say than ever before. These people have always treated us with the greatest generosity. Daff's little speech (prepared for her by me) is a great success.

We return for the night to the Raven Hotel relieved that the painful function is over and very sad at parting with our friends.

On 9 September Harmsworth travelled to the spa town of Harrogate to undertake a course of treatment.

15 September
Harrogate

In the afternoon we all go to York. Lunch and tea at Terry's. The Minster is easily among the three or four finest buildings I have ever seen. I was greatly interested to see so much ancient glass. We also visited the old Merchants' Hall – a place of historic interest maintained in a depressing state of squalor. With all its picturesqueness and its well-nigh incomparable Minster York is not a cheerful place. I could not help thinking all the time of Seebohm Rowntree's[52] scientific calculation that one-third of the population live on the 'hunger line'. There are dismal courts running out of important streets and there is,

---

[51] Thomas Barclay (1853–1941): Lib. MP Blackburn Jan.–Dec. 1910; authority on economics and international law; knighted 1904.
[52] Benjamin Seebohm Rowntree (1871–1954): businessman and social investigator, author of numerous books including *Poverty: A Study of Town Life* (London: Macmillan, 1901).

obviously to the naked eye, a stratum of the population extraordinarily low in civilisation and character.

8 October
Dublin.

Delightful morning in Trinity College. – The Chapel, the Dining Hall, the Kitchen and the Library. Such old memories revived! It is a noble place, if the atmosphere is a little cold.

After lunch to call on the Swift MacNeill's[53] at 17 Pembroke Road. S. MacN. is Nationalist Member for Donegal and as good-hearted, hot-tempered a Celt as ever lived. He is a cousin of E.'s and they are in the same relation to Dean Swift's[54] family. He has many fine relics of Swift – a replica of the Bindon portrait [now in my possession. C.H. 20 VII 1927] of which examples are in the Deanery of St. Patrick's and at Howth Castle. He has also a fine miniature of Swift – the one, he says, that Stella[55] used to wear. Also a silver snuff-box of Swift's in the shape of a three-cornered hat. There is a further-portrait of Swift in his old age – a copy by Pratt Swift of his original which is at Swift's Heath. A less desirable curiosity of Swift MacN.'s is a round early-Victorian settee in red plush that was made by John Walsh,[56] Master of the Rolls, (his and E.'s cousin) when a briefless barrister.

1 November
[London]

To see R.C. Hawkin,[57] Secretary of the 80 Club, and to discuss the political situation with him.

---

[53] John Gordon Swift MacNeill (1849–1926): Protestant Irish Nat. MP South Donegal 1887–1918; lawyer, QC 1893; became Professor in Law at National University of Ireland 1909.

[54] The author Jonathan Swift (1667–1745): Dean of St Patrick's Cathedral, Dublin 1713–1745.

[55] Esther Johnson (1681–1728): a close friend of Swift.

[56] John Edward Walsh (1816–1869): Attorney General for Ireland 1866; Master of the Rolls in Ireland 1866–1869.

[57] Robert Crawford Hawkin (1872–1939): called to the Bar 1904; an expert on international law.

8 November

Eighty Club[58] Smoking At Home at the Criterion Restaurant, and discussion on 'Federal Home Rule'.

On 10 November The Times reported that Harmsworth had told the executive committee of the Mid-Worcestershire Liberal association that he had 'definitely given up all intention' of being their candidate again, adding that Harmsworth's 'severe illness' in the spring had left him 'unable to undertake the fatigue of a contested election in such a scattered constituency'.

11 November

Em and I dine at the Charles Henry's[59] in Carlton Gardens. Present Mr. and Mrs. Lloyd-George,[60] Mr. S.O. Buckmaster, Sir T. Lipton, Mr. and Mrs. Donald Maclean,[61] Mr. and Mrs. Ellis Griffith,[62] Sir J.D. and Lady Rees and others. Lloyd-George announces the break-up this day of the Conference (between 4 Liberal and 4 Conservative leaders) to settle, if possible, the question of the Lords' Veto. The talk is all of another, early General Election.

Em says that after dinner at the Henry's the ladies, excepting herself, rose to their feet when Lloyd-George engaged them in conversation. I happened not to notice it myself but is this in any case a precedent? I have read somewhere that when Disraeli[63] was at the zenith of his power and reputation duchesses rose from their chairs when he entered a room! Ll.-G. certainly does not shine brilliantly in private society.

He is insignificant in appearance and undistinguished in conversation. I have never heard him make a remark or use a phrase

---

[58] A Liberal-aligned club founded in 1880.

[59] Charles Solomon Henry (1860–1919): Australian merchant; Lib. MP Wellington 1906–1918; Coalition Lib. (Co. Lib.) MP The Wrekin 1918–1919; cr. baronet 1911; m. 1892 Julia Lewisohn (d. 1927), American heiress. Close friends of Lloyd George.

[60] Margaret Lloyd George, née Owen (1866–1941): m. 1888; cr. Dame 1920.

[61] Donald Charles Hugh Maclean (1864–1932): Lib. MP Bath 1906–1910, Peebles and Selkirk 1910–1918, Peebles and South Midlothian 1918–1922, Cornwall North 1929–1932; acting leader of Liberal party in Parliament 1918–1920; President of the Board of Education 1931–1932; m. 1907 Gwendolen Margaret Devitt (1880–1962).

[62] Ellis Jones Ellis-Griffith (1860–1926): Lib. (then Co. Lib.) MP Anglesey 1895–1918; Carmarthen 1923–1924; Under-Secretary of State, Home Department 1914–1915; m. 1892 Mary Owen (c.1864–1941).

[63] Benjamin Disraeli (1804–1881): Conservative Prime Minister 1868, 1874–1880; cr. Earl of Beaconsfield 1876.

[in private conversation] worth recording. He has in full measure the vivacity of the Welsh Celt but gives no sign of the qualities that have made him a foremost debater in the H. of C. and a really splendid speaker on the platform.

12 November

H.S.H. [Rothermere] to lunch with us and to discuss the political situation.

16 November

With H.D. Harben[64] to the Whips' Office 12 Downing Street. A scene of bustle and excitement with many prospective Liberal Candidates attending on the Junior Lords of the Treasury.

With E. to the marriage of Hamar Greenwood's[65] sister Florence[66] to L.S. Amery,[67] Editor of the *Times* History of the Boer War. At St. Margaret's, Westminster.

28 November

To town with Em, and in the afternoon to Droitwich to preside at meeting in the Salter's Hall in favour of Dr. Clifford Brookes[68] the new

---

[64]Henry Devenish Harben (1874–1967): Con. candidate for Suffolk North-East 1900; Lib. candidate for Worcester 1906 and for Portsmouth December 1910; a wealthy funder of progressive causes, including the suffragettes, the *Daily Herald* and the *New Statesman*.
[65]Hamar Greenwood (1870–1948): Lib. MP York 1906–Jan. 1910; Lib/Co. Lib. Sunderland Dec. 1910–1922; Constitutionalist/Con. Walthamstow East 1924–1929; Under-Secretary of State, Home Department 1919; Secretary for Overseas Trade 1919–1920; Chief Secretary for Ireland 1920–1922; cr. baronet 1915, Baron 1929, Viscount 1937.
[66]Adeliza Florence Louise Hamar Greenwood (1885–1975).
[67]Leopold Charles Maurice Stennett Amery (1873–1955): Lib. Unionist/Con. MP Birmingham South 1911–1918, Birmingham Sparkbrook 1918–1945; Under-Secretary of State for the Colonies 1919–1921; First Lord of the Admiralty 1922–1924; Secretary of State for the Colonies 1924–1929, and Dominion Affairs 1925–1929; Secretary of State for India 1940–1945.
[68]Clifford Brookes, Lib. candidate for Droitwich December 1910.

Liberal candidate. Dr. Brookes unfortunately detained in town by the sudden and serious illness of his wife.

3 December

Speech for Mr. Spokes[69] Liberal candidate for W. Marylebone in the Portman Rooms. Midday to Henley to superintend planting of roses. Everything very dreary.

5 December

In the evening: I take chair for Mr. E.A. Strauss,[70] Liberal candidate for W. Southwark at the Lavington Street Baths. Great and enthusiastic gathering. Speech by Winston Churchill who had a tremendous reception. The boy Statesman not so fine as usual.

6 December

Out to Henley to vote for George Nicholson.[71] Find that the Poll is on the 13th! Lunch at the Red Lion. [...]

Sunderland goes Liberal and Labour – Hamar Greenwood the Liberal candidate. Sunderland and Stafford were both offered me when I as ill, and have been true to Liberalism.

To Rotherhithe at night to hear the result. Hubert C[arr]-G[omm] returned by an increased majority. Great enthusiasm.

---

[69] A.H. Spokes (1854–1922): Recorder of Reading; Lib. candidate for Marylebone Dec. 1910.

[70] Edward Anthony Strauss (1862–1939): Lib. MP for the Abingdon division of Berkshire 1906–January 1910, Southwark West Dec. 1910–1918; Co. Lib. MP for Southwark North 1918–23; Lib. MP for Southwark North 1927–1929; and served again as a Liberal National 1931–1939.

[71] George Crosfield Norris Nicholson (1884–1916); the only son of Charles Nicholson; Lib. candidate for Henley December 1910; served in the RFC during the First World War and attained the rank of Captain; killed in a flying accident in England.

7 December

To Stourbridge by the 4.45 from Paddington to address a meeting in the Town hall for Dr. Brookes. At the Paddington booking office I meet Lord Beauchamp who explains that at the last moment and at the urgent request of the Chief Whip he is going down to Stourbridge on a like errand. He has stipulated that he is to have a special train to Stourbridge and back again at the expense of the Whips' Office, and he invites me to share it with him. Lord B. as First Commissioner of Works brings with him a beautiful new dispatch box in sealing-wax red. It appears to contain little else than Liberal Publication Dept.'s booklets and other raw material for political orations.

We are splendidly received in the packed Town Hall and I am given a great and most affecting ovation by my old friends. In less than an hour and a half we are out of the town again and journeying Londonwards in our special train. An ample hot dinner put on board for us at Worcester, and so to Paddington without another stop. Home at 12 o'clock. I suppose that few meetings during the Election have cost so much.

9 December

Result in Mid-Worcestershire:-
   Hon. J.C. Lyttelton   4880
   Dr. Clifford Brookes   4808
                             72

10 December

Fifty-third Annual Dinner of the Savage Club[72] at the Hotel Cecil, Sir George Reid,[73] High Commissioner for Australia, in the Chair. I attend as guest of Mr. E.W. Roper[74] and in obedience to an urgent invitation of the Committee two days ago I propose the toast of the 'Savage Club coupled with the name of Sir G. Reid'. A brilliant assembly

---

[72] A 'gentleman's club' formed in 1857.
[73] George Houston Reid (1845–1918): Australian politician, premier of New South Wales 1894–1899; Prime Minister of Australia 1904–1905; Australian High Commissioner to the UK 1910–1916; Con. MP for St George, Hanover Square [Westminster St George's] 1916–1918.
[74] Probably E.W. Roper of Christchurch, New Zealand; President of the New Zealand Naval League in 1908; involved in the English Speaking Union after 1918.

including General French[75] and Field Marshal Lord Grenfell.[76] We adjourn afterwards to the Club house in the Adelphi.

13 December

Again to Henley to vote for young George Nicholson. Depressing array of Tory blue everywhere. [...] E.'s birthday. We dine snugly together, using the old china-handled knives and forks, best dessert service and dinner service and the tall wine-glasses. Afterwards, a good evening's work addressing Christmas cards.

15 December

Take chair at meeting of the Amalgamated Press Ltd. Profits for the year £259, 590. 15. 1d. Dividend for the year 40%.

Afterwards to Mr Bruce-Joy's[77] Studio, W. Kensington, to see his huge statue of Lord Kelvin[78] for Belfast. I sat next Lord K. at a public dinner for a whole evening once – a sweet-mannered modest old man. Statue very like.

---

[75] John Denton Pickstone French (1852–1925): General 1907, Field Marshal 1913; Inspector-General of Army 1907–1912; Chief of Imperial General Staff 1912–1914; Commander of the British Expeditionary Force 1914–1915; Lord Lieutenant of Ireland 1918–1921; cr. Viscount French 1916, Earl of Ypres 1922.

[76] Francis Wallace Grenfell (1841–1925): General 1904, Field Marshal 1908; retired 1908; cr. Baron 1902.

[77] Albert Bruce-Joy (1842–1924): sculptor, whose works included the sculpture of John Bright in Albert Square, Manchester.

[78] William Thomson (1824–1907): Belfast-born mathematician and physicist; Fellow of Royal Society (FRS) 1851, President 1890–1895; cr. Baron Kelvin 1892.

1911

2 January
Brighton.

In the early afternoon I take E. to see Dr. Johnson's house[1] – not very willingly because I have not wished her to form the worst impression of my intended purchase. Mr. Burr,[2] agent for the Calthorpe estates, goes with us. Happily some attempt has been made by the care-taker to clean up the windows and sweep the house down a bit and it looks a little less dreary than when I saw it some weeks since.

8 January

Back to Montagu Square – my companion in the railway carriage being John Lyttelton [afterwards Lord Cobham], my former opponent in Mid-Worcestershire and the present Member. We get on together famously as usual.

16 January

To Totteridge walking from Child's Hill. St. J. much better and we go out for a run to Damson Hall. [. . .] Alfred (Northcliffe) to stay night. Very full of his improvements to *The Times*.

3 February

Back to town. Whitefriars Club dinner in the evening with Hubert Carr-Gomm. Sir Robert Hudson[3] in the chair – Sir Courtenay

---

[1] See the introduction to this volume.
[2] Alfred Burr (1855–1952): architect; took charge of the restoration of Dr Johnson's house.
[3] Robert Arundell Hudson (1864–1927): secretary of Liberal Central Association and National Liberal Federation 1893–1927; married Northcliffe's widow, Mary Elizabeth Harmsworth, 1923.

Ilbert,[4] Clerk of the H. of Commons, as chief guest. Other guests include Mr. Erskine,[5] the Serjeant-at-Arms and Mr. Vaughan Nash[6] the Prime Minister's principal private secretary. Admirable discursive speech by Sir C. Ilbert on 'How Parliaments Differ'. Mr. Erskine told a very effective story of the most exciting, incident he had ever witnessed in the House – the appearance of a black beetle at the Bar of the House, its attempts to find shelter first on the Govt. and then on the Opposition side and its ultimate annihilation by a short-sighted Irish member who planted his flat foot on it amidst a storm of laughter from all members. Mr. Erskine's story made all the stronger impression because we all thought he was going to refer to the occasion when, in the course of the Home Rule debates of —, there was a free fight on the floor of the House and several Irish Members wore carried out by the police.

4 February

At night to Mrs. Asquith's[7] reception at 10 Downing Street. The Liberal Party in its glory and in high spirits. I meet Sir Samuel Evans, President of the Divorce Court, and remind him that he owes me £2. Late in the Session of 1909 he bet me 2 to £10. the Lords would *not* throw out the Lloyd-George Budget [Sam never paid me]. For the purposes of this reception the Prime Minister's House, that of the Ch. of the Excheqr. and the Whips office are thrown into one. Many long passages and a considerable segregation of people into groups but the general effect excellent.

---

[4] Courtenay Ilbert (1841–1924): Clerk of House of Commons, 1902–1921.

[5] Henry David Erskine (1838–1921): Serjeant-at-Arms of the House of Commons 1885–1915.

[6] Vaughan Robinson Nash (1861–1932): journalist; an assistant private secretary to Prime Ministers Campbell-Bannerman and Asquith 1905–1908; principal private secretary to Asquith 1908–1912; commissioner then vice-chairman of the Development Commission 1912–1915, 1919–1929; worked on reconstruction 1915–1919.

[7] Emma Alice Margaret 'Margot' Asquith, née Tennant (1864–1945): m. 1894 (Asquith's second wife).

21 February

Larry[8] and I to town. In the afternoon I see Mr. Culpin[9] [E.G. Culpin, afterwards Alderman and Vice Chairman of the L.C.C.] Secretary of the Garden Cities Assn. of which body I have been chosen Chairman of the Council.

3 March

Dine with F.W. Maude[10] at Cadogan Gardens to meet Mr. Haldane[11] Secretary for War. Quite a revival of old Liberal League times. Also present Lord Willingdon,[12] Neil Primrose,[13] Cecil Beck, Sir C.D. Rose,[14] Sir Robt. Perks,[15] Sir Clifford Cory,[16] Sir West Ridgeway, Lord Justice Fletcher Moulton.[17]

5 March

Golf at Ranelagh with Alfred [Northcliffe]. He has played only a short time but in his second round were 10 fives. After many vicissitudes I ended the same round with 4 fours.

[8]The nickname of Henry Telford Maffett (1872–1914): twelfth of the Maffett children; a captain in the Leinster regiment; killed in action.
[9]Ernest Gladstone Culpin (1877–1946): architect; secretary, Garden Cities Association.
[10]Frederick William Maude (1857–1923): Baron of the Cinque Ports and sometime Mayor of New Romsey.
[11]Richard Burdon Haldane (1856–1928): Lib. MP Haddingtonshire 1885–1911; Secretary of State for War 1905–1912; Lord Chancellor 1912–1915, 1924; leader of Labour party in House of Lords 1924–1928; cr. Viscount 1912.
[12]Freeman Freeman-Thomas (1866–1941): Lib. MP Hastings 1900–1906, Bodmin 1906–1910; Governor of Bombay 1913–1918, Madras 1919–1924; Governor-General of Canada 1926–1930; Viceroy of India 1931–1936; cr. Baron Willingdon 1910, Viscount 1924, Earl 1931.
[13]Neil James Archibald Primrose (1882–1917): son of Lord Rosebery (Lib. Prime Minister 1894–1895); Lib. MP Wisbech 1910–1917 (Co. Lib. 1916–1917); Under-Secretary of State for Foreign Affairs 1915; Joint Parliamentary Secretary to the Treasury (Chief Whip) 1916–1917; died of wounds received in action 1917.
[14]Charles Day Rose (1847–1913): Lib. MP Cambridgeshire East 1903–1913; cr. baronet 1909.
[15]Robert William Perks (1849–1934): Lib. MP Louth 1892–1910; businessman; leading lay Wesleyan Methodist, and co-founder and chairman of the Nonconformist Parliamentary Council, 1898–1908.
[16]Clifford John Cory (1859–1941): Lib. MP St Ives 1906–1922 (Co. Lib. 1916–1922), 1923–1924; Welsh colliery owner; cr. baronet 1907.
[17]John Fletcher Moulton (1844–1921): Lib. MP Clapham 1885–1886, Hackney South 1894–1895, Launceston 1898–1906; Lord Justice on the Court of Appeal 1906–1912; organised Explosives Supply Department under War Office in Great War; cr. Baron 1912.

6 March

Golf on the Merrow Downs Links with Alfred and lunch afterwards at Sutton Place. He much pleased with his new great room under the long Gallery, and keenly interested in his private links in the park row in process of formation.

13 March

In the morning with Reggie Maffett to Henley to arrange for the sowing of annual seeds, etc. Lunch at the Red Lion. In the evening to the Annual Dinner of the Marylebone Liberal Club, Sir Victor Horsley[18] in the chair. The great surgeon in fine form – a strong Liberal well acquainted evidently with all the political questions of the day. The young lady who responded for the ladies spoke fluently for a few minutes and then broke down saying 'There, you see I can't speak and I told you I couldn't.' This reminded Sir Victor of an Irishman who went to a doctor and complained that he had lost the power of speech 'Sure, doctor dear, I can't speak a word.' DOCTOR: 'Rubbish man, pull yourself together. Pronounce some common word that you are always using. Say 'horse', for instance.' PATIENT: 'Indeed, doctor, but 'horse' is one of the very words I can't say at all.'

15 March

A vile day with driving sleet and rain. Alfred (Northcliffe) turns up nevertheless for a round of golf on the Totteridge links. We are the only enthusiasts who brave the elements today. The heavy clay soil of Totteridge is not suited to winter golf and the recent rains have reduced the links to a quagmire.

[. . .]

I return to town in time for the Executive Committee meeting of the Garden Cities and Town Planning Association. Mr. Ebenezer Howard,[19] the pioneer of the whole movement, present – a simple,

---

[18] Victor Alexander Haden Horsley (1857–1916): physiologist and surgeon; Vice-President, National Temperance League, and President, British Medical Temperance Association; unsuccessful Lib. candidate 1910 and prospective candidate 1911–1914.

[19] Ebenezer Howard (1850–1928): author, *Garden Cities of To-morrow* (London: Swan Sonnnenschein, 1902) [1st edn as: *To-morrow: A Peaceful Path to Real Reform* (London: Swan Sonnnenschein, 1898)]; founder, Garden Cities Association 1899.

fresh-coloured man with the glow of health about him that rightly belongs to an inhabitant of First Garden City.

27 March

Today I conclude the negotiations for the purchase of Numbers 17 and 16 Gough Square at the offices of Messrs. Walters, 9 New Square, Lincoln's Inn, I hand over a cheque for £4,000., sign the contract and receive the keys in the evening.

After dinner with E. and Reggie to Mrs. Scott's[20] reception at her studio in Buckingham Palace Road. Mrs. Scott is wife of Capt. Scott, R.N.,[21] who is at present in the Antarctic. First official news of the expedition since it arrived in the Antarctic came this evening.

28 March

Visit to Dr. Johnson's house with Mr. A.P. Nicholson[22] the very able 'Lobby' representative of *The Times*. We go over the dilapidated old residence with great care, noting every feature of (presumably) contemporary interest. Mr. Nicholson is to publish a detailed account of this transaction in *The Times* on the day following a purely formal announcement (stating that I have bought the house) in the whole of the Press.

2 April
[28 Montagu Square]

CENSUS DAY. Twelve people sleeping here tonight – C.B.H., E.A.H., Daff, Bud, Gol, Con Baker, Reggie Maffett, Mrs. Parkes (nurse),

---

[20] Kathleen Scott, née Bruce (1878–1947): sculptor; m. R.F. Scott 1908; m. secondly the politician Edward Hilton Young 1922; became Baroness Kennet 1935.
[21] Robert Falcon Scott (1868–1912): Royal Navy officer and polar explorer.
[22] Arthur Pole Nicholson (1869–1940): journalist and author; parliamentary correspondent of *The Times* 1908–1913.

1911

Lena Guy (cook),[23] Lister (parlourmaid),[24] Reading (housemaid)[25] and Kate Sumner (kitchenmaid).[26]

11 May

Annual Dinner of the 'T.C.D.' Dining Club at the Grand Hotel, Sir Edward Carson[27] M.P. in the chair. A most enjoyable evening with the renewal of many old acquaintanceships. I propose the toast of the 'Guests', responded to by F.E. Smith K.C. M.P. in a speech of much humour and eloquence. The best speech of his I have heard since his memorable maiden speech in the H. of Commons in 1906.

18 May

Annual Dinner of the Sylvan Debating Club. Lord Robert Cecil[28] chief guest. Also present Harold Cox,[29] Lord Northcliffe, and H.S.H. Lord R.C. makes a speech, well-reasoned and searching, which seemed to justify the claim I have always made for him that, of the coming men on the Tory side in the Parliament of 1906–10, he shared the honours with F.E. Smith.

---

[23] Selina Guy (b. *c.*1871).
[24] Grace Lister (b. *c.*1885).
[25] Daisy Reading (*c.*1886–1926).
[26] Kate Sumner (b. *c.*1892).
[27] Edward Henry Carson (1853–1935): Unionist MP University of Dublin 1892–1918; Belfast Duncairn 1918–1921; Solicitor General for Ireland 1892; Solicitor General for England and Wales 1900–1905; Attorney General for England and Wales 1915; First Lord of the Admiralty 1916–1917; Minister without Portfolio 1917–1919.
[28] Edgar Algernon Robert Gascoyne-Cecil (1864–1958): Con. MP Marylebone East 1906–1910, Hitchin 1911–1923; Under-Secretary of State for Foreign Affairs 1916–1919; Minister of Blockade 1916–1918; Lord Privy Seal 1923–1924; Chancellor of the Duchy of Lancaster 1924–1927; cr. Viscount Cecil of Chelwood 1923; awarded Nobel Peace Prize 1937.
[29] Harold Cox (1859–1936): Lib. MP Preston 1906–1910; economist and ardent free trader; editor, *Edinburgh Review* 1912–1929; author of works such as *Economic Liberty* (London: Longman's, Green & Co., 1920).

19 May
Montagu Square

To see the Master of Elibank at 12 Downing Street about a Seat that is coming vacant in consequence of the election of a Liberal Member (unnamed) to the Peerage.

Afterwards to 38 Berkeley Sq. to call for Lord Rosebery and to take him to see Johnson's house. Lord R. not less unaffected and friendly than I have ever known him. He is not, think, a close student of Johnson nor has he the highest opinion of his literary qualities. 'Irene' in his opinion the worst tragedy ever written – so poor as to verge almost on comedy. The Dictionary probably his most memorable work. He is much pleased with the house, not having expected to find it in such good and *original* condition. [...] On our way home he refers to Harold's giving up Chatham's House at Hampstead. Asks very kindly after St. J. and after my own health. Spoke of his having had influenza when he was 'First Minister' and of the insomnia that crippled him then.

I notice again at Berkeley Square the scores of walking-sticks in the hall, the many tall hats on a side table, and the countless pairs of gloves. The rooms are full of fine pictures, presentation photographs from Kings and Queens, and splendid furniture, but it is a particularly unhomelike home even for a great London house.

20 May

Mr. E.G. Culpin, Secretary Garden City Association, and I to Letchworth. Mr. Ebenezer Howard meets us at the station. A most interesting day with him viewing the whole estate. The great experiment may now be regarded as a triumphant success – about 1200 houses already built; population estimated at nearly 5,000; factories 25, most of them now in the process of enlargement. The central square is, of course, planned and groups of young trees are planted, but there are no municipal or other public buildings. We visit the printing and book-binding establishment of Messrs. Dent and note the cheerful, healthy appearance of the workers. The population of the Garden City would be considerably larger but for the fact that many of the workers come from the surrounding villages which, Mr. Howard says, have been greatly revived by this contact with Letchworth. (Mr. Dent[30] told us he had observed an improvement in

---

[30]Joseph Malaby Dent (1849–1926): publisher, known for the highly successful *Everyman's Library* Series.

21 May

E. and I to Sutton Place to the opening of Alfred's golf course by Mr. Balfour. I suppose that a more original or interesting afternoon party has rarely been given. Among those staying at Sutton Place for the weekend or visiting for the afternoon – Mr. A.J. Balfour, Mr. Gerald Balfour,[31] Mr. Alfred Lyttelton,[32] the Bishop of Pretoria (Dr. Furse),[33] Mr. G.H. Elwes (who sings so sweetly) and Lady Winefride Elwes,[34] Sir Joseph, Lady and various young Leese's,[35] Mr. and Mrs. Colefax,[36] Mr. Garvin,[37] Mrs. Furse (widow of the artist),[38] Mrs. Pennant,[39] Mr. Marlowe[40] (editor of the D. Mail), Mr. and Mrs. St. Loe Strachey,[41] Mr. P.A. Laszlo,[42] the artist, etc., etc. Four aeroplanists, Messrs.

---

[31] Gerald William Balfour (1853–1945): Con. MP Leeds Central 1885–1906; Chief Secretary for Ireland 1895–1900; President of the Board of Trade 1900–1905; President of the Local Government Board 1905; younger brother of A.J. Balfour, whom he succeeded as 2nd Earl of Balfour in 1930.

[32] Alfred Lyttelton (1857–1913): Con. MP Warwick and Leamington 1895–1906; St George Hanover Square 1906–1913; Secretary of State for Colonies 1903–1905.

[33] Michael Bolton Furse (1870–1955): Bishop of Pretoria 1909–1920; Bishop of St Albans 1920–1944.

[34] Gervase Henry Elwes (1866–1921) distinguished English tenor, one of the most popular singers of the day; gave the first performance Vaughan Williams's *On Wenlock Edge* in 1909; m. 1889 Winefride Mary Elizabeth Fielding (1868/9–1959): daughter of the Earl of Denbigh.

[35] Sir Joseph Leese (1845–1914): Lib. MP Accrington 1892–1910, cr. baronet 1908; m. 1867 Mary Constance Hageans (d. 1928).

[36] Henry Arthur Colefax (1866–1936): Con. MP Manchester South-West 1910; lawyer; knighted 1920; m. 1901 Sybil Halsey (1874–1950): later, as Sybil Colefax, became a noted interior designer.

[37] James Louis Garvin (1868–1947): journalist and author; editor, *The Observer* 1908–1942.

[38] Katherine Furse, née Symonds (1875–1952): widow of the painter Charles Wellington Furse (1868–1904), m. 1900; founded the Voluntary Aid Detachment in the Great War; Director of the World Association of Girl Guides and Girl Scouts, 1928–1938.

[39] Possibly Violet Blanche Douglas-Pennant (1869–1945): who briefly served as commandant of the Women's Royal Air Force (WRAF) in 1918 before her controversial dismissal. Harmsworth undertook an official post-war inquiry into the episode. However, Douglas-Pennant was unmarried, and so may not be the 'Mrs. Pennant' mentioned here.

[40] Thomas Henry Marlowe (1868–1935): editor, *Daily Mail*, 1899–1926.

[41] John St Loe Strachey (1860–1927): editor, *The Spectator*, 1887–1925; m. 1887 Henrietta Mary Amy Simpson (1866–1957).

[42] Philip Alexius de Laszlo (1869–1937): Hungarian-born portrait artist, domiciled in London from 1907.

Grahame-White, Snowden Smith,[43] Astley,[44] and Hewitt[45] arrive in biplanes or monoplanes from Hendon and Brooklands. I follow Mr. Balfour and Mr. Lyttelton round the links for some time and help to look for (but not to find) Mr. Balfour's ball when he pulls into the rough. The two statesmen – tall thin figures in loose tweed suits and with large spectacles – playing as well as one might expect considering the state of the course. It seems to be quite true that Mr. Balfour's golf language never goes beyond 'Bother!' and 'Oh, dear!' He tells me that he thinks very well of the possibilities of the course and is surprised to find so much natural sand.

22 May

We dine at the Emile Mond's[46] – afterwards to the Foreign Office reception to meet the Colonial Premiers assembled for the Colonial Conference.

27 May

With Harold [Rothermere] Lil and E. to the Granard's[47] reception in their fine house in Halkin Street. The interior is all new stone which 'comes off' on one's clothes. As I am proceeding up the grand staircase with E. to make my bow to Lord and Lady G. I am plucked by the sleeve and somebody brushes my coat vigorously with his hands. – It is Winston Churchill. I am relieved to find other people's clothes powdered in the same way. A crowded reception – said by *The Times* to be the most brilliant for two seasons. Indian Princes, inexpressibly gorgeous, Colonial Prime Ministers, Ambassadors, Cabinet

---

[43] Richard Talbot Snowden-Smith (1887–1951): lieutenant, aviator; became first officer on the Active List to be awarded a pilot's licence, 15 November 1911.
[44] Henry J Delaval Astley (1888–1912): aviator; died flying a Bleriot in an exhibition flight at Belfast.
[45] Vivian Hewitt (1888–1965): aviator; first person to fly from Holyhead to Dublin, April 1912.
[46] Emile Mond (1865–1938): scientist; member of board of Brunner-Mond, chemical company.
[47] Bernard Arthur William Patrick Hastings Forbes (1874–1948): soldier and Liberal politician; Lord-in-Waiting 1905–1907; Master of the Horse 1907–1915, 1923–1926; succ. as 8th Earl Granard 1889.

Ministers – most people in court dress or uniform, having come on from the King's Birthday dinners.

19 June

Interview with the Master of Elibank (Chief Whip) in regard to the vacancy in South Beds and satisfactory talk with a deputation from Luton in Sir Jesse Herbert's[48] room.

20 June

A hitch in the S. Beds business. Hemmerde[49] intervenes and finds favour with some of the Luton people. Elibank compels him to withdraw. I meanwhile knowing nothing of all this and wandering round the streets looking at the Coronation decorations and the armies of sightseers blocking every thoroughfare. Then a hurried visit to the H. of C, to see Elibank and to find the difficulty smoothed over.

Then an anxious and wearisome meeting trying to get on the telephone to Luton and Droitwich (to ask Mr. Hobson, my late Chairman, to send a message of recommendation to the S. Beds people).

21 June

Adopted, unanimously and enthusiastically, Liberal Candidate for S. Beds at the Liberal Club Luton. Bye-Election owing to Mr. Gair Ashton's[50] elevation to the peerage. Return to town at night.

22 June

Coronation Day. Harold having got me a ticket for the Press Gallery I arrive at the Abbey at about 8 o' clock, leaving Dora and Cuthbert

---

[48]Jesse Herbert (1851–1916): political secretary to the Liberal Chief Whip from 1890s; knighted 1911.
[49]Edward George Hemmerde (1871–1948): Lib. MP East Denbighshire 1906–1910, North-West Norfolk 1912–1918; Lab. MP Crewe 1922–1924.
[50]Thomas Gair Ashton (1855–1933): Lib. MP Hyde 1885–1886, Luton 1895–1911; industrialist; chairman of Cotton Exports Committee in Great War; cr. Baron 1911.

Maffett[51] at the H. of Commons stand in Palace Yard (tickets given us by the Carr-Gomms). By a dark and narrow circular staircase I make my way up to the N. Triforium which proves to be an unexpectedly broad gallery affording many points of view along the N. Transept and the Nave to the W. door. A company of journalists in constant touch with telegraph messenger boys, and Westminster boys with their masters. One or two trim hospital nurses are in charge of a stretcher and 'first-aid' equipment. By standing in my place I get a good view of the H. of Commons gallery just below – occupying the whole of the 'upper floor' of the transept (and the other transept) – the altar with Edward the Confessor's chapel beyond, the old chair (under which is the stone of destiny) and the two chairs of estate ranged in front of the tomb of Anne of Cleves, and the Royal box. The Abbey has undergone a remarkable transformation. The fine old grey pillars and arches remain but the tombs and statues have disappeared under the elaborate staging, and the great Church is seen to be strictly cruciform. The woodwork is covered for the most part in dove grey material. The floor of the theatre (the centre part of the cross) is carpeted in dark blue with a rich Persian carpet under the old Throne and another, much larger, is spread before the altar and up the altar steps. There is a magnificent display of gold vessels and plate on the altar and on the tomb of Anne of Cleves. At first only a few ecclesiastics – bishops, and the Dean and Canons of Westminster, in rich copes – move here and there about the theatre. Gradually ladies in court dress and men in uniform fill up the boxes and stagings. The judges of the High Court are massed in a great box in the archway below my general point of view – the Peers occupy the ground floor under the H. of Commons stagings in the two transepts.

The first event of supreme interest is the procession of the Princesses of the Blood with immense long trains of purple velvet edged with gold and ermine, their coronets borne by officers and their trains carried by ladies. Then there is the procession of the P. of Wales[52] in garter robes and with a great towering plumed hat and a coronet carried by a page. At each royal approach there is a fanfare of trumpets with other music from the Orchestra on the choir screen.

---

[51] Dora Harriett Maffett, née Fenwick (1868–1944): m. 1893 Charles Hamilton Maffett (b. 1866); their son Cuthbert William Maffett (1894–1982). Dora and Cuthbert were visiting from Ireland, and had unveiled a Classical Water Carrier in memorial to her father, Robert Fenwick, at Wandle Park, Croydon, on 14 June 1911.
[52] Edward Albert Christian George Andrew Patrick David, Prince of Wales (1894–1972); reigned briefly as King Edward VIII (1936).

23 June

Meet Mr. Cotchin[53] and other officials at Luton.

24 June

Meet Mr. Cotchin again at Luton to arrange plan of campaign. Go round Leighton Buzzard, Dunstable, Toddington, etc., with him.

26 June
Leighton Buzzard.

Fine meeting.
    We come down to Luton to stay at Mr. Cotchin's house very kindly lent by him:
    Wardenhurst
    Ashburnham Road
    Luton.

28 June

Meetings at: – Chalton Milton Bryant and Toddington.
    ...
    Over Mr. Davis's[54] Diamond works (iron foundry, stoves, ranges, etc.) in the morning with Mr. Inwards.[55]

---

[53] Charles Cotchin (*c.*1856–1923): at different times held various positions in the South Bedfordshire Liberal Association.
[54] The Diamond Foundry, Luton, owned by the David Gas Stove Co. Ltd.
[55] Harry Inwards (*c.*1863–1943): Luton manufacturer and active Liberal; author of *Straw Hats: Their History and Manufacture* (London: Pitman, 1922).

29 June
Luton

Great meeting in the Plant Hall. Speakers F. Kellaway[56] M.P. for Bedford and Milner Gray.[57]

3 July

To Luton by train (via Paddington and St. Pancras). Round the shops and warehouses of Luton with Mr. George Warren.[58] After lunch to Dunstable round the shops with Mr. Inwards.
Meetings: – Houghton Regis and Dunstable.
Speakers: Mr. Milner Gray at both places. Mr. T.W. Dobson[59] ex-M.P. for Plymouth at Dunstable. [He was gifted with one of the finest voices I have heard on the platform – a clarion voice overriding tumultuous mass gatherings and the hubbub of market-place meetings. He was one of the regular speakers for the Liberal Party and was so acceptable and effective at Dunstable that I arranged with headquarters that he should be with me during the bye-election for as many meetings as he could spare. C.H. Oct. 1936.]

5 July

Meeting in Vauxhall Works 1.40. Deputation of chemists 2.15.
Evening meetings: –
Stondon (poor)
Shillington (splendid)
Leagrave (excellent)

---

[56] Frederick George Kellaway (1870–1933): Lib. MP Bedford 1910–1922 (Co. Lib. from 1916); Parliamentary Secretary to Ministry of Munitions 1916–1920; Secretary for Overseas Trade 1920–1921; Postmaster General 1921–1922; later Managing Director of Marconi.

[57] Milner Gray (1871–1943): chairman of Frank Harden Ltd of Luton (ladies' hat makers) and a director of the United Match Industries; subsequently Lib. MP Mid-Bedfordshire 1929–1931; chairman of National Liberal Federation 1934–1936; Chairman of Liberal party 1937–1939.

[58] George Warren (b. c.1849): Straw hat and plait merchant; Mayor of Luton 1897–1899.

[59] Thomas William Dobson (1853–1935): Lib. MP Plymouth 1906–1910.

and look in at Plait Hall mass meeting addressed for 2 hours (!) on Insurance Bill by L.G. Chiozza-Money, M.P.[60] and Mr. Dobson.

6 July
Luton.

12.30 Balmforth's Works.
1.30 Kent's Works.
2.15 photographed by Mr. Cox.[61]
3.0   "   " Mr. Thurston.[62]
8.0 small (very small) meeting at Hyde.
9.30 Show myself at outdoor meeting in front of Corn Exchange, previously addressed by Mr. Dobson and George Nicholls, farmer agricultural-labour candidate and M.P.
10.0. Meeting of workers at Club. Great alarm as to position of small hat-manufacturers under Insurance Bill.

7 July

Daff's birthday.
Luton.
Meeting at Brown's Works 11.55.
    "   " Commercial Cars 1.40.
Gathering of Life Assurance Workers at Liberal Club 2.30.
Evening meetings: –
Eggington 7.0.
Billington 7.30.
Heath (large and interrupted freely by a dozen noisy youths) 8.0.
Hockcliffe (very rowdy, but I secure a decent hearing) 8.0.

14 July
Luton.

Nomination at the Town Hall.
Gas Works 1.55.

---

[60] Leo George Chiozza Money (1870–1944): Lib. MP Paddington North 1906–1910, Northamptonshire East 1910–1918; economist and author.
[61] Probably Joseph Cox: local photographer.
[62] Frederick Thurston (c.1855–1933): photographer and art dealer.

Deputations: –
  Free Church Council 2.30.
  Extreme Suffragists 3.30.
  Doctors 4. 0.
Mass meeting Park Square at 8. Triumphal return to Club.

19 July
Luton.

Final meetings at Leighton Buzzard and Dunstable. Speakers Silvester Horne[63] and Chiozza Money. Splendid enthusiasm.

20 July

Luton. Polling day.
  Blazing day. All round the Constituency in our Vauxhall car gaily decorated with light blue and yellow flags – Daff and Bud with us most of the day.

21 July

Anxious time in the counting room – the Council Chamber of the Town Hall, Luton. At one time (near the five-thousands) Hickman[64] and I were neck and neck and for a moment he had even forged ahead!
Result: –

Harmsworth (L.)	7619
Hickman, J.O. (C.)	7006
	615

Magnificent scene when I emerge on the balcony on the right-hand of the Under-Sheriff.

---

[63] Charles Silvester Horne (1865–1914): Lib. MP Ipswich 1910–1914; Congregationalist Minister, and first serving minister of religion to sit as an MP since Praisegod Barebones.

[64] John Owen Hickman (1870–1949): barrister; brother of the Conservative MP Thomas Edgecumbe Hickman (1859–1930).

1911

Tremendous throng in the Liberal Club and outside. After lunch in the Club triumphal procession accompanied by four other motor-cars round the Constituency.

24 July

Alfred arrives Poynters about 6 A.M. after seeing the airmen go North from Hendon on the £10,000. *Daily Mail* flight. My re-entry into the H. of C. The Master of Elibank and Leicester[65] my sponsors. The House packed in every part and buzzing with excitement. The Prime Minister to move the rejection of the Lords' Amendments to the Veto Bill. Refused a hearing by the Tories! Scene of indescribable uproar during which the P.M. vainly attempted a dozen times to make himself heard. Speaker's appeals absolutely ignored. Mr. Balfour, replying for Opposition, given a polite hearing by Liberal, Labour and Irish parties. After that a stately little speech of rebuke to Tory rowdies from Sir E. Grey.[66] Then F.E. Smith attempted to speak but our people would not listen to him. Eventually Speaker adjourned House under Standing Order 21.

25 July
H. of Commons.

Education and other votes.

Innumerable congratulations from Members, Liberal, Tory, Irish and Labour – including Lloyd George, Winston Churchill, John Redmond, Willie Redmond,[67] Swift McNeill, T.P. O'Connor,[68] Pike

---

[65]Robert Leicester Harmsworth (1870–1937): 4th son of Alfred and Geraldine Harmsworth, younger brother of CBH; Lib. MP Caithness 1900–1918, Caithness and Sutherland 1918–1922.
[66]Edward Grey (1862–1933): Lib. MP Berwick-upon-Tweed 1885–1916; Under-Secretary of State for Foreign Affairs 1892–1895; Foreign Secretary 1905–1916; leader of Liberals in House of Lords 1923–1924; succ. as baronet 1882; cr. Viscount 1916.
[67]William Hoey Kearney Redmond (1861–1929): Irish Nat. MP Wexford Borough 1883–1885, Fermanagh North 1885–1892, Clare East 1892–1917; younger brother of John Redmond.
[68]Thomas Power O'Connor (1848–1929): Irish Nat. MP Galway Borough 1880–1885, Liverpool Scotland 1885–1929; Father of the House at the time of his death.

Pease,[69] Ramsay MacDonald,[70] C.W. Bowerman,[71] Sidney Buxton,[72] John Burns, F.E. Smith, Arthur Lee,[73] Stanley Baldwin,[74] Jerry MacVeagh,[75] Ellis-Griffith, J.P. Boland,[76] Sir W.P. Byles,[77] H.W. Carr-Gomm, W. Clough,[78] S. Collins,[79] Herbert Craig, Sir H. Dalziel,[80] Eustace Fiennes,[81] Hamar Greenwood, G.G. Greenwood,[82] Silvester

[69] Hubert Pike Pease (1867–1949): Lib. Unionist (later Unionist) MP Darlington 1898–1910 and 1910–1923; Assistant Postmaster General 1915–1922; cr. Baron Daryngton 1923.

[70] James Ramsay MacDonald (1866–1937): Lab. MP Leicester 1906–1918, Aberavon 1922–1929, Seaham 1929–1931; Nat. Lab. Seaham 1931–1935, Combined Scottish Universities 1936–1937; Labour party secretary 1900–1912, chairman of parliamentary Labour party 1911–1914; leader of Labour party 1922–1931; Prime Minister and Foreign Secretary 1924; Prime Minister 1929–1935; Lord President of the Council 1935–1937.

[71] Charles William Bowerman (1851–1947): London Society of Compositors general secretary 1892–1906, Parliamentary Secretary 1906–1911; Lab. MP Deptford 1906–1931; Secretary of Trades Union Congress 1911–1923.

[72] Sidney Charles Buxton (1853–1934): Lib. MP Peterborough 1883–1885, Poplar 1886–1914; Under-Secretary of State for the Colonies 1892–1895; Postmaster General 1905–1910; President of the Board of Trade 1910–1914; Governor-General of South Africa 1914–1920; cr. Viscount 1914, Earl 1920.

[73] Arthur Hamilton Lee (1868–1947): Unionist MP Fareham 1900–1918; Civil Lord of the Admiralty 1903–1905; Minister of Agriculture and Fisheries 1919–1921; First Lord of the Admiralty 1921–1922; donated Chequers for use of British prime ministers 1917; cr. Baron 1918, Viscount 1922.

[74] Stanley Baldwin (1867–1947): Unionist/Con. MP Bewdley 1908–1937; joint Financial Secretary to the Treasury 1917–1921; President of the Board of Trade 1921–1922; Chancellor of the Exchequer 1922–1923; leader of Conservative party 1923–1937; Prime Minister 1923–1924, 1924–1929, 1935–1937; Lord President of the Council 1931–1935; Lord Privy Seal 1932–1934.

[75] Jeremiah McVeagh (1870–1932): Irish Nat. MP Down South 1902–1922.

[76] John Pius Boland (1870–1958): Irish Nat. MP Kerry South 1900–1918.

[77] William Pollard Byles (1839–1917): Lib. MP Shipley 1892–1895, Salford North 1906–1917; owner of the *Yorkshire Observer*; knighted 1911.

[78] William Clough (1862–1937): Lib. MP Skipton 1906–1918.

[79] Stephen Collins (d. 1925 at age 77): Lib. MP for Lambeth Kennington 1906–1918; knighted 1913.

[80] James Henry Dalziel (1868–1935): Lib. MP Kirkcaldy Burghs 1892–1921 (Co Lib. from 1916); editor, *Reynolds's News* 1907–1920, and owner 1914–1922; attributed with bringing Northcliffe and Lloyd George together in 1909; organised Lloyd George's purchase of *Daily Chronicle* in 1918, and thereafter its chairman and political director; cr. baronet 1918; Baron 1921.

[81] Eustace Twisleton-Wykeham-Fiennes (1864–1943): Lib. MP Banbury 1906–1910, 1910–1918; PPS to Churchill as First Lord 1912–1914; Governor of Seychelles 1918–1921, of Leeward Islands 1921–1929; cr. baronet 1916.

[82] Granville George Greenwood (1850–1928): Lib. MP Peterborough 1906–1918; knighted 1916.

Horne, Rufus Isaacs,[83] Sir J. Simon,[84] H.L.W. Lawson,[85] P.A. Moltino,[86] A.A.W.H. Ponsonby,[87] C.P. Trevelyan, A.J. Sherwell,[88] and scores of others.

26 July

E. India vote.
Dinner with Mr. and Mrs. Ellis Griffith and John Burns in the Harcourt Room. John full of stories of his early life. – Hampton Court was mentioned and John told us how he was chosen to conduct the late King (Edward VII.) over the old Palace on account of his special knowledge of it. How had he come to be so familiar with the Palace? He had spent his one-day honeymoon there!

27 July

Garden party at the Prime Minister's Downing Street. The pretty old garden gay with a distinguished throng. The P.M. good enough to say he was very glad to see me back.
Foreign Office vote in the House and important statement by the P.M. on German policy in Morocco.

---

[83] Rufus Daniel Isaacs (1860–1935): Lib. MP Reading 1906–1913; Solicitor General 1910; Attorney General 1910–1913; Lord Chief Justice 1913–1921; British Ambassador to USA 1918–1919; Viceroy of India 1921–1925; Foreign Secretary 1931; leader of Liberals in House of Lords 1931–1935; knighted 1910; cr. Baron Reading 1914, Viscount 1916, Earl 1917, Marquess 1926.

[84] John Allsebrook Simon (1873–1954): Lib. MP Walthamstow 1906–1918, Spen Valley 1922–1940 (as Lib. Nat from 1931); Solicitor General 1910–1913; Attorney General 1913–1915; Home Secretary 1915–1916, 1935–1937; leader of Liberal National party 1931–1940; Foreign Secretary 1931–1935; Chancellor of the Exchequer 1937–1940; Lord Chancellor 1940–1945; knighted 1910; cr. Viscount 1940.

[85] Henry Lawson Webster Levy-Lawson (1862–1933): Lib. Unionist MP St Pancras West 1885–1892, Cirencester 1893–1895; Tower Hamlets Mile End 1905–1906, 1910–1916; succ. as Baron Burnham, and inherited the *Daily Telegraph*, on death of father 1916; cr. Viscount 1919; sold *Telegraph* to Berry brothers 1927; served as chairman of numerous important public bodies.

[86] Percy Alport Moltino (1861–1937): Lib. MP Dumfriesshire 1906–1918; shipping magnate and philanthropist born in Cape Colony.

[87] Arthur Augustus William Harry Ponsonby (1871–1946): Lib. MP Stirling Burghs 1908–1918; Lab. MP Sheffield Brightside 1922–1930; Parliamentary Under-Secretary of State for Foreign Affairs 1924; Parliamentary Secretary to the Ministry of Transport 1929–1931; Chancellor of the Duchy of Lancaster 1931; leader of Labour party in House of Lords 1931–1935; cr. Baron 1930.

[88] Arthur Sherwell (1863–1942): Lib. MP Huddersfield 1906–1918.

PARLIAMENTARY LETTER.
MR. HARMSWORTH TAKES HIS SEAT.
TORIES AND THE PRIME MINISTER.
MONDAY'S DISORDERLY SCENES.

The new Member of Parliament must keep within the Bar of the House until he has formally taken his seat. Immediately after questions, the Speaker, standing in his place, says: 'Members desiring to take their seats', and the blushing novice, with the Chief Whip of his party on one side and another member on the other, advances up the floor of the House to the table, to the accompaniment of loud cheers from his own side. The little procession makes a profound bow at the Bar, another half way up the floor, and another at the table; and then the new Member takes the oath, signs the roll, shakes hands with the Speaker, and disappears from view behind the Speaker's chair. My sponsors on Monday were the Master of Elibank, M.P., and my brother, Mr. Leicester Harmsworth, M.P.

The moment I entered the House on Monday I felt conscious that the atmosphere was heavily charged with electricity. The House was packed in every part, and there was a buzz of conversation that drowned the voices of Members who were asking questions and of Ministers who were replying to them. Now and again there were wild disorderly shouts from one side of the House to the other. The excitement reached a high pitch when the Prime Minister came in from behind the Speaker's chair. The Liberal, Labour, and Nationalist Members rose as one man to their feet and cheered him rapturously for some moments. A like ovation was accorded to Mr. Balfour by his own friends when he entered a minute or two later. It required no great experience of the House of Commons to realise that a thunderstorm was brewing. Indeed, with the exception of the occasion when Mr. Ure, the Lord Advocate, made his memorable reply to Mr. Balfour's attacks on November 3rd, 1909, I have never seen the House in so excited a mood.

The order for Monday was the consideration of the Lords' amendments to the Parliament or Veto Bill. The Prime Minister rose from his place on the Treasury Bench, spread out his notes on the brass bound box, and prepared himself to make a statement that had been eagerly anticipated not only by Members of both Houses of Parliament, but by the great world outside. Mr. Asquith was not allowed to make his statement! To the dismay and to the intense indignation of all Members of the House of Commons who are jealous of the good name of the House, the Prime Minister was shouted down by the rowdies on the Tory side. Shouts of 'Traitor!' derisive cheers, and continuous cries of 'Vide' 'Vide' 'Vide' rose from the Opposition benches, and generally such a disgraceful hubbub as has never before, so far as I am aware, affronted the dignity of the First Minister of the Crown. Mr. Asquith kept his temper perfectly and essayed a dozen times to begin his speech. Each fresh attempt on his part led merely to another outburst from the Tories. Mr. Asquith was at the table, I suppose, for the best part of three quarters of an hour, and there was practically no lull in the uproar throughout that time. Conspicuous among the malcontents was Lord Hugh Cecil,[89] whose cries of 'Vide!' were maintained without intermission during the whole period. It is said that a group of the younger and less responsible Tories had resolved to get themselves 'named' by the Speaker, and suspended. That the conduct of the Opposition on this occasion may be properly judged, let it be remembered that they insulted not only the Prime Minister but the Chair as well. Twice or three times Mr. Lowther rose in his place and appealed to them for order. His efforts were wholly unavailing. Mr. Lowther is by all admissions the ablest and most influential Speaker of modern times, but the Tories treated his appeals with complete indifference and disrespect. Meanwhile, it was impossible to form any notion of what Mr. Asquith was saying, and we who were in the House at the time were obliged to turn to the newspapers of Tuesday morning for information. In the end Mr. Asquith rolled up his notes, resumed his seat on the Treasury Bench, and made way for Mr. Balfour.

My friends in South Beds will have noted already that Mr. Balfour was given a perfectly courteous hearing by Liberal, Labour and Nationalist members. Never before have I had so much reason to be proud of my Party. We were angry, too, and passionately indignant at the insult offered to a Chief who commands our affectionate loyalty, but we did not forget our manners nor the respect that is due to the Chair and to the Mother of Parliaments. I think that the sharp contrast between their own conduct and ours went home to the Tories. They expected to be repaid in their own coin. Very likely they hoped to be able to say afterwards that if they had treated our leader badly we had retaliated in kind on theirs. Little by little a look of shame crept over the faces on the other side of the House as Mr. Balfour proceeded with a speech that, rambling and inconsequential as it was, was listened to with polite attention. After Mr. Balfour came Sir Edward Grey, who administered a stately rebuke to the Opposition. Sir Edward occupies a position of almost unequalled authority in the House of Commons. The fact that he is Foreign Secretary keeps him in some degree aloof from many of the more heated controversies of the day. He speaks rarely in the House on matters outside his own department,

---

[89] Hugh Richard Heathcote Gascoyne-Cecil (1869–1956): Unionist/Con. MP Greenwich 1895–1906, Oxford University 1910–1937; author of *Conservatism* (London: Williams and Norgate, 1912); cr. Baron Quickswood 1941.

and never intervenes in ordinary debates without making a profound impression. By the time he had finished his few dignified remarks the temperature of the House had fallen nearly to normal, and the debate, as was intended, might have been adjourned without further incident. Unhappily, however, Mr. F.E. Smith stood up to speak after Sir Edward had resumed his seat, and the storm broke out afresh, Our people were in no mood to listen to Mr. Smith. The methods of controversy, whether in the House or on the platform, adopted by this remarkable young politician, are anything but conciliatory. If he had been allowed to speak there might have been a scene of physical violence on the floor of the House. The blood was up again on both sides.

At this point Mr. Lowther intervened again. By Standing Order 21, the Speaker is empowered to adjourn the House 'without Question put' in circumstances of grave disorder. Mr. Lowther adjourned the House, and, after some noisy recriminations on both sides, we adjourned to the Terrace to cool our fevered brows.

So ended one of the most discreditable episodes in the history of the House of Commons. I fear that I have not conveyed to the minds of my friends in South Bedfordshire any adequate notion of the vulgarity on this occasion of the turbulent section of the Tory party. I have been present at many hostile political meetings, but I have never been treated with the disrespect that was meted out to the Prime Minister on Monday by the Tories in the House of Commons. I am far from saying that every Tory member in the House sympathised with the methods of the more disorderly section. For all I know these methods may have been resented by the quieter members. There was, however, no attempt made on that side to quell the disturbance, and Mr. Balfour, flushed and embarrassed, kept to his seat while the storm raged, uncontrolled, around him.

The Tories know that as regards the Veto Bill their game is up. The Prime Minister has the whip hand of them. This explains their outrageous conduct on Monday. They have been defeated hip and thigh, and must be conscious that, but for their own folly in the past in using the House of Lords for their own party purposes, they need never have met with so humiliating a reverse. They are in reality more angry with themselves and their leaders than they are with us, and their only refuge is in violent abuse and recrimination. But they are going to swallow the leek. Mr. Asquith will 'forcibly feed' them if necessary.

Let me add that my colleagues in the House are delighted with the result in South Beds. They think we have done exceedingly well in difficult circumstances. I tell them that we are not satisfied with 615, and mean to do much better next time.

CECIL HARMSWORTH.
Luton News, July 27th, 1911.

1 August
H. of C.

Short speech on Medical Institutes under Insurance Bill in a thin House at dinner-time. Very well received.

2 August
H. of C.

Insurance Bill in Committee. My amendment accepted.

4 August
H. of C.

Last day of Insurance Bill in Committee before Autumn session, Explanatory statement by Lloyd-George.
To Henley with Babes by 6 o'clock train.

7 August
Henley.

To town in the morning. Balfour's Vote of Censure against the Government on account of advice given by them to H.M. to create Peers, Rejected by 119. Exciting debate. House insufferably warm.

8 August
H. of C.

Lords amendments to Parliament Bill considered and, in the main, rejected. E. and Con Baker to dinner. Hugh Edwards, M.P.,[90] with us.

---

[90] John Hugh Edwards (1868–1945): Lib. MP Mid-Glamorgan 1910–1918, Neath 1918–1922, Accrington 1923–1929.

9 August
H. of C.

Finance Bill. The centre of interest is, however, in the H. of Lords where the Parliament Bill is under discussion. The gilded chamber packed in every part and the atmosphere stifling. I am unlucky enough not to hear any of the important speeches. Alfred comes to me at the Bar and we adjourn to the Terrace. The speculation is all as to whether the rebel Lords (the 'Die Hards') I will succeed in voting down the Parliament Bill in spite of the abstention of the more responsible peers. The Die Hards and our Liberal peers are said to be neck and neck.

10 August

VETO BILL carried in the H. of Lords by 131 votes to 114. Thirty-seven Tory Lords voted with the Government and 15 Bishops.

PAYMENT OF MEMBERS resolution carried in the Commons by 256 to 159. I did not vote although in favour of the principle – my view that the measure should not be carried by resolution but by a Bill and that it should not apply to Members of this Parliament.

17 August

Gloomy day in the H. of C. Rumours and counter rumours all day long as to the negotiations about the labour troubles on the Railways. Late in the afternoon it is reported that all attempts at a settlement have fallen through. The Government have offered the men a Royal Commission and the offer has been flatly refused. Asquith is said to have taken a very high hand with the men. Labour Members very angry with him.

Strike notices issued. Much depends on how far the Non-Union men will co-operate with the Trade Unionists.

18 August

Royal Assent to the Parliament Bill in the H. of Lords. Liberal Members at the Bar and in the side galleries of the Lords raise a hearty cheer. [. . .]

Adjournment of Parliament postponed on account of the railway strike.

19 August

Liberal Demonstration at Bedford to celebrate the passing of the Veto Bill. By road to Bedford with F. Kellaway, MP [Afterwards Postmaster General.] for the Borough. A procession with banners through the streets to the Park where a mass meeting is held. We look in at the Liberal Clubs at Bedford and Luton. Back again by motor-car at night. Most fatiguing day.

22 August
H. of C.

Adjourned meeting of the H. of C. Names of Royal Commissioners to enquire into men's grievances announced. Some silly provocative speeches made by Labour Members and two or three Radicals – another proof afforded that it is not advisable to summon Parliament when delicate negotiations, national or international, are proceeding. Parliament adjourned until October 24th.

13 September

Stone-laying at new Baptist School, High Town, Luton. Ceremony considerably marred by rain.
    In the afternoon to Heath to open new Liberal Institute. Afterwards Liberal Club at Leighton Buzzard. Local Liberals greatly perturbed by revived rumour that I am about to be promoted to the H. of Lords!

15 September

Eighty Club Tour. [This was a tour in Ireland of unofficial Liberals, members of the 80 Club, to study conditions in Ireland, with special reference to Home Rule. Em and I were amused to be taken round many places that were very familiar to us. Some of our co-tourists had not been in Ireland before. C.H. Octr. 1936.]
    Em and I from Euston for Ireland by special express at 8.30 A.M. Reception by Mr. and Mrs. John Redmond at the Gresham Hotel.

16 September
Dublin.

Breakfast at the Royal Albert Farm Glasnevin. Speech by Rt. Hon T.W. Russell,[91] V.P. Board of Agriculture. Lunch 2 o'clock by Capt. Cooper and leading Unionists at Hibernian Hotel. Dinner by National Club of Ireland, Rt. Hon. Michael Cox, M.D.,[92] presiding. I respond to toast of Eighty Club – everybody very complimentary.

17 September
Dublin.

Motor to Col. Sir Nugent Everard's,[93] Randlestown, Navan, to lunch and to see his tobacco Farm. One of the most interesting things in Ireland.

19 September
Belfast.

Grand Central Hotel – excellent. A remarkably full day. Address at *breakfast time* (Hubert C.-G. in the chair) by Miss Galway[94] on conditions of labour in the textile trades of Belfast. Then to Harland & Wolff's[95] – a magnificent example of industrial enterprise. Lunch with Ulster Liberal Association. Great reception by Mr. Joseph Devlin M.P.[96] (Nationalist) in the evening. ['Joe' Devlin, the pocket Demosthenes of the Irish party and the youngest of its prominent members. A fierce and fiery orator – and one of the prime favourites of the H. of C. of

---

[91] Thomas Wallace Russell (1841–1920): Lib. Unionist MP Tyrone South 1886–1906; Independent Unionist 1906–1910; defeated as Lib. 1910; Lib. MP Tyrone North 1911–1918; Parliamentary Secretary to the Local Government Board 1895–1900; Vice-President of the Irish Department of Agriculture and Technical Instruction 1907–1918; cr. baronet 1917.
[92] Michael Francis Cox (1852–1926): distinguished Irish physician; friend and doctor to John Redmond and John Dillon; sworn of Irish Privy Council 1911.
[93] Nugent Talbot Everard (1849–1929): Lord Lieutenant of Meath 1906–1922; cr. baronet 1911; elected to Irish Senate 1922.
[94] Mary Galway (c.1864–1928): organiser of the Irish Textile Operatives' Society.
[95] A major shipbuilding firm based in Belfast.
[96] Joseph Devlin (1871–1934): journalist; Irish Nat. MP Kilkenny North 1902–1906, Belfast West 1906–1918, Belfast Falls 1918–1922, Fermanagh and Tyrone 1929–1934; leader of the Irish Nat. MPs at Westminster 1919–1921; leader of Nationalist party in Northern Ireland parliament 1922–1934.

my time. Called 'Joe' by everybody. As great a master of vituperation almost as Tim Healy – eloquent, sincere, warm-hearted – he was of the type of Irish leader that the blockheads of Dublin Castle could never understand. C.H. Octr. 1936] Each of the ladies of the Eighty Club party presented with a beautiful bouquet.

21 September
Belfast to Galway.

Special train early from Belfast. Addresses and speeches all the way along! First ceremony at Armagh where addresses are presented to us in the Town Hall by various bodies. First-class reply by Prof. Morgan.[97] Then to the R.C. Cathedral to hear few words from Cardinal Logue[98] – a short ruddy old gentleman in a red skull—cap and with a typically Irish face. One of our party, Murray Hyslop,[99] President of the Congregational Union or something of the kind, so overcome by H.E.'s graciousness that he rapturously kisses his ring for all the world as if he were a good Roman Catholic. (We were greeted at Armagh by a picturesque body of Irish pipers in ancient national costume.) Addresses also at Cavan, Mullingar, and Athlone. Band at Galway station and much enthusiasm. Another address after dinner! A full but pleasant day.

22 September

Various groups of our party to various congested districts. We thoroughly explore Galway with Mr. Murphy,[100] Solicitor. This must be the most decayed town in the British Islands. Flour mills, distilleries, warehouses, woollen mills (except one) all tumbling to ruin. There is supposed to have been at one time a population of 40,000. Now it

---

[97] John Hartman Morgan, KC (1876–1955): Professor of Constitutional Law at University College, London; Lib. candidate for Birmingham Edgbaston Jan. 1910 and Edinburgh West Dec. 1910; entered the army 1914 and retired with the rank of Brigadier-General 1923; legal adviser to the American war crimes commission at Nuremberg 1947–1949.

[98] Michael Logue (1840–1924): Catholic Archbishop of Armagh and Primate of All Ireland 1887–1924; cr. Cardinal 1893.

[99] Robert Murray Hyslop (1858–1935): industrialist; leading Congregationalist, and for many years Treasurer of the Congregational Union of England and Wales; chairman of West Kent Liberal Association 1910–1918, and of Home Counties Liberal Council 1920; knighted 1917.

[100] Probably Henry Murphy (b. c.1867), of Kilcorkey.

is 14,000. The few remaining fine old houses and numerous coats of arms testify to a former great prosperity.

We also visit the Claddagh – not for the first time (for Em and me). Strange that such conditions should still exist, but some of the cabins are relatively clean and comfortable. 'You're all very welcome' and 'God speed your honours' are the universal salutations. We eat delicious oysters in one cabin and commission a griddle-cake in another.

Included in our round is the Industrial School conducted by Christian Brothers where boys are taught tailoring, boot-making, carpentry, baking, etc., etc., and then to the Queen's College a most pleasant foundation (not residential) in Tudor style. [. . .]

The Industrial boys play for us, and very well too, during dinner and I stand them cakes and lemonade.

23 September

Most interesting expedition by the S.S. Granuail to the Aran Islands – to the largest of them, Inishmore. A sea trip of about 3 hours. Enthusiastic greeting by the islanders with green banners bearing mottoes 'We want Home Rule', Cead Mille Failthe etc. etc. There are said to be but three outside cars and one road on the island. We drive to Dun Angus a wonderful fort on the edge of a precipice. [. . .] I buy a pair of the native raw-hide shoes which are too raw, however and soon become so offensive that they have to be thrown away. In general, conditions on Inishmore resemble those on the mainland opposite, at Costello.

25 September
Galway to Killaloe.

An early start by train to Athlone. Here we are first inconvenienced by the railway strike. Considerable difficulty and delay in getting our mountainous luggage from the train to the Shannon steamer. The Shannon scenery in these upper reaches by no means unattractive – fine grazing lands mostly with white-washed farms. In any case the drenching rain mitigates our delight in such scenery as presents itself. Clonmacnoise with its 2 Round Towers and ruins compensates us in some degree. Address at Portumna. Weather clears when we reach the Lake and we have a fine view of it. Most picturesque reception at Killaloe. A score or more bonfires at various points and candles in all the windows of the cottages by the water's edge. Every man woman and child in the town on the quay, and a band! Great enthusiasm and shrill cheers (Irish crowds can't cheer properly). After dinner addresses from County Councils, Boards of Guardians and the like, and an excellent response from Artemus Jones[101] of our party.

28 September
Killaloe to Cork.

By char-a-banc to Limerick. Railway strike in lull swing and station thronged with constabulary men and soldiers. No signs of disorder. Our train the only one of the day, I think. At Cork we repair to the Imperial Hotel. The Lord Mayor goes off to the station to meet the Killarney contingent who arrive at the Hotel about 7 o'clock amidst tremendous popular enthusiasm. Responses from Hotel windows by P.W. Wilson[102] and Isaac Foot[103] – very good. Reception by the Mayor. Mrs. Crawshay-Williams[104] arrives and the C.W.' s, C.G.' s and ourselves drink fizz in honour of my birthday. Case for shaving papers from darling Daff and delightful letters and drawings from Bud and Gol.

29 September
Cork.

Interview in the morning with 6 sturdy Protestant and Unionist farmers of the county. One, Mr. Kingston,[105] a victim at present of boycotting and going everywhere with 4 armed constabularymen. He is in possession and has been for over 2 years of a farm from which the previous tenant was evicted. A *son* of the evicted tenant has returned from America and Mr. Kingston is expected to resign his farm in

[101] Thomas Artemus Jones (1871–1943): Welsh barrister, KC 1919; unsuccessful Lib. candidate 1922, 1923, 1924; North Wales County Court Judge 1929–1942.
[102] Philip Whitwell Wilson (1875–1956): author and journalist; Lib. MP for St. Pancras South 1906–Jan. 1910; Lib. candidate for Westmorland (Appleby) Dec. 1910.
[103] Isaac Foot (1880–1960): solicitor; Lib. Councillor Plymouth 1907–1927; unsuccessful Lib. candidate 1910; Lib. MP Bodmin 1922–1924, 1929–1935; President of Methodist Conference 1937–1938; President of Liberal party 1947–1948.
[104] Alice Crawshay-Williams, née Gay-Roberts (b.1887); divorced Eliot Crawshay-Williams (1879–1962) in 1913 following the latter's affair with Mrs Carr-Gomm and his resignation as Lib. MP for Leicester which he had won in 1910.
[105] Richard Kingston, of Curraclough, County Cork. The boycott was still going on in 1914.

favour of the evicted man's son. He resolutely declines of course. We entertain our farmers at lunch and then a party of us accept the invitation of the President, Dr. Windle,[106] to visit the University College (formerly Queen's College). The main building is constructed of the local beautiful white limestone and is charming. Both sexes and all religions attend the College – even Franciscan Friars! One of these is Prof. of Scholastic Philosophy. The College is surprisingly progressive and up-to-date. An item in its equipment is a seismograph and a wonderful hydraulic engine for testing ironwork, concrete and other building materials. All the materials of a new bridge at Waterford are now being tested at the College.

Tea with Dr. and Mrs. Windle.

Reception at night by the United Irish League in a vast bare Town Hall. A rather cheerless entertainment in spite of patriotic songs and admirable speeches by two of our young men – Isaac Foot, and Dodds[107] who by the way has made some very clever caricatures of members of the party.

**30 September
Fishguard.**

Very rough passage from Rosslare. E. goes on with the main body of Eighty Club to Paddington. I remain here to keep my Welsh appointments with Hugh Edwards, M.P.

**4 October
Neath. Castle Hotel.**

Comfortable old-fashioned Hotel with a room that Nelson once occupied. Interviews during the day with Nonconformist divines and others about the forthcoming Disestablishment Bill. It is indeed astonishing that a whole people – or a huge majority of them – should find in the Disestablishment and Disendowment of the Church the most ardent expression of nationality.

---

[106]Bertram Alan Coghill Windle (1858–1929): anatomist and archaeologist; President, Queen's College (from 1907, University College), Cork 1904–1919; emigrated to Canada 1919.
[107]George Elliott Dodds (1889–1977): at this time a student at Oxford; author of various works on Liberalism; Lib. candidate for York 1922 and 1923; Halifax 1929; Rochdale 1931 and 1935; President of the Liberal Party, 1948, editor of the *Huddersfield Examiner* 1924–1959.

Through Maesteg to Nantymoel where I open the new Liberal Institute, and they present me with a silver key.

**22 October
Garden City Letchworth Hall Hotel.**

In the morning a walk over the golf-links and a tour of the estate in the motor-car with Mr. Williams.[108]

After lunch to call on Mr. Pearsall[109] one of the directors of the Garden City Company – tea at Mr. Gaunts[110] the estate agent – and then to Ebenezer Howard's cottage. The author of the Garden City in gold-rimmed spectacles, fresh as ever in colour, diffident in manner and benignant as Mr. Pickwick, greets us with great warmth. He is now for embarking on an active campaign to secure the establishment of a second Garden City We are afraid that the promotion of a second venture would tend to distract attention from First Garden City and to divert into the new channel capital badly needed for the fuller development of Letchworth. Williams suggests rather that Ebenezer should write a new book to be called something like 'The Garden City as it is' and describing the success that has attended the great experiment. Mr. Howard explains that the arduous nature of his work – that of shorthand-writer in the High Court and before Parliamentary Private Bill Committees, Royal Commissions, etc. gives him but little spare time and exhausts him too much for substantial literary effort. Not that but his profession has been a useful and congenial one, he assures us. It has put him in the way of acquainting himself with many aspects of public life and of forming a silent judgment on important social and economic questions. Still the profession is exacting and fatiguing, and the great reformer shakes his head ruefully over the prospect of another book to be written in the spare moments of a busy life.

How many members of Lords & Commons Committees and of Royal Commissions and how many Judges of the High Court have realised that the fresh little man with the gold-rimmed spectacles and the delicate aquiline features, transcribing with feverish haste the

---

[108] Aneurin Williams (1859–1924): Lib. MP for Plymouth 1910, Durham North-Western 1914–1918, Consett 1918–1922; Chairman of First Garden City Ltd., Letchworth.

[109] Howard Devenish Pearsall (1845–1919): Hampstead borough councillor; director of First Garden City Ltd., Letchworth; member of Fabian Society.

[110] Walter Henry Gaunt (1874–1951): president of the National Housing and Town Planning Council in the 1930s; served on Lord Reith's committee on New Towns 1946.

evidence given before them, was one of the most notable men of their time!

Mr. H. dines with us at the Letchworth Hall Hotel.

He, Mr. Williams and Mr. Pearsall press me strongly to become a director of First Garden City Ltd. I demur on three grounds: – (1) that I am too busy; (2) that, however busy, I am not a 'business' man; and (3) that I made it a rule when I became a candidate for Parliament not to accept any directorate other than that of our own Amalgamated Press. But I promise to consider the matter.

23 October

Sir Henry Dalziel's lunch at the Savoy Hotel to Lloyd-George.

24 October

Government resolution claiming all the time of the House for Government business during the Autumn Session. The Babes home from Eastbourne – in highest spirits.

27 October

Insurance Bill in Committee.

Proportional Representation meeting at the National Liberal Club – Lord Courtney of Penwith[111] chief speaker. They want me to be responsible for the Bill in the H. of C.

28 October
Sutton Place.

To stay at Sutton Place for the week-end. Alfred [Northcliffe] better in health than I have seen him for years and full of enthusiasm for his new golf-links.

---

[111] Leonard Henry Courtney (1832–1918): Lib. MP Liskeard 1876–1885, Bodmin 1885–1900; Under-Secretary of State, Home Department 1881; Under-Secretary of State for Colonies 1881–1882; Financial Secretary to the Treasury 1882–1884; President of Royal Statistical Society 1897–1899; cr. Baron 1906.

15 November

Mr. Runciman[112] [President Board of Agriculture and Fisheries] asks me to be his Parliamentary Secretary (unpaid) and I accept after several hours hard thinking. Don't see how I can refuse. Insurance Bill in Committee. Grand Committee B.

17 November

First morning at the Board of Agriculture & Fisheries.
In the H. of C. Scottish Small-Holders Bill – 3rd Reading.

18 December

I dine with J.M. Mullaly[113] at the Devonshire Club. Among those present General R.S.S. Baden-Powell[114] and Col. D.M.T. Lumsden.[115] I tell Baden-Powell of the children's interest in Boy Scouts and carry him messages from them. A very enjoyable evening.

---

[112] Walter Runciman (1870–1949): Lib. MP Oldham 1899–1900, Dewsbury 1902–1918, Swansea West 1924–1929, St Ives 1929–1937 (as Lib. Nat from 1931); Parliamentary Secretary to the Local Government Board 1905–1907; Financial Secretary to the Treasury 1907–1908; President of the Board of Education 1908–1911; President of the Board of Agriculture 1911–1914; President of the Board of Trade 1914–1916, 1931–1937; Lord President of the Council 1937–1939; cr. Viscount 1937.

[113] Possibly the scientist of that name.

[114] Robert Stephenson Smyth Baden-Powell (1857–1941): army officer 1876–1910; founded Boy Scouts 1908, Girl Scouts 1909; Chief Scout of the World 1910–1937; cr. baronet 1921.

[115] Dugald McTavish Lumsden (d. 1915 at age 64): raised a volunteer corps of Europeans in India to fight in the Boer War; given the honorary rank of lieutenant colonel and gazetted CB.

1912

6 January
St. Helena[1]

With Mr. R.A. Anderson,[2] Father Finlay[3] and L.S. Amery, M.P., to Boyle Co. Roscommon to attend a Conference of the Irish Agricultural Organisation Society.

12 January
St. Helena

To the Vicarage with Eric to see Mr. Ardagh,[4] the fine old Church plate, and the very interesting Vestry Book going back beyond Commonwealth times. Many interesting signatures including several of the old Settle family.

In the afternoon to town *[Dublin]* to see Sir Henry Robinson[5] head of the L.G.B. *[Local Government Board]* in Ireland and to discuss with him (for Runciman) the working of the Labourers Cottages Act in Ireland, Home in time to tell the babes Peggy and other stories before bed.

---

[1] Property of the Harmsworths in Finglas, County Dublin, originally owned by CBH's father-in-law, William Hamilton Maffett.

[2] Robert Andrew Ramsay Anderson (1860–1942): Secretary of the Irish Agricultural Organisation Society, a successful co-operative organisation founded by Horace Plunkett in 1894.

[3] Thomas A. Finlay (1848–1940): entered the Jesuit order 1866; a professor at University College Dublin 1883–1930; Vice-President of the Irish Agricultural Organisation Society and a close collaborator of Plunkett and Anderson.

[4] Arthur William Ardagh (c.1858–1925): Vicar of Finglas 1891–1919.

[5] Sir Henry Augustus Robertson (1857–1927): Irish civil servant; Vice-President of the Irish Local Government Board 1898–1920; knighted 1900, cr. baronet 1920.

13 January
St. Helena

The babes riding as usual – Giltrap[6] 'ringing' the cob on a long rope. Daff getting on extremely well.
In the afternoon Aunt Marcella,[7] Em and I call on the Swift McNeills at 17 Pembroke Road. [...]
Also there T.W. and Mrs. Russell. T.W.R. apprehensive that Home Rule may be ship-wrecked on one of two rocks – the recent Papal proprio motu decree[8] and or the fiscal question. The Government, to judge by what T.W.R. says, determined not to give an Irish Parliament control of Customs. Many important Nationalist influences in favour of fiscal autonomy — including the *Daily Independent*, the Healy-O'Brienite section,[9] and the old *Freeman* leaning that way.

15 January
St. Helena

Lunch at the Kildare Street Club with Sir H. Robinson. We discuss further the working of the Labourers (Ireland) Acts under the Irish L.G.B.
Afterwards with Em to call on old Mr. Deane in Mount Street and to see his very fine old Waterford glass.

---

[6] John Giltrap (b. *c*.1867): coachman and domestic servant.
[7] Presumably Marcella Deane, aunt to CBH's children.
[8] In December 1911 Pius X issued a decree 'Quantavis diligentia' which subjected to excommunication any private individual who summoned a member of the clergy before a tribunal of laymen without first seeking the permission of the ecclesiastical authorities. In other words, he was attempting to discourage people from suing clerics.
[9] Timothy Michael Healy, (1855–1931): Nationalist MP for Wexford 1880–1883, Monaghan 1883–1885, Londonderry South 1885–1886, North Longford 1886–1892, North Louth 1892–December 1910, North-East Cork 1911–1918; first Governor-General of the Irish Free State, 1922–1928. William O'Brien (1852–1928): journalist and author; founder of the anti-sectarian All-for-Ireland League; Nationalist MP for Mallow 1883–1885; Tyrone South 1886, North-East Cork 1887–1892; and Cork City, 1892–1895 and 1901–1918. By the time of this entry, Healy and O'Brien, who favoured a conciliatory approach to the quest for Home Rule, had broken away from the Irish Parliamentary Party under the leadership of John Redmond and had obtained a small following of MPs.

16 January
St. Helena

To the office of the Congested Districts Board in Rutland Square to discuss with Mr. Doran[10] the working of the Board's schemes for building homesteads for small farmers.
    E. and I lunch at the Mitchells – the children go to the Museum. We dine at Sir C. Nixon's[11] 2 Merrion Square[...] Afterwards to our dance at Roebuck. A delightful affair. Lots of fresh, pretty young people[...]
    To sleep at St. Helena as the old clock in the hall strikes 4.

22 January
Montagu Square

To the War Office to see Sir E.W.D. Ward[12] about Fred Spencer.[13] Sir E.W.D. very good about it but not certain that he can do anything.
    In the afternoon to the Old Masters at Burlington House and then to a Committee meeting of the Proportional Representation Society at Lord Courtney's, Cheyne Walk.
    Bishop of Ossory (Dr. Bernard) dines with us. Just off with the Speaker's party to Russia.
    Em and the children home from Ireland by the express arriving at Euston at 11 P.M. All well but very tired.

24 January

To discuss affairs of the Garden Cities Association with E.G. Culpin the Secretary. Afterwards to Carmelite House to see Harold [Rothermere]

---

[10] Henry Francis Doran (1856–1928): Irish civil servant; Inspector of the Congested Districts Board for Ireland 1892–1910; a Statutory Permanent Member of the Board from 1910.

[11] Christopher John Nixon (1849–1914): prominent Irish physician and academic, holding a series of senior posts at National University of Ireland; founder of Royal Veterinary College of Ireland.

[12] Edward Willis Duncan Ward (1853–1928): army officer; Permanent Under-Secretary of State at the War Office 1901–1914; knighted 1900; cr. baronet 1914.

[13] Frederick A. Spencer: later a Captain in the Royal Tank Corps, m. 1925 CBH's niece Sophie Geraldine ('Chirrie') King (b.1902).

25 January

Board of Agriculture in the morning to report results of my enquiries as to the working of the Labourers (Ireland) Acts. Lunch with Bonch at the Cavendish Hotel. Turkish Bath at the Automobile Club.

29 January

Finance & General Committee Garden City Association. After dinner to the Sylvan Debating Club. Discussion on Welsh Disestablishment.

30 January

Lunch at 22 St. James's Place with Alfred and Mary.[14] Also there Mr. Scott,[15] engineer at Grand Falls, and Arthur Lee [Lord Lee of Fareham], Tory MP for Fareham. Then to meeting of National Insurance Committee, 12 Downing Street, the Master of Elibank, Chief Whip, in the chair. Dine in Hall, Middle Temple, with Dudley Stewart Smith, K.C., a Bencher.[16] Port, wonderful old sherry, and dessert in the Parliament Room. A delightful evening. I meet several old friends of my father who was a member of this Inn. Mr. Henry R. Beeton[17] recalled with much pleasure my father's 'charming humorous speeches' at the Sylvan Debating Club.

31 January

Meeting of Council Garden Cities Association, 3 Grays Inn Place. Afterwards Turkish Bath at the R.A.C.

---

[14] Mary Elizabeth Harmsworth, née Milner (1867–1963); Baroness Northcliffe, wife of Northcliffe.
[15] William Scott (d. 1922): civil engineer, Grand Falls, Newfoundland.
[16] Dudley Stewart-Smith (1857–1919): Lib. MP Kendal 1906–1910; knighted 1917.
[17] Henry Ramie Beeton (1850/1–1934): pioneer of the electricity supply industry; founder and chairman of the Brompton and Kensington Electricity Supply Company and its predecessors for 45 years.

1 February

Committee meeting Commons & Footpaths Preservation Society, Lord Eversley[18] in the chair.

5 February

Annual Meeting of the Garden Cities & Town Planning Association at Carpenters Hall (very splendid) Mr. Justice Neville[19] in the chair. Mr. Ebenezer Howard on the platform by my side and with characteristic modesty taking a shorthand note of the proceedings in place of a reporter who had failed. Prof. Adshead[20] gives a Lecture on the Improvement of London.

6 February

Finance Committee at Millbank House of the National Insurance Committee. In the afternoon Turkish Bath at the Automobile Club. Bonch dines with us – and Mr. and Mrs. Hamar Greenwood,[21] Mr. and Mrs. H.D. Harben,[22] Miss McCheane,[23] Mr. Hankey,[24] Ruth, Bayly[25] and Fred Spencer.

---

[18] George John Shaw-Lefevre (1831–1928): Lib. MP Reading 1863–1885, Bradford Central 1886–1895; Civil Lord of the Admiralty 1866; Parliamentary Secretary to the Board of Trade 1868–1871; Under-Secretary of State, Home Department 1871; Parliamentary Secretary to the Admiralty 1871–1874, 1880; First Commissioner of Works 1881–1885, 1892–1894; Postmaster General 1884–1885; President of the Local Government Board 1894–1895; co-founder and first chairman of the Commons Preservation Society 1865, and its president 1905; cr. Baron Eversley 1906.

[19] Ralph Neville (1848–1918): Lib. MP Liverpool Exchange 1887–1895; QC 1888; judge in Court of Appeal from 1906.

[20] Stanley Davenport Adshead (1868–1946): architect and town planner; Associate Professor, later Professor of Civic Design, University of Liverpool, 1909–1914; Professor of Town Planning, University of London, 1914–1935; first editor of *Town Planning Review*.

[21] Margery Greenwood, née Spencer (1887–1968): m. 1911; cr. Dame 1922.

[22] Agnes Helen Harben, née Bostock (1879–1961).

[23] Ethel Agnes McCheane (1864–1928): dog enthusiast and shower.

[24] Maurice Pascal Akers Hankey (1877–1963): Naval Assistant to Committee of Imperial Defence 1908–1912; secretary to Committee of Imperial Defence 1912–1938; secretary to War Council 1914–1916; secretary to Cabinet 1916–1938; Chancellor of Duchy of Lancaster 1940–1941; Paymaster General 1941–1942; cr. Baron 1939.

[25] Probably Oswald Bayly Maffett.

9 February
Leighton Buzzard

With Handel Booth, M.P.,[26] a great authority on the Insurance Act. Dinner in comfort at the Swan – Mr. W.H. Smith[27] with us. Large and very keen audience in the Town Hall. We motor back to town – too much of a journey altogether.

10 February

Walk from Hampstead, through the Garden Suburb and on to Totteridge to see Mother. [...]
Members of the Council of the Garden Cities Association to dinner – Messrs. Warwick Draper,[28] Fremantle,[29] Montagu Harris,[30] Warren[31] and Pepler[32] – and to discuss points of policy.

12 February

E. and I to Lloyd-George's great meeting of the Insurance Act in the London Opera House, Kingsway. An embarrassing moment for me when Ll.-G. in referring to what is known as the 'Harmsworth Amendment' (that relating to medical institutes 15 (4)) turned round and indicated me, sitting two rows behind him, with outstretched hand!

---

[26] Frederick Handel Booth (1867–1947): industrialist; Lib. MP Pontefract 1910–1918; led government inquiry into Marconi Scandal 1912; convicted of fraud in *Gruban v. Booth* 1917.

[27] Probably the W.H. Smith who had previously served as clerk to the Leighton Buzzard Board of Guardians; appears not to be part of the newsagent family.

[28] Warwick Herbert Draper (1873–1926): lawyer and town planner; chairman of the Garden City Association; leading figure in the foundation of Letchworth in 1905.

[29] Francis Edward Fremantle (1872–1943): physician; Medical Officer of Health for Hertfordshire 1902–1916; Con. MP St Albans 1919–1943.

[30] George Montagu Harris (d. 1951): secretary of the County Councils Association; civil servant in the Ministry of Health during the 1920s; latterly honorary president of the International Union of Local Authorities; OBE 1918.

[31] Thomas Herbert Warren (1853–1930): President of Magdalen College, Oxford, 1885–1928; Vice Chancellor of the university, 1906–1910; knighted 1914.

[32] George Lionel Pepler (1882–1959): a key figure in the town planning movement and a civil servant with responsibility for planning 1914–1946; a major influence on the Town and Country Planning Act (1947); CB 1944; knighted 1948.

13 February
Luton.

By motor-car to Luton immediately after lunch to open Sale of Work in connection with the Parish Church.
    Afterwards to tea with Mr. Alderman Oakley[33] and then to a meeting at the Liberal Club to discuss the Insurance Act.
    A Lady at the Sale of Work did a silhouette of me for 1/-.

14 February

Opening of Parliament.
    E. and Ruth Spencer[34] view the State Procession in the Royal Gallery. I have an excellent seat in the front row of the gallery of the H. of Lords on the right of the clock reserved for Members of Parliament. The House of Lords not more than 2-thirds full. I have never before seen any vacant places on such an occasion as this. [It was said at the time that very many 'Die Hard' Lords absented themselves because of their disgust at the King's promised action in the matter of the creation of Peers, to outvote them on the Veto Bill. (C.H. 1936)] The King[35] husky but audible, and sunburned after his Indian tour. The Queen[36] wearing the wonderful Cullinan diamonds rippling in liquid fire down the front of her dress.

15 February

Debate on the Address. Ramsay MacDonald's Amendment – Minimum Wage etc. E., Ruth Spencer and Bayly dine H. of C.

17 February

By road with E. and Ruth to the Harbens. Delightful day. Eric H. and Agnes in great form. [. . .] Ramsay MacDonald, M.P., to tea.

---

    [33] Edwin Oakley (1852–1930): Mayor of Luton 1891, 1984, 1906; his brother, Albert Arthur Oakley (1854–1917) was mayor 1903.
    [34] Ruth Spencer: sister of Frederick Spencer, m. 1913 the civil servant Henry Gascoyen Maurice (1874–1950).
    [35] King George V (1865–1936): reigned 1910–1936.
    [36] Queen Mary (1867–1953): m. George V 1893.

19 February

Debate on the Address – F.E. Smith's Amendment alleging generally that it is incompetent for the Government to proceed with highly contentious measures – Home Rule, Welsh Disestablishment etc. – before the H. of Lords is reformed and while H.M.'s faithful subjects are deprived of their usual Constitutional safeguards. Bright speech from F.E. and brilliant rejoinder by Simon.

20 February

Debate on Address – F.E. Smith's Amendment, 2nd Day. Splendid debating speech by the P.M. who is easily head and shoulders above any other Parliamentarian in force, language and everything else.

I make a little speech in a very thin House which people profess to like.

21 February

Committee Meeting Liberal (late *National*) Insurance Committee. I dine with Alfred [N.] at 22 St. James's Place. Fred Wood there.[37] [Fred Wood, a very old and affectionate friend of my Father's and of N.'s] Em to Luton with Ruth to attend Women's Liberal Association.

22 February

Address – Fiscal Reform debate. Deputations with Runciman.

23 February

Address – Mr. Stanier's[38] Amendment on Small Holdings etc. To the Kinemacolor exhibition of Durbar incidents at the Scala Theatre.

---

[37] Fred Wood: childhood friend of Alfred Harmsworth Senior; maintained a close friendship with Northcliffe; head of the Mercantile Marine Department of the Board of Trade, for which Rothermere worked as a boy; died during the First World War.

[38] Beville Stanier (1867–1921): Con. MP Newport 1908–1918, Ludlow 1918–1921; cr. baronet 1917.

Children's little party with Mary's [Mary Northcliffe's] Christmas tree.

26 February

Agricultural Deputations at the H. of Commons – Supplemental Estimates.

27 February

Agricultural deputations. H. of C.
Supplemental estimates continued. Meeting Liberal Insurance Committee in Committee Room 11.

1 March

H. of C. debate on Mr. Baker's[39] Plural Voting Bill.
Em and I dine at Lord Granard's. A Liberal party. The P.M. and Sir E. Grey the principal guests. After dinner the P.M. and Sir E.G. play Bridge.
The Militant Suffragettes make a raid on the plate glass windows of Bond Street, Regent Street and Piccadilly. We drive round after dinner at the Granards to view the damage. Brown paper patches on windows everywhere and many shops barricaded. After dinner Asquith says across the table to Grey – 'Well, Grey, your friends have been breaking my windows again.'
Sir E.G. is a champion of the cause.

4 March

Army estimates. Suffragettes make an ineffectual attack on the H. of C. One young woman dashes into Palace Yard and is ejected by 5 policemen. The crowd seems less friendly to the Suffragettes than on former occasions. Another window-smashing campaign, this time chiefly among the big shops at Brompton.
Statement about the Coal Strike by the P.M.

---

[39] Harold Trevor Baker (1877–1960): Lib. MP Accrington 1910–1918; Financial Secretary to the War Office 1915–1916.

8 March

Great luncheon at Covent Garden Opera House to the Prime Minister to celebrate (somewhat late in the day) the passing of the Parliament Act. The floor of the theatre and the stage covered with small tables. A brilliant scene and an excellent lunch. The P.M. (Mr. Asquith) in noble voice and language. The party is unanimously devoted to him.

12 March

Prof. Morgan lunches H. of C. with me to discuss my proposed chapter for his Home Rule book.[40]

15 March

Em helping at the Irish Industries Sale at Londonderry House.

H. of C. – Discussion on Sir A. Griffith-Boscawen's[41] Housing of the Working Classes Bill – a feeble little Bill, aptly described by John Burns in his great voice as 'a wooden nutmeg'.

Meeting at Luton with Jeremiah MacVeagh – Jerry devoting himself to the wrongs of Ireland, and I to the Insurance Act.

18 March

Naval estimates. Speech of great range and power by Winston Churchill. Conference in W. Runciman's room with Lord Lucas[42] [Parly. Secy. Ed. of Agriculture & Fisheries. A romantic and splendid

---

[40] J.H. Morgan (ed.), *The New Irish Constitution: An Exposition and Some Arguments* (London: Hodder & Stoughton, 1912. This book was published under the auspices of the Eighty Club. CBH's chapter was entitled 'The State of Public Business'.

[41] Arthur Sackville Trevor Griffith-Boscawen (1865–1946): Con. MP Tonbridge 1892–1906, Dudley 1910–1921, Taunton 1921–1922; Minister of Agriculture 1921–1922; Minister of Health 1922–1923.

[42] Auberon Thomas Herbert (1876–1916): succ. as 9th Baron Lucas 1905; Under-Secretary of State for War 1908–1911; Under-Secretary of State for Colonies 1911; Parliamentary Secretary to the Board of Agriculture and Fisheries 1911–1914; President of the Board of Agriculture and Fisheries 1914–1915; served in the RFC in Great War; missing in action, presumed killed, 1916.

person. A face like Byron's. There was universal regret when in the Great War he flew over the enemy lines and was no more heard of [...] He used to amuse us both by suggesting that I should buy or rent his great uninteresting seat of Wrest Park in the midst of my Bedfordshire constituency with its famous gardens and over 40 gardeners. (C.H. 1936)] Mr. Middleton and Mr. Maurice on Mr. Middleton's draft Scheme for the organisation of agricultural education.

19 March

Mr. Asquith introduces Minimum Wage Bill for Coal Miners. Nobody likes it but nobody has a better remedy to offer.

Dinner and presentation of portrait and cheque to Mr. Ebenezer Howard at the Holborn Restaurant. Earl Grey[43] in the Chair. Numerous tributes to E.H. from all over the world.

20 March

Naval estimates.

Further conference on agricultural education with W. Runciman, Lord Lucas and Mr. Middleton.[44]

Rumours tonight that the Miners will not accept the Wage Bill unless it contains their Schedule of minimum rates for the several districts.

26 March

Report Stage of Minimum Wage Bill. The P.M., greatly moved, announces that all efforts to settle the Coal Strike by negotiation have failed. Wage Bill carried between 2 and 3 o'clock in the morning and sent direct to the Lords who have been in attendance.

---

[43] Albert Henry George Grey (1851–1917): Lib. MP Northumberland South 1880–1885, Tyneside 1885–1886; succ. as 4th Earl Grey 1894; Governor-General of Canada 1904–1911.

[44] Thomas Hudson Middleton (1863–1943): Professor of Agriculture, University of Cambridge, 1902–1906; Assistant Secretary to the Board of Agriculture 1906–1919; member, Development Commission (under the Development and Road Improvement Acts) 1919–1941; first recipient of the Royal Agricultural Society's Gold Medal 1933; FRS 1936; Chair of Agricultural Research Council 1938–1943; knighted 1913.

28 March

Mr. Ebenezer Howard to tea with me at the H. of C. and to expound a new scheme of his for a Garden City or rather a properly planned sea-port. A feature of the scheme is the construction of a great semi-circular dam open at both ends to the sea (with locks) and the utilisation of the tides for creating electric power. It seems a wild notion but E.H.'s enthusiasm is irresistible as his eyes flash through his gold-rimmed spectacles.

2 April

Lloyd-George introduces his Budget. Hon. Ernest Allsopp,[45] the Socialist younger son, lunches with me at the H. of C.

8 April

By motor to Luton to lunch with the Friendly Societies' Medical Alliance. Enthusiastic reception. All on account of the Amendment to Clause 15 Sec. 4 [National Insurance Act] that I moved immediately after my return for S. Beds in last July.

Back to Henley by Dunstable, Tring, Wendover, Watlington and Stonor.

11 April

HOME RULE BILL. Introduction in two hours' speech by the P.M. House packed. H.S.H. [Rothermere] in the gallery. P.M.'s speech wonderfully concise and clear.

Dine with Runciman and executive committee of League of Young Liberals in the H. of C.

Meeting of Departmental Committee on Small Holdings in morning at Royal Commissions House.

---

[45] Frederick Ernest Allsopp (1857–1928): 9th of the 11 children (6th of the 8 sons) of the 1st Baron Hindlip; army officer.

12 April

To Letchworth with other members of Departmental Committee on buildings for Small Holdings. We examine houses in concrete and inspect several small holdings. Mr. Gaunt, the estate agent First Garden City Ltd., takes us round. Among our members Mr. Raymond Unwin[46] who practically planned Garden City and Mr. Christopher Turnor,[47] the chairman of the Committee.

13 April

To Sunningdale to see the Chief Whip (Master of Elibank) who provisionally offers me the vacant Junior Lordship of the Treasury. Discussion as to whether S. Beds would stand by us through a Bye-election. I do not disguise my fear that the experiment would be a very risky one. The continuing unpopularity of the Insurance Act – the possible resentment of the electors at a fourth election in little more than two years, etc., etc. I am to sound opinion in the Constituency by way of Mr. Milner Gray, Liberal Candidate for St. Albans Division and one of my chief Luton supporters.

The Master of E. tells me that of the 'dummy peers' who were to have overborne the H. of Lords if they had defeated the Parliament Bill only 4 were to have been taken from the H. of Commons.

In regard to the Home Rule Scheme he divulges a plan whereby certain Counties of Ulster are to be allowed to contract out of the H.R. Act and to remain under direct Government of the British Parliament. This scheme to be forced on the Government by *The Times* and *Daily Mail* bringing it forward as their own!

14 April

Anxious discussions during the day with E. as to our prospects in S. Beds in the event of an election.

---

[46] Raymond Unwin (1863–1940): engineer, architect and town planner; planning career included Letchworth and Hampstead Garden Suburb; strongly influential in inter-war planning in Britain and the USA.

[47] Christopher Hatton Turnor (1873–1940): owner of extensive lands in Lincolnshire; agricultural and social reformer; co-founder of Central Landowners Association.

15 April

Mr. Milner Gray lunches with me at the H. of C. In regard to the proposed Bye-election in S. Beds he agrees with me that though we might pull it off, the risk is very considerable. Later, Alec Murray (Master of Elibank) informs me that from private intelligences from S. Beds the Government has virtually decided not to invite a contest there. So the day dream is over! Most kindly references by Alec Murray to my attitude in this affair. [It is a little hard that this is perhaps the first occasion in the history of S. Beds that a Bye-election might not have been risked.]

First Reading (2nd day) of H. Rule Bill. I spend fruitless day trying to catch Mr. Speaker's eye.

Wreck of the Titanic, the largest ship in the world, by icebergs in the Atlantic.

16 April

I write a letter of grateful thanks and duty to the Prime Minister for his kindness in considering my name in connection with the vacant Jr. Lordship of the Treasury and expressing my profound regret that the present condition of affairs does not justify an appeal to the electors. This letter I hand to C.H. Lyell,[48] the P.M.'s private Parliamentary Secretary and soon afterwards I receive the following note:-

'10 Downing Street,
Whitehall, S.W.
'My dear Harmsworth

Very many thanks for your letter. I much regret that, for the moment, we are not to have the advantage of your co-operation as a colleague, but I hope that the opportunity may not be long deferred.

'Yours sincerely
(Sgd.) H.H. ASQUITH.'

To which I send a note expressing my deep obligation to the P.M.

---

[48] Charles Henry Lyell (1875–1918): Lib. MP Dorset East 1904–1910, Edinburgh South 1910–1917; died of pneumonia while serving as Assistant Military Attaché to the USA.

17 April
Luton.

In the H. of C. Motion of the Ch. of the Excheqr. to set up a Select Committee on Estimates.

Em, Ruth Spencer and I to Luton to attend Annual Meeting of S. Beds Liberal Association. Presentation of handsome inkstand to Lord Ashton of Hyde and of a pair of candlesticks to Lady A.[49]

Eclipse of the sun. Everybody (including our babes) peering at the sun through smoked glass. Most curious effect during the transit as of yellow moonlight.

Mr. Henry Webb,[50] Member for the Forest of Dean, with a majority of over 3000 appointed Jr. Lord of the Treasury.

18 April

Quiet day in the H. of C. Discussion (on Estimates) on general working of Insurance Act. I pair with young John Lyttelton my successful opponent in Mid Worcestershire, for today and tomorrow.

Dine at home. Ruth and G. Sheppard.

Lord Lytton[51] asks me to cut the first sod for the Co-partnership cottages and open some completed houses at Knebworth Garden Village – in place of Earl Grey who is unwell. I accept.

19 April

I walk out from Golders Green to Totteridge to see Mother recently returned from her trip with Alfred (Northcliffe) to the South of France.

Back to town for the first of the town-planning lectures at the office of the Garden Cities Association.

---

[49] Eva Margaret James (1855–1938): Baroness Ashton.
[50] Henry Webb (1866–1940): Lib. MP Forest of Dean 1911–1918, Cardiff East 1923–1924; Junior Lord of the Treasury 1912–1915.
[51] Victor Alexander George Robert Bulwer-Lytton (1876–1947): succ. as 2nd Earl of Lytton 1891; supporter of Garden Cities Movement; Civil Lord of the Admiralty 1916, 1919–1920; Parliamentary Secretary to the Admiralty 1917–1919; Parliamentary Under-Secretary of State for India 1920–1922; Governor of Bengal 1922–1927.

20 April
Knebworth

To Knebworth House by road with Em to cut the first sod of Lord Lytton's new Garden Suburb. [...] Sod cut by E. Speeches by Sir Sydney Lea,[52] Lord Robert Cecil and myself. Immediately afterwards we hasten back to town – I to take Chair at the 22nd Annual Dinner of the Readers' Pensions Committee at the Trocadero. A very successful dinner.

23 April

With Em, Ruth and Sheppard to the Ideal Homes Exhibition of the *Daily Mail* at Olympia. A delightful Show.
  In the H. of C. introduction of the Welsh Disestablishment Bill by Mr. McKenna.[53] A very unpopular Bill, I think, on our side.

30 April

H. of C. Home Rule Bill — 2nd Reading. An unhappy day trying vainly to catch Mr. Speaker's eye. I spent the three days of the First Reading in the same unprofitable task.

1 May

Home Rule Bill Second Reading.

2 May

Departmental Committee on Buildings for Small Holdings. With the Deptl. Committee to Swindon. We inspect Col. Calley's concrete

---

[52] Thomas Sydney Lea (1867–1946): Worcestershire magistrate, supporter of garden cities movement.
[53] Reginald McKenna (1863–1943): Lib. MP Monmouthshire North 1895–1918; Financial Secretary to the Treasury 1905–1907; President of the Board of Education 1907–1908; First Lord of the Admiralty 1908–1911; Home Secretary 1911–1915; Chancellor of the Exchequer 1915–1916; chairman of Midland Bank 1919–1943.

farm-buildings at Burderop. Then to Dumbleton to see an excellent example of covered yard in creosoted wood.

9 May

Last day of 2nd Reading Debate and DIVISION on HOME RULE BILL. Noble speech by the P.M., not inferior, I am sure, in manner, in voice and in language above all, to anything in our Parliamentary history. House full to congestion. 640 Members present out of 670. The halt and maimed summoned from their beds of sickness. Majority of 100 exactly on the Closure and of 101 on the Motion that 'now' stand.

The inside of the day among the D. of Bedford's[54] Small Holders at Maulden near Ampthill.

T.C.D. Dinner at the Grand Hotel. A delightful function as usual.

10 May
Highcliffe Castle.

Miscellaneous little Bills in the H. of C. House counted out and an early adjournment.

To Highcliffe by 4.30 train[...]

11 May
Highcliffe

Sea mist in the morning turning sunny and warm after lunch. We see the land at Upper Highcliffe that Harold [Rothermere] has purchased and where he is to establish a seaside garden suburb.

13 May

Back to town. Welsh Disestablishment Bill – 2nd Reading (1st Day).

---

[54] Herbrand Arthur Russell (1858–1940): succ. 1893 as 11th Duke of Bedford.

16 May

Welsh Disestablishment Bill 2nd Reading carried, I vote very reluctantly, with reservations as to Disendowment.

17 May

Meeting of Liberal Churchmen H. of C. to discuss amendments to Disendowment proposals.

22 May House rises for Whitsuntide Recess.

By evening train to Hook to stay with Alfred (Northcliffe) for two or three days Mayfly fishing on the Lyde.

14 June

H. of C. Dull private members' Bills, so I take a day off. [. . .]
The Bishop to a great Anti-Home Rule demonstration at the Albert Hall. Em and I to the Government's India Office Reception. A splendid gathering. Lilian Harmsworth with us and all have supper at the Whips' Table (with the Master of Elibank) in the Royal Supper room.

21 June

Departmental Committee
Round the Staffs C.C.S. Holdings – almost entirely devoted to dairying. Return to town with Mr. Cheney,[55] Senior Small Holdings Commissioner.
Dinner at 10 Downing Street. Forty or fifty at round tables in the fine pannelled dining-room. Opposite me the striking but, I fear, rather indifferent portrait of Nelson.[56] We notice a fine pencil drawing by Sargent of Mr. Asquith's youngest boy. The P.M. tells us that Sargent

---

[55] E.J. Cheney (1862–1921): civil servant, at this time Assistant Secretary at the Board of Agriculture and Fisheries and, in that capacity, Smallholdings Commissioner.
[56] Admiral Lord Nelson (1758–1805).

did it in two hours. A similar portrait of the youngest girl, also by Sargent. The P.M. exceedingly pleasant and simple.
10 DOWNING STREET.
Diner du 21 Juin, 1912.
Melon.
Consommé Paysanne.
Filets de Sole Cubat.
Soufflé de Cailles.
Selle d'Agneau.
Jambon.
Crème Glacée Pralinée.
Biscuits Diable.

25 June

H. of C. Woods & Forests Vote. Bedford College for Women, Regent Street Quadrant, Forest of Dean, Scotch Crown Salmon-fishings and miscellaneous points. Scene in the House. Lansbury,[57] the Socialist Member for Bow & Bromley, waxes uncontrollable over the 'forcible feeding' of women suffragist prisoners. Shakes his fist (having advanced up the floor of the House) in the P.M.'s face. Withdraws on the earnest entreaty of Mr. Speaker and some of his friends.

26 June

H. of C. Supply Board of A. & F. Admirable speech by Runciman.
Alexandra Day in commemoration of Queen Alexandra's landing in England as 'Sea-King's daughter from over the Sea' – forty-nine years ago. Ladies sell artificial wild-roses made by cripple girls in aid of the Hospitals in which Queen Alexandra is interested. Em told off to sell in the Ladies Gallery H. of C. but finding little or nothing doing there goes out to Westminster Bridge and Waterloo Station and plies a roaring trade. Sells flowers to 13 sweeps!

---

[57] George Lansbury (1859–1940): Lab. MP Bow and Bromley 1910–1912, 1922–1940; resigned seat 1912 to fight (and in the event lose) by-election on issue of women's suffrage; editor, *Daily Herald*, 1913–1922; First Commissioner of Works 1929–1931; leader of Labour party 1932–1935.

Two in three members of the H. of C. wearing roses.

29 June 1912

With Percy Illingworth, M.P.[58] to Hook to fish Alfred's Water (the Lyde). A day of many showers, Fish rising well off and on. Bag 6 Brace not up to the best standard of the water in size.

1 July

Departmental Committee on Buildings for S. Holdings. We hear evidence at Royal Commissions House.
    H. Rule Bill. 5th Day Committee.

6 July
Henley Regatta.

The King and Queen at Henley. They proceed from the Station in their State barge to the specially-built pavilion a little lower down than our lawn on the other side of the river. The barge itself with its high stern and scarlet canopy, its royal standard and watermen in quaint red tunics and peaked caps, is a most picturesque feature of a memorable Henley. [...] Sixty or seventy to lunch. [...] Hundreds on our lawn after lunch and to tea.
    I run up to town in the motor-car to the annual dinner of the Amalgamated Press. Alfred in the Chair.

9 July

Naval Inspection.

The Lords & Commons to Southampton to join the 'Armadale Castle' (the ship in which we went to S. Africa) and to inspect the Fleet. Most delightful day. Several fine flights by hydroplanes. An attack

---

[58] Percy Holden Illingworth (1869–1915): Lib. MP Shipley 1906–1915; Parliamentary Secretary to Treasury and Liberal Chief Whip 1912–1915.

by destroyers. Submarines. The only official function of the year I thoroughly enjoy.

17 July
Luton.

Interview with lady suffragists at the house of Mrs. Lewis,[59] Luton.
 Garden-party at Mr. Edwin Oakley's.

18 July

Royal garden-party at Windsor. Em and I there and back by train very comfortably. A brilliant scene – the women in beautiful frocks, the men as dingy as modern fashions can make them.

19 July

State Ball at Buckingham Palace. A splendid affair. A young dinner-party at Montagu Square for the Public Schools dance at the Savoy. I take Em there after the State Ball and then return home.

23 July

At Stafford with W.R. [Walter Runciman], Lord Lucas and Mr. Middleton on Agricultural education conference.

24 July

Agricultural Education Conference – Wye College district – at Winchester House, St. James's Square, with W.R. and Lord Lucas and Mr. Middleton.
 Council meeting Garden Cities Association.
 Lunch with Em at Lady St. Davids.

---

[59] Possibly Ellen Lewis (b. c.1850): listed in the 1911 census as 'Chairwoman'.

25 July

With W.R. and Mr. Middleton to Agricultural Conference at Bristol.

26 July

Flitwick. Liberal fête and meeting. Tea at Mr. Goodman's,[60] the miller's.

30 July
H. of C.

Deputation of cattle-salesmen from Drogheda to see W.R [Walter Runciman] and to argue about the closing of that port to the export of cattle on account of the outbreak of Foot & Mouth at Drogheda. W.R. sympathetic but inflexible.

31 July
Shillington.

Opening of new Liberal Hall. The parson having imposed conditions as to what subjects should be discussed at Liberal meetings in the village schools, the local Liberals – 'Boys of the bull-dog breed' – have transformed a discarded Wesleyan Chapel into a Liberal meeting-place. An enthusiastic and most cheerful gathering, preceded by tea and cakes. Em with me and a considerable party from Luton – Col. and Mrs. Carruthers,[61] Mr. and Mrs. Milner Gray, Mr. Edwin and Mr. and Mrs. Albert Oakley, Mr. George Warren, Mr. Field,[62] Mr. Cotchin and others.
I pair for the day.

1 August

An almost all-night sitting. I walk home about 4.30 – London beautifully fresh and bright at this hour of the morning.

---

[60] Richard Goodman (b. *c.*1853): flour miller and cow merchant.
[61] Lt Col. Andrew Carruthers (b. *c.*1848): Luton magistrate; m. Emily (1855–1932).
[62] Probably George Field (b. *c.*1865): manure and seed agent.

2 August

In the House at 12 this morning. In spite of a telegraphic Whip the Government majority on the first Division is only 26.

7 August
H. of C.

Motion for Adjournment. In the evening with W. Runciman and Charles Nicholson to dinner at the Automobile Club and afterwards to the Palace Theatre.

Resignation announced of the Master of Elibank, the best Chief Whip the Liberal party or any other party ever had. He has been very kind to me. Percy Illingworth succeeds him.

8 August

Shopping for Newfoundland and a visit to the dentist. The Babes home in the afternoon from Henley. [. . .]

To 'Gipsy Love' at Daly's – a pretty piece. Master of Elibank (and his brother Arthur)[63] in a box. I go up to see him and to congratulate and condole with him. He does not like leaving the H. of C.

12 August

To Poynters to dine with Mother. Alfred [N.] arrives full of victory over Winston Churchill at golf on Princes Links. He is to play Bonar Law[64] in a day or two. Much talk about Newfoundland.

---

[63] Arthur Cecil Murray (1879–1962): Lib. MP Kincardineshire 1908–1918, Kincardineshire and Aberdeenshire West 1918–1923; PPS to Sir Edward Grey 1910–1914; served in army in Great War; succ. as 3rd Viscount Elibank 1951.

[64] Andrew Bonar Law (1858–1922): Con. MP Glasgow Blackfriars and Hutchesontown 1900–1906, Dulwich 1906–1910, Bootle 1911–1918, Glasgow Central 1918–1923; Parliamentary Secretary to the Board of Trade 1902–1905; leader of Conservative party 1911–1921, 1922–193; Secretary of State for Colonies 1915–1916; Chancellor of the Exchequer 1916–1919; Leader of House of Commons 1916–1921; Lord Privy Seal 1919–1921; Prime Minister 1922–1923.

13 August

To see Alfred at Carmelite House and to discuss the Newfoundland trip with him.
On 16 August, Harmsworth departed on a trip to Newfoundland. He returned on 11 October.

14 October
H. of C.

I spend the morning at the Board of Agriculture.
Discussion in the H. of C. resumed and concluding Debate on the Home Rule Bill Guillotine Resolution. Following my usual practice I do not vote on the main question [My view was that the guillotine was destroying the House of Commons as a deliberative Assembly. C.H.]
Dinner at Brooks's with Hubert Carr-Gomm, Albion Richardson[65] and Herbert Craig.

17 October

A talk with Sir Edward Grey in Palace Yard. He has been so busy with foreign affairs this Autumn that he has had but little time for fishing. His bag has been only one 'red old salmon'.

19 October
Luton.

Deputation of the small manufacturers to present their case in regard to the Insurance Act and married women outworkers. Lunch at the Liberal Club. Then a County round with Mr. Cotchin and Mr. E. Oakley – Leagrave, Limbury Chalton and Toddington. All very pleased to see us.

---

[65] Albion Henry Herbert Richardson (1874–1950): Lib. MP Camberwell Peckham 1910–1922 (as Co. Lib. 1916–1922); knighted 1919; KC 1930.

20 October

A large party to the Zoo. [. . .] An amusing rencontre in the elephant house. The children are feeding the elephants with cake and buns and all of a sudden I notice that next to Daff leaning on the rail is Lloyd-George with a little girl. Daff whispers to me: 'Isn't that gentleman very like Mr. Lloyd-George?' I come up against Ll.-G. a few minutes afterwards and tell him of the incident. I am not quite sure whether he was exactly pleased. In these days of furious Suffragettes a Cabinet Minister does not much relish being recognised even by a child who has never seen him before. (But Daff had – at Droitwich. C.H.)

21 October

Home Rule Bill in Committee.
Short speech against Amendment to exclude T.C.D. from the jurisdiction of the proposed Irish parliament.

22 October

Sir J. McFadyean[66] and Mr. G. Thatcher[67] call on me at Montagu Square to discuss the Veterinary Surgeon's Act Amendment Bill.
H. of C. Home Rule Bill in Committee.

24 October

Lunch with Christopher Turnor at Automobile Club and discuss with him draft Report of our Committee on Buildings for Small Holdings.
Dine with the Crawshay-Williams's H. of C.

26 October
Luton.

With Mr. W.H. Smith and Mr. Cotchin round some of the country districts visiting friends – Woburn, Woburn Sands, Aspley

---

[66] John McFadyean (1853–1941): Principal of Royal Veterinary College 1892–1927.
[67] Possibly of Messrs G. Thatcher and Son, Solicitors.

Guise (the printing works burnt down last Christmas now rebuilt and in full working order) and Eversholt. Deputation of Industrial Co.'s Assurance agents (Prudential) at the Liberal Club Luton.

4 November

H. Rule Bill in Committee. Discussion on Proportional Representation for the Irish H. of Commons. I speak in support of P.R.

7 November

Opening of Fleetway House, the new home in Farringdon Street of the Amalgamated Press. The house wonderfully transformed by Sir Joseph Lyons'[68] firm and the dining-room as gay as the Savoy on a gala night. Banquet a magnificent success in every way, the dinner being cooked on the premises. Fine speech by A.C.H. [Northcliffe] and one of the wittiest I have ever heard by Sir Thomas Dewar[69] [Afterwards Lord Dewar].
At noon with W. Runciman to the Horticultural Society's headquarters in Vincent Square to discuss the proposal that the Bd. of A. & F. and the R.H.S. should establish a Diploma as part of a joint scheme.

11 November

Exeter. Devon & Cornwall Enquiry.
The Devon & Cornwall Sea Fisheries Committee having petitioned the Development Fund Commissioner for grants of £10,000, each with the object of assisting fishermen to instal motor-power in their boats, the board of A. & F. has hung up the application pending an enquiry into the whole question of the Inshore Fisheries of the two Counties. Runciman has nominated Messrs. Stephen Reynolds

---

[68] Joseph Nathaniel Lyons (1847–1930): caterer and founder of J. Lyons and Co. Ltd. 1894, opening a chain of teashops in London; knighted 1911.
[69] Thomas Robert Dewar (1864–1930): whisky blender; Con. MP Tower Hamlets, St George 1900–1906; cr. baronet 1917, Baron 1919.

[the author of admirable Fisheries books];[70] Selwyn Fremantle[71] [of the Indian Civil Service] and myself, with E.T. Atkinson[72] as Secy., to enquire.

Reynolds, Atkinson, and I call on Mr. Harry Ford,[73] Solicitor, Secretary of the Devon Sea Fisheries Committee at his office in Exeter. Afterwards by motor to Beer (Dolphin Hotel). Before dinner we spend some time in the bar of the Anchor talking to the fishermen.

The Dolphin Hotel most comfortable. Herrings caught today, and cutlets, for dinner. Fremantle to join us tomorrow.

– Govt. defeated by 22 early today on financial clause of H. Rule Bill.

13 November
Sidmouth

In Stephen Reynolds' motor boat to Sidmouth with the other members of the Committee, and Harry[74] and Tom Woolley.[75] A fine fresh morning. The coast line here is most attractive – the cliffs sometimes of chalk and sometimes warm red sandstone with delightful green coombes or chines in between.

We put up at the comfortable Bedford Hotel – old-fashioned and snug, with *English* waiters. Sidmouth lying prettily between high red headlands presents a charming Georgian sea front. It is perhaps the pleasantest small seaside town I have seen anywhere.

We summon a meeting of fishermen at the Anchor Inn. [. . .] A small gathering. The question of the £10,000 grant fully discussed, with other matters.

After dinner we go to S. Reynolds' diggings where we meet Mr. Peile,[76] medical officer of health, Uncle Sam Woolley,[77] Harry and

---

[70] Stephen Reynolds (1881–1919): author of *A Poor Man's Home* (London: J. Lane, 1908) and *Seems So! A Working-Class View of Politics* (London: Macmillan,1911), written in collaboration with Robert and Tom Woolley, with whom he lived in Sidmouth from 1907 until shortly before his death; member of Harmsworth Committee 1912–1913, and of Inshore Fisheries Committee 1914; fisheries adviser to Development Commission; resident fisheries inspector for Board of Agriculture and Fisheries during the Great War.

[71] Selwyn Howe Fremantle (1869–1942), Indian civil servant 1890–1925; knighted 1925.

[72] Possibly Edward Tindall Atkinson (1878–1957): lawyer; Director of Public Prosecutions 1930–1944; knighted 1932.

[73] Henry Ford (*c*.1868–?1937): of Messrs Ford, Harris and Ford, Exeter.

[74] Harry Woolley (b. 1873): Sidmouth fisherman; younger brother of Robert.

[75] Tom Woolley (1878–1953): Sidmouth fisherman; younger brother of Robert and Harry.

[76] William Hall Peile (1869–1919): qualified in Dublin as a medical doctor.

[77] Samuel Joseph Godfrey Woolley (1845–1919): Sidmouth fisherman, younger brother of Robert's father; uncle of Robert, Harry and Tom.

Bob.[78] An open shingle beach here – the river Sid and the former harbour at the E. end of the town almost completely silted up with shingle.

Today there was a furious scene in the H. of C. – the Tories refusing to hear the Attorney-General. The Speaker suspended the sitting.

14 November
Budleigh Salterton & Exmouth.

By motor-boat to Budleigh Salterton – a delicious day and wonderfully warm for the time of year. The cliff scenery even more entrancing than that between Beer and Sidmouth. But Salterton does not compare in charm with Sidmouth. There is a very long open shingle beach – the river which enters the sea at the E. end of the town badly silted up as at Sidmouth and Seaton. One old salt tells us that he has seen ships of over 100 tons lying in the now non-existent harbour.

We find Salterton all agog with a carnival. We hold an informal meeting with a handful of fishermen on the sea front. They seem anxious to have motors in their boats. We visit the Coastguard Station.

In the evening by train to Exmouth (Imperial Hotel).

H. of C. meets today and adjourns until Monday with a view to the establishment of a modus vivendi between the parties.

16 November
Montagu Square

With S.H. Fremantle to town. Stephen Reynolds returns to Sidmouth and G.T. Atkinson stays at Exeter over the weekend.

Romps and stories with the children after tea. E. and I dine with the Courtneys of Penwith at their interesting old house 15 Cheyne Walk. Also there 'Tim' Healy and the Hugh Laws.[79] Also Dickinson, M.P.[80] and his wife.[81] Old Lord Courtney in his characteristic coat with gold buttons and famous buff waistcoat. He is almost the last of the old

---

[78] Robert William Woolley (1865–1947): Sidmouth fisherman; older brother of Harry and Tom.

[79] Hugh Alexander Laws (1872–1943): Irish Nat. MP Donegal West 1902–1918; Cumann na nGaedheal member of Irish Dail 1927–1932.

[80] Willoughby Hyett Dickinson (1869–1943): Lib. MP St Pancras North 1906–1918; knighted 1918; joined Labour party 1930; cr. Baron Dickinson 1930.

[81] Minnie Elizabeth Gordon Cumming Dickinson, née Meade (1865–1967): m. 1891.

stagers, if not the last, to sport a low-crowned tall-hat of the John Bull pattern.

17 November

A quiet day at home. Storytelling with the children.
<ins>ONE OF THE ABSENTEES.</ins>
You may search through the lists of the lobby in vain,
He was not among the M.P.'s
Who voted, his friends must have noted with pain,
He *was* one of the absentees.
It could surely not be, one so docile and bland
Had rebelled against party and got 'out of hand'?
Was he still so intent on recording the deeds
Giving fame to his holiday trip,
Too busy to bother with the Party needs
Or respond to the crack of the Whip?
You could hardly imagine it one of those cases
Where, hard driven, at last he'd 'kicked over the traces'.
In the last of his letters to come to hand,
He vaguely addressed it, 'At Sea'.
Was it possible that he had never reached land?
Had there been some catastrophe?
Or had he returned to the 'Isle of the Mist',
That, as 'missing' his name appeared in the list?
Such thoughts must have filled his friends with chagrin,
But they know now the reason why
He was not in the wreck of the Party machine –
He had other fish to fry!
Piscatorial exploits in his late expedition
Have gained him a seat on a Fishery Commission!
JINGLE.
Verses in the *Luton Reporter* (Tory) on my absence from the fateful Division of Monday Novr. 11th.

18 November

Brixham. Devon Fisheries Enquiry.
By midday train to Brixham – the most important fishing port on the S. Coast. It is a quaint little place climbing steeply round the small inner harbour and owes its picturesque-ness not to its buildings but to

its situation. The houses are as ugly almost as those of the back streets of Marylebone.

Brixham clings tenaciously to its beautiful sailing trawlers but its leading citizens are anxious that the Government should aid the fishermen in installing motor power. The sentiments of the harbour and the quays seem generally hostile to the proposal.

22 November
Leighton Buzzard.

Albion Richardson and I speak in Town Hall. A surprisingly good meeting. Albion [Sir Albion R., K.B.E., K.C.] in first-rate form.
We dine previously in the good old-fashioned 'Swan' Hotel.
All day on the Departmental Committee on S. Holdings discussing our Report.

24 November

With E. and the babes to St. Paul's in the afternoon. Excellent sermon by Canon Simpson.[82]

26 November

Lunch at the Prime Minister's [Mr. Asquith] in the fine pannelled dining-room with portraits of Nelson, Wellington, Charles James Fox, the younger Pitt and others. Present: the P.M., Mr. and Mrs. Granville Barker,[83] Colonel Seely, Secretary for War, Mr. G. Spencer Pryse,[84] the artist and Mr. Bonham-Carter,[85] private Secretary. (Mrs. and Miss

---

[82] James Gilliland Simpson (1865–1948): Anglican priest; Canon of Manchester 1910–1912, of St Paul's 1912–1928; Dean of Peterborough 1928–1942.

[83] Harley Granville Barker (1877–1946): actor-manager, director, producer, critic and playwright; in 1912 directed *A Winter's Tale* and *Twelfth Night* at the Savoy Theatre; Lillah Barker, née McCarthy (1875–1960): actress and theatrical manager; m. 1908, div. 1918.

[84] Gerald Spencer Pryse (1882–1956): Welsh artist, contributor of lithographs to journals including *Punch*; member of Fabian Society.

[85] Maurice Bonham Carter (1880–1960): principal private secretary to the Prime Minister 1910–1916; knighted 1916.

Asquith[86] away attending the funeral of a member of the Strutt family.) Delightful conversation about plays and books. The P.M. in most genial mood. Said that he desired to recommend Dr. Richter[87] the musician and composer, and Mr. J.S. Sargent, R.A., the great painter, for honours but was debarred by the fact that neither has become a naturalised British subject.

Afternoon train to Plymouth in connection with the Devon Fisheries Committee. Meet Reynolds, Fremantle and Atkinson at the Central Hotel (quite comfortable).

28 November
Plymouth.

The fish market before breakfast. A fair catch of dog-fish, now among the most valuable harvests of the Plymouth fishermen. The dog-fish, skinned and cleaned, go to London under the name of 'flakes' and are used in the fried fish shops.

To town in time for the opening of the H. of C. Debate on Guillotine Resolution Welsh Disestablishment Bill.

All night sitting. Supper (devilled bones) about 3 o'clock with T.P. O'Connor and 'Long' John O'Connor.[88]

To bed at 6 A.M.

3 December

Market Gardeners Bill in Grand Committee 15th day.

In the afternoon to meet Lord Robert Cecil in Committee Room 12 to discuss how best the iniquitous system of the guillotine can be obviated. Lord R.C. elaborates a plan.

---

[86] Helen Violet Asquith (1887–1969): daughter of H.H. and Helen Asquith; m. Maurice Bonham Carter 1915; president of Women's Liberal Federation 1923–1925, 1939–1945; president of Liberal party 1945–1947; cr. Baroness 1964.

[87] Hans Richter (1843–1916): Austro-Hungarian conductor; director of Halle Orchestra 1899–1911, London Symphony Orchestra 1904–1911.

[88] John O'Connor (1850–1928): called 'Long' on account of his great height; an active Fenian in his youth, he later became a strong supporter of Charles Stewart Parnell; Nationalist MP for Tipperary 1885; South Tipperary 1885–1992; North Kildare 1905–1918; called to the English Bar (Middle Temple) 1893; KC 1919; no relation of T.P. O'Connor.

5 December

In the morning to Kelmscott House, Hammersmith, to meet Warwick Draper and G. Spencer Pryse, the painter, and to go over Hampshire House, the remarkable social enterprise on the lines of Toynbee Hall etc. that has been established by Draper and a few friends in this surprisingly poor part of London.

The district, especially that part which fronts on the river, is one of the quaintest in London. Kelmscott House is a very interesting specimen of the Queen Anne style and has many literary associations. William Morris[89] lived here. Two of the rooms are illustrated in the Life by J.W. Mackail.[90]

6 December
H. of C.

Stephen Reynolds, Selwyn Fremantle and Atkinson with me all day long in Runciman's room discussing our interim Report on the Devon Sea Fisheries Committee's application.

7 December

Busy all day over the new clause dealing with the position of T.C.D. under the H. Rule Bill.

In the evening to dine with Warwick Draper at Kelmscott House Upper Mall Hammersmith to meet some of the Trustees of Hampshire House and to discuss ways and means in connection with proposals to establish a Settlement on Toynbee Hall lines. Present: Messrs. Draper, F. Rowntree,[91] Spencer Pryse, H.D.C. Pepler,[92] J.P. Bren[93] and myself.

---

[89] William Morris (1834–1996): artist, designer, writer and socialist.
[90] J.W. Mackail, *The Life of William Morris*, 2 vols (London: Longmans, Green & Co, 1899).
[91] Frederick Rowntree (1860–1927): architect influenced by the Arts and Crafts Movement; Quaker background; related to the confectionary family.
[92] Harry Douglas Clark Pepler (1878–1951): printer, writer, poet; Quaker background.
[93] Unidentified.

12 December

Last day Committee H. Rule Bill. I move T.C.D. amendment. Campbell,[94] junior member for T.C.D., responds very pleasantly, while Birrell, J. Redmond and Simon all make most friendly speeches. My Amendment negatived on the understanding that Birrell will move something more generally acceptable on Report.

13 December

E.'s Birthday.

H. of C. Debate on Clause 4 Welsh Disestablishment Bill. Partial revolt of Liberal Churchmen on Gerald France's motion to reserve to the Church in Wales everything but the tithe. Admirable speeches by France[95] and young Gladstone.[96]

21 December

House of Commons rises for the Christmas recess. E. calls for me with children. We all go to Camberwell to see Lady Lever's[97] Insurance Act play.

30 December

Back to town this morning.
    1st Day Report Stage H. Rule Bill. Amendment Safeguarding T.C.D., and Queen's University Belfast. I make a short speech.

---

[94] James Henry Mussen Campbell (1851–1931): Irish Unionist MP Dublin St Stephen's Green 1898–1900, Dublin University 1903–1917; Solicitor General for Ireland 1903–1905; Attorney General for Ireland 1905, 1916–1917; Lord Chief Justice of Ireland 1917–1918; Lord Chancellor of Ireland 1918–1921; cr. Baron Glenavy 1921; member and chair of Irish Free State Senate 1922–1928.

[95] Gerald Ashburner France (1870–1935): Lib. MP Morley 1910–1918, Batley and Morley 1918–1922; businessman and leading lay Wesleyan.

[96] William Glynne Charles Gladstone (1885–1915): grandson of W.E. Gladstone (1809–1898) and son of William Henry Gladstone (1840–1891): Lib. MP Kilmarnock Burghs 1911–1915; killed in action 1915.

[97] Elizabeth Ellen Lever, née Hulme (c.1851–1913): m. William Hesketh Lever, industrialist, 1874; he was knighted 1911 hence her title.

31 December

H. Rule Bill Report Stage 2nd Day.

Walter Runciman and I play truant, dine at Brooks's and go to see 'Doormats', an exceedingly well-acted little serio-comedy, at Wyndham's. We in our workaday H. of Commons clothes find ourselves among the smartest crowd I have seen at the theatre for a long time.

Off to Cornwall by mid-night train from Paddington with G.T. Atkinson to begin our enquiry into the fisheries of Cornwall. Fremantle and Reynolds to follow.

Atkinson and I wish one another all sorts of happy New Years as the train steams out of the station.

1913

12 January
St. Ives.

Lovely day. In the afternoon Reynolds, Atkinson and I walk over to Lelant where most of the big St. Ives boats lie up between seasons. Many of them, I fear, will never leave their moorings again. A mournful spectacle – 80 sail or so of the once brilliant fleet of St. Ives. Can motor-power avail to save them?

[When we had completed our enquiry in Devon and Cornwall and agreed on our Recommendations Stephen Reynolds was left with a free hand in writing our Report [Cd 6752]. His passage on the St. Ives' boats at Lelant was widely quoted in the Press at the time. He said:—

'On a grey Sunday afternoon, near about sundown, we walked to Lelant, where the St. Ives boats are laid up. There, on one side of the broad sand and mud flats of Hayle Harbour, we saw a fleet of seventy or eighty boats, mostly luggers, moored up with old chains and rotting ropes to rusty railway lines of the old broad-gauge along a grass-grown quay. In local phrase, they were the St. Ives boats that have died. The unpainted hulls of many were ripe and rotten. On their still standing masts, the running gear, left as it returned from sea for another season that never came, had flapped in the wind until it parted. Only one boat of all the laid-up fleet was being repaired, perhaps not for the St. Ives fishing. The picture of that silent dead boats' graveyard remains vividly in our minds. It impressed upon us, more than all the sometimes contradictory representations we had heard, far more than angry protests, the decline of the West Cornish fisheries. In no light spirit we began our investigations. With a deep sense of the tragedy of the present situation we ended them.]

15 January

House of Commons. Home Rule Bill Third Reading. Superb oration by the Prime Minister – the finest speech, I think, I have yet heard in the H. of C.

16 January

House of Commons. 3rd Reading Home Rule Bill carried by majority of 110.

17 January

House of Commons. Welsh Bill Committee. Dinner N.L.C. given by Percy Illingworth, Chief Whip, to members of Liberal Insurance Committee. Sparkling speech by Lloyd George.

19 January

At work all day on the Draft Report on our enquiry in Devon & Cornwall.

20 January

H. of C. Committee Welsh Bill. Great deputation of the Irish Nationalist party to W.R. in Committee Room 14. Subject: the proposed 'quarantine' of 12 hours on all cattle from Ireland.

22 January

All other interests in the H. of C. dwarfed by the Woman's Franchise question. The Government has promised to give the House full licence to insert a Woman Franchise Amendment into the Franchise Bill. The P.M. is invincibly hostile to the enfranchisement of women and a fair half of the Cabinet are with him. The Constitutional question is what is to be the position of the P.M. and the members of the Cabinet who agree with him if an Amendment in favour of the women *is* carried? An even more important question is – What right has this Parliament to pass any measure enfranchising women? The informal undertakings in this regard given by Members in former days are coming home to roost with a vengeance. My own attitude is neutral. I have much sympathy with the claims of women but I don't think that this Parliament has any right whatever to give them votes.

24 January

Woman Suffrage Debate. Alfred Lyttelton opens in favour of the women. Lewis Harcourt[1] replies in a speech of epigrams at the expense of Lloyd George and other members of the Cabinet.

On 27 February, Runciman announced the appointment of a departmental committee on the state of the inshore fisheries, following the more limited enquiry in Devon and Cornwall. Harmsworth was appointed to the committee, which was chaired by Sir E. Stafford Howard[2] and which also included T.H.W. Pelham,[3] Sir K.S. Anderson,[4] Sir Sam Fay,[5] J. Beaumont Pease,[6] S. Bostock,[7] C. Hellyer,[8] D.H. Lane[9] and Stephen Reynolds, plus the MPs Sir N.W. Helme,[10] N. Craig,[11] and W. Brace.[12] A.T.A. Dobson[13] of the Board of Agriculture and Fisheries acted as its secretary.

[1] Lewis Vernon Harcourt (1863–1922): Lib. MP Rossendale 1904–1916; First Commissioner of Works 1905–1910, 1915–1916; Secretary of State for Colonies 1910–1915; cr. Viscount 1917; known as 'Lulu'.
[2] Edward Stafford Howard (1851–1916): Lib. MP Cumberland East 1876–1885, Thornbury 1885–1886; Under-Secretary of State for India 1886; Senior Commissioner of Woods, Forests and Land Revenues 1908–1912; Mayor of Llanelli 1913–1916; Ecclesiastical Commissioner 1914–1916; knighted 1909.
[3] Thomas Henry William Pelham (1847–1916): Assistant Secretary of the Board of Trade 1895–1913.
[4] Kenneth Skelton Anderson (1866–1942): manager of the Orient Steam Navigation Company; knighted 1909, cr. baronet 1919.
[5] Samuel Fay (1856–1953): general manager of the Great Central Railway 1902–1917; knighted 1912 by King George V at the opening of Immingham Dock.
[6] John William Beaumont Pease (1869–1950): deputy chairman of Lloyds Bank 1910–1922, chairman 1922–1945; cr. Baron Waddington 1936.
[7] Samuel Bostock (1868–1938): leading figure in the Agricultural Organisation Society (formed 1901); later a promoter of the Women's Institute movement.
[8] Charles Pickering Hellyer (1876–1930): of Brixham and Hull, owner of the Hellyer Steam Fishing Company, Hull.
[9] D.H. Lane, formerly Inspector of Irish Fisheries.
[10] Norval Watson Helme (1849–1962): Lib. MP Lancaster 1900–1918; mill owner and leading lay Wesleyan.
[11] Norman Carlyle Craig (1868–1919): Con. MP Isle of Thanet 1910–1919, when succeeded by Esmond Harmsworth; KC 1909.
[12] William Brace (1865–1947): Vice-President of South Wales Miners' Federation 1898–1911, President 1911–1920; Lib.-Lab. then Lab. MP Glamorgan South 1906–1918; Lab. MP Abertillery 1918–1920; chief labour advisor to Ministry of Mines 1920–1927.
[13] A.T.A. Dobson (1885–1962): civil servant at the Board of Agriculture and Fisheries; later a leading international figure in marine conservation.

8 February

To Shrewsbury to respond for the Bd. of A. & F. at the annual Dinner of the Shrewsbury branch of the National Farmers Union. A gathering of 200 or more in the Music Hall.
Vile dinner and bad speeches.

12 February

This week we have news of the disaster to Captain Scott and his little party at the S. Pole. He was a most simple, unaffected sailor man. Stayed, and Mrs. Scott, with us at Henley not long before he left on his last journey of exploration.

14 February

House rises after having sat for exactly a year. This has been one of the most fatiguing sessions on record. [...]
First meeting at Winchester House, St. James's Sq., of the Inshore Fisheries Committee.
(H. of C.) We have sat pretty late every day this week but this day. My hours for going to sleep have been Monday 3 A.M.., Tuesday 4, Wednesday 3 and Thursday 3.30.

21 February
La Dragonnière. Cap Martin.

On the whole a very tolerable journey from Calais.
I sleep most of the night. Leicester (staying with Annie at the Victoria Hotel) meets us at Monte Carlo Station. I consign my charges to his care and proceed in a little Victoria the 3 or 4 miles to Cap Martin. [...] Alfred and G.A. Sutton[14] (from Grasse) over for lunch. Alfred remarkably well and gay.
I go into Monte after lunch with Harold, leave him at the 'tables', wander round the town and then walk back to Cap Martin. Bridge after dinner.

---

[14]George Augustus Sutton (*c.*1869–1947): began working for *Answers* in 1888; held important roles in the Amalgamated Press and Associated Newspapers, Ltd.; cr. baronet 1919; a trusted associate of Northcliffe and an executor of his will.

24 February
La Dragonnière Cap Martin.

After lunch Harold and I over the magnificent Corniche road to call on Lloyd-George and T.P. O'Connor staying at Nice at the Negresco Hotel. Ll.-G. and T.P. come in with Sir Charles and Lady Henry from playing golf just as we are leaving cards. Ll.-G. T.P. and Henry had had a mild adventure among the mountains as they came through in a motorcar. They were snowed up and had to stay the night at a dirty little Inn. Ll.-G. has the priceless gift of sleep at any moment and in any place and he got through the night pretty comfortably in the only available bed. T.P. and Henry had to content themselves with chairs, and were still sore in the recollection of their troubles.

Ll.G. fresh and gay. The first time he came to Monte Carlo, he said, he was in the Casino and at one of the tables he found Sir Edward Carson, then Solicitor-General, laying on his money. Carson's confusion was manifest when he caught the eye of one of his most formidable opponents. Ll.-G. saved the situation, however, and put Carson entirely at his ease by himself putting on a small sum immediately opposite to where Carson was sitting. So were they tarred with the same brush – and Carson most grateful.

5 March
Montagu Square.

In the country between Paris and Calais the year is less advanced than between Dover and London. The boat full of M.P.'s, Radical and Tory, returning to their patriotic duties at Westminster.

6 March

Meeting of the H. of C. – the last day but one of the Session of 1912! The Lords amendments to various Bills including the Scottish Temperance Bill and the Railways (No. 2) Bill considered. House rises about 6.30.

New works in progress at the H. of C. including the grand staircase down to the Terrace in place of the old narrow and mean back-stairs.

10 March

Opening of Parliament by the King and Queen. I view the Scene from the H. of C. gallery. The King wears his crown – an innovation on former ceremonials. King Edward and King George until now wore a Field Marshal's hat with feathers. Again, the former custom of keeping the King and Lords waiting for the faithful Commons was abandoned on this occasion, the Commons being in waiting at the Bar for the King.
Meeting at Aspley Guise. Packed and enthusiastic.

12 March
Flitwick.

Good meeting in School. Mr. Albert Oakley with us and Mr. Goodman in the chair. Dreadful village songs and music. [...]
All day on the Inshore Fisheries Deptl. Committee at Winchester House.

18 March
Luton.

Great meeting in the Plait Hall with Alexander Ure, Lord Advocate, who holds the audience spell-bound, as they say, for about an hour and a quarter, speaking without a note. We return to town by road.

22 March
Poynters Hall.

In the morning I write my chapter for the forthcoming book on the Garden City at Letchworth. [...]
A little story of Basil Burton.[15] His Uncle Alfred (Northcliffe) had got wet through on the Totteridge Golf Links and appeared anon in a suit lent him by Mansell, Mother's butler. Basil (taking his father aside and whispering in his ear) 'Dad, has Uncle Alfred got Mansell's job?'

---

[15] Percy Basil Harmsworth Burton (1906–1970): eldest child of CBH's sister Christabel Rose Harmsworth (1880–1967) and Percy Collingwood Burton (d. 1953).

27 March

Em home early this morning from Ireland. Alfred (Northcliffe) comes for me about 11 o'clock in his motor car and we go up to Hampstead. Walk over the Heath and then in to town, first to Fleetway House and then to *The Times* office, Printing House Sq. Lunch in the comfortable old-fashioned Georgian house of the Walters, two ancient parlourmaids in attendance. A unique experience.

To the H. of C. Long talk with Winston Churchill.

8 April

Dined with Stephen Gwynn[16] at the H. of C. in one of the small rooms downstairs. Of the select party were John Redmond, T.P. O'Connor, Sir W. Nugent[17] and the great Profr. Mahaffy,[18] who is said to exhibit leanings to Home Rule and to be anxious to occupy a seat in the Irish Senate – when it meets. The Profr. is a man of witty and inexhaustible conversation; knows everything and everybody; a scholar eminent in Greek, Latin, German, French, Italian and in English Literature; a translator of Kant; a Doctor of Music as well as of Divinity; a cricketer (in earlier days) a shot and an angler. He is not above using a d–n word on occasion but then he is only a clergyman under the old academic regime. Lucas and Geraldine who have travelled with him in Greece say that he is a perfect companion on such a trip – imperturbably good-tempered, kind and thoughtful.

11 April

Vere Harmsworth lunches at the H. of C. with me and I secure him a place under the Gallery. After pointing out the celebrities to him I go down to Walter Runciman's private room and fall asleep in the big chair before the fire. I awake to the dread reality of influenza. Home as quickly as possible in a taxi-cab, and to bed.

---

[16]Stephen Lucius Gwynn (1864–1950): Irish Nat. MP Galway Borough 1906–1918; Protestant; writer; the son of John Gwynn, the Regius Professor of Divinity at TCD during Harmsworth's time there.
[17]Walter Richard Nugent (1865–1955): Irish Nat. MP Westmeath South 1907–1918; succ. as 4th baronet 1896.
[18]John Pentland Mahaffy (1839–1919): classicist and musicologist; Fellow, then Professor, TCD, 1864–1919 (Provost 1914–1919).

25 April

A fortnight's 'flue'. High temperatures have given place to low ones. Much better.
    Arthur Murray [Lt. Col. Hon. Arthur C. Murray, M.P.] to see me.

2 July

First day of Henley Regatta but we do not receive visitors. All day discussion and all night sitting on the Plural Voting Bill. I stay at the House until 6 a.m. when I make for Paddington and catch the 6.50 for Henley.

30 July

Ebenezer Howard to lunch. Full of his co-operative housekeeping scheme, Homesgarth, at Letchworth.
    Abortive attempt of Tory party to spring a 'snap' Division in the H. of C. on the Army Vote. They turned up from everywhere and located themselves on the Terrace and in all sorts of nooks and crannies until 10.55. Got us down to 33 amidst much cheering and laughter. Some of them hid in the bathrooms attached to the Members' dressing-rooms. This was their whip for this occasion:
    Private and Confidential.
    Please come 10.55 Wednesday, July 30.
    Come straight to the Terrace without going upstairs. It is vital not to mention this to anyone.
    It was signed 'H.P.P.' (H. Pike Pease, one of the Tory Whips) [Always called 'Pike' by Libs as well as Tories. Afterwards Lord Daryngton.]

1 August

Busy day in the H. of C. Acting as Lloyd-George's parliamentary Secretary in place of J.H. Whitehouse,[19] absent. Also, by a fortunate coincidence, in charge of several amendments to the Revenue Bill in behalf of the Garden City at Letchworth. 'L.G.' accepts amendments.

---

[19] John Howard Whitehouse (1873–1955): Lib. MP Mid-Lanarkshire 1910–1918; subsequently a prominent educationalist.

20 August

In the afternoon Em and I to Madresfield (Malvern Link) to stay with Lord and Lady Beauchamp. They and their sweet family of 6 children (Elmley, Lettice, Hugh, Sybil and two other little girls) greet us very cordially. [...] The grounds opposite the drawing-room windows are full of marquees, merry-go-rounds, cokernut shies and other preparations for tomorrow's gathering of the Liberal clans of Worcestershire.

21 August

A little after midday the Liberal visitors begin to arrive and they assemble eventually to the number of something between four and six thousand. We are greeted everywhere by old Mid-Worcestershire friends with affecting warmth. We shall never forget them or they us. There is all the fun of the fair until about 6.30 when we inflict speeches on [...]

22 August
Madresfield.

We catch the 11 something train to town. [...]
   I dine with the foreign Town-Planning tourists at the Grafton Hotel, Tottenham Court Road, and we form an International Garden Cities & Town-Planning Association. French, German, Polish, American and Japanese representatives present. Ebenezer Howard with us and the recipient of compliments calculated to turn the head of a less modest man.

15 September
Henley.

We are, it appears, the centre of large military movements. A Brown Army is pursuing a White Army which has retreated N. of the Thames, having taken care to destroy (theoretically) the bridges at Henley and Marlow. Every lane swarms with men in khaki or is congested with transport wagons and guns. Two or three aeroplanes perform their wonderful evolutions over us in the morning. In the afternoon we row down to Aston Ferry just below Hambleden lock. The soldiers are taking their horses, stores and guns across river in great broad ferry boats, a laborious and leisurely occupation. We hope for an attack of the enemy but he does not show himself, Tea at the humble Flower Pot Inn which is for the time being the home of the Headquarters Staff of the Brown Army. Generals with double rows of medal ribbons jostle us in the passages of the Inn.

24 September
Luton.

I open the splendid new baths of the Luton Corporation[...] A lovely day and an exceedingly well-managed function. Unhappily I bend the handsome silver-gilt key and it has to be sent back to the manufacturers to be straightened.

5 October
Montagu Square.

Busy in the morning with my Report on the Decrepit Horse trade for Runciman.

6 October

Busy all day with correspondence and other matters. Dine with Harold at the Ritz Hotel.
[Decrepit Horses.
The trade in decrepit horses (for food and sometimes for further use on farms, etc.) from Gt. Britain to the Continent (generally Belgium and Holland) is carried on under the inspection and licensing of the Dept. of Agriculture & Fisheries. At this time there was a Bill (in the name of my friend Col. Arthur Murray) designed still further to restrict this unhappy trade, if not altogether to suppress it. I was acting at the time as Private Parly. Secy. to Walter Runciman, President of the (then) Ed. of A. & F. Angry questions were being asked in the House. Walter knew nothing about it. I offered to go myself to investigate the trade, from the various ports of embarkation in England to the arrival of the animals in Belgium and Holland, and this I did very thoroughly. My enquiry brought out in relief the incurable Pecksniffism of the British peoples – our worst national vice. Whereas the R.S.P.C.A. and our Dumb Friends' League were lurid in their denunciations of

the treatment of these poor creatures on shipboard and the ports of Belgium and Holland, they had no condemnation for the conditions under which it was possible to bring such decrepit horses down to *our* ports. Some I saw that well-nigh brought tears to my eyes – broken draught horses, discarded hunters and even, children's pet ponies!

It is a long story. If I remember aright my main recommendation was that if conditions could not be improved by a more effective inspection *here*, we should shut down the trade altogether. Even so, there was the risk that in the lack of a Continental outlet, *our* decrepit horses would be worked on our own farms etc. to a still further and more painful state of decrepitude! My friends in the H. of C. blazing with fury against the d—d foreigner were impatient of my view. But not one of them had taken the trouble to investigate the conditions of the trade, at home or abroad.]

9 October

First meeting at offices of A.O.S. *[Agricultural Organisation Society]* of provisional Committee of proposed Fisheries Organisation Society. Present: Stephen Reynolds, Sir Kenneth Anderson, S. Bostock, Col. Cotton[20] and myself. We decide that such a body should be formed.

11 October

Opening of Lloyd-George's Land campaign. Em and I go down by the 10.5 train from St. Pancras as we are entertaining at Lunch the statesmen (other than Ll.-G.) M.P.'s, candidates and other important people associated with the Libl. Party, and desire to assure ourselves as to the adequacy of the arrangement. 73 acceptances. Ll.-G. lies doggo somewhere in the vicinity, at Sir John Barker's,[21] Bishop's Stortford, I think. The town agog with excitement and the fine old Swan Hotel, where the Luncheon is to take place, swarming with police and detectives. After lunch we make through a dense crowd for the Drill Hall and soon afterwards Ll.-G. arrives with Sir John. A comfortable well-carpeted ante-room. Ll.-G. partakes of pounded liquorice from an envelope and offers me some. A vast meeting – a sea of pink

---

[20] Edward Thomas Davenant Cotton-Joddrell (1847–1917): lieut. col. in the territorials; Con. MP for the Wirrall 1885–1900; knighted 1911. Known until 1890 as Edward Cotton, he had shown some interest in fisheries during his parliamentary career.

[21] John Barker (1840–1914): Lib. MP Maidstone 1900–191, Penryn and Falmouth 1906–1910; founder of Barker's department store in Kensington; cr. baronet 1908.

bald people – a delirious reception for Ll.-G. and an atmosphere that thickens momentarily. Ll.-G. speaks 2 hours and twenty minutes, Kellaway for 5 minutes and I, perceiving that people have had enough, for 1¼ minutes. Ll.G. diagnoses the disease but omits to prescribe the remedies.

Afterwards a select party – including Em and myself – dine with the Kellaways at the Swan. Present: Ll.-G., Miss and two Masters Ll.-G.,[22] Mrs. Ll.-G. (a pleasant unaffected little lady), the C.F.G. Mastermans,[23] Dr. Macnamara[24] [...]

Then an evening meeting – the same vast array of pink faces. Admirable speeches by Kellaway, Ll.-G, Masterman, Trevelyan and Mac[namara]. Suffrage interruptions quite negligible.

We get home at about 12.30, more dead than alive.

14 October
Hitchin.

I debate the question of the Referendum with Lord Robert Cecil in the Town Hall, Hitchin. Lord R.C. moves that:

'Irreconcilable differences between the two Houses of Parliament can only be settled satisfactorily by an appeal to the Electorate and that the Referendum is the only method by which such an appeal can be satisfactorily decided.' A decorous company of some 150 persons who, as I understand, have paid for their seats. Lord R.C. speaks for 40 minutes – I follow for 40 minutes too. Then we have 10 minutes each to reply. Lord R.C. not quite up to his usual formidable debating strength. Very polite to me – indeed we are scrupulously polite to one another. Motion carried but a good bunch of hands are held up for me.

---

[22] At this point the Lloyd Georges had four children: Richard (1889–1968); Olwen (1892–1990); Gwilym (1894–1967); and Megan (1902–1966).
[23] Charles Frederick Gurney Masterman (1873–1927): author and journalist; Lib. candidate Dulwich 1903, Lib. MP West Ham (North) 1906–1911, Bethnal Green South-West 1911–1914, candidate West Ham (Stratford) 1918, Manchester Rusholme 1923–1924; Parliamentary Secretary to the Local Government Board 1908–1909; Under-Secretary of State, Home Department 1909–1912; Financial Secretary to the Treasury 1912–1914; Chancellor of the Duchy of Lancaster 1914–1915.
[24] Thomas James Macnamara (1861–1931): Lib. MP Camberwell North 1900–1918; Co. Lib. MP Camberwell North-West 1918–1924; Parliamentary Secretary to the Local Government Board 1907–1908; Parliamentary and Financial Secretary to the Admiralty 1908–1920; Minister of Labour 1920–1922.

16 October

Round the County Council holdings at Barton – well-named Barton-in-the-Clay. Heavy, sticky land in a shocking condition of neglect. Small Holders mostly village tradesmen. Only two or three agricultural labourers.
Afterwards to Markyate. Meeting of 70 people or so in the billiard room of the Liberal Club. The Club occupies the old Toll Gate house.

24 October

A visit to the Union House[25] Luton with Mr. Primett,[26] Mayor-elect of Luton, Mr. George Field and A. Earle. A clean, hygienic, entirely sanitary institution and depressing withal. Tea with the Master and Matron – Mr. and Mrs. Richmond.[27]
Then to Eaton Bray. Second tea with Mr. Gaius Batchelor[28] fine old Radical farmer (reputed wealthy) with land of his own and misgivings about Lloyd-George's land policy. Aged 81 and bright as a button. Farm (a poor modern building) surrounded by a moat. Formerly a castle here.

29 November
Letchworth.

I spend the inside of the day with Mr. Ebenezer Howard at Garden City. He is now living at Homesgarth, the centre of his Co-operative Housekeeping Scheme. Homesgarth consists of a little community of middle-aged and elderly people who have flats and take their meals in a common room. We lunch (at a separate table) with the Homesgarthians. E.H. beaming benignantly through his gold-rimmed spectacles and dreaming dreams of a working-class settlement with common kitchen, crèche, laundry and work-rooms. He is still heavily employed at his profession of shorthand writing. Recently his working hours (for the London County Council I think) were 12, 14, 14, and 10 for four consecutive days shorthand writing and transcribing. He does not complain but wishes he were freer to work for his ideals. He tells me

---

[25] i.e. the workhouse run by the local Poor Law Union.
[26] Walter James Primett (1864–1939): Mayor of Luton 1913–1915.
[27] Arthur Bridgwater Richmond (c.1868–1935); m. 1900 Amelia Goodall (c.1869–1932).
[28] Gaius Batchelor (b. c.1833). He had been a farmer at Park Farm, Eaton Bray since at least 1882. He appears to have slightly exaggerated his age to CH.

that he is often able to think of other matters when taking shorthand notes so natural and habitual has the practice of stenography become with him. This occurs when the subject matter is very familiar.

We look over a cheap cottage, inspect the Noel convalescent home and visit a man, one Mr. Clack,[29] a printer, who makes money out of a small plot of garden and a number of thoughtfully-bred fowls.

Tea at the Letchworth Club.

1 December

With Alfred [N.] at St. James's Place. Afterwards with him to the Sylvan Debating Club, Tavistock Hotel, Covent Garden. Excellent attendance.

Alfred offers me presidency of Anglo-Newfoundland Development Coy.

2 December

Inside of day with Sir Stafford Howard and Mr. Pelham considering draft Report of Inshore Fisheries Committee.

Dine with Harold [Rothermere] at Claridge's Hotel.

3 December

Report Inshore Committee again. Dinner of Proportional Representation Committee at Holborn Restaurant. Many people of all parties present and members of foreign parliaments. Fine sonorous speech from Lord Courtney, now 81 years of age. A grand old boy he is – straight-backed, hale and vigorous.

8 December

First meeting of the Cottage Committee – Christopher Turnor, Raymond Unwin, Laurence Weaver[30] and myself. [This was a Committee set up by Walter Runciman to enquire and make plans

---

[29] Thomas Henry Clack (b. *c.*1878): linotype operator.
[30] Laurence Weaver (1876–1930): writer on architecture, influenced by the Arts and Crafts Movement; knighted 1925.

for rural cottages on the most efficient lines and with regard to the local building materials etc. We hadn't met more than two or three times before I suggested that a good common-sensible woman should be added to our number, which was accordingly done. She was worth the lot of us when it came to matters of kitchens, bedrooms, washtubs and the like.

We had several models to scale made (at our own expense) with removable roofs so that you could inspect the indoor arrangements, and we issued early in 1914 an admirable Report, with estimates, plans, illustrations of recommended types and other practical details, which was lost sight of altogether in the Great War and has never been resuscitated.

C.H. 18/1/1934.]

9 December

Deputation of members of the Farmers' Union to W.R. at Whitehall Place.

Dinner of the Central Land & Housing Council (formed to organize Lloyd-George's Land Campaign) at the National Liberal Club.

12 December

Breakfast with Harold at Claridge's Hotel. Mr. Mallaby-Deeley,[31] M.P. to see me about his Northern Junction Railway Bill. We defeated this Bill in the H. of C. this Session because it decapitated the Hampstead Garden Suburb. Mr. M.D. assures me that it has now been planned so as to avoid all injury to the Suburb. We shall see.

13 December

Luncheon of the Central Land & Housing Council at the National Liberal Club. I sit next to Lloyd-George and inform him of the progress the land policy is making in S. Beds.

Afterwards Lord Beauchamp carries me off to Stafford House where the London Museum collection is now being installed (Lord B. is a trustee).

---

[31] Harry Deeley Mallaby-Deeley (1863–1937): Con. MP Harrow 1910–1918, Willesden East 1918–1923; cr. baronet 1922.

22 December

Christmas shopping with the children. Mr. Myers,[32] M.P. (New Zealand) and Messrs. E.G. Culpin and Reade[33] of the Garden Cities Association to dinner and to discuss Australasian Town-Planning tour.

[32] Arthur Mielziner Myers (1868–1926): Ind. then Lib. member of New Zealand House of Representatives 1910–1921; government minister 1912, 1915–1919; knighted 1924.

[33] Charles Compton Reade (1880–1933): New Zealand-born journalist working mainly in Britain and becoming a leading member of the Garden Cities and Town Planning Association, before working in New Zealand 1911–12; selected to promote the garden cities movement in Australia and New Zealand with W.R. Davidge in 1914; became a very influential figure in Australian town planning.

1914

3 January

In the evening to the National Sporting Club to present prizes in place of Alfred (Northcliffe) at an Assault of Arms of the Northcliffe Sports Association. The theatre packed with people from the Amalgamated Press, *Daily Mail* & *Daily Mirror*. A really inspiring sight. Great enthusiasm and excellent boxing and wrestling.

4 February

Dinner of the Luton Chamber of Commerce – Mr. Harry Inwards in the chair. I sit next Mr. George Elliott,[1] K.C. [who was greatly loved in the Constituency, by Liberals & Tories alike. C.H. 2nd Febry. 1934], former Conservative candidate for S. Beds, and, as it turns out, an old friend of my Father of whom he speaks very warmly in the course of a brilliant speech proposing the Luton Chamber of Commerce. I propose 'Luton & its industries'.

9 February

Em and I attend the Prime Minister's reception at Downing Street taking Lilian (Lady Rothermere) with us. A brilliant and very cheerful assemblage. Mrs. Asquith receives her guests sitting down. The P.M. in his uniform as a Brother of Trinity House looking more like Oliver Cromwell than ever.

10 February

The King and Queen open Parliament – H.M. wearing his crown as the new custom is, and the Queen a blaze of diamonds. Em in feathers

---

[1] George Elliott (d.1916); successful criminal and licensing lawyer; called to the Bar 1882; Unionist candidate for South Bedfordshire 1900 and Jan. 1910.

and lappets surveys the scene from one of the side galleries in the H. of Lords. I have a seat in the strangers' gallery.
In the H. of Commons the debate turns immediately on Home Rule.

11 February

Resumed debate in the H. of C. on Home Rule. Most impressive speech by Sir Edward Carson.

17 February

Dinner party H. of C. given by me to representative Australians in London in aid of the projected Town-Planning tour in Australasia. Ewart Culpin, Mr. Davidge,[2] Chas. Reade and four or five Australasians. We secure the guarantee for the tour.

18 March

Harold takes the oath and signs the Roll in the House of Lords as Baron Rothermere. I go into the Moses Room and find him in his robes and with his cocked hat. With him are Alfred (Northcliffe), Lords Lincolnshire[3] & Colebrook,[4] Garter King in his tabard, Black Rod and assistant Black Rod. Afterwards the quaint ceremony of traversing the floor and the gangways of the House. Mother witnesses the ceremony, the only woman, it is said, who has ever seen two sons take their places in the H. of L. as first peers of their line.

22 March

Breakfast with Harold (Rothermere) at Claridge's and discuss the Irish crisis with him.

---

[2] William Robert Davidge (1879–1961): architect and surveyor, with an early interest in the garden cities movement; travelled to Australia and New Zealand with Reade in 1913–1914 to popularise town planning; President of the Royal Town Planning Institute 1926–1927.

[3] Charles Robert Wynn-Carrington (1843–1928): Lib. MP Wycombe 1865–1868; succ. as 3rd Baron Carrington 1868; cr. Earl Carrington 1895, Marquess of Lincolnshire 1912; President of the Board of Agriculture 1905–1911; Lord Privy Seal 1911–1912.

[4] Edward Arthur Colebrook (1861–1939): Lib. peer; succ. as baronet 1890; cr. Baron 1906; Lord-in-Waiting (government whip in House of Lords) 1906–1911; Captain of the Honourable Corps of Gentlemen-at-Arms 1911–1922.

25 March

Greater Excitement in the House this week than I have ever known. The Tory plot to incite officers of the Army to refuse to serve in Ulster comes to a head in a virtual ultimatum of General Gough[5] and the officers of the Brigade at the Curragh to the Government. Seely, Secy. of State for War, seriously embarrasses the Government by adding an unauthorised rider to a Cabinet Memorandum dealing with this question. Liberal members all over the House gathering in gloomy knots and anxiously canvassing the situation. On Friday (March 27th) I find Winston (Churchill) singing blithely to himself in the lavatory behind the Speaker's Chair.

I thank him for his reassuring cheerfulness and he tells me that it is his habit to confront difficult situations with an outward serenity of aspect.

Much talk of a general election and the usual chatter about 'Cabinet dissensions'.

30 March

Fierce debate in the House on the situation in the Army. Resignation of Col. Seely as Secretary for War. The Prime Minister announces that *he* is to be the new Secretary of State!

31 March

First day of the Second Reading of the Home Rule Bill – the third Second Reading under the Parliament Act. An atmosphere of conciliation.

1 April

Still the Home Rule debate. I spend most of the day vainly endeavouring to catch the Speaker's eye – a nerve-shaking process that, often and unsuccessfully repeated, has driven many an

---

[5] Hubert Gough de la Poer Gough (1870–1963): army officer of Anglo-Irish aristocratic background; Brigadier-General commanding Third cavalry brigade at the time of the Curragh incident; commanded British Fifth Army 1916–1918.

aspiring Member into permanent silence and obscurity on the back benches.

3 April

H. of C.
 Decrepit Horse Bill. Brief speech based on my experiences of last autumn.

8 April
Henley

Adjournment of the H. of Commons for the Easter Recess. Immense number of Blocking Motions put down by our side.

Last day (for the signing of the Report) of the Inshore Fisheries Committee. I am unable to attend it owing to the threatened difficulties in the H of C. over the Motion for Adjournment.

[As a Member of Parliament I spent far too much of my parliamentary time on Committees outside the House – Fisheries Committees, Housing Committees, and others – and, again, as Private Parly. Secy. to a Minister. I hope I did useful work, but the place of a. Member of Parliament is *the House of Commons*. To know the House; the characters and moods of its members; its rules (which not one Member in fifty ever understands); the moods of the House as a whole as distinguished from its individuals; to be on the spot and ready to take part in debates and not to be too timid to do so – to play your part in short as a Parliamentarian, that is the true business of a Member of Parliament. In the arena of the H. of C. the fate of Empires is decided and not in outside activities however interesting and important. (C.H. 23.VI.1936)]

28 April.

Tory Vote of Censure on the Government in connection with the movement of troops in Ireland. Winston Churchill's offer to Sir E. Carson.

29 April

Second day of the Vote of Censure. Mr. Balfour acknowledges that all his work of thirty years against H. Rule seems likely to prove abortive. Sir E. Carson makes a definite approach to peace.

I dine with the Free Trade Union sitting next to Mr. Henry Gladstone,[6] son of the great Statesman, a fresh, jolly clean-shaven gentleman.

11 May
Luton.

Meeting of workers in the Liberal Club to inaugurate the land Campaign in S. Beds.

21 May

Great row in the House. The Tories refuse to discuss the 3rd Reading of the Home Rule Bill. Bonar Law at loggerheads with Mr. Speaker. Sitting adjourned until Monday.

25 May

In the H. of C. the Tories decline to discuss 3rd Reading of the Home Rule Bill and we proceed immediately after Questions to a Division. Later, Motion for adjournment for Whitsuntide holiday carried.

6 June
Henley.

With us for the week-end – Mr. [Walter Runciman's private secy.] and Mrs. A.D. Sanderson. [...] Sanderson and I walk to Wargrave to see the church burnt down by the Suffragettes. A melancholy ruin.

---

[6] Henry Neville Gladstone (1852–1935): 3rd son of W.E. Gladstone; businessman and financier; cr. Baron 1932.

9 June

A very full day for me, as thus:
With W.A.W[hite][7] to the Horse Show in the morning after some correspondence. Lunch with the *Country Life* people at the Carlton Hotel then to the opening of their Cottage Exhibition (by Runciman) at the Alpine Club.
House of Commons.
Home to dinner and then to the Royal Ball at Buckingham Palace. Gorgeous scene. The royal circle dancing as awkwardly as ever. Fewer scrubby foreign Princes than usual. H.M. in red uniform of the Black Watch. The Queen healthy and glowing. A blaze of gold plate in the supper-room. Beefeaters, scarlet uniforms, diamonds and splendour. Em delightful in a fashionable mauve dress.

'Mrs. Cecil Harmsworth – Parma violet and silver brocade the bodice softened with tulle and adorned with silver embroideries.'

14 June

To Poynters to see Mother and St. John. [. . .] A great gathering the clan – Harold, Vi and Wilfrid, Leicester, Hildebrand, Christabel and Percy and a crowd of grandchildren of all ages.

6 July

To town by early train. I attend the Memorial Service to Joseph Chamberlain[8] in St. Margaret's Church. Everybody there: Asquith, Balfour, Bonar Law, Lord Roberts,[9] Rudyard Kipling,[10] the H. of Lords and the H. of Commons. A simple, beautiful Service.

House adjourns after a noble tribute from Asquith and speeches from B. Law and Balfour. Balfour astonishingly feeble as he customarily is on these ceremonious occasions.

---

[7] Probably William Augustus White (1843–1927): an American book collector acquainted with the Harmsworth family.

[8] Joseph Chamberlain (1836–1914): Lib. MP Birmingham 1876–1885, Lib. then Lib. Unionist MP Birmingham West 1885–1914; former cabinet minister and leading tariff reformer, had died on 2 July 1914.

[9] Frederick Sleigh Roberts (1932–1914): Field Marshal.

[10] Joseph Rudyard Kipling (1865–1936): celebrated writer and poet.

7 July

Government majority today only 23. This was on the Resolution allocating the time for the remaining stages of the Finance Bill. I was among those who abstained. I have an intense objection to the 'Guillotine' and have never yet voted for a Guillotine Resolution.

8 July

Discussion on the Guillotine Resolution continued. The situation being so serious for the Govt. I very reluctantly vote for the Resolution – on the main question being put.

9 July

A rather more than average H. of C. day. On Standing Committee 'B' (Milk & Dairies Bill) at 11.30. On Committee 'C' (Exportation of Horses Bill) at 12 and after an hour or so back to 'B'!

After lunch meeting of Provisional Committee Fisheries Organization Society at the A.O.S. office.

Then to begin the day in earnest at the H. of C.

10 July

Before that to see Harold at Claridge's. Harold is busily engaged with Murray of Elibank in trying to arrange the Ulster difficulty. He has seen the 'P.M.' two or three times, L.-George, Redmond, Carson and Birrell.

13 July

Harold asks me to tell W. Runciman of the Ulster negotiations which I do. W.R. quite unaware of what has been going on. He is greatly impressed.

The Ulster demands for the moment are the exclusion of:
Co. Antrim
Co. Londonderry
Co. Down (except perhaps a small part)

Co. Armagh (except perhaps a part of the S.)
Co. Tyrone
N. Fermanagh
Londonderry City
(The excluded area to vote as a whole and not by Counties as under the Government's offer.)
Tyrone is the bone of contention. There are isolated groups of Covenanters in considerable numbers whom Carson will not give up. On the other hand 55.4 [per cent] of the population is said to be R. Catholic and returns 2 Nationalist members, the one and only Irish Liberal member (T.W. Russell) and the Orangeman. A.C. Murray tells his Chief Edward Grey of the Ulster negociations. Astonishing that E.G. should have had no knowledge of them!

17 July

W.R. [Walter Runciman] tells me that the Housing Bill is to be taken on Monday.

18 July

Busy again in the morning with preparations for the 2nd reading of the Housing Bill which is set down for Monday.

20 July

Announcement in *The Times* and *Daily Mail* today that the King has summoned a conference of Party leaders at Buckingham Palace. Asquith and Ll.-G., Lansdowne and B. Law, Redmond and Dillon,[11] Carson and Captain Craig.[12]

The House agog with excitement. Ardent Radicals and stalwart constitutionalists all very critical of the King's action.

After all, the Housing Bill does not come on. Tories object to taking so important and contentious a Bill at short notice. We discuss the Criminal Law Amendment Bill instead. A thin House. Members of all

---

[11] John Dillon (1851–1927): Irish Nat. MP Tipperary 1880–1883, Mayo East 1885–1918.

[12] James Craig (1871–1940): Unionist MP Down East 1906–1918, Mid-Down 1918–1921; leader of Ulster Unionist party and prime minister of Northern Ireland 1921–1940; cr. baronet 1918, Viscount Craigavon 1927.

parties putting their heads together in the lobbies and in the smoking-rooms and on the Terrace in eager discussion of the new development.

21 July
H. of C.

First meeting of the Buckingham Palace conference.
Report stage of the Budget (1st day) in the thinnest and most listless of Houses. Everybody out in the lobbies and on the Terrace talking about the Conference. Members generally very pessimistic as to its results and Liberals still alarmed at and suspicious of the King's intervention.

22 July

Second meeting of the Buckingham Palace conference. Terms of the King's Speech published today. Greater excitement still among Liberals and, it is said, disapproval of many Tories. The critics fail to discover in the Speech any trace of the Asquithian style. Is it H.M.'s own unaided effort?
In answer to questions the P.M. says that the Speech was in his hands the night before it was delivered, and that he accepts full responsibility for it.

24 July

H. of C. Government's Housing Bill – 2nd Reading.

30 July

War having been declared between Austria and Servia, Mr. Asquith announces in the H. of Commons that it has been arranged between the Government and the Opposition not to proceed for the time being with the highly contentious Amending Bill to the H. Rule Bill.
The papers today full of rumours of a European War. If Russia comes to the aid of Servia and Germany to the aid of Austria then a general conflagration may ensue. Hence the importance of our presenting a united front as a nation.

31 July

Mr. Asquith informs the House that Germany has announced a state of martial law throughout the empire. Russia reported to he mobilising on her S.W. frontier with a view, presumably, to assisting Servia. The Germans threaten to mobilise, too, if the Russian movement extends along Germany's frontier. The London and provincial Stock exchanges declared closed. Bank rate raised yesterday from 3 to 4 and today to 8%.

1 August
Henley

Worse news than ever of the European situation. All the armies of Europe, including even Holland and Belgium, said to be mobilising. Bank rate 10%! In the newspapers appeals to well-to-do householders not to buy up stores because of the result on prices and consequent effects on the poor.

2 August
Henley.

To church with the children and Helen Hamilton. In the afternoon (Sir) Charles Nicholson comes in from Phyllis Court with the news that Germany is reported to have marched into Luxembourg and that heavy gun-firing has been heard in the N. Sea. Charles has motored into town for the news. Hears that there have been two Cabinet councils today.

3 August

Sir E. Grey's great speech in the H. of C. explaining our position. It amounts to this that in view of the obligations to France we have already incurred in connection with the Entente Cordiale and our long-standing obligations in regard to the independence of Belgium the Government has found it necessary to make a firm stand. We have therefore assured France that we shall protect the coast towns on her northern and western shores from naval aggression and we have undertaken to protect Belgium. A most remarkable scene in the House. Four rows of chairs in the floor – Questions postponed and the 'Moratorium' Bill rushed through both Houses in a few minutes.

4 August

The P.M. announces in the House that the Government have sent an Ultimatum expiring at 12 o'clock tonight requiring that Germany shall respect the neutrality of Belgium. The news comes along in the course of the day, however, that Germany has already penetrated the Belgian frontier.
All the outstanding Votes passed in a few minutes.
Practically all parties in the House are now united. The small group who pleaded for our neutrality yesterday is now silenced. The invasion by Germany of the rights of Belgium has brought everybody into line.
Lord Morley[13] and John Burns have definitely resigned.
Runciman tells me that he has been appointed President of the Board of Trade in John Burns' place. Lord Lucas to be President of the Board of A. & F.
Remarkable crowds in all the chief streets and outside Buckingham Palace.

5 August

The Germans refuse to comply with our ultimatum and we are at WAR. And we are in to the thick of it very soon too. A German liner is sunk today while she is engaged in mine-laying – am not sure where but not far from Harwich. German army held in check at Liege and said to have suffered heavy losses.
Lord Kitchener[14] appointed Secretary of State for War.
The papers full of rumours as to the military and naval incidents all over the vast theatre of war.
The fact that we are at War brought home to us in many ways. Soldiers bustling off in every direction – large holiday crowds patrolling the chief thoroughfares – little Union Jacks and tricolours sold by all the street hawkers – cheering multitudes outside Buckingham Palace – public-houses crammed.

---

[13] John Morley (1838–1923): Lib. MP Newcastle upon Tyne 1883–1895, Montrose Burghs 1896–1908; cr. Viscount Morley 1908; Chief Secretary for Ireland 1886, 1892–1895; Secretary of State for India 1905–1910, 1911; Lord President of the Council 1910–1914.

[14] Horatio Herbert Kitchener (1850–1916): Field Marshal; cr. Baron 1898, Viscount 1902, Earl 1914; Secretary of State for War 1914–1916.

The H. of C. meets each day for a few hours – passes emergency Bills through all stages and adjourns early.

6 August

H. of C. We pass three astonishing votes without a murmur in any part of the House.
1. A vote for £100,000,000.
2. A vote for 500,000 more men for the Army.
3. A vote for 67,000 more men for the Navy.

Liege still holds out with immense heroism. Sinking of H.M.S. Amphion by a mine laid by the German ship destroyed yesterday. Feverish activity at the Board of A. & F. and at the Board of Trade in connection with enquiries as to food-supplies, relief projects, etc.

I spend the day with Arnold Rowntree[15] and Mr. Cross[16] trying to revive our Housing Bill. I interview Walter Long,[17] Lord Robert Cecil, Charles Bathurst[18] and Arthur Henderson[19] chairman of the Labour Party.

7 August

Further negociations in connection with the Housing Bill.

[15] Arnold Stephenson Rowntree (1872–1951): Lib. MP York 1910–1918; Quaker; opposed to the war.

[16] Elihu Richard Cross (1864–1916): Scarborough solicitor; friend and political associate of Arnold Rowntree.

[17] Walter Hume Long (1854–1924): Con. MP Wiltshire North 1880–1885, Devizes 1885–1892, Liverpool West Derby 1893–1900, Bristol South 1900–1906, Dublin County South 1906–1910, Strand 1910–1918, Westminster St George's 1918–1921; Parliamentary Secretary to the Local Government Board 1886–1892; President of the Board of Agriculture 1895–1900; President of the Local Government Board 1900–1905; Chief Secretary for Ireland 1905; President of the Local Government Board 1915–1916; Secretary of State for Colonies 1916–1919; First Lord of the Admiralty 1919–1921; cr. Viscount 1921.

[18] Charles Bathurst (1867–1958): Con. MP Wilton 1910–1918; cr. Baron Bledisloe 1918, Viscount 1935; Governor-General of New Zealand 1930–1935.

[19] Arthur Henderson (1863–1935): succeeded MacDonald as chairman of the parliamentary Labour party on 4 August 1914; Lab. MP Barnard Castle 1903–1918, Widnes 1919–1922, Newcastle East 1923, Burnley 1924–1931, Clay Cross 1933–1935; Labour party secretary 1912–1934; chairman of parliamentary Labour party 1908–1910, 1914–1917; leader of Labour party 1931–1932; President of the Board of Education 1915–1916; Paymaster-General 1916; Minister without Portfolio in War Cabinet 1916–1917; Home Secretary 1924; Foreign Secretary 1929–1931; president of World Disarmament Conference 1932–1934.

I go with W.R. to the Board of Trade.
The names of the Nord Deutscher Lloyd and Hamburg Amerika lines[20] pasted over at their fine offices in Trafalgar Square.

8 August

H. of C. sits today. Housing Bill Money Resolution and First Reading taken.
While I am sitting in the evening in W. Runciman's room at the Board of Trade John Burns comes in. He is the retiring President having resigned from the Ministry because of his opposition to the War. He has come to remove his dispatch boxes and papers which he does very ruefully. I tell him I hope he will soon be back with us again. Poor JB. He has always been very kind to me.
Harry Verney[21] appointed to the place I looked for at the Bd. of A. & F. – that of Parliamentary Secretary. Runciman has pressed me to go with him to the Board of Trade.

10 August

The H. of C. adjourns for a fortnight after passing the Housing Bill through all its remaining stages.
Early in the morning I attend a conference at the L.G.B. with Herbert Samuel,[22] Lord Lucas, Ld. Robert Cecil, Walter Long and others to agree finally on the details of the Housing Bill.

11 August

We are expecting a great battle in Belgium. It is now privately known that a part at least of our Expeditionary force is over there.

---

[20] German shipping companies.
[21] Harry Calvert Williams Verney (1881–1974): Lib. MP Buckingham 1910–1918; Parliamentary Secretary to the Board of Agriculture and Fisheries 1914–1915; succ. as 4th baronet 1910.
[22] Herbert Louis Samuel (1870–1963): Lib. MP Cleveland 1902–1918, Darwen 1929–1935; Under-Secretary of State, Home Department 1905–1909; Chancellor of the Duchy of Lancaster 1909–1910, 1915–1916; Postmaster General 1910–1914, 1915–1916; President of the Local Government Board 1914–1915; Home Secretary 1916, 1931–1932; High Commissioner for Palestine 1920–1925; cr. Viscount Samuel 1937.

I take the 3 children to the Hampstead Baths in the morning and to Lords Cricket Ground in the afternoon. A surprisingly large attendance at Lords (Surrey v. Kent the Oval having been requisitioned for military purposes), our 'flannelled fools' delighting an appreciative crowd just as highly as if the fate of Europe were not in the balance.

I decide after a most pressing request from Runciman to go with him to the B. of T. as his Parliamentary Secy.

12 August

We are on the eve of what may prove to be as great a battle as Waterloo. [...]

The fate of Europe trembles in the balance. Yet we take it very calmly. There is an extraordinary bustle about the War Office and recruits are drilling in the Temple Gardens and in every vacant space. A brisk demand for newspapers and unusual holiday-like crowds in the streets. On the Admiralty arches, and, I think, on the Foreign Office high-angle guns have been mounted behind screens so coloured as to attract as little notice as possible. Yet, I say, we are wonderfully quiet. Perhaps we rely too confidently on our fleets in the N. Sea and on our Allies and our Expeditionary Force in Belgium. What ever happens we cannot believe that Germany will ultimately prevail. I see no signs of boastfulness or swagger anywhere but only the orderly mobilising of a whole nation to resist German arrogance to the death. I attend meetings with shipowners at the Bd. of T. and at the L.G.B. a meeting to decide how best to make use of the provisions of the Housing Act during the bad period of unemployment that may be coming.

13 August

I am busy all day at the Bd. of Trade. One deputation after another dealing with shipping risks, the cotton trade, the corn supply, Argentine Beef and the national commissariat generally. Later to confer with Mr. Betham[23] in regard to Rural Housing under the new Act.

---

[23] Ernest Burton Betham (1864–1938): involved in the Garden City movement and published on topics related to housing; one of the architects of the Tatchbrook Estate, Westminster, which opened in 1935.

14 August

Another day without *new* news. The newspapers industriously furbish up for us again the accounts of the fighting round Liege. I spend the day finding out for Runciman at the Custom House and of the Admiralty Marshal what exactly is the jurisdiction in the matter of Prizes. It appears that the Marshal has full control, making use of Collectors of Customs as local agents or substitutes. The Board of Trade has no jurisdiction at all. Shipping and food supply Conferences at the Bd. of T. all day.

The Bd. of T. is now in control of all the railways of the country. The Government has bought vast quantities of sugar (for the general consumer and not merely for the W.O. and Admiralty) and quantities also of Canadian wheat.

15 August

Henley in the afternoon. A delightful day. The Babes and I indulge in an evening bathe. Such is the spirit of the times that one cannot altogether avoid a sort of guilty feeling in deserting the post of duty in London and taking refuge in the country even for a short week-end.

24 August

News this afternoon of the fall of Namur. This fortified place seems to have been expected to give a better account of itself even than Liege and its surrender is a serious matter.

It is now certain that our Expeditionary Force has been operating in the neighbourhood of Mons and has been obliged to fall back to lines of defence on the French frontier in company with our French Allies. The Prime Minister announces in the House that the retreat has been accomplished in good order but with 2,000 casualties to our troops.

The House meets after its brief recess and rises for the day after a number of urgency Bills have been given a Second Reading.

Conferences all day at the B. of Trade in respect of shipping, food-supplies, finance of industries, etc.

26 August

In the House today a batch of small emergency Bills are introduced and advanced various stages. There is a discussion as to the action of the banks – some are described by Ll.-G. as behaving well in the matter of providing credit to traders, others as deserving censure.

28 August

Short gloomy day at the H. of C. The P.M. announces that our soldiers on the Cambrai–Le Cateau lines have been fiercely engaged with 5 German Army Corps, 2 Cavalry Divisions, 1 Cavalry Reserve and 1(second) Cavalry Division and that our casualties have been 'very heavy'. What is to be the end of it all? It is pretty clear that ever since Namur and Mons we have been fighting a series of terrific rear guard actions. We seem to have fallen back some forty miles in a few days.

British marines land at Ostende to guard the town. Lord Crewe[24] in the Lords announces that we are bringing Indian troops to fight in France – which I greatly regret in spite of the circumstances.

29 August

I spend the morning at the Bd. of Trade and carry a message for Runciman to the War Office. Proud boy scouts as messengers everywhere in the great Dept.

The 12.5 to Henley. Our garden brilliant with flowers. This lovely riverside scene seems almost unnaturally remote from the tremendous events taking place not more perhaps than 150 miles from so tranquil a spot. How did our ancestors comport themselves just before Waterloo? I cannot avoid a sort of guilty feeling that I should be rusticating so easefully here while our men *out there* are struggling against terrific odds for the liberties of Europe.

---

[24] Robert Offley Ashburton Crewe-Milnes (1858–1945): Lib. peer; succ. as 2nd Baron Houghton 1885; succ. as 4th Baron Crewe 1894; cr. Earl of Crewe 1895, Marquess 1911; Lord Lieutenant or Ireland 1892–1895; Lord President of the Council 1905–1908; Leader of House of Lords 1908–1916; Secretary of State for Colonies 1908–1910; Secretary of State for India 1910–1915; Lord Privy Seal 1910–1911, 1912–1915; Lord President of the Council 1915–1916; President of the Board of Education 1916; Secretary of State for War 1931; leader of the Liberals in the House of Lords 1908–1923, 1936–1944.

31 August

To town by early train. The official news today is reassuring. We and our Allies are firmly established in our new lines nearer Paris. A persistent rumour that a large body of Russian troops (via Archangel, no doubt) have passed through Scotland and England on their way to the Continent.

Mischievous discussion in the H. of C. on Ireland, and Welsh Disestablishment. With Runciman and McKenna on discussions relating to the supply of wheat and meat.

I offer myself as a veteran to the C.O. of the Artists, 8th London Rifles.

1 September

Busy with W.R. at the Bd. of Trade. Mr. Neville Chamberlain[25] (a son of Joe's and much more like him in appearance than Austen)[26] comes along to advocate the spending of Govt. money on improving Canals in order to find employment.

2 September

Deputation to W.R. today of East End women workers headed by Miss Sylvia Pankhurst,[27] the younger of the formidable militant sisters.

---

[25] Arthur Neville Chamberlain (1869–1940): younger son of Joseph Chamberlain and half-brother of Austen; businessman and industrialist; Birmingham City Councillor from 1911, and Lord Mayor 1915–1916; Director-General of National Service 1916–1917; Unionist MP Birmingham Ladywood 1918–1929, Birmingham Edgbaston 1929–1940; Minister of Health 1922–1923, 1924–1929; Chancellor of the Exchequer 1923–1924, 1931–1937; leader of Conservative party and Prime Minister 1937–1940.

[26] Joseph Austen Chamberlain (1863–1937): elder son of Joseph Chamberlain and half-brother of Neville; Unionist MP Worcestershire East 1892–1914, Birmingham West 1914–1937; Civil Lord of the Admiralty 1895–1900; Financial Secretary to the Treasury 1900–1902; Postmaster General 1902–1903; Chancellor of the Exchequer 1903–1995, 1919–1921; Secretary of State for India 1915–1917; Lord Privy Seal 1921–1922; leader of the Conservative party 1921–1922; Foreign Secretary 1924–1929; First Lord of the Admiralty 1931; knighted 1925.

[27] Estelle Sylvia Pankhurst (1882–1960): daughter of Emmeline Pankhurst; suffragette; broke with the Women's Social and political Union in 1914 to form the East London Federation of Suffragettes, which later became in turn the Women's Suffrage Federation, the Workers' Socialist Federation and finally, in 1920, the Communist Party (British Section of the Third International); the last joined the Communist party of Great Britain in 1921 but Pankhurst was expelled soon afterwards.

The discussion is mainly about the cost of food in the East End and the competition of amateur lady needlewomen with the shirt-makers, etc. Sylvia states the main case with admirable precision and force and, later, when W.R. has left the room one of the women lectures the astonished permanent officials on the advantages of Woman Suffrage.

3 September

W.R. assures me today that there is not a word of truth in the rumour about Russian reinforcements coming from Archangel and passing through Scotland and England. He suggests that the supposed Muscovites must have been Lord Lovat's Gaelic-speaking gillies who have been enrolled for the War! Thus perishes one of the most widely and persistently circulated rumours in history.

4 September

Great speeches by the P.M. and Bonar Law at the Guildhall. Kitchener's new army already between 200,000 and 500,000 men.

I receive a letter from Lt. Col. May[28] of the Artists (28th London) Battn. saying that he fears I am too old to rejoin and asking me to visit the Headquarters which are now at Lords Cricket Ground.

7 September

Em and I go at night to meet Larry at Victoria Park station, N.L.R., beyond Bethnal Green. The Leinster Regt. has been stationed provisionally for some time at Cambridge and later at Newmarket. Now on its way by this unobtrusive route to the South Western Ry. and so to Southampton. The N.L.Ry closed to ordinary traffic but the station officials at Victoria Park allow us on to the platform. Larry's train, packed with cheering Tommies in their shirt sleeves, is even before its time. We are able to give him a latest pattern service revolver obtained by special permit from the Tower of London.

---

[28] Henry Allan Roughton May (1864–1930); commanded the 28th Battalion of the London Regiment (Artists Rifles) from 1912–1915, 1919–1920; in the interval he was Commandant of the Officers' School of Instruction at Tidworth.

9 September

The H. of C. reassembles alter a brief adjournment. Glowing and picturesque account of the loyal offers of the Princes of India. [It is impossible to describe the emotion and enthusiasm with which this message from India was received by the House.]

10 September

I address with J.O. Hickman, the Tory candidate,[29] recruiting meetings at Luton and Shillington.

11 September

War news today better and better. [...]
    To Lords Cricket Ground to see my old Corps, the Artists, at their temporary headquarters. They occupy the range of summer-houses round the practice ground. The actual cricket ground itself is left undisturbed. Col. May is good enough to walk round with me. He tells me they have had a wonderful rush of recruits of the best sort – Oxford and Cambridge men, old Blues, public school boys, etc. A slap-up lot.

14 September

This evening Em and I motor round the town to see the preparations that have been taken against attacks by German Zeppelins and other aircraft. They are putting a searchlight on the arches at Hyde Park Corner next to Apsley House. Two very powerful lights on Charing Cross Station that play on the clouds and search every space of the sky. The order has gone forth that all bright lamps, electric advertisements, etc. are to be put out. Even the blinds on the Embankment trains are drawn. Avenues of acetylene lamps in the Parks with a view, it is thought, to deceiving hostile aviators as to the topography of London by night.

---

[29] Although Hickman had been re-adopted as the prospective Con. candidate for Luton, he did not fight the seat in 1918.

20 October

Deputation today at the Board of Trade to consider the present gloomy condition of the whole cotton industry of Lancashire. The only helpful suggestion is that perhaps woollen khaki may be woven on some of the Lancashire looms.

21 October

Today Mlle. Ophelie Vertroost[30] of Ghent, a Belgian refugee, comes to stay with us. She got away from Ghent to Ostende by tram – Ghent then being in the hands of the Germans. [Mlle. Vertroost stayed with us all the years of the War and became a great favourite with us and the family generally. We were indeed very lucky in our merry roundabout little Mademoiselle. Many of the Belgian refugees taken hospitably into English homes were terrors.]

24 October

Lamentable news this evening that Larry has been killed in action – on the 21st [on the 20th as we learn from his Colonel (Col. Reeve)[31]]. A telegram from the War Office with this bare information. Poor dear Em in terrible distress. Her favourite brother and one of my dearest friends. How he used to worry me in the early days of the War to exercise influence to get him sent out to the front.

11 November

Opening of 5th Session of this Parliament.
Board of Trade and H. of Commons. I follow Mr. Speaker to the H. of Lords to hear the King's Speech. H.M. husky and very brief. Splendid in his scintillating crown and royal robes. Her M. a fine figure in the famous Cullinan diamonds and other jewels.

---

[30] No further information on her is available beyond that provided in this entry.
[31] William Tankerville Moneypenny Reeve (c.1866–1915): Lt Col., Commander of the Leinster Regiment's Second Battalion.

23 November

In the H. of Commons we are and have been ever since the outbreak of war a united family. There are no whips on the doors and the Division bells have not sounded for months. It is a joy to be able to get home most days for dinner.

8 December

To Newport (Mon.) with Henry Webb, M.P., G. Hay-Morgan,[32] M.P., and Sir G.H. Pollard,[33] M.P. to consider the question of raising Forest of Dean Battn. of the Gloucestershire Regt. We stay the night at Webb's house Llwynarthen, Castleton, between Newport and Cardiff.

Webb presses me to accept a Commission in the new Battn.

14 December

Down to Newnham on Severn to speak at meetings for the Forest of Dean Battn. My two places are The Sladd and Drybrook. Excellent gathering of miners at the latter.

The Sladd has apparently been drained pretty dry of young men.

21 December

Christmas shopping with Em and the babes in the morning. In the afternoon to the Board of Trade. Conference with Runciman and R. McKenna on the purchases of wheat by the Government.

24 December
Mother's Birthday.

To Poynters to dine with mother. Our dinner party consists of Alfred (Northcliffe), Harold (Rothermere), Leicester and Anne,

---

[32] George Herbert Pollard (1864–1937): Lib. MP Eccles 1906–1918.
[33] George Hay Morgan (1866–1931): called to the Bar 1899; KC 1913; Lib. MP Truro-Helston 1906–1918; Co. Lib. candidate in the Abertillery by-election 1920.

St John, Esmond H.,[34] Christabel and Percy [Burton] and Dr. Hall of Hatfield.

I return in Harold's car in a fog that deepens as we get nearer to town. The obscuring of all lights in and about London adds greatly to the fog difficulty. We take refuge in the Hampstead Tube railway and I arrive home very late for filling the children's stockings with Em.

31 December

Board of Trade. I send in my application for membership of the Old Boys Corps.

At midnight Em and I stand at the door steps to welcome the New Year in – conversing at the same time with the policeman on the beat as to the likelihood of a Zeppelin raid. The police have orders to make for the nearest telephone and ring up the Admiralty if they sight Zeppelins or other aircraft.

---

[34] Esmond Cecil Harmsworth (1898–1978): third son of Harold Harmsworth and succeeded as his heir after both his brothers Vyvyan and Vere were killed; served in the army during the First World War; ADC to Lloyd George at the Paris Peace Conference 1919; Con. MP Isle of Thanet 1919–1929; Chairman of Associated newspapers 1932–1971; succ. as 2nd Viscount Rothermere, 1940.

1915

1 January

My first squad drill for the old Boys Corps.

2 January

My second and third squad drills – the first at the Corps' dingy premises 6 Upper Baker Street, the second at the camp at Wembley Park. A fine bright day but plenty of mud at Wembley. The corps has here a range of sleeping huts made very ingeniously out of old railway carriages. The main body marches from the Regent's Park and arrives just as we conclude our drill.

3 January

Day of Intercession – observed in all the Churches of the Allies. E, I and the children to old Marylebone Church.

6 January

Two drills this morning. At 2.30 to the Memorial Service to Percy Illingworth, Chief whip, at the Presbyterian Church in Upper George Street. A great many members of all parties present [. . .] A Dignified and impressive service.
    Board of Trade.

8 January

Daily Mail private show (at the Ambassadors Theatre) of the German Govt. Films especially designed for exhibition in neutral countries.

Excellent films but little calculated, I think, to excite sympathy with the German cause.

13 January

Board of Trade before and after lunch. Runciman tells me that I am one of the three on the Prime Minister's short list for the vacant Under-Secretaryship Home Office and that McKenna is backing me strongly. The Liberal newspapers nominate me pretty definitely.

14 January

Runciman surprised that I have not yet heard from the P.M. McKenna tells him again today that so far as he knows there can be no doubt about the appointment.

15 January

Still no news from the P.M. Is it a case of the cup and the lip I wonder?

19 January

Board of Trade. Important conferences on the railways and on wheat supplies. [...]
No news of the H.O. appointment. Runciman tells me that this office is regarded as a 'plum' and may go to a junior Minister who has worked hard in some other department. Meanwhile I remain McKenna's nominee.

29 January

It gets on to the 'tape' from the Central News that I am to be appointed under Home Secretary next week. Meanwhile I have no official information.

2 February

The House of Commons reassembles today. I receive many hearty but premature congratulations on my appointment to the Under-Secretaryship of the Home Office. Meanwhile have no news from the P.M.
    Charles Masterman's resignation of the Duchy of Lancaster confirmed.

4 February

This morning I receive the following letter from the Prime Minister:-
    10, Downing Street
    Whitehall, S.W.
    3 Feb. 1915
My dear Harmsworth,
    It will give me much pleasure if you can see your way to accept the Under- Secretaryship of the Home Office, vacated by E. Griffith.
    Yours sincerely,
    H.H. ASQUITH
I repair early to Downing Street to thank the P.M. in person and he being busily engaged I leave a note. In the anteroom I meet Runciman, Lord Lucas, Peter Murray[1] and Harold Baker[2] all of whom congratulate me warmly. Em and I go to Poynters to tell dear Mother. [...]
    The rest of the afternoon I spend at the Bd. Of Trade – my last day there. It is not without sincere regret that I leave the President's splendid old room – formerly I suppose the dining-room of the Earls of Pembroke – with its ornate stucco ceiling, gilded cornices and pendant chandelier and above all its view of a spacious lawn and trees and the river with all its busy traffic beyond. These amenities will be sadly impaired when the new Bd. of Trade building is erected.

5 February

My first day at the HOME OFFICE. I lunch first with McKenna and Mrs. McK. at 36 Smith Square, their beautiful new Lutyens house.

---

[1] Unidentified.
[2] Harold Trevor Baker (1877–1960): called to the Bar 1903; Lib. MP Accrington 1910–1918; Financial Secretary to the War Office 1912–1914; Warden of Winchester College 1933–1946.

Sir E. Troup,³ K.C.B., also one of the party. Afterwards McK, Troup and I repair to the Home Office where we meet Ellis J. Griffith, the retiring Under Secretary, who inducts me into my dignified but gloomy apartment.

Shoals of congratulatory letters and telegrams with which I grapple during the rest of the day.

6 February

Home Office in the morning. My H.O. Secretary, Mr. A. Locke,⁴ goes over the business with me.

8 February

My first question in the H. of Commons. Lots of cheers which reduced me to a state of almost complete inaudibility. Neil Primrose (Under-Secy. F.O.) makes his debut at the same time and is almost equally voiceless.

12 February

Home Office in the morning and afternoon. My chief executive function just now is to consider applications for naturalization. Very few granted.

H. of C. not now sitting on Fridays.

23 March

First meeting (in my room at the H.O.) of the newly appointed Committee to enquire as to best means of stimulating recruiting in shops.

---

³Charles Edward Troup (1857–1941): Permanent Under-Secretary at the Home Office 1908–1922.

⁴Arthur Locke (d. 1932 at age 59): civil servant.

29 March

I attend as representative of the Home Office at the Treasury where Lloyd-George and Mackinnon Wood[5] receive a deputation of shipbuilders who come to urge the Government to prohibit the sale of drink during the War. The meeting takes place in the handsome Board Room with its vaulted ceiling and fine heavy Chippendale furniture. Ll.G. very grave and worn, his long grey hair more dishevelled than ever. He is greatly impressed by what the ship-builders tell him.

31 March

Third meeting of the Shops Committee. We consider and pass our first draft interim Report – so speedily must work be done in these days.

13 April

Recruiting Conference at the H.O. with the biscuit manufacturers of the U. Kingdom. All the familiar famous names well represented – Huntley & Palmer; Peek, Frean; McVitie Price; Macfarlane, Lang; Jacobs and the others. I address them in the conference room.

14 April

H. of Commons reassembles. At the H.O – a meeting of our Shops Committee, now happily reaching the end of its labours.

I am busy also with our little emergency Mental Treatment Bill which I am to take charge of in the House. The Bill is to enable officers who have been mentally upset for the time being by wounds and shocks at the Front, to receive treatment without being 'certified' or put into asylums.

---

[5] Thomas McKinnon Wood (1855–1927); London County Council 1892–1909; Lib. MP Glasgow St Rollox 1906–1918; Parliamentary Secretary to Board of Education 1908; Under-Secretary of State for Foreign Affairs 1908–1911; Financial Secretary to the Treasury 1911–1912; Secretary of State for Scotland 1912–1915; Chancellor of the Duchy of Lancaster and Financial Secretary to the Treasury 1916.

15 April

Busy all day with work connected with the Shops Recruiting Committee and the Mental Treatment Bill. [...]

Sad news today in the House of the death in action of W.G.C. Gladstone, M.P., the very promising grandson of the G.O.M. He made admirable speeches in the house on the Welsh Church question. I have several times walked home with him to his house in Berkeley Sq. and had a great liking for him.

17 April
Liverpool.

A visit in the morning from the Lord Mayor to discuss the Liverpool meeting in connection with the Shops Recruiting Committee.

Then Em and I go out in a taxi to the Red Cross Military Hospital at Moss Side, Maygull [Maghull]. At this hospital private soldiers and N.C.O.'s are receiving the sort of treatment we propose to make possible for officers under our Mental Treatment Bill. [Bill subsequently withdrawn on account partly of differences of opinion as to its desirability among Members of Parliament and partly because the War Office undertakes to extend as far as possible the Moss Side system to commissioned officers.]

22 April

R. McKenna offers today to bet me 15 to 1 that the Germans have evacuated Brussels (but not Antwerp) by the end of May.

23 April

Very busy day at the H. Office. Discussions about the Mental Treatment Bill, the second reading of which I am to move on Tuesday.

In the afternoon a Recruiting Conference with the Hotel and Restaurant Proprietors of the country. They think that they have but very few men of military age still in their service.

4 May

Great meeting of the Distributing tradesmen in the Westminster Palace Hotel addressed by the Prime Minister whose speech is almost entirely based on notes furnished by me. I take the Chair.

5 May

To Bath to address the local tradesmen in the afternoon and the Grocers Federation in the evening. Bath full of visitors and enjoying something like a return of its old time prosperity.

6 May

Conference in Committee Room 9 with members and permanent officials with a view to agreement on the Mental Treatment Bill. Bill left in a very delicate state of health.

8 May

News today of the sinking of the great liner 'Lusitania' by murderous German submarine. Over 1,000 men, women and children drowned.

12 May

Grievous news today that Geraldine's eldest boy Luke has been killed in the trenches.[6]

15 May

H.O. and then after lunch to see Alfred at St. James's Place. He is full of the delinquencies of the Govt. – the lax authority of the Prime Minister, the 'muddling' of Kitchener and the general ineptitude the whole body. He tells me that one of the most important of our Ministers

---

[6] Lucas Henry St Aubyn King (1895–1915): CH's nephew; of the Fourth Battalion King's Royal Rifle Corps; killed by shellfire near Ypres.

(Winston as I guess, but he does not say so) has been at him trying to get him to attack McKenna and Runciman. I reason with him on the folly of undermining one individual Minister after another, there being no other Ministry, Coalition or otherwise, in sight.

17 May

To Birmingham for a Recruiting Meeting in connection with the Shops Committee. Met grandly at New [Street] Station by the Lord Mayor.

This week beginning May 17th will prove, I suppose, one of the most momentous in our political history. On Monday a Liberal Govt. of great achievements and high prestige in full power on Friday everything in the melting pot and active measures being taken for establishing a Coalition Government.

I have set forth how this came about in another book – the details being too many for this diary.[7]

20 May

To Hull to address a meeting of local tradesmen in connection with the Shops Committee. Met grandly again at the station by the Lord Mayor and the Sheriff. March past at the Town Hall of a large number of the new recruits. I am called upon to take the salute!

21 May

H.O. I suggest to McKenna that it will be best for me and for everybody if he will accept my resignation. [In view, that is, of the general ill-feeling (and particular resentment on our Liberal side) excited by Northcliffe's savage onslaught on Kitchener in the *Daily Mail*.] He refuses to hear of it.

---

[7] Harmsworth's fuller account of the fall of the government appears to have gone missing within his own lifetime.

22 May

I write to McKenna formally tendering my resignation.

24 May

At lunch at the Reform Gulland[8] (Chief Liberal Whip) tells a group of us that probably the following Liberals will be found in the Coalition Cabinet in addition to the P.M. and Sir E. Grey: McKenna, Runciman and Mackinnon Wood.
Gulland confirms the rumour that a large number of Liberal M.P.s have expressed an emphatic opinion that Winston should on no account be a member of the new Cabinet.
After dinner, also at the Reform, Stanley Buckmaster informs me that Winston has been intriguing for a Coalition (of course with his bosom friend F.E. Smith in it) ever since the War began.

25 May

McKenna accepts my resignation.
Cabinet-making proceeding.

26 May

Before going to the H.O. I pay a visit to Dr. Johnson's house. The library room a great success and all in perfect order.
R. McKenna Chancellor of the Exchequer! I congratulate him. He decides not to show my letter of resignation to the P.M. unless it becomes clear that I must in any case yield place to a Tory Undersecretary. The Cabinet appointments gazetted today.

---

[8] John William Gulland (1864–1920): Lib. MP Dumfries Burghs 1906–1918; Junior Lord of the Treasury 1909–1915; Parliamentary Secretary (later joint) to the Treasury and Liberal Chief Whip 1915–1916.

27 May

John Simon's first day as Home Secretary. He is very nice to me when I congratulate him but there is something in his manner that suggests to me that my fate is already sealed.

I preside at the H.O. over a committee of 3 – the others being Will Crooks,[9] M.P. and H. Nield,[10] K.C., M.P. – to consider whether the topographical examination for taxi drivers is not too severe.

28 May

Simon takes me aside at the H.O. this morning and tells me that, greatly to his regret, I am on the proscribed list. The junior Ministers of most recent appointment are to be sacrificed. William Brace, a Labour M.P., is to succeed me.

Another meeting of the little cab committee. The famous Ebenezer Howard takes a verbatim note – his pen flying with great speed over the paper.

29 May
Lambourne.

My first day's fishing of the year. I take darling Daff with me for company. [. . .]

Truth to tell, it as not possible these sad days to relish any recreation – even fishing. One's mind *will* revert to the trenches in Flanders. It is nevertheless a sweet peaceful day.

31 May

I say goodbye to the permanent chiefs at the Home Office.

I dine with the McKenna's at 36 Smith Square. It is a dinner of farewell on McKenna's part to the H.O. chiefs and of greeting to John Simon. The new Lord Chancellor (Buckmaster) is the only guest present who is not associated with the H.O. As we are talking after dinner a message comes that a Zeppelin is fast approaching London

---

[9] William Crooks (1852–1921): elected to London County Council 1892; Lab. MP Woolwich 1903–1918, Woolwich East 1918–1921.
[10] Herbert Nield (1862–1932): Con. MP Ealing 1906–1931; knighted 1918.

by way of the Thames. Mrs. McKenna instantly thinks of bringing her children down to the cellarage and I make home with all speed. We fetch the children down to the dining-room while the maids repair to the basement. In an hour or so all to bed.

1 June

A long talk with Harold at the Ritz Hotel where he is now staying. He tells me that he has been in close touch with Bonar Law and that if B.L. had been appointed to the Admiralty he (Harold) was to have been Minister of Munitions! The furious *Daily Mail* attack on Kitchener upsets all such plans.

My painful duty today to introduce my successor, Wm. Brace, to the H.O.

The Zeppelin attack on London results in four deaths. The Admiralty is very secretive about the parts of London visited by the airship but rumour is very strong that Shoreditch and Stoke Newington are among them. Over 90 explosive and incendiary bombs dropped.

2 June

I preside over meeting of the governors of the Fisheries Organization society.

Another long talk with Harold at the Ritz. Sir Max Aitken,[11] Bonar Law's confidant has told Harold that Kitchener intends to raise the question of Alfred's attack on him, in the Lords. [. . .]

A letter from Gulland, Chief Liberal Whip, expressing his regret at my retirement from office and saying that I am to sit on the front bench to the left of the Speaker's chair.

---

[11]William Maxwell Aitken (1879–1964): Canadian businessman; newspaper magnate, owner of *Daily Express* from 1916 and founder of *Sunday Express* in 1918; Con. MP Ashton–under-Lyne 1910–1916; knighted 1911, cr. baronet 1916, Baron Beaverbrook 1917; Minister of Information 1918; Chancellor of the Duchy of Lancaster 1918; Minister of Aircraft Production 1940–1941; Minister of Supply 1941–1942; Minister of War Production 1942; Lord Privy Seal 1943–1945.

3 June

The H. of Commons reassembles with the Coalition Ministers – a certain number of them rather – on the Treasury Bench. Simon introduces a Bill to obviate the necessity for new Cabinet Ministers etc. to stand for re-election.

The Liberals and Irish seething with discontent. Why was a Coalition formed without preliminary party conferences? What was the need for it? Where will Liberalism and H. Rule be at the end of it?

T.P. O' Connor takes me along in his cab from the House and tells me that he is plunged in the depths of despair. Carson Attorney and in the Cabinet! Campbell bidding strong for the Irish Lord Chancellorship!

4 June

In the afternoon Em, Gol, Earle and I to Stoke Newington to see the houses damaged by Monday's Zeppelin (or Zeppelins, for nobody seems certain whether there was one or more). It is well-nigh miraculous that more human life was not lost. Both explosive and incendiary bombs were dropped. [. . .]

No apparent panic in this district. A policeman or so and a few women, children and interested visitors like ourselves outside each house.

I preside (after returning from S. Newington) at meeting of General Council of the Old Boys Volunteer Corps. Col. Grant hears at the War Office that we may soon be called on to perform duties usually assigned to the Territorials.

7 June

The Coalition now in full force on the Treasury Bench. It is odd to see Bonar Law, Robert Cecil and H.W. Forster[12] bobbing up among our old Liberal Ministers to answer Questions. Carson cheek by jowl with Simon and the P.M. and B. Law conferring amiably on points as they arise.

---

[12] Henry William Forster (1866–1936): Con. MP Sevenoaks 1892–1918, Bromley 1918–1919; Financial Secretary to the War Office 1915–1919; cr. Baron 1919; Governor-General of Australia 1920–1925.

Bill for creating a Minister of Munitions.

The Irish Party raging because of the proposal to appoint Campbell, Carson's colleague in the representation for T.C.D., Ld. Chancellor of Ireland.

Runciman invites me to return to him as Private Parly. Secy. Tells me, however, to go to McKenna at the Exchequer if he wants me.

8 June

McKenna asks me to become his Private Secy. and I accept.

14 June

A long pow-wow in the Board Room at the Treasury on the anxious financial problems of these unhappy times – McKenna, Edwin Montagu, Lord Reading[13] and Sir John Bradbury,[14] the Governor or the Bank of England (Lord Cunliffe)[15] and the Deputy-Governor[16] look in for a few minutes. Most of the discussion is metaphysics to me.

15 June

At McKenna's request I discuss with Hartley Withers[17] the question of an extra tax on War profits. [He had been City Editor of *The Times* and was Editor afterwards of *The Economist*. He was working now at the Treasury as 'Director of Financial Enquiries'. We used to sit in a little room over the passage that runs under Treasury Chambers thinking out schemes of taxation for McKenna. None of them were

---

[13]Rufus Daniel Isaacs (1860–1935): called to the Bar 1887; Lib. candidate for North Kensington 1900; MP for Reading 1904–1913; Solicitor General 1910; Attorney General 1910–1913; Lord Chief Justice 1913–1921; Viceroy of India 1921–1926; Foreign Secretary 1931; knighted 1910; cr. Baron Reading 1914; cr. Marquess of Reading 1926.

[14]John Swanwick Bradbury (1872–1950): economist and civil servant; Joint Permanent Secretary to the Treasury 1913–1919; cr. Baron 1925.

[15]Walter Cunliffe (1855–1920): merchant banker; Governor of the Bank of England 1913–1918; cr. Baron 1914.

[16]Brien Cokayne (1864–1932): Deputy Governor of the Bank of England 1915–1918, Governor 1918–1920; cr. Baron Cullen of Ashbourne 1918.

[17]Hartley Withers (1867–1950): City editor, *The Times* 1905–1910, *Morning Post* 1910–1911; merchant banker 1911–1915; Director of Financial Inquiries at the Treasury 1915–1916; editor, *The Economist*, 1916–1921.

new devices, so far as I remember – I mean of our devising. (C.H. 6th Feby. 1934) (See 9th August)]

16 June

To see Harold (Rothermere) at the Ritz Hotel. He is just back from a second or third visit to the front in Flanders and is, for the moment at least, as pessimistic as he was formerly sanguine. He says that the important soldiers at the front whom he has seen do not believe that we shall ever be able to dislodge the Germans. Further, that they have little confidence in French (Sir J.). H. takes too a very gloomy view of our financial position. He walks with me to the Treasury and makes some suggestions to McKenna.

17 June

I dine with the McKennas at Smith Square. Also of the party the Walter Runcimans and Harold Baker. Some amusing political gossip – how that Simon is very unpopular with his colleagues in the Cabinet partly because of his huge vanity – and of Arthur Balfour's subtle workings to consolidate his position in his own party and to keep Bonar Law out of the reversion to the leadership of the Tory Party. There is talk too of Lloyd George's machinations which are supposed to have for their object the ousting of the P.M. and the putting of Ll. G. in his place. The P.M. reported to be very firm in the saddle and keeping a tighter rein than formerly.

18 June

Another talk with Hartley Withers about the proposed tax on War profits and methods for popularising the War Loan which McKenna is to announce in the H. of C. on Monday.

21 June

We are feverishly busy at the Treasury with the War Loan and with plans for popularising it.

Today McKenna makes his great War Loan speech in the House – surpassing all his previous achievements and, it must be added, the most sanguine expectations of his friends, by the lucidity of his Statement. He aims at a loan reaching to the stupendous figures of perhaps 900 millions – but will be well satisfied with 500 or 600.

22 June

Our constant visitors at the Treasury are: the Governor of the Bank, Lord Cunliffe, a large jovial John Bull of a man whose levity of manner is only the thinnest disguise for one of the astutest minds in the country: Lord Reading, Lord Chief Justice, with his splendid handsome face and deep musical voice – the only member of his race I have ever really liked: Chisholm,[18] the financial editor of *The Times*: Alfred Spender[19] of the *Westminster Gazette*: *The Economist*, *The Statist*, and all manner of people skilled in high finance.

At my instance, McKenna invites Northcliffe to the Treasury with a view to enlisting the largest circulations in active support of the loan. They get on famously together.

23 June

The H. of C. sits but we are very little there except at question time. Hartley Withers and I are to knock out a scheme for popularising the Loan. We decide to ask for the assistance of the Parliamentary Recruiting Committee.

24 June

The best part of the day with Hartley Withers in the room that has been taken for him at the Bd. of Education. His nominal post is that of Director of Financial Intelligence or something of that kind.

We draw up a letter addressed to John Gulland, Chief Liberal Whip and Chairman of the Parly. Recruiting Committee, asking the Committee to lend their valuable assistance to the War Loan movement.

---

[18] Hugh Chisholm (1866–1924): financial editor of *The Times* 1914–1920.
[19] John Alfred Spender (1862–1942): prominent Liberal journalist; editor of the *Westminster Gazette* 1896–1922; biographer of Asquith and Campbell-Bannerman.

These several days McKenna receiving all sorts of deputations about the Loan.

25 June

Meeting of the Parliamentary Recruiting Committee in the long room at 12 Downing Street. Hartley Withers and I asked to be present. Of the Committee itself the following members:
J. Gulland, Lord Edmund Talbot[20] (Chief Tory Whip), Steel-Maitland,[21] E.S. Montagu, Herbert Samuel (Post Master General), Sir Jesse Herbert, Boraston[22] (Chief Tory Agent), Arthur Henderson (Chairman of the Labour Party and President Board of Education), Lord Colebrooke and Arthur Peters.[23] It is agreed to create a second War Savings Committee to work through and on parallel lines, with the Recruiting Committee.

Montagu and I walk away from the meeting together and go through No. 10 to the Treasury. Mrs. Asquith drives up as we are knocking at the door. I carry in her parcels – among them a broken cardboard box revealing a pair of blue satin shoes.

All the rest of the day with McKenna in the Board Room and working with Hamilton[24] (principal private secretary).

27 June

How quickly these delicious week-ends pass! It is only in such happy intervals that one really lives. And yet since the War began it has not been possible fully to enjoy a respite from work. Always in the

---

[20] Edmund FitzAlan-Howard (1855–1947): styled Lord Edmund Talbot 1876–1921; 2nd son of the 14th Duke of Norfolk; Con. MP Chichester 1894–1921; joint Parliamentary Secretary to the Treasury and Chief Whip 1915–1921; Lord Lieutenant of Ireland 1921–1922; cr. Viscount FitzAlan 1921.

[21] Arthur Herbert Drummond Ramsay Steel-Maitland (1876–1935): Con. MP Birmingham East 1910–1918, Birmingham Erdington 1918–1929, Tamworth 1929–1935; Chairman of Unionist party 1911–1916; Under-Secretary of State for the Colonies 1915–1917; Secretary for Overseas Trade 1917–1918; Minister of Labour 1924–1929; cr. baronet 1917.

[22] John Boraston (1851–1920): assistant secretary of Liberal Unionist organisation 1887–1891; Liberal Unionist Chief Agent 1891–1912; Principal Agent for combined unionist party 1912–1920.

[23] Arthur Peters: Labour party national agent 1908–1919.

[24] Horace Perkins Hamilton (1880–1971): civil servant; Permanent Secretary to the Board of Trade 1927–1937; Permanent Secretary to the Scottish Office 1937–1946; knighted 1921.

background of one's mind is the life and death struggle in Flanders and in Gallipoli. It seems unworthy to rest at such a time.

8 July

To Manchester with M.H. Whitelegge[25] of the Home Office to attend a Conference of the Cotton industry to discuss what means should be taken to release a larger number of men for enlistment. With Gerald Bellhouse,[26] also of the H.O., we spend the afternoon going over a spinning mill.

9 July

In the morning we visit a weaving mill.

After lunch the Conference of employers and operatives at the Town Hall. I take the chair. An amicable discussion. It is agreed on both sides that everything must be done – whether by substituting women for men in some branches, by the relaxing of Trade Union rules etc., and by assurances from employers that any such readjustments shall be purely temporary – to facilitate recruiting.

16 July

Em's first night as a nurse at Lady Mountgarret's private military Hospital 18 Cadogan Gardens.

20 July

In H. of C. the P.M. moves a Vote of Credit for £150,000,000 bringing the total voted since the outbreak of War to £1,012,000,000.

Veiled references of the P.M.'s to possible loans to Powers which are not in alliance with us revive hopes that Bulgaria, Roumania and Greece may be coming in. A fantastic rumour in the lobbies that Turkey is going to join us!

---

[25] Maurice Horsley Whitelegge (1889–1978): civil servant.
[26] Gerald Bellhouse (1868–1946): civil servant; Chief Inspector of Factories 1922–1932; knighted 1924.

22 July

I am now installed at the Treasury in a little room of my own almost exactly over the tunnel under the Treasury house and looking through some green pleasant trees to Downing Street. The room has been cut out of a much larger one and boasts a very handsome carved marble mantel-piece and a beautiful mahogany door. McKenna is on the other side of the narrow passage in the fine old Board Room.

23 July

The deadlock continues on the Western front and there seems to be little doing at the Dardanelles, but every day has its grievous casualty list. We are awaiting with anxiety the outcome of the Germans' third great thrust for Warsaw. A terrible struggle is proceeding.

29 July
Ongar Camp.

I go into Camp for a few days with the Old Boys who rejoice on ceremonious occasions in the fuller title of the 3rd Battn. (Old Boys) Central London Regt. (Volunteer). We make quite a brave show in spite of our years as we muster at 6 o'clock in the evening on the platform at Liverpool Street.

Our camp is in a meadow within a stone's throw of Blakehall railway station and consists of 4 lines of bell tents, a huge mess marquee, a smaller marquee for the officers, and quarters for the cooks, waiters and other details. Straw is spread thick on the floors of the bell tents and water is laid on from the station.

9 August

I spend the afternoon with Hartley Withers considering taxation proposals for McKenna's Autumn Budget. We decide to recommend the doubling of all existing taxes and licences and of inland postages and receipt and cheque duties. New taxes also on tickets for theatres, cinemas, race-meetings, football matches, etc. [. . .]

News today that Harold's eldest boy Vyv.[27] has been wounded again – this time in the face. We do not know how seriously. Harold at Boulogne where Vyv. is in hospital.

10 August

Treasury. A talk this morning at the War Office with General Montgomery,[28] Director-General of Recruiting, about the trades or departments of trades in regard to which the W.O. recognises that further recruiting is inadvisable. Such occupations are certain branches of work in engineering and agriculture, and 'piecers' in the woollen and cotton industries.

Discussion with Hartley Withers on the proposed memorandum to McKenna with suggestions for his forthcoming Budget.

11 August

(Vyv had a very narrow shave of it this time. A bullet glanced from his left eyebrow to the bridge of his nose leaving scars that he will probably carry with him all his life.)

18 August

My little room at the Treasury is also the waiting-room for important visitors to McKenna.

Today while McKenna is presiding over the first meeting of the Retrenchment Committee Lord Reading comes in and we discuss gloomily the latest phase of the War on the eastern front – the reported fall of Kovno and other cheerless details. Then Edward Grey is shown in wearing his great smoked-glass spectacles. He tells us that by the use of these glasses he will retain his power of eyesight but that any loss of power must be permanent. He has no actual improvement to look for. All this he explains philosophically – with a quiet heroism

---

[27] Harold Alfred Vyvyan St George Harmsworth (1894–1918): eldest of the three sons of Harold Sidney Harmsworth; killed in action.

[28] Robert Arthur Montgomery (1848–1931); retired in 1910 after a long military career but was re-employed upon the outbreak of war and served as Director-General of Recruiting in 1915.

that is admirable and characteristic. A sad misfortune indeed to fall on a fine sportsman, the beau ideal of English statesmen.

19 August

Treasury again today. Lord Reading comes in again and we continue our doleful talk about the War. Suppose after all that a material part of the Grand Duke's forces is surrounded by the Germans? What if the Russians grow weary of the War and decide on a separate peace? Again, what is the use of this agitation for compulsory service, seeing that it is not so much largely-increased numbers of men we want as rifles and machine-guns for the hundreds of thousands now in training? If the Allies fail, shall we go on squeezing the Germans by means of our sea-power? And so on in melancholy strain until Reading, tired of waiting for McKenna who is again busy with the Retrenchment Committee, goes in to No. 11 to see Lloyd-George who is suffering from a bad cold.

14 September

Reassembling of Parliament. A few Questions – chiefly on the vexed question of Compulsory Service – and then some talk on the Adjournment.

I walk back to the Treasury with McKenna who is full of his Budget speech on Tuesday.

15 September

The P.M. moves another vote of credit for £250,000,000 and Kitchener makes a general statement in the H. of Lords. He stands up at the table and reads through his big spectacles from a manuscript. He looks like a great big foot-guardsman and is red and bronzed and healthy as vigorous a man at 65 as you will find anywhere. A thin attendance of their Lordships who murmur polite applause two or three times.

In the H. of C. we have a warm discussion on Compulsory Service.

I never quite know whether the P.M. recognises me but he called to me by name behind the Speaker's chair this afternoon and asked me to find Gulland (the Chief Whip) for him which I accordingly did.

16 September

A story current just now:

Lord Rosebery was dining at Buckingham Palace where, in accordance with the King's pledge of abstinence during the War, temperance drinks only found place on the royal table. The conversation turned on Zeppelin raids. 'I suppose,' said H.M., 'if they come about here we shall all have to bolt for the wine-cellars.' Rosebery, fingering somewhat ruefully a glass of barley-water: 'May I start now, Sir?'

21 September

McKenna introduces the biggest Budget that ever was in a speech of admirable lucidity. Heavy increased taxation on most of the old lines and a new little tariff on imported manufactures which greatly pleases the 'Tariff reformers'. The proposal to raise the charges on Press telegrams received with the loudest cheer of all by a House that does not love the Press.

My part in the proceedings consists in sending along the front Bench to McKenna a small glass containing egg flip with which he moistens his parched lips from time to time. I have never before known him so nervous.

House rises about 9 o'clock. On my way home I call in at the Ritz to see Harold. He has just returned from another visit to the Front and is full of interesting news from the British and French lines. He says that the French are just as confident as our people are depressed. Our officers full of complaints of our generals.

Harold tells me that the P.M. and Ll.-George have been scarcely on speaking terms of late. The rumours quite true that Ll.-G. is or has been leading a revolt against the P.M. and in favour of a more energetic conduct of the War, together with Compulsory Service and other vigorous policies.

Murray of Elibank, the former Liberal Chief Whip, busily employed in bringing the two great men together.

23 September

Budget in Committee. I receive for McKenna a deputation of motor agents and retailers who protest vigorously against the $33\frac{1}{3}\%$ Tariff on imported cars, bicycles and accessories. My memories of the old

'Tariff Reform' controversy vividly awakened. British manufacturers who are now mainly occupied on munitions of war want foreign cars etc. kept out – the agents declare that they will be ruined if the duty is imposed. (They are interested chiefly in the small American cars against which the duty has been mainly designed with a view (1) to restoring the balance of trade between the U.S.A. and ourselves and (2) to checking the extravagance of our people.)

24 September

Another lesson in Tariff mongering. The Managing director of our chief manufactory of ball-bearings, his most important works being in Sweden, wants to know if the 33 1/3 duty is to apply to ball-bearings. If so he must forthwith decline Government and other orders. Ball-bearings are used in a hundred different kinds of machinery and he cannot separate those used in motor-cars and bicycles from those required for the many other purposes.

Another visitor represents the French and Italian motor-manufacturers. A few cars are still coming to us from our Allies. Are we going to dash their enthusiasm by imposing on them a duty which is directed against the huge import of small American cars? This visitor is only too willing that American cars should be penalised but French and Italian cars are quite another matter.

(On Thursday night I went to Islington start a 'War Savings' movement on behalf of the Parliamentary War Savings Committee.)

27 September

Treasury. Interview with Luton people about the duty on hats. What are hats from the Budget point of view? If only complete hats are to be taxed then the staunchest Free Traders amongst my Luton friends are prepared to accept the 33 1/3 tariff with resignation – the 'hoods' and forms and shapes are another matter. I ring up the Commissioners of Customs & Excise and find that 'hats' means hats in all stages of evolution. This is a sad blow to my visitors.

A Member of Parliament comes in to complain that the doubled duty on Patent medicines has thrown the whole trade into confusion and that the abolition of the halfpenny postage for circulars will cost him £250 a year.

'Broadening the basis of Taxation' has its disadvantages after all.

28 September

My birthday. A card from dear Mother who is touring round the West Country still – kept away from Poynters by fear of Zeppelins. Not that she is afraid of Zeppelins but that Alfred is apprehensive on her behalf. [. . .]
    H. of C. and Treasury. Deputations today about watches and hats. Everybody enthusiastic for a tariff on somebody else's commodities.
    Dinner given by H.M. Government to M. Bark,[29] Russian Minister of Finance, who has been in and out of the Treasury for days trying to raise the wind, as I understand, for his suffering government. The London Museum is the scene of the banquet. A very splendid gathering the P.M., Kitchener, Simon, Winston Churchill (sitting immediately opposite me), McKenna, Ld. Chr. Buckmaster, Walter Long, Lord Crewe, Lord St. Aldwyn,[30] Sir John Bradbury, Sir Edward Grey (in his great black spectacles), the Russian, French and Italian Ambassadors, the Servian, Belgian and Greek Ministers, Walter Runciman, Lulu Harcourt, Sir Guy Laking[31] (curator of the Museum) and a fringe of Secretaries of Legations, private secretaries (like myself) and other small fry. Dinner excellent – cigars even better.

30 September

Better news of our forward movement. Many German guns and prisoners taken. Protective tariffs debated in H. of C. Hat tax laughed out of the House.

1 October

To see Sir Edward Troup at the Home Office. They want me be Chairman of another recruiting committee – to enquire how best clerks can be released for military service.

---

[29] Pyotr Lvovich Bark, later Peter Bark (1869–1937): Russian Minister of Finance 1914–1917; exiled to London after the revolution; knighted 1935 for services to banking.

[30] Michael Edward Hicks Beach (1837–1916): Con. MP for East Gloucestershire 1864–1885; Bristol West 1885–1904; Chief Secretary of Ireland 1874–1878 and 1886–1887; Secretary of State for the Colonies 1878–1880; Chancellor of the Exchequer and Leader of the Commons 1885–1886 and 1895–1902; President of the Board of Trade 1888–1892; cr. Viscount St. Aldwyn 1906 and Earl St. Aldwyn 1915.

[31] Guy Francis Laking (1875–1919): first Keeper of the London Museum from 1911 until his death; succ. as 2nd baronet 1914.

2 October

To Luton to take part in a big recruiting 'rally'. A procession through the town – soldiers, Volunteers, hospital nurses, Boy Scouts and two field guns. Mass meeting outside the Town Hall.

3 October

With Daff to Poynters to see Mother and St. John. Alfred comes later from *The Times* office a little more cheerful about the War.

11 October

I attend Lord Derby's[32] recruiting conference at the Chief Whip's office 12 Downing Street. (Lord Derby is the newly-appointed Director General of Recruiting). Parliamentary Recruiting Committee and Labour leaders present. Lord Derby is to give the voluntary system a final trial and then – ?

The rest of the day at the H.O. and the Treasury arranging *our* new recruiting campaign in the clerical employments.

12 October

At tea time to the H.O. to receive two members of the Amalgamated Society Union of Co-operative Employees. It is charged against their Union that action taken by them is hindering recruiting.

In the morning to 22 St. James's Place to see Northcliffe who is indoors with a chill. I find him in bed flanked by a telephone on either side and partially submerged under piles of newspapers. He was to have told me of fresh Cabinet disruptions but a War Correspondent from the Western front and another visitor occupy his attention, and I hear nothing. N. is more dreary than ever about the War. There is nothing for it but a brand new Government!

---

[32] Edward George Villiers Stanley (1865–1948): Con. MP for West Houghton 1892–1906; Junior Lord of the Treasury 1895–1899; Financial Secretary to the War Office 1901–1903; Postmaster General 1903–1906; Director-General of Recruiting 1915–1918 and author of the so-called 'Derby Scheme' to promote enlistment; Ambassador to France 1918–1920; succ. as 17th Earl of Derby 1908; known as the 'Uncrowned King of Lancashire' because of his importance to the county's political and associational life.

What Government and where from? – I should have heard something of this but for the interlopers before-mentioned.

13 October

Quarterly supper of the Johnson Club at Dr. Johnson's House. After supper a paper (an excellent one) with the unpromising title of 'The Cynicism of Dr. Johnson' is read by a visitor and we are discussing it when of a sudden there are three or four tremendous reverberating crashes and lesser sounds of gunfire. We rush to the windows and there poised almost immediately overhead is a Zeppelin. White and beautiful with the beams of searchlights full upon it. Though probably at a great height I distinguish its huge flat fish-tail quite clearly. The shells from our air-craft guns break like stars round the great vessel with only a faint popping sound.

Whether any of the shells are anywhere within range of the Zeppelin we cannot tell. The airship remains poised over St. Paul's for some two or three minutes – for such time at least as enables Mr. Birrell and me to escape from the press of Johnsonians at the windows of the Dictionary Attic and to make for one of the rooms below. Here we have an uninterrupted view of the Zeppelin which lingers for some time before eventually it fades away in a S. Easterly direction. The fusillade of the aircraft guns has meantime been briskly maintained. Long after the departure of our murderous visitant two military gentlemen of our company keep their gaze fixed on the constellation Pleiades and stoutly assert that it is the vanished airship.

After these sensational events we return to the discussion of Johnson's cynicism. Birrell's contribution to the debate is less happy than usual what could be expected even of the most brilliant after-dinner orator in London who has been engaged at a stormy Cabinet meeting all the afternoon and the train of whose reflections has been broken by a Zeppelin raid? [. . .]

Renewed rumours in the H. of C. today of troubles in the Government. There is a Cabinet Council from 4 o'clock in the afternoon until past half-past 6. Carson ostentatiously dissociates himself from his colleagues and sits in the smoking room gossiping with friends while the Council is taking place in the P.M.'s room behind the Speaker's Chair.

14 October

In the H. of C. there is much talk about the Cabinet dissensions. Carson is said to be profoundly dissatisfied with the Dardanelles situation and with the Allied landing of troops at Salonica.

15 October

Treasury. Lord Fisher,[33] recently First Sea Lord, comes into my room to wait for McKenna. 'Jackie' Fisher, as he is called, is sometimes described as the maker of our modern navy and is brisker at 74 than most men of half his age, a bantam for size with an indescribably clever face. He has just time to express wonder that none of our generals have been shot when McKenna comes in to fetch him away.

19 October

First meeting of the Clerical employments Committee. [Committee, that is, for the substitution of women for men in banks, insurance offices, etc. When I think of it, how the H.O. and the Departments piled these committees on me during the War! I ought to have stuck to my place in the House. C.H. 23/10/1935.]

23 October

At the H.O. in the morning with Delevingne[34] and Whitelegge. We go to the Board of Education to see Sir L.A. Selby-Bigge[35] in connection with proposals for training girls for clerical employments.

---

[33] John Arbuthnot Fisher, (1841–1920): became a full Admiral in 1901 after a long naval career, and an Admiral of the Fleet in 1905; Second Sea Lord 1902–1904; First Sea Lord 1904–1910, 1914–1915; chairman of the Board of Invention and research 1915–1918; cr. 1st Baron Fisher 1909. His recall as First Sea Lord by Churchill upon the outbreak of war was followed by a disastrous clash between the two men, which helped trigger the creation of the Asquith coalition in May 1915.

[34] Malcolm Delevingne, (1868–1950): entered the civil service 1892, rose to be Permanent Secretary at the Home Office 1922–1932; knighted 1919.

[35] Lewis Amherst Selby-Bigge (1860–1951): Permanent Secretary at the Board of Education 1911–1925; knighted 1913.

I [go] to the Scottish Office to discover whether they want our Committee to operate in Scotland. I am not surprised to find that Scotland prefers to manage her own affairs.

1 November

The McKennas and Harold (Rothermere) lunch with us at Gough Square. An excellent repast, including a small edition of the famous beefsteak pie, served piping hot from the Cheshire Cheese. It is a snug and harmonious little party – the McKennas greatly enjoying their novel experience.

Afterwards Reggie hurries off to a Cabinet Council and I to a Conference on the subject of my Committee with certain Lord Mayors at the H.O.

2 November

Alfred rings me up early to announce that he is coming to take me for a walk round Hyde Park. He is in a more equable mood than usual but is full of the crimes and shortcomings of the Government. The only Minister he has a really good word for is my chief McKenna. I leave him in Trafalgar Square and he proceeds on his way to Printing House Square.

5 November

After lunch at the Reform today I find a small knot of people gathered round the still-veiled statue of Captain Scott in Waterloo Place. It is about to be unveiled by Arthur Balfour. Gradually the crowd increases in size, and admirals and other high personages assemble. At last Mr. Balfour arrives and from a small platform proceeds to address us. He pulls the tape and the very picturesque statue, the work of Lady Scott, is revealed. It ought to be more like the original than any statue in London but I should not have known it was meant for Captain Scott if I had not been told. Perhaps the lights on the new green bronze of the face are deceptive.

6 November

News today that Kitchener has gone abroad on important business connected with the War. The Prime Minister takes over the War Office in his absence.

9 November

Lord Mayor's Show Day. Em on duty with other St. John's nurses in the street. I meet Mrs. McKenna at the H. of C. in the evening and she tells me that Em has saved two lives in the crowd – one that of a woman who falls in a fit. Mrs. McKenna is Commandant of Em's detachment.

17 November

Simon asks me to take charge of a Committee to consider the general Question of substituting women for men in employment luring the War. A gigantic task!

25 November

These apparently blank days[36] I have spent at the Home Office engaged on work of the Clerical Employments Committee and of the new Committee on women's employment generally. The question is how best to mobilise the reserves of woman labour so that the gaps in industrial and other employment caused by enlistment may best be filled. This problem and that of National economy are the two most anxious domestic questions of the War.

My attendances at the H. of C. few and far between these days.

[Later: I hope that my time on these Committees was usefully spent but even in wartime an M.P.'s proper place is the House of Commons, if he is not on active service. As it was, most parliamentary hours were occupied by snipers who harassed the Government continually with but few members to talk back to them and to put the Government and national case. The life of a Government always depends in the long run on the House of Commons and in wartime it is more than

---

[36] i.e. 22 and 23 November.

ever necessary that it should be a friendly, reassured and contented House. C.H.]

2 December

Conferences at the H.O. of manufacturing clothiers and operatives of the U.K. The operatives desire certain assurances if women are to be introduced into departments hitherto reserved to men. No agreement reached but I do not despair.
    Afterwards Conference with Bankers at the H.O. – they greatly alarmed at the prospect of losing their indispensable men under Lord Derby's recruiting scheme.

3 December

Conferences at the H.O. all day long with great associations – Accountants, Corn Exchange and Shipping Federation with a view to securing them better safeguards under Lord Derby's recruiting scheme.
    I seem to live at the H.O. these days. [...]
    To Poynters. Harold comes in later.

13 December

First meeting of the new War Loan Committee from which McKenna would not let me escape. [The Committee that devised and recommended War Savings Certificates. The idea was Lord Bradbury's.]

16 December

Second meeting of the War Savings Committee in Birrell's room at the H. of Commons. Our problem is to devise a scheme of saving that will really attract the working classes. We toy with suggestions for a lottery on Continental lines!
    To Paddington, first of all, to meet Gol returning from his first term at Summer Fields.[37] The little lad in an absurd bowler hat and a bright

---

[37] Oxford preparatory school.

red tie is in the very pink of condition and brings with him a prize — Scott's Poems — for Latin.

20 December

I forget what day it was but earlier in the Session I had a long talk on the Terrace with John Burns about the War. Since his resignation in August of last year he has taken no part in the proceedings of the House nor has he had anything to do with Peace movements but he is as strong as ever in his conviction that we should have kept out of the War. 'The result will be – you mark my words – the loss of 500,000 of our best, a debt of 3,000 millions, two years stagnation and a draw!'

24 December
Totteridge.

Mother's birthday. [. . .] Alfred, Harold and Vyv come in time for dinner.

Our talk is all of the newest Government Crisis. The P.M.'s repeated promise that unmarried 'slackers' should be compelled to enlist before the married men are taken seems likely to prove very awkward, if, as it is beginning to be alleged, the number of slackers is considerable. The results of the Derby canvass are now being made up. The P.M.'s pledge must of course be kept yet it would be a violent thing to bring in compulsion merely in order to redeem a pledge somewhat hastily and heedlessly given.

27 December
Poynters.

Alfred in after dinner with fresh news of the Cabinet Crisis. Resignations are threatened on the one side if Compulsion is insisted on and on the other if it is not!

28 December

To town today with Alfred, and busy at the Home Office with Delevigne considering the Report of our Committee on the general question of substituting women for enlisted men.

In the evening to Totteridge. Alfred comes in before dinner and says that the Cabinet have decided to adopt Compulsion. He does not know how far any Ministers on the one side or the other are standing out. He goes to bed very early and I read to him and translate passages out of a batch of German Christmas numbers of periodicals he has with him.

29 December

Bud and I come in to town early in St. John's car – the others following later.
After lunch I walk to Westminster Abbey to hear the carols. [. . .]
Afterwards to the Treasury. H.P. Hamilton, McKenna's Secretary, all agog with excitement and wondering whether McK. is still Ch. of the Excheqr. He has all McK.'s affairs in order and merely awaits marching orders.
McK. himself looks in for a moment. He is very cheerful but sphinxlike as to his intentions.
It seems that he, Runciman and John Simon are the strongest anti-conscriptionists in the Cabinet and McK.'s resignation is actually in the P.M.'s hands. The die appears not to be irrevocably cast, however.

30 December

All the afternoon with the Women's Occupations Committee. We consider our Report. A 4 hours' session!
Afterwards to the Treasury for a few moments. McKenna looks in and I have just time to say that I hope he is not going to shake the dust of the Treasury off his feet when he goes out again.

31 December

For an hour to the Treasury where I hear that Simon has left the Government but that there is a good chance of McKenna and Runciman remaining. Cabinet councils morning and afternoon.

1916

5 January

Introduction by the P.M. of the Compulsory Service Bill in the fullest House since the first few weeks of the War. A large number of members in khaki.

6 January

First reading of the Compulsion Bill carried by 405 against 105. A notable feature of the debate is a fervent speech supporting the Bill by John Ward,[1] the navvies' member now a Colonel in the Army. The 3 Labour members of the Government including Brace,[2] my successor at the H.O., resign their offices.

11 January

Last meeting (I hope) of the Women's Employment Committee. It has been a very weary job composing the endless differences of the H.O. and Bd. of Trade members of this Committee.

---

[1] John Ward (1866–1934): trades unionist; MP for Stoke-upon-Trent and a successor constituency 1906–1929, first as a Lib-Lab, as a Lib. Coalitionist from 1918, and as Constitutionalist from 1924, rejoining the Liberal Party later that year. During the First World War he served in France with the 21st Middlesex regiment, of which he was lieutenant colonel.

[2] William Brace (1865–1947): Lab. MP for South Glamorgan 1906–1918 (initially Lib-Lab), Abertillery 1918–1920; Under-Secretary for Home Affairs 1915–1919. The other Labour ministers were Arthur Henderson, President of the Board of Education, and George Henry Roberts (1868–1928), Lord Commissioner of the Treasury. The resignations were rescinded after assurances were given that the proposed Military Service Act would not be used for the purposes of industrial conscription.

19 January

Eric back to Summer Fields in charge of Antony Asquith[3] and young Runciman.[4] Mrs. Asquith at the station to see her boy off. She brings us all back to Montagu Sq. in her motor car discussing excitedly Northcliffe's attacks on the P.M. She evidently thinks that N. has some personal grudge against the P.M. – a mistaken impression that we do our best to dispel. She tells us that the P.M. works at his papers for two or three hours after his game of Bridge in the evening.

15 February

Opening of the new Session of Parliament. The King presented by a Commission of five peers in the H. of Lords and his speech read by the Lord Chancellor.

16 February

Short speech in the H. of C. in favour of the establishment of a department or Ministry for Air Service.

23 February

Conference at the H.O. with a view to settling a dispute in the clothing trade.

29 February

To the Board of Trade to arrange with Walter Runciman the personnel of the new public committee (superseding the recent inter-departmental committee) to consider the substitution of women for men in industries during the War.

---

[3] Anthony Asquith (1902–1968): youngest son of H.H. and his second wife Margot; became a successful film director.
[4] James Cochran Stevenson Runciman (1903–2000): third child of Walter Runciman; known as Steven; became an historian; knighted 1958.

3 March

First meeting of the new Committee on Women's employment at the Board of Trade.

In the afternoon Turkish bath at the Automobile Club where I meet three men whose names in their several ways are as well-known as any in England – Sir John Dewar,[5] the head of the great whiskey firm, John Redmond (eagle-like and still dignified even in the scanty blue cotton wrapper of the hot rooms) and Winston Churchill, just back from the Front. In Winston's case the care that sits on the faded cheek of the statesman has been lost in the trenches and he has a fine healthy colour. He asks after Northcliffe and Rothermere and takes a cheerful view of the Allied prospects on the West front. Referring to the great fight now raging round Verdun [he] is always willing to exchange so many yards of ground for so many German bodies. 'I have always been against these local offensives,' he says. He has some thought of taking part in the debate on Naval estimates on Tuesday.

7 March

Winston is as good as or better than his word. He makes a sensational attack on Admiralty policy, following Balfour's introductory speech on the estimates.

Em and Daff to Luton for annual meeting of Liberal Women.

8 March

Correspondence at home before lunch. At 2 o'clock I preside at annual meeting of the Fisheries Organization Society (a legacy from my Board of Agriculture & Fisheries days); at 3 I attend meeting of Labour Exchange officials; at 5 I preside at Council meeting of the Garden Cities Association, and I have just time to get back to the H. of C. to meet the employers in the Wholesale Clothing trade whose men are threatening to strike. I who formed a resolve early in public life that I would not be rushed about from one committee meeting or other engagement to another!

---

[5] John Alexander Dewar (1856–1929): whisky blender; brother of Thomas Dewar; Lib. MP for Inverness-shire from 1900–1916; cr. baronet 1907; cr. 1st Baron Forteviot 1916.

18 March

Daily Mail office to see Mr. Basil Clarke.[6] The D.M. is taking much interest in the question of substituting women for enlisted men.
On my way home after lunching at the Reform I walk through Hyde Park where there is a demonstration of married attested men.[7] They are demanding: (1) that unmarried exempted men shall be taken out of Munitions works etc. and put into the Army; (2) that the unattested married men of military age shall be compelled to join; (3) that adequate financial provision shall be made for enlisted married men. Their spokesmen threaten the Government with all sorts of difficulties unless these things are done.

21 March

I dine this evening with Alfred and Mary to meet Mr. William Morris Hughes[8] the Labour Prime Minister of Australia. He has made a great impression here with his finely expressive speeches on the War. He is a small delicate man and very deaf.

22 March
Luton.

Annual meeting of the South Beds Liberal Association where, in the evening, I make a speech on the War – party politics being wholly barred at this time.
During the day I visit two large engineering firms – Kent's and Davis's – both now chiefly engaged in making fuses (Kent's) and shells, hand-grenades and rifle-grenades (Davis's). Both places buzzing with activity. Hundreds and hundreds of girls in blue overalls and caps at Kent's, working with great skill on the machines used in the many processes of fuse-making.

---

[6]Basil Clarke (d. 1947 at age 68): journalist and subsequently public information official; knighted 1923.
[7]Under the Derby recruiting scheme of 1915, married men were encouraged to 'attest' their willingness to join up if the war situation were to demand it.
[8]William Morris Hughes (1862–1952): Prime Minister of Australia 1915–1923, initially as leader of the Labor Party and subsequently as leader of the Nationalist Party, which he founded. A member of the British delegation to the Paris Peace conference in 1919.

Kent's have a great new works at Chaul End outside Luton for fuse-filling.

29 March

A painful incident in the House today. Just as Percy Harris,[9] the new member for Market Harborough, was taking the oath at the table, an officer began clambering over the railing of the Ambassadors Gallery to the left of the clock. His movements were swift and athletic and in a moment he was hanging by his hands looking about for a clear spot to drop among the group of members behind the Bar. We were all too much astonished even to exclaim. The officer let himself go, and fell, out of my sight, among the members. He was on his feet in an instant with some words about calling on the H. of C. to protect the heads of our soldiers against shrapnel. He was led out unresistingly. He seems to be a Lieut. Turnbull, R.A.M.C.[10]

4 March

McKenna makes another of his short and brilliantly clear Budget statements. It is my duty as his Parliamentary Secy. to send him along a glass of something for his voice – this time it is white and thick with perhaps a suspicion of rum in it. His butler is late with it and keeps me very fidgety until he arrives.

Such figures! Estimated total revenue for 1916–17: £502,275,000. Estimated Expenditure: £1,825,380,000.

6 April

Budget resolutions. Desultory debate all day. About 9.30 I go home with McKenna and dine with him, Mrs. McK., Lady Jekyll and J.H. Whitehouse, M.P.

---

[9] Percy Alfred Harris (1876–1952): Lib. candidate for Harrow Jan. 1910; Lib. MP for Market Harborough 1916–1918; Bethnal Green 1922–1945; Chief Whip 1935–1945; cr. baronet 1932.

[10] Dr Arthur Turnbull (? b.1884): a lieutenant in the Royal Army Medical Corps. He subsequently wrote to *The Times* apologising for his course of action; fought three by-elections as an Independent during 1916.

McKenna shows me the King's cheque for £100,000 – H.M.'s 'War Savings' to be devoted to any purpose approved by the Govt. The King banks at Coutts's.

10 April

H. of C. Second Reading of the Bill embodying the new taxes on mineral waters, amusements, matches and railway tickets.
At 8 o'clock to the Sylvan Debating Club at the Tavistock Hotel. A larger attendance than I have ever seen at the Club to hear Alfred (Northcliffe) speak on his experiences during his 6 visits to the Front and on the shortcomings of the two successive War Governments. A most interesting discourse.

11 April

I go down to Lancashire to preside at a Conference of employers and operatives in the Cotton trade – the object being to devise means for bringing back to the trade married women weavers who have left it. There are other women temporarily unemployed because the mills in which they ordinarily work are shut down.

17 April

Cabinet crisis at its height. The question is whether conscription shall be extended to (1) the unattested married men and (2) young men of 18. The P.M.'s pledge that he will not remain head of a Government that makes itself responsible or an extension of the compulsory principle is thought to be an insurmountable difficulty.

18 April

In the House today the P.M.'s statement in regard to the recruiting crisis is postponed owing, as he says, to there being some outstanding points without which his statement would be 'incomplete and inadequate'. The House adjourns very early and I go home with Walter Runciman to tea. He tells me that but for Ll.-George the Cabinet difficulties would have been accommodated – that Ll.-G.

assailed the P.M. very bitterly in a recent Cabinet. W.R. is far more deeply concerned himself about the shipping and shipbuilding questions than about recruiting. He shows me urgent memoranda on these questions circulated by him to the Cabinet.

19 April

The P.M.'s statement again postponed – this time until Tuesday next. He speaks now frankly of Cabinet dissensions that threaten the break-up of the Government. A crowded and excited House (many soldier members having been called back from the Front) and such a 'Lobby' as has scarcely been seen since the War began.

Sitting next Carson on the Front Opposition Bench he tells me of the P.M.'s fine courtesy and great patience in Cabinet but also of his utter lack of initiative, his main object on all occasions of difficulty being to contrive a formula that would cover difference of opinion instead of putting his foot down and insisting on having his way. The House rises early again and I go over to the Treasury to talk to McKenna. I point out to him that the best friends of the P.M. are distressed and uneasy and that most of them know nothing about the actual state of affairs except what they read in the accounts of Lobby correspondents in the papers. I urge strongly that the Government should have the matter discussed in the House sitting with closed doors and that the House should be taken frankly into the confidence of the Government. There can be no more danger in this, I suggest, than in the bruiting abroad of all sorts of rumours in newspapers pretty accurately primed by Ll.-George and his supporters.

20 April

At lunch at the Reform today, I sit with Alfred Spender, editor of the *Westminster Gazette*, and McKenna,[11] the Chancellor's brother. I take up my parable about the desirability of the Government's holding a sitting of the House with closed doors and telling members the plain truth about the situation. My suggestion is scouted as wholly impracticable and I am overwhelmed with a *great* wealth of arguments. We grow quite warm about it in fact and have not left our places at the table when Mackinnon Wood, the Scotch Secretary, comes along to tell us that the crisis is over and that the sitting on Tuesday is to be *in camera*!

[11] McKenna had four brothers; it is unclear which one is referred to here.

25 April

This is the day of the Secret Session of Parliament and of much sensational news. The first thing we hear at the H. of C. is that the Sinn Feiners have broken loose in Dublin, have taken possession of the G.P.O., the railway stations and other strategic points and are virtually in control of the Capital. There are rumours that the Under-Secretary, Sir M. Nathan,[12] is a prisoner in Dublin Castle and that even the Lord Lt. is in the hands of the insurgents. Mr. Redmond looking very haggard, and deep gloom generally prevails among the Nationalist members. It is felt that once again the fruition of national aspirations has been frustrated by the folly of the Irish people themselves.

The Secret Session is a comparatively tame affair. After strangers have withdrawn on the P.M.'s intimation to the Chair members overflow into the Peers', Distinguished Strangers' and Press Galleries and the P.M. makes a long statement of which only two or three points are of a really confidential nature. Carson, who replies, is critical enough but seems not inclined to carry his motion of censure to a Division. By dinner-time the House is nearly empty though excellent speeches continue to be made from time to time.

Of other sensational events a Zeppelin attack on the E. Coast and the bombardment of Lowestoft and Yarmouth by a German light squadron are the most important.

26 April

Communications with Dublin still interrupted. Em sends three prepaid telegrams to various relations and none are answered.

In the H. of C. the news is that Sir M. Nathan is really a prisoner but finds means in some way not fully explained to communicate by wireless with the Government. Some officers, returning from the races at Fairyhouse, taken as hostages by the rebels. Liberty Hall, near the Custom House, the headquarters of the insurgents, shelled to pieces by a gunboat operating in the river. Minor outbreaks reported from Swords and Lusk, from Ardee and from Drogheda.

In the House the depression of the Nationalists is set off by the unconcealed elation of the Ulster men.

---

[12] Matthew Nathan (1862–1939): Under-Secretary for Ireland 1914–1916, having previously held various colonial governorships; Governor of Queensland 1920–1925; knighted 1899.

T.W. Russell tells me that the Irish Civil Service and especially the Post Office is packed with Sinn Feiners.

Second day of the Secret Session. A great deal of very frank criticism of the Government but again no real secrets are divulged.

2 May

P.M. announces that the Cabinet have decided to complete the circle of military compulsion.

3 May

At Question time Birrell appears sitting at the corner above the gangway on the bench immediately behind Ministers. He makes a frank explanation of the causes that have led to his resignation and is heard with much sympathy in every part of the House. The P.M., Carson and Redmond all make generous little speeches – Carson's coming with special grace from that dark incarnation of the Ulster spirit.

The P.M. introduces the Second Compulsory Bill – bringing in, that is, the unattested married men, the lads of 18 and making other minor provisions.

General Maxwell[13] announces that all the surviving Irish rebels have surrendered. It is also officially announced that Patrick Pearse,[14] Thomas MacDonagh[15] and Clarke,[16] three of the ringleaders, have been shot this morning.

I spend the afternoon with McKenna at the Treasury.

9 May

H. of C. Second Military Service (Compulsion) Bill. We sit late.

---

[13]John Grenfell Maxwell (1859–1929): army officer; Major General 1906; appointed as commanding officer with dictatorial powers following the Easter Rising of 1916; responsible for the disastrous decision to shoot fifteen of the rebels; knighted 1915.

[14]Patrick Henry Pearse (1879–1916): President of the provisional Irish Republic that the rebels declared.

[15]Thomas Stanislaus MacDonagh (1878–1916): poet, one of seven signatories to the proclamation of the Republic.

[16]Thomas James Clarke, (1858–1916): a significant figure in the Irish Republican Brotherhood, first signatory to the proclamation of the Republic.

I find myself in mixed company on the front Opposition Bench these days. There is the grim-visaged Carson who is so gentle and even communicative in private conversation: Winston fresh from the trenches and full of hostility to the Government of which he was so recently a member: Sir F. Banbury,[17] the arch-obstructionist in old party days and now so impatient of the speeches of members below the gangway on the other side: Ellis Griffith, an ex-Under Secretary Home Office like myself, a brilliant critic of the unfortunate Government: Sir James Dougherty, formerly permanent Under Secretary in Ireland and full of inside information about Irish affairs: C.E.H. Hobhouse[18] who was once unaccountably a Cabinet Minister and whose bitterness against the Government is only restrained by his eagerness for another job: 'Tommy' Lough,[19] H.M.L.[20] for County Cavan (why?), an impulsive Irish tea-merchant who was 'stellenbosched'[21] in the early days of the 1906 Government: J.M. Robertson,[22] one of the junior ministers who like myself was displaced at the formation of the Coalition, a profound authority on Free Trade and Elizabethan literature: Sir Alfred Mond,[23] an 'Hebrew Jew', and with all his thick utterance and swarthy appearance well-nigh as able a man as there is in the House: Duke, K.C.,[24] the 'heavy father' of our group: Lord Claud Hamilton,[25] who was a junior Lord before I was born and who is one of the few aristocratic-looking aristocrats of our time: Sir

[17]Frederick George Banbury (1850–1936): Con. MP for Peckham 1892–1906; City of London 1906–1924; cr. baronet 1903; privy councillor 1916; cr. 1st Baron Banbury of Southam 1924.
[18]Charles Edward Henry Hobhouse (1862–1941): Lib. MP for Wiltshire East 1892–195; Bristol East 1900–1918; Under-Secretary of State for India 1907–1908; Financial Secretary to the Treasury 1908–1911; Chancellor of the Duchy of Lancaster 1911–1914; Postmaster General 1914–1915; succ. as 4th baronet 1916.
[19]Thomas Lough (1850–1922): Lib. candidate for Truro 1886; Lib. MP for West Islington 1892–1918; Parliamentary Secretary to the Board of Education 1905–198.
[20]His Majesty's Lieutenant, or Lord Lieutenant, a largely honorific position.
[21]i.e. dismissed for inadequacy. During the Boer War incompetent British officers were sent to a camp at Stellenbosch in order to await transport to Britain. In his ministerial role, Lough had handled the government's Education Bill poorly.
[22]John Mackinnon Robertson (1856–1933): freethinker and rationalist author; independent Radical candidate for Northampton 1895; Lib. MP for Tyneside 1906–1918; Parliamentary Secretary to the Board of Trade 1911–1915.
[23]Alfred Moritz Mond (1868–1930): industrialist; Lib. MP for Chester 1906–1910; Swansea 1910–1923, 1924–1928 (joining the Conservative Party in 1926); First Commissioner of Works 1916–21; Minister of Health 1921–1922; cr. baronet 1910; cr. Baron Melchett of Landford 1928.
[24]Henry Edward Duke (1855–1939): called to the Bar 1885; served as a judge from 1897–1933; QC 1899; Unionist MP for Plymouth 1900–1906; Exeter Jan. 1910–1918; Chief Secretary for Ireland 1916–1918; cr. Baron Merrivale of Walkhampton 1925.
[25]Lord Claud John Hamilton (1843–1925): Con. MP for Londonderry City 1865–1868; King's Lynn 1869–1880; Liverpool 1880–1885; Liverpool West Derby 1885–1888; South

George Reid, an Australian statesman and as round as a barrel: Sir R. Finlay, K.C.,[26] a dour old Scotsman who has been a Tory Law Officer and who has been disappointed of the Woolsack: Stuart Wortley,[27] a third Home Office Under Secretary: and half a dozen other ex-Ministers and Privy Councillors. We are united by one sentiment only – namely, that, if only we had continued in such and such an office, such and such egregious blunders would not have been committed. There is a flutter of expectancy amongst us when any ministerial office falls vacant. When the appointment is made we relapse into our customary attitude of critical observation of the Government. In less anxious times than these it would be a delight to hob-nob day by day with this ill-assorted but entirely friendly crowd of greater or lesser political derelicts.

10 May

In the House the Irish members call for a discussion on the Military executions now taking place in Ireland. The debate is set down first order for tomorrow.

11 May

Discussion on the rebellion in Ireland. Dillon makes a characteristically bitter speech.

Military Service Bill in Committee. Having nothing more useful to do I sit out the Debate and make 3 small speeches.

17 May

The House rises early today. John Simon takes me to the Garrick Club where we dine pleasantly in the fine room full of handsome pictures.

Kensington Jan. 1910–1918; served as Lord of the Treasury 1868; Chairman of the Great Eastern Railway.

[26] Robert Bannatyne Finlay, (1842–1929): called to the Bar 1867; QC 1882; Lib. candidate for East Lothian 1883; Lib. then Lib. Unionist MP for Inverness Burghs 1885–1892, 1895–1906; Edinburgh and St. Andrew's Universities Jan. 1910–1916; Solicitor General 1895–1900; Attorney General 1900–1905; Lord Chancellor 1916–1919; knighted 1895; cr. Baron Finlay 1916; cr. Viscount Finlay 1919.

[27] Charles Beilby Stuart-Wortley (1851–1926): called to the Bar 1886; QC 1892; Con. candidate for Sheffield 1879; Con. MP for Sheffield 1880–1885; Sheffield Hallam 1885–1916; Under-Secretary at the Home Office 1885–1886, 1886–1892; cr Lord Stuart of Wortley 1916.

Simon is a varied and resourceful talker with a touch of pedantry. He tells me that it is at 'The Club'? of which he is a member that the best modern conversation is heard. He has been present when the P.M. and two ex-P.M.'s (Rosebery and Balfour) were capping one another's stories in delightful style.

18 May

Lunch today at the McKenna's. Lord and Lady Pirrie,[28] Mr. and Mrs. Runciman[29] and Vaughan Nash there. The talk on the scribbling and other meditative tricks of members of the Cabinet in Cabinet. Balfour draws very pretty little ink sketches of Scotch scenery with groups of pines, using blue and red pencils for some of his effects. F.E. Smith produces a coin from his pocket, places a piece of paper over it and takes a 'rubbing' of it with a lead pencil. Bonar Law covers sheet after sheet of official stationery with spirals [...] McKenna draws endless carefully balanced geometrical designs. Winston Churchill's trick was to roll neat cylinders of paper and to tuck the open ends into one another, generally in a triangular form. The PM is always writing letters supposed to begin invariably 'Dearest —'. [Later: Letters to 'Hilda' no doubt.[30] C.H. 6/2/1934.] Much laughter at this.

19 May
Shelbourne Hotel, Dublin.

Lovely May morning. No signs of the late Rebellion save a Martial Law Proclamation here and there, some bullet holes in the lower windows of the Shelbourne and I see from my window long mounds of newly-turned earth in St. Stephen's Green – the parapets, I suppose, of the Sinn Fein trenches. (No – these are only road-mending materials. The

---

[28] William James Pirrie (1847–1924): Chairman of the Belfast shipbuilders Harland and Wolff from 1895; Comptroller of the Household of the Lord Lieutenant of Ireland 1907–1913; cr. Baron Pirrie 1906; cr. Viscount Pirrie 1921; m. Margaret Montgomery Carlisle (1857–1935) 1879.
[29] Hilda Runciman, née Stevenson (1869–1956): m. Walter Runciman 1898; Lib. MP for St. Ives 1928–1929; Lib. candidate for Tavistock 1929; became Viscountess Runciman of Doxford in 1937 when her husband was elevated to the peerage.
[30] Hilda Harrisson (1887–1972): widow of Captain Roland Harrisson (1882–1917); painter; one of several Asquith confidantes.

'trenches' were no more than shallow scrapes among the trees at the corners of the Green.)

Em and Daff arrive two or three hours after me by the North Wall boat.

We go off to Sackville Street to see the ruins. The E. side completely wrecked as far as Nelson's Pillar. On the W. side there is a much shattered block standing and then ruins as far as the G.P.O., the outer shell only of which stands still complete. The devastation extends far down the side streets and is of much greater extent than I had imagined.

Lucas,[31] Dot, Enid and Lady Castlemaine[32] lunch with us. Afterwards I tour round the city with the Kings in their car, visiting. King Street where some of the fiercest fighting took place and the Linenhall Barracks now a gigantic ruin. The number of houses riddled with bullets is beyond counting in different parts of the city the College of Surgeons and houses adjoining, the Four Courts and many houses on that side of the river, together with almost every house in King Street.

21 May

To Roebuck Hall to lunch. [. . .] Dr. Mahaffy full of the exploits of the T.C.D. Officers' Training Corps a handful of whom manned the front of the College and saved the Bank and the heart of the City. They had a machine gun on the roof of the northern abutment and swept Westmoreland Street, Carlisle Bridge and Lower Sackville Street. All this under the skilful direction of Alton F.T.C.D.,[33] whom Mahaffy has recommended to the P.M. for the D.S.O. Dr. Mahaffy very scornful of the 'minor poets' who led the Rebellion and attributing much of their fatal enthusiasm to the study of the Irish language.

22 May

Lunch with Lucas in the Fellows' Common Room T.C.D. With us Alton and Prof. Starkie.[34] All agree that the present regime must go

---

[31] i.e. Lucas White King.
[32] Annie Evelyn Barrington (d. 1955): m. Albert Edward Handcock, 5th Baron Castlemaine 1895.
[33] Ernest Henry Alton (c.1873–1952): Fellow of TCD from 1905; Chair of Latin 1921–1942; Provost 1942–1952.
[34] William Joseph Myles Starkie (1860–1920): President of Queen's College, Galway, 1897–1899; Resident Commissioner of National Education in Ireland 1899–1920.

and that in some way Irishmen must be associated with Irish Govt. Lord Macdonnell is mentioned as a possible Chief Secy. but there is the difficulty that he is a peer.

(I forgot to mention that Asquith told Mahaffy the two things that most pleased him during his visit to Ireland were the Provost's House and the beautiful gorse of County Cork!)

After lunch we fetch Em and Daff from the Shelbourne and all in the motor-car on a further tour of inspection of the damaged parts of the City – the City Hall, Four Courts, the City of Dublin Distillery and Boland's bread factory.

We dive with Lucas into sundry musty old curiosity shops on and about the Quays, looking for rebellion relics. No Sinn Fein stamps or rebel Proclamations to be had for love or money. A belt, a copy of the 'War News', and two or three Irish Volunteer and republican buttons comprise our bag.

24 May

We dine with the Archbishop and Mrs. Bernard. John Dublin's[35] view is that two first steps are necessary at the present unhappy juncture in Irish affairs (1) the maintenance of a very strong garrison and (2) the pardoning of the rank and file of the rebels now in prison in Ireland and England while at the same time and as a part of the same policy making it clear that the imprisoned ringleaders will not be amnestied but must work out their sentences to the bitter end.

I receive a telegram from Alfred Northcliffe saying that he has shown my recent letter to Lloyd-George and asking me to stay on in Dublin for some days longer. He is busy in London trying with Ll.-G. to solve the Irish problem.

A story of the Rebellion. While the populace were looting a shop in Henry Street a woman who was vainly struggling to carry away groceries and other goods beyond her physical capacity was heard to exclaim – 'Glory be to Mary, why didn't I bring me ass an' cart!'

25, 26 & 27 May

I have no daily record of this period. On Thursday Em and Daft went down to spend the night with the Bernards of Bernard Castle,

---

[35] i.e. Bernard. The Church of Ireland Archbishop of Dublin signed himself 'John Dublin'.

Kinnety while I stay in Dublin to track down Wm. M. Murphy,[36] the great tramway magnate and owner of the *Daily Independent* whom Alfred and Ll.-G. regard as an essential element in the negociations now going on for the settlement of the Irish question. The role of Pacificator has been assigned to Ll.-G. by the Cabinet and he has not only Liberal opinion with him but almost the whole of British Unionist opinion too. Murphy's newspaper has all along maintained an attitude aloof from that of the regular Nationalist party. It has been severely critical of the Home Rule Bill and has usually been less than cordial to the Nationalist leaders. With its circulation of 120,000 a day it is a power to be reckoned with, especially if it is assumed that large numbers of its readers share its opinions. Clearly, Murphy and the *Independent* cannot be left out of account in any proposals for 'settling' Ireland.

29 May

We spend the morning at the Hardinge (Rebellion) Commission[37] now sitting in one of the rooms of the Shelbourne. We hear the evidence of two ex-police officers, Sir J. Ross[38] of Bladensburg and Mr. Harrel.[39] Their evidence strengthens the impression that during recent years there has been no government in Ireland, Castle or other.

2 June

A telegram from Alfred saying that he and Ll.-G., want me to see prominent Dublin business men and sound them as to the present situation. I see Mr. George Stewart,[40] Governor (last year) of the

---

[36] William Martin Murphy (1844–1919); tramway entrepreneur and press magnate; Irish Nat. MP for St. Patrick's, Dublin 1885–1892; candidate for Kerry South 1895; Mayo North 1900.
[37] The Royal Commission on the Rebellion in Ireland, chaired by Lord Hardinge of Penshurst, reported in June 1916.
[38] John Foster George Ross (d. 1926 at age 77); Chief Commissioner of the Dublin Metropolitan Police 1901–1914; resigned in protest at the dismissal of W.V. Harrel (see following note); knighted 1903.
[39] William Vesey Harrel (1866–1956); Assistant Commissioner of the Dublin Police for twelve years prior to 1914, when he was dismissed in the wake of the Howth gun-running affair, in which a Nationalist attempt to land weapons was followed by the shooting of unarmed civilians by the authorities.
[40] George Francis Stewart (1851–1928): land agent; Irish Unionist.

Bank of Ireland and Sir Wm. Goulding, Bart.,[41] Chairman of the Irish Railway Clearing House and of the Great S. & W. Railway etc. Both mild Unionists but agreed that Home Rule must ultimately come. They deprecate, however, any instalment of H.R. at this present juncture – Mr. Stewart because such a concession would be regarded as a triumph for the Sinn Feiners, Sir Wm. Goulding rather because he thinks Redmond has lost so much influence that he could not govern Ireland. The exclusion of the recalcitrant Ulster counties necessary in any case. Both much prefer a *governing* Lord Lieutenant, with a nominated Council of Irishmen.

3 June

I call this morning at the Castle on Herbert Samuel, Home Secretary, who is over to settle the question of compensation to property owners in Dublin for damage caused during the Rebellion and on Sir Robert Chalmers[42] of the Treasury who has been over here as Under Secretary since just after the Rebellion. Poor Chalmers by no means happy in his novel and difficult position. He regards himself as exiled and is visibly delighted to have a Minister from England to support him. He greets me with effusion as a comrade from the Treasury. Chalmers *is* the Irish Government so far as it is not in the hands of General Maxwell.

I lunch with Samuel, Chalmers and Sir J. Barran, M.P.,[43] Samuel's parliamentary fag, at the Hibernian Hotel, and we then drive out in a military car to see the rhododendrons at Howth Castle. We trudge to the top of the hill, Chalmers toiling up the rugged path in a big overcoat and mighty glad to rest on the turf with a splendid view before him of Dublin Bay, Clontarf, Sutton, Portmarnock and even of the Mourne Mountains. [. . .]

Samuel and Barran are dreadfully 'English' in their opinions of Ireland and know as much about it as I do of Ceylon, and Chalmers frankly loathes his job. The P.M. sent him here and he will stay, I suppose, until it has been decided how Ireland is to be governed. He

---

[41] William Joshua Goulding (1856–1925); member of the Irish Convention 1917–1918; subsequently member of the Irish Free State Senate; cr. baronet 1904.

[42] Robert Chalmers (1858–1938): Treasury civil servant 1882–1919, including a period as Permanent Secretary (1911–1913): and with a break during which he served as Governor of Ceylon (1913–1915). From May to September 1916 he served as Under-Secretary for Ireland. Knighted 1900; cr. Baron Chalmers of Northiam 1919.

[43] John Nicholson Barran (1872–1952); Lib. MP for Hawick Burghs 1909–1918; Lib. candidate for North-West Hull 1922, 1923 and 1924; succ. as 2nd baronet 1905. During his Commons career he served as PPS to a succession of ministers, including Samuel.

wishes to Heaven I were to come to Ireland as Chief Secretary thinking that with my views and my knowledge of Ireland we together would have no difficulty in managing the country – which shows that he too knows very little about it. The distinguished statesmen *will* pronounce the 'th' in Howth and Louth hard. These little things count in Ireland.

5 June

Lucas fetches me off in the morning and introduces me to some important business men at the Chamber of Commerce. We discuss the proposed H. Rule settlement, all my new friends being resolutely opposed to the exclusion of Ulster as well on business as on other grounds.

After lunch the Archbishop calls for me and we go to the Palace and smoke a pipe or two together. Again the topic is the 'settlement' of Ireland. John Dublin has been asked to send his views to Ll.-George and has done so.

10 June

We leave Dublin for London by the morning mail. As wet and dreary a June day as ever I saw.

20 June

To 11 Downing Street at 9.15 to breakfast with the Minister of Munitions. I find Ll.-G. bending over a map of the Western Front, looking for the places where his sons are. He greets me cordially and tells me that he is much obliged for the information which I sent to him through Alfred from Ireland and that he found it perfectly accurate. Referring to the negotiations for the Irish settlement he says that there is trouble with some of the Unionist members of the Government. I urge him to *force* a settlement if it comes to – that to 'jump with both feet' on obstruction.

We repair to the breakfast room where Mrs. Ll.-G. ('Maggie', Ll.-G. calls her), one of their daughters in nurse's uniform, and Prof. Pares,[44]

---

[44] Bernard Pares (1867–1949): professor of Russian language, literature and history at London University 1919–1936; spent much time in Russia during and after the First World War, becoming an adviser to the anti-Bolshevik forces during the civil war; knighted 1919.

the great authority on Russia, join us. It is a simple domestic party, each of us fetching his or her fish, or bacon and eggs from a side table. Ll.-G. is as brisk at this early hour as most other people are when the world is well-aired and hums a cheerful stave as he moves to and from the side-table. He drops the Irish question when Pares comes in and discusses the prospects of the Russian offensive in Buchovina with much animation. He doubts whether the Russians have yet munitions sufficient for a campaign all along their extended front.

The conversation turns on the similarity between Russian and some of the Balkan languages. Pares says that a Russian can understand these cognate languages (Serbian was specially mentioned, I think) with a little practice. Ll.-G. says that when he has heard the Bretons talk it was as if he were listening to Welsh spoken indistinctly. He thinks he could pick up Breton in a month or so.

Immediately after breakfast and a small cigar Ll.-G. goes next door to see the P.M. There is direct communication through between No. 11 and No. 10. His parting words to me are to supply him with any further Irish information that comes my way and mine to him to stand no nonsense and to compel if necessary a settlement of Ireland. The breakfasts at No. 11 are famous and I quite enjoyed the experience though I am not myself good for much so early in the day. They do say that many a political plot has been hatched over the bacon and eggs at No. 11.

4 July

Small business in the H. of C. All the talk in the smoking-room is of the great British offensive and of the still pending Irish settlement. Lord Lansdowne, Walter Long and Lord Robert Cecil said to be still recalcitrant.

5 July

Lunch with Harold at 10A Duchess Street. With him are Lord Charles Beresford[45] and Lord Murray of Elibank. 'Charlie' Beresford gives us an interesting account of the part he played on Sunday August 2 1914 when it was yet uncertain whether we should join in or not. On that

---

[45] Charles William de la Poer Beresford (1846–1919): high-ranking and controversial naval officer; Conservative MP for East Marylebone 1885–1992, Woolwich, 1902–1903, Portsmouth 1910–1916; cr. Baron Beresford 1916.

day he called two or three times on the French Ambassador (Cambon)⁴⁶ and the Russian Ambassador (Benckendorff)⁴⁷ and found them both ringing their hands at the prospect of our standing put. He called, too, on Balfour, the only leader of the Opposition in town. Learning that Bonar Law was 'week-ending' at his riverside place near Reading the vigorous old sailor proceeded there immediately and found B.L. and F.E. Smith playing tennis! He had some difficulty in persuading B.L. of the extreme gravity of the crisis but he was successful at last in getting him to confer without delay with Lord Lansdowne. The result was the famous letter signed by Lord L. and B.L., assuring the Liberal Government of the whole support of the Opposition in any action they chose to take. [But Charlie Beresford's stories were always taken by those who knew him with many a grain of salt.]

7 July

An emergency meeting at the Board of Trade of the Women's Employment Committee. The question is whether the Government should be advised by us to interfere (by administrative action or otherwise) to prevent women in poorly-paid employments from going into munitions works. A typical case is that of Carlisle where women's wages are low and where they are only waiting until the Government munitions works at Gretna is opened to transfer their services. We fail to agree and decide merely to state the case for the powers that be.

10 July

In the H. of C. the P.M. makes his formal statement as to the result of the negociations for the settlement of Irish affairs.

Then the 2nd Reading of the Small Holding Colonies Bill which comes down to us from the Lords and which affects to cope with the huge problem of putting on the land our soldiers and sailors after the War by providing in Great Britain 8,000 acres for experimental small holding colonies! I join in the chorus of dissatisfaction at these meagre proposals.

---

⁴⁶Paul Cambon (1843–1924): French Ambassador to Britain 1898–1920.
⁴⁷Count Alexander Konstantinovich Benckendorff (1849–1917): Russian ambassador to Britain 1903–1917.

Jesse Collings[48] at 85 years of age takes an effective part in the debate. The famous old champion of the agricultural labourer reads his notes and quotations from Reports etc. without the aid of glasses.

24 July

A hot Irish debate in the H. of C. The Lloyd-George settlement has broken down and the Nationalists talk of going into vigorous opposition to the Coalition. Fine conciliatory speech by Carson – one of the half dozen utterances in point of importance and effectiveness of my time in the House.

31 July

In the H. of C. the P.M. announces the definite break-down of Ll.-G.'s Irish negociations and the re-establishment, for the time being, of Castle Government.

9 August

At the Treasury there is a discussion – McKenna, Mackinnon Wood, and Sir Thomas Heath[49] – as to whether it is possible to relieve the Lord Lieutenant *[of Ireland]* of a part of the Income Tax charges on his official salary of £20,000 a year. Income Tax and Super Tax come to 8/6 in the £1 and there is besides a standing charge of £2,000 a year and more for the gardens of the Viceregal Lodge. His Excellency is very hard hit by War taxation. It is decided to enquire whether £15,000 of the salary may be regarded as an 'allowance' and so relieved of taxation.

---

[48] Jesse Collings (1831–1920): advocate of land reform and follower of Joseph Chamberlain; Mayor of Birmingham 1878–1880; Lib. MP for Ipswich 1880–1886; Lib. Unionist MP for Birmingham Bordesley 1886–1918; Under-Secretary to the Home Office 1895–1902.

[49] Thomas Little Heath (1861–1940): civil servant; joint Permanent Secretary to the Treasury 1913–1919; knighted 1909.

17 August

It is just as well we are breaking up in the H. of C. in a few days. The House is tired and tempers are rising especially among my colleagues on the front Opposition bench. Carson is snappy and Winston positively rude to his late friends on the Treasury bench. I think he must feel that he has made a mess of things. His retirement from the Admiralty a year ago evoked no popular emotion. People thought he was doing a sporting thing when he joined his Regiment at the Front and they don't understand why he so soon deserted the trenches. Meanwhile neither wing of the Coalition seems anxious for his return to office indeed I hear that the Tories have flatly refused to have him back. His manner is specially offensive to the P.M. and Bonar Law.

21 August

McKenna and I walk over from the House to the Treasury and I spend the rest of the afternoon there with him Lord Reading and Sir John Bradbury. The talk is all of the measures that have been and must be taken to keep the exchanges right between us and the U.S.A. Lord, what financial burdens we are bearing, and yet some people still complain that we are not pulling our full weight in this War!

29 August

Archbishop and Mrs. Bernard arrived [at Henley] last evening at 6.15. [...]
Bernard and I discuss the political situation an Ireland. One of the questions is, whether liberal-minded Irish Unionists like B. himself, Horace Plunkett,[50] Lord Desart,[51] Sir Hutcheson Poë[52] and others should issue a manifesto declaring their willingness to work with Redmond and other loyal Irishmen for the good of Ireland. I

---

[50] Horace Curzon Plunkett (1854–1932): Unionist MP for South County Dublin1892–1900; founded the Irish Agricultural Organisation Society 1894; chaired the Irish Convention 1917–1918; Irish Free State Senator 1922–193; knighted 1903.
[51] Hamilton John Agmondesham Cuffe (1848–1934): Director of Public Prosecutions 1894–1908; Treasury Solicitor 1894–1909; knighted 1898; succ. as 5th Earl of Desart 1898; cr. Baron Desart 1909.
[52] William Hutcheson Poë (1848–1934): army officer, landowner and magistrate; Irish Free State Senator 1922–1925.

suggest that such a declaration might (1) embarrass Redmond and (2) result in these influential Unionists being labelled 'Nationalists' with the inevitable loss of their influence as moderators of opinion in Ireland. B. shows me letters he has received from Plunkett, Desart, Poë, etc.

3 October

I dine with Harold at the Ritz. [...] Among those present are Bonar Law, Winston Churchill and F.E. Smith. Winston, as usual, talks for himself and everybody else. He is exceedingly pessimistic about the prospects of a war in the direction of which he has now no part. F.E. is gloomy and, when he secures a conversational opening, sententious – so much so, that Bonar congratulates him slyly on having recovered his platform manner. Bonar's occasional thrusts are highly effective.

4 October

Harold has just been appointed Director General of the Army Clothing Dept. at Pimlico.

10 October

House reassembles.
[...] I attend a lunch of the Aldwych Club at the Connaught rooms where Alfred gives an 'uncensored' address on his experiences and views of the War. About 500 lunchers, some 1500 more having failed to secure tickets. Business men, M.P.'s of all parties, and journalists. Alfred has a reception that would not be accorded, I think, to any one of our statesmen with the possible exception of Ll.-G.
More men and still more men, says Alfred; no twaddle about Peace as long as the Huns remain in France, Belgium, Poland and Servia; no interference by politicians with the Army; conscription for Ireland; watch narrowly the arch mischiefmaker Lord Haldane; look out for the democratic tendencies of our men in the trenches who will demand high wages and land for themselves – these are some of the points of his very interesting discourse.

14 October

Dinner with Mother at 'Northcliffe' where she has been staying [...]. Alfred there – in most amiable mood. He tells us that he has given Ll.-George warning not to interfere with strategic affairs. He is said to be worrying Sir William Robertson[53] and even to have another little military expedition of his own in view – A Gallipoli, it may be, or a Mesopotamia!

16 October

Alfred comes early for me and takes me off to Princes Golf Links at Sandwich, a splendid natural course of great difficulty. Alfred has with him a young pro., Cole, from Kingsgate who seems able to put in any amount of vigorous golf but has been adjudged by the Tribunal as too delicate for military service. We speculate as to how these things are arranged.

Quick and splenetic as he is ordinarily Alfred is one of the most placid golfers I have seen. Today he did describe one lie as damnable but he eschews bad language with wonderful fortitude. Getting into the rough at one hole (and the rough at Prince's is rough indeed) he ambitiously tried a wooden club with disastrous results. 'There's no fool like a fat fool' was his only comment.

The 8th at Princes is a very celebrated hole, long and extremely difficult. 'He did the 8th hole at Princes in 4', is to be part of Alfred's epitaph. Today it is 7 or 8.

19 October

A great deputation of Irish members at the Treasury to urge McKenna to grant War bonuses to the very badly paid elementary school teachers in Ireland. However acute Irish political differences may be there are two occasions when Irish members of all sections dwell together in perfect amity (1) when a raid is to be made on the Exchequer and (2) when whiskey is threatened with higher taxation. So we have today Redmond and Carson sitting cheek by jowl and conferring as to how most successfully to squeeze McKenna, with

---

[53]William Robert Robertson (1860–1933): army officer; Chief of the Imperial General Staff 1915–1918; Field Marshal 1920; cr. baronet 1919.

Tim Healy's brother[54] (as representing the Cork faction) regarding them appreciatively from a back chair. Carson is not less insistent than the others in voicing the wrongs of the teachers and his remarks are punctuated by warmer applause (from Orangemen and Nationalists alike) than the stately Board Room is accustomed to. In the end McKenna offers the same War bonuses to the school teachers as are being conceded to members of the regular Civil Service.

23 October

Sir Hutcheson Poë to dine with us this evening. He is the leading spirit among those 'Southern' Irish Unionists who desire to live on friendly terms with the Nationalists and who having made up their minds that Home Rule is certainly coming are disposed to fall cheerfully into line and to work the new system to the best advantage of their country.

26 October

I spend the afternoon at the Treasury with McKenna, Mackinnon Wood and Sir R. Chalmers. Lord Reading looks in. The talk is of course all of War finance.

Chalmers tells me that Duke, the Irish Secy., wants me to go with him as his parliamentary private fag. [Later: I was acting in that capacity to McKenna at the time and decided not to change. I was always sorry afterwards I didn't go with Duke. In fact, however, I was getting impatient of this sort of ministerial subordination and thinking it high time I had a Government job of my own. It is unwise for an aspiring young politician to serve for more than a short term as Private Parliamentary Secy. to a Minister. The position gives him a close insight into a great government Dept. of which he has the full run and brings him in immediate contact day by day with his own and other Ministers, but it has severe limitations. It deprives him of his liberty of action in the House and of most of his chances of speaking, since he can make no use of his special knowledge gained in the Dept. nor criticize his Govt. –, any more than if he were a member of it. C.H. 6th Feby. 1934.]

---

[54] Maurice Healy (1859–1923): Irish Nat. MP For Cork City, 1885–1900, 1909–1910, 1910–1918.

8 November

A concert at Summer Fields. Daff and I leave Gol and walk to the station and so home. I have to go to the H. of C. at 10 to vote [the Carsonites having challenged a Division involving a vote of Censure on the Govt.].

10 November

With the Parliamentary Air Committee to Hendon to see the splendid works of the Aircraft Manufacturing Coy. At the beginning of the War about 50 people were employed – now there are 2,500. Aeroplanes are made here, all parts of them except engines and propellers. The great shops are scenes of varied and ceaseless activity – delicate carpentering, brazing of parts, wire-drawing, canvassing wings, beating out and shaping aluminium bodies and assembling.

I go for a flight (Mr. Birchenough,[55] pilot) in an aeroplane. A glorious sensation! Strange to say, though I have the poorest of heads for dizzy heights I am not a bit nervous when we mount over the patchwork fields and see trains looking like toys. The finest sight of all is when the new fast 'Havilland' (130 miles an hour) circles and manoeuvres beneath us like a beautiful great hawk.

The noise is deafening, not unlike that of one of the huge Daily Mail presses at full speed or a train rushing in a rocky cutting. The pilot and I cannot converse but he turns in his seat every now and then and smiles at me reassuringly. [. . .]

In the afternoon I take the Chair at a Council meeting of the Old Boys' Corps, now the 3rd Battalion of the London Volunteer Regt. The Army Council is taking over the Volunteers and our civil management will soon be a thing of the past.

11 November

To the official cinema pictures of the Somme battles after lunch. A sad but intensely interesting record. The operator must have gone into the thick almost of the battles. We see our wounded soldiers returning from the fights and dazed German prisoners still holding up both hands in token of surrender. There are dead men too, our own and German, lying out in the open or huddled in the almost obliterated

[55] William Birchenough: test pilot.

trenches. I could scarcely bring myself to look at some of the scenes. Yet it is right that we stay-at-homes should get even a faint idea of what this war really means. No doubt these films will be preserved and will be shown to future generations who will marvel at the mad horrors of these unhappy times.

21 November

Sad news today of the death in action of my very dear nephew and godson Vere. I go to see poor Harold. Alfred and Leicester, Vyv and Esmond with him.

24 November

This is one of the gloomiest periods of the War. Though Haig[56] has made recently good progress on the Somme and the Servians have just taken Monastir there is for the moment a bleak prospect in every other direction. My own thoughts are coloured no doubt by the loss of Vere, but depression rules in the H. of C. and everywhere I go. The Germans seem to be overrunning Roumania going through it like brown-paper – and have sunk our great hospital ship the 'Britannic' by mine or torpedo together with an ever rising list of cargo vessels belonging to us the Allies and the neutrals. A Russian Dreadnought is said to have gone down in the Black Sea and indeed Russia fails us at every point.

In the House there is an almost general dissatisfaction with the Govt. which is always late and piles blunder on blunder.

We have had moments like this before but I have never seen so many people shaking their heads over our chances of winning the War.

3 December

Rumours all this week-end of a Cabinet crisis with confident statements in some of the Sunday papers that a War Council of four or five is to be set up and to be charged with full responsibility

---

[56] Douglas Haig, 1st Earl Haig (1861–1928): army officer; Commander-in-Chief (C.-in-C.) of the British Expeditionary Force 1915–1918 and of the Home Forces 1918–1921; Field Marshal 1917; cr. Earl Haig 1919.

for prosecuting the War with all possible vigour. The members of the Council are said to be:
The P.M. (Mr. Asquith)
Mr. Lloyd George
Mr. Bonar Law
Mr. Balfour and
Sir E. Carson
with Sir J. Jellicoe[57] and Sir W. Robertson as Naval and Military assessors.

In some forecasts the P.M. and Mr. Balfour are left out and a Labour Minister included.

For some time past the P.M. and the Coalition have been criticised severely for their lack of vigour and resolution and this not only in the 'Northcliffe Press' but in faithful Radical sheets also. Alfred (Northcliffe) has been actively at work with Ll.-G. with a view to bringing about a change.

4 December

The following official statement was issued at 11.45 last night:–
'The Prime Minister, with a view to the most effective prosecution of the war, has decided to advise his Majesty the King to consent to a reconstruction of the Government.'
Times Dec. 4th.
Alfred on the telephone early today. 'Who killed cock robin?' he cries. 'You did' I reply.

Later at the Treasury McKenna tells me that in view of the P.M.'s announcement (above) there is now no Chancellor of the Exchequer and no Government. He seems not to view his own position with much concern. He agrees that the P.M. cannot possibly hold on if he is not to be in the War Council. We can't have two Prime Ministers!

Later again I see Alfred at St. James's Place. He tells me that he was with Lloyd-George yesterday and that the two clever Hebrews Samuel and Montagu – both of whom owe their political fortunes to Asquith – were already there staking out claims. N. says they greeted him (N.) with positively oriental salaams.

In the H. of C. confusion and bewilderment. Most people have been growing uneasy under the nerveless direction of the P.M. but most people also regard the possible premiership of Ll.-G. with dismay. It

---

[57] John Rushworth Jellicoe (1859–1935): naval officer; commander of the Grand Fleet 1914–1916; First Sea Lord 1916–1917; Admiral of the Fleet 1919; Governor-General of New Zealand 1920–1924; knighted 1907; cr. Viscount Jellicoe 1918; first Earl Jellicoe 1925.

is not exactly a case of better the divvle you know than the divvle you don't know – (for we know both divvles intimately. But Ll.-G.'s erratic record!

And while we are absorbed in the excitements of a domestic political crisis the Germans are thundering at the gates of Bucharest!

5 December

The Times announces this morning that a state of deadlock as regards the political crisis exists. I go to the Treasury and find McKenna's Secretaries, H.P. Hamilton and Alan Parsons,[58] packing up. The belief is that Herbert Samuel is to succeed our chief. I see McKenna later and represent to him strongly that he and other good Liberals should not desert the Govt. that is to be formed. He says that as regards himself: (1) He could not serve under Ll.-G. and (2) That Ll.-G. wouldn't have him anyway. To the Ritz Hotel to see Harold. I find him with Winston who walks rapidly up and down the room talking at the top of his voice. All the swiftly-changing aspects of the crisis are heatedly discussed.

Home to dinner leaving Winston declaiming.

Tonight the P.M. resigns and Bonar Law is sent for by the King.

6 December

Things move rapidly today. Bonar informs the King that he is not in a position to form a Ministry.

The King summons the 'elder statesmen' of the former Coalition to a Conference at Buckingham Palace with a view no doubt to securing agreement. The upshot is that Ll.-G. is invited to try his hand at Cabinet making.

The London Liberal daily papers all this time are full of denunciations of Northcliffe whom they regard as the arch wrecker of the Asquith Govt. There is truth in this of course but not all the truth. Grave dissatisfaction with the P.M.'s leadership has been growing apace among Liberals in the House and has found expression in such staunchly Liberal papers as the *Manchester Guardian* and *The Nation*.

---

[58] Alan Leonard Romaine Parsons (1889–1933): civil servant and drama critic of the *Daily Mail*.

7 December

The shortest sitting of the H. of C. on record I should think. I am only 3 or 4 minutes late at the House but the business of the day is already over. Gulland, the Chief Liberal Whip, has moved the adjournment until next Tuesday and members are all out in the Members' Lobby which is densely packed and hums like a bee-hive.

It is said that Liberal ex-Cabinet Ministers have resolved to stand out of the Bonar – George Ministry en bloc. I write to Runciman who is confined to his house urging that this is an unwise and even an unpatriotic policy.

Meanwhile, Ll.-G. is reported to have made generous offers of ministerial appointments to the Labour Party and to have secured their support by a narrow majority.

Of Liberal Members, so far as I have had any talk with them, about half are burning with indignation at the way the P.M. (Asquith) has been treated by Ll.-G. and Northcliffe while the other half think that his habits of delay and indecision – the policy of 'wait and see' – have been the main cause of merited misfortune.

8 December

The 'Court Circular' last night contained the following:

The Right Hon. D. Lloyd George, M.P., had an audience of the King this evening, and accepted his Majesty's offer of the post of Prime Minister and First Lord of the Treasury, and kissed hands upon his appointment.

A party meeting under Mr. Asquith's Chairmanship at the Reform Club today which neither Leicester nor I attend. I doubt the expediency of holding such a meeting, am a little afraid that rival resolutions may be moved and in any case have no wish to hear what may be said in criticism of Northcliffe who has had so large a share in the present upheaval. In fact, however, nothing embarrassing seems to have happened at the meeting.

Some Cabinet appointments announced [. . .]

Harold has been offered the First Commissionership of Works and has declined.

11 December

Women's War Work Committee at the Board of Trade.

Chief offices in Govt. are now filled with the exception of some of the new Ministries. The elder Tory statesmen mostly retained but the Liberal Ministers are generally new men. A good sprinkling of Labour representatives.

12 December

First meeting of H. of C. under Lloyd-George's Govt. Bonar Law moves the adjournment of the House until Thursday. Ll. -G. and Asquith both in bed with had colds.

The House crowded and in a very excitable mood. The proceedings last less than an hour and then all Members stream out into the Lobby which hums again like a bee-hive.

I have a long talk with Winston and John Dillon in the Smoking-room.

All the Cabinet posts in the Govt. are now filled.

26 December

I take the two boys to see their Uncle Northcliffe at *The Times* office. We find the King maker in the handsome Georgian parlour of the oldest fashioned house in London. N. presents each of the boys with a one pound note and promises them copies of his Red Cross book 'At the War'.[59] He takes us into the great machine room where everything is ready for printing tonight's *Times*. N. is to spend two hours this evening with the Prime Minister (Ll.-George).

---

[59] Lord Northcliffe, *At the War* (London, 1916). Published by Hodder & Stoughton for the Joint War Committee of the British Red Cross Society and the order of St John of Jerusalem in England.

1917

3 January

I call on Hodge,[1] Labour Minister, at Montague House Whitehall and find him sitting a little incongruously in one of the State parlours of the D. of Buccleuch.[2] I discuss with him the relations of my Committee to his Dept. and find him most friendly.

We dine with the Reggie McKenna's at Smith Square. The other guests are Mr. and Mrs. – McKenna and Sir Hedley Le Bas.[3]

McK. looks all the better for his release from office and is very cheerful and not a little malicious about the Ll.-G. Govt. (To say that there is no love lost between the two statesmen is putting it very mildly.) McK. has had a visitor from Germany and another from the United States, the one having been in touch with the German Chancellor Bethmann Hollweg[4] and the other with President Wilson[5] who both, strange to say, give the following as Germany's minimum or ultimate Peace terms:

> Evacuation of Belgium with return by Germany of tribute exacted.
>
> Evacuation of N. France, with restoration of machinery, etc., removed.
>
> Independence of Russian Poland.
>
> Restoration to Germany of her Colonies except S.W. Africa and the Pacific islands.
>
> Internationalisation of Constantinople, Trieste and Fiume.
>
> Freedom for German commerce, meaning, I suppose, undertakings not to penalise her by differential tariffs.

[1] John Hodge (1855–1937): trades unionist; Lab. candidate for Gower 1900 and Preston 1903; Lab. MP for Gorton 1906–1923; Minister of Labour 1916–1917; Minister of Pensions 1917–1919.
[2] John Charles Montagu-Douglas-Scott (1864–1935): Unionist MP for Roxburgh 1895–1906; succ. as 7th Duke of Buccleuch and 9th Duke of Queensbury 1914.
[3] Hedley Francis Le Bas (1868–1926): founder of the Caxton Publishing Company; advised the government on propaganda during the First World War; knighted 1916.
[4] Theobald von Bethmann-Hollweg (1856–1921): Chancellor of Germany 1909–1917.
[5] Thomas Woodrow Wilson (1856–1924): US President 1913–1921.

Balkan affairs to be settled by arrangement and conference (!!)

McK. and Sir H. Le Bas think these terms worth considering. I say, – but how can we leave the Balkan situation obscure? and what about shipping?
Sir H. prophesies that Northcliffe will be Prime Minister before the year is out.

4 January

In the evening I see Harold (Rothermere) at the Ritz. He foretells Peace in 3 or 6 months.

29 January

G. Lyster Todd,[6] a temporary officer with the Fleet, having told me of his misgivings in regard to the very free telegraphic facilities from H.M.S. Cyclops at Scapa, I go to see Sir John Jellicoe by appointment at the Admiralty. The famous admiral is an alert little man who but for the many rings of gold braid on his sleeves and his three rows of medal ribbons might pass any day for the excellent Vicar of a parish. He has the odd pinched in corners of the mouth of his portraits, brown eyes and coal black hair with only a grey hair or two above his ears. He was very simple and friendly and after some talk handed me on to Commodore Halsey,[7] 4th Sea Lord. They both said that they had no reason to suspect that any leakage of important news from the Grand Fleet had ever taken place but were not nearly so comfortable in their minds about other Naval stations near large centres of population.

Commodore Halsey said the rumours that information was given to the Germans leading to the blowing up of the Hampshire with Ld. Kitchener on board were all nonsense. Only 4 people in the Fleet knew of the precise movements of the Hampshire and these did not even include the Captain of the ship [before sailing. (C.H.)]

---

[6] George H. Lyster Todd: otherwise unidentified.

[7] Lionel Halsey (1872–1949): naval officer and royal official; Fourth Sea Lord 1916–1917; Third Sea Lord 1917–1918; knighted 1918.

7 February

Opening day of new Session. Fine speech by Asquith of whom in his reply Bonar Law speaks involuntarily as 'Prime Minister' to the delight of many Members. B. Law is Leader of the House and Ll.-G. does not even take the trouble to come down for the first hours of the Debate on the Address.

12 February

To the Ministry of National Service, St. Ermin's Hotel, to see Miss Violet Markham[8] the assistant Director of the Women's department. I find Miss M. high up in a barely furnished room and amidst much confusion. It appears that Neville Chamberlain, new to departmental life, has omitted to set up a registry of correspondence and poor Miss M. spent the best part of Saturday answering urgent letters that had been mislaid a week in the department!

15 February

Debate in the H. of C. on the Ministry of Natl. Service. I make a hot little speech deprecating nagging criticism of these new ministries and am warmly complimented by Bonar Law and others.

16 February

Welfare Conference at the Home Office. [. . .]
Addison,[9] Minister of Munitions, meeting me at the Club tells me he wants me to take on the job of Director of Welfare work with full

---

[8] Violet Rosa Markham (1872–1959): Deputy Director of the Women's Section of the National Service Department 1917, and also fulfilled a wide variety of other public service roles; Lib. candidate for Mansfield 1918; Companion of Honour 1917.

[9] Christopher Addison (1869–1951): Lib. (then Coalition Lib) MP for Hoxton 1910–1922; Independent Lib. candidate for Shoreditch 1922; Lab. candidate for Hammersmith South 1924; Lab. MP for Swindon 1929–1931, 1934–1935; Minister of Munitions 1916–1917; Minister of Reconstruction 1917–1918; President of the Local Government Board 1919; Minister of Health 1919–1921; Parliamentary Secretary for Agriculture 1929–1930; Minister of Agriculture 1930–1931; Dominions Secretary and Leader of the House of Lords, 1945–1951; cr. Baron Addison 1937, Viscount 1945.

powers. But I shan't be able to do it. My new fisheries job will fully occupy me.

23 February

Lloyd-George comes down to the House and makes his great speech on the measures necessary for winning the War – import restrictions, land cultivation, etc. [...]

The speech was the best, I think, I have ever heard Ll.-G. make in the House – as well-arranged and clear as one of Asquith's, and with eloquent passages.

W.R. [Walter Runciman] at the top of his form too in reply.

27 February

In the H. of C. Dillon moves a new clause excluding Ireland from the National Service Bill. I make a short speech (well-liked) warning him of the danger of seeking to contract Ireland out of her Imperial obligations. Dillon says nice things about me but persists and goes to a Division. New clause badly defeated.

7 March

Motor Committee all the morning. In the H. of C. a great debate on Ireland, the Irish members, led by John Redmond, marching solemnly, if a little sheepishly, out of the House. Fine, broad, conciliatory speech by Willie Redmond, a Major now in H.M. Army.

15 March

In the H. of C. general debate on Vote of Credit.

Bonar Law announces that the Czar[10] has abdicated and that his brother the Grand Duke Michael[11] has been appointed Regent. This is a triumph for the pro-War and anti-German party in Russia.

---

[10] Nicholas II (1868–1918).
[11] Grand Duke Michael Alexandrovich (1878–1918). He never took up the throne and was later murdered by the Bolsheviks.

16 March

With the Parliamentary Air Committee to Wool in Dorset to see the great training camp for 'tanks'. The camp is situated on a rugged heath, the softer parts of which are churned up into huge furrows by the mysterious craft that suggest immense antediluvian beetles as they crush their way through and over everything that lies in their path. We are afforded some surprising demonstrations of their power. In one case the tank advanced to a small deep shell crater, poised itself on the edge plunged heavily into it through the bottom and then laboriously but irresistibly up the other side. One is shot backwards and forwards violently as the tank plunges into a hollow or gathers its strength for an upward climb. They are very greasy inside and there is nothing much to hold on to, and the engines make a great noise. I travelled on the outside of one over a broad stretch of barbed wire, the wire and its posts going down like rough grass under a garden-roller. We butted into a sturdy pine-tree not much less than a foot thick at the roots and after two or three attempts laid it flat. [. . .]

The secret of the tanks was extraordinarily well kept. It is believed that they were a complete surprise to the Germans when they appeared at the Front last year, and I can well imagine that they would strike terror into the hearts of men in the trenches on which they advanced in their slow, methodical, remorseless way.

22 March

Leicester tells me in great confidence that Ll.-G. is seriously thinking of offering me the position of Chief Liberal Whip to the Coalition and is only deterred by the fact of the formidable Harmsworth name! This is news indeed to me, and L. won't say where he heard it. It seems certain that Neil Primrose is resigning the post and equally certain that there are 5 or 4 others in the running for it – Freddie Guest,[12] Hamar Greenwood, E. Shortt, K.C.,[13] and Illingworth, the Postmaster

---

[12] Frederick Edward Guest (1875–1937): army officer; cousin of Winston Churchill; Lib. candidate for Kingswinford 1906, Cockermouth 1906, Brigg 1907; Lib. (then Coalition Lib) MP for East Dorset 1910–1922, Stroud 1923–1924, Bristol North 1924–1929; Con. MP for Plymouth Drake 1931–1937; Lord of the Treasury 1911; Treasurer of the Royal Household 1912; Coalition Chief Whip 1917–1921; Secretary of State for the Air 1921–1922.

[13] Edward Shortt (1862–1935): called to the Bar 1890; KC 1910; Recorder of Sunderland 1907–1918; Lib. MP for Newcastle upon Tyne 1906–1918; Newcastle West 1918–1922; Chief Secretary for Ireland 1918–1919; Home Secretary 1919–1922; President of the British Board of Film Censors 1929–1935.

General.[14] Well, I hope they are all as unconcerned about the event as I am!

28 March

The work of our Fish Food and Motor Loan Committee falls into two departments. We have first to promote by every means in our power the fitting out of the inshore fishing boats with motor-power so as to increase their catching capacity, it being estimated that on an average the fishing boat so equipped brings in three times as much fish as a boat dependent on sails and oars alone. Two difficulties arise in this connection – (1) the shortage of marine motors due to the fact that the makers generally are up to their eyes in Admiralty and War Office work and (2) the unwillingness of the fishermen in some places (as at Poole) to adopt motor-power.

The other branch of our work is more onerous and more responsible. We are charged with the duty of advising the Food Controller as to the best use to be made of the vast quantities of pickled herrings and pilchards and dried cod that are usually sent abroad and are so heavily salted as to be unacceptable in the home market. Pilchards, for instance, are not eaten fresh in this country. The bulk of the catch is salted down and exported to Italy in times of peace. Of the British herring catch 85 per cent is normally salted down and sold to Germany, Russia, etc. In addition to our own heavy stocks the Govt. has been buying large quantities of these pickled herrings in Norway, Holland, etc. in order to prevent the Germans getting them and has now in hand or in sight 150,000 tons of them.

How best to desalt and render these pickled herrings more palatable is an important object of our enquiry and we are getting all sorts of people to make experiments. Further, we must try to arrange things so that the herrings etc. of this season's harvest are not put into brine but are either marketed fresh or are kippered, 'redded' or bloatered. All this means in effect the upheaving of a great and complicated trade.

The tantalising circumstance is that here we have a huge supply of nutritious food that our people won't eat in its present condition unless indeed they are driven by severe privation to doing so.

---

[14] Albert Holden Illingworth (1865–1942): industrialist; Lib. (then Coalition Lib) MP for Heywood 1915–1918; Heywood and Radcliffe 1918–1921; Postmaster General 1916–1921, cr. Baron Illingworth 1921.

3 April

Today with a group of Liberal Members headed by Walter Runciman to see Bonar Law in the Prime Minister's room and discuss the submarine menace with him. Bonar confirms the disquieting conclusions we had already arrived at. It may become a neck and neck race between us and the Germans in the escape from famine. Our shipping losses lately have been most serious and Bonar tells us frankly that the Admiralty have not got the situation in hand.

19 April

This last week I have been fully occupied with my Fish Food problems and very little in the H. of Commons, finding that the duties and hours of an (unpaid) Civil Servant are hardly compatible with those of a Member of Parliament. I begin to think that an *increase* in the fish supply is not to be expected and that we must be content to make the best use of fishing fleets severely reduced by the Admiralty restrictions on seafishing and in consequence of their demands for patrol boats and minesweepers and, again, by their exactions in the matter of fishermen recruits for Naval services. We shall not get more fish but must catch and market all we can.

20 April

Great service at St. Paul's to celebrate the entry of the United States into the Alliance. Union Jack and Stars & Stripes flown together on the Houses of Parliament.

26 April

I walk into town with Bernard and meet Lord Rosebery, Lord Fisher and Neil Primrose in Pall Mall. Neil detaches himself from the others and tells me that the Prime Minister wants me to be Chief Whip. I indicate my dislike for this particular office, but promise to let him know. Walking later in Horse Guards parade I meet Ll.-G. with one of his Secretaries, Philip Kerr.[15] Ll.-G. makes me go along with him and we make a round of St. James's Park. He asks me first if Neil has spoken to me and presses the appointment on me. I ask him if I may give him my views quite frankly and on his assenting very readily I do so. (People recognise Ll.-G. all along as we go and touch their hats.) I explain my dislike of the Chief Whip's office. Ll.G. is good enough to say that I am popular with his Liberal colleagues in the Coalition and generally in the House and that he wants 'eyes' and 'ears' in the House to keep him informed. I express my deep obligation to him and ask him for leave to consider the proposal. My ground of objection is my invincible repugnance to that part of the Chief Whip's work that relates to the conferring of honours and titles. It is a pity and a disappointment and I am a fool – but there it is.

27 February

I call for Neil Primrose and we walk to Downing Street. I say again what I said before and implore him to beg me off. There is a man cleaning the windows at No. 10 and I tell Neil to tell Ll.-G. I will do that or anything for him that will help him on with the War.

1 May

With Neil Primrose to No. 10 to lunch with the Prime Minister. We are a party of three in a snug little pannelled room. I explain my position quite frankly to the P.M. who thinks things can be arranged by getting a trusted somebody else to share the financial responsibilities of the Chief Whip's office with me. A very interesting talk. Ll.-G. says he must go off again to France on Thursday. He doesn't want to go, but must. He makes light of the submarine danger but says that he should regard drowning as the most unpleasant of deaths.

There is much fun over a big brown jar of John Jameson's whisky that some Irish admirer has sent him. It is opened for us and we must all try it. Addison, Minister of Munitions, comes in and there is all sorts of confidential talk. Addison has to try the whisky too.

---

[15]Philip Henry Kerr (1882–1940): a key figure in Lord Milner's South African 'kindergarten'; founding editor of *The Round Table*; private secretary to Lloyd George 1916–1921; managing editor of the *Daily Chronicle* 1921–1922; Chancellor of the Duchy of Lancaster 1931; Under-Secretary of State at the India Office 1931–1932; Ambassador to the USA 1938–1940; Companion of Honour 1920; succ. as 11th Marquess of Lothian 1930.

I tell Ll.-G. that if I am an obstinate radical in some things he is to some extent answerable I having sat at his feet as a humble disciple for years; and that I have twists in my moral structure just as other men have. We sit long and smoke excellent cigars out of a box that looks like a golf prize of Ll.-G.'s. What a wonderful creature he is! He has just come from a prolonged War Cabinet and is as fresh and keen on my political foibles, the stone jar of 'J.J.' and Addison's more weighty problems, as if he had no other responsibilities in life.

Afterwards in Neil's room in the H. of C., and subsequently to a talk with the other man, I unburden myself fully to Neil and say that I cannot go on. We argue the subject of the traffic in titles earnestly and I plead that I never could share in that work. Both of us much agitated. Neil doesn't like the business himself and confesses that his dislike of it is one of the reasons of his giving up the Chief Whip's office and joining his regiment in Palestine. I beg him to help me to get out of an impossible position. [. . .]

I write my apologia to Ll.-G., begging leave definitely to decline.

2 May

To my Fish Committee. Neil Primrose telephones to say that the Prime Minister would like to see me at 3, just before the meeting of the War Cabinet and that I am to be offered a place in his Secretariat. I present myself at 10 Downing Street at the appointed time. I wait in the passage to the Cabinet Room and Ll.-G.'s youngest girl, a pretty child of about 12 or 13 years of age [Megan], comes along with her pet dog in her arms. She greets her Father affectionately who comes from seeing the King at Buckingham Palace. Lloyd-George tells me that he wants me to join his Secretariat and I thank him warmly and accept with alacrity. As Ll.-G. goes into the Cabinet room I have a fleeting vision of that illustrious conclave. Then I descend to the 'Garden Suburb', the waggishly named temporary building in the garden of No. 10 where the Secretariat is established. It is a structure of light concrete and match-boarding and has the pleasant fresh smell of a wooden shack in Newfoundland. My room is airy and cheerful with budding hawthorns and fig-trees outside the window, and, inside, a huge safe containing all the Cabinet secrets. All specially confidential documents are lodged in this safe before we leave at night. Twice I am summoned to the Prime Minister whom I find I in the Cabinet room with the table still covered with the fresh red blotting-paper provided for the recent Cabinet meeting. On the first occasion Northcliffe is with him, and Mr. Alfred Butt[16] of the Ministry of Food who has been since January planning a scheme of compulsory rationing and who dwells woefully on the dilatoriness of the great Food Controller, Ld. Devonport.[17]

The Prime Minister asks Prof. Adams[18] and me to take pot luck with him and his family at dinner. It is a pleasant domestic scene at one end of the fine dining-room and a most frugal War time meal. There are Mrs. Ll.-G, a grown-up daughter and the newly married Major Ll.-G.[19] and his pretty wife (one of the Miss McAlpines of Totteridge).[20] The P.M. is as fresh as a daisy and at one moment breaks into a stave of two of a song, in Welsh.

Adams and I sit with him smoking until late although Ll.-G. is off to France at 8 o'clock tomorrow morning. We discuss the ever anxious food question and agree that it is not quite as gloomy as some people think it. Bonar Law comes in, a bit tired after a Budget speech. He leaves us early to play Bridge which he finds the best of tonics for his mind.

Ll.-G. maintains the old-fashioned habit that I like so much myself of taking tea instead of coffee after dinner.

3 May

The Prime Minister off to France this morning. I am busy all day in the 'garden suburb', devoting myself industriously to the three important questions he has assigned to me – food, shipping and National Service.

---

[16] Alfred Butt (1878–1962): Director of Rationing at the Ministry of Food, 1917–1918; Unionist MP for Balham and Tooting 1922–1936; theatrical figure and racehorse owner; resigned from the Commons after he was implicated in the scandal that brought down J.H. Thomas; knighted 1918; cr. baronet 1929.

[17] Hudson Ewbanke Kearley (1856–1934): grocery magnate; Lib. MP for Devonport 1892–1910; Parliamentary Secretary to the Board of Trade 1905–1909; Chairman of the Port of London Authority 1909–25; Minister of Food Control 1916–1917; cr. baronet 1908; cr. Viscount Devonport 1917.

[18] William George Stewart Adams (1874–1966): Gladstone Professor of Political Theory and Institutions 1912–1933; member of Lloyd George's Secretariat 1916–1918; Warden of All Souls 1933–1945, Companion of Honour 1936.

[19] Richard Lloyd George (1889–1968): served in the Royal Engineers during the First World War; succ. as 2nd Earl Lloyd-George 1945.

[20] Roberta Ida Freeman Lloyd George, née McAlpine (1868–1966); m. Richard Lloyd George 1917, divorced 1933.

5 May

The business of the Secretariat in the temporary building ('garden suburb') in the garden of No. 10 is to digest the vital questions of the day and to prepare memoranda for the P.M. We Secretaries are liaison officers between the Ministers and those Govt. Departments that are not represented in the War Cabinet of five. We see all secret documents of state and are in a position to make ourselves felt in all questions of high policy.

10 May
Secret Session.

The proceedings are opened in a gloomy speech by Winston Churchill who receives a more than adequate reply from Ll.-G. In the course of his speech Ll.-G. dwells on the Food question and gives a confident view of our position up to this year's harvest and is scarcely less reassuring about the situation in 1918. I gather subsequently from Lobby gossip that a good many Members and some Ministers regard his statement as too rosy and there is even some talk of his having misled the House. [A great deal of such talk, I remember. There were Members who roundly charged Ll.-G. with being a damned liar. In fact, the figures he gave were on the strictly conservative side.] This part of his speech is in fact based on our exhaustive enquiries in the Garden Suburb.

11 May

Secret Session. 2nd Day.
    Adams, Astor[21] and I see Ll.-G. early this morning and impress on him the importance of his speaking again today in the H. of C. on the food question so that all misgivings may be dispelled. Ll.-G. furiously angry when he hears that even Ministers are reported to have questioned his sanguine account of the food situation. He damns liberally and even uses the word 'bloody' in apostrophising the disloyalty of his colleagues.

---

[21] Waldorf Astor (1879–1952): Con. MP for Plymouth 1910–1919; proprietor of *The Observer*; member of Lloyd George's prime ministerial secretariat; PPS to Lloyd George 1916–1918; Parliamentary Secretary to the Ministry of Food 1918–1919; Parliamentary Secretary to the Ministry of Health, 1919–1921; succ. as 2nd Viscount Astor 1919.

He makes the desired re-statement in the House. Fine Admiralty speech by Carson.

12 May

In the Garden House Downing Street all the morning. Adams and I to see Lord Milner[22] in his pleasant old house in Great College Street (overlooking a fine old garden with tennis lawns) and talk about Food Economy with him. A man of power, Lord Milner, I think, with a surprisingly gentle manner considering his formidable reputation. He has the air of an ascetic – and is elderly and faded beyond his 65 years.

At night Alfred [Northcliffe] presides over the Annual Dinner of the Newspaper Press Fund at the Mansion House. A thronged gathering and a record subscription list.

18 May

Much of my time these last few days has been taken up by the repeated Conferences at the Ministry of Food (Grosvenor House) on the question of compulsory rationing. Lord Milner present at two of the Conferences and Lord Devonport usually in the Chair.

Should we ration compulsorily?

Arguments against:

Encouraging effects on Germans and depressing effects on our own people.

Doubtful if necessary.

Arguments for:

Best means of ascertaining facts as to populations and consumption, and of satisfying a section of anxious opinion.

Only really satisfactory means of initiating scheme of general rationing should it ever be necessary – and needed quickly.

---

[22] Alfred Milner (1854–1925): Lib. candidate for Harrow 1885; High Commissioner in South Africa 1897–1905; member of the War Cabinet without portfolio 1916–1918; Secretary of State for War 1916–1918; Secretary of State for the Colonies 1918–1921; cr. Baron Milner 1901; cr. Viscount Milner 1902.

24 May

My days are very fully employed what with the H. of C., my Fish Food Committee and my work at No. 10. Here I am very happily situated in a bright, airy room with hawthorns and laburnums blooming outside and a fig-tree spreading its big emerald leaves on the old wall. Prof. Adams [Afterwards Warden of All Souls], David Davies [Lord Davies],[23] Philip Kerr [Marquis of Lothian], and young Astor [Lord Astor] and I form a happy, friendly little party, and I think we are really helpful to Ll.-G. [And (Sir) Joseph Davies,[24] Secy.]

Food prices and Ireland engage the best part of our attention this week.

30 May

It is a function of members of the secretariat to attend Cabinet Councils when any subject with which they are specially concerned comes up for discussion. There is a shipping matter today and I attend for the first time. Ll.-G., of course, in the chair and present also Bonar Law, Lord Curzon,[25] Barnes,[26] Lord Milner, Sir E. Carson, Lord R. Cecil, Addison and others.

I am irreverent enough to think that the long Cabinet table with its green baize is very like one of the roulette tables at Monte Carlo.

---

[23] David Davies (1880–1944): industrialist; Lib. MP for Montgomeryshire 1906–1929; PPS to Lloyd George 1916; member of the prime minister's secretariat 1916–1917; cr. Baron Davies 1932.

[24] Joseph Davies (1886–1954): industrialist; member of the prime minister's secretariat (and from 1917 its secretary) 1916–1920; Co. Lib. MP for Crewe 1918–1922; knighted 1918.

[25] George Nathaniel Curzon (1859–1925): Con. candidate for South Derbyshire 1885; Con. MP for Southport 1886–1898; Under-Secretary for India 1891–1892; Under-Secretary of State at the Foreign Office 1895–1898; Viceroy of India 1899–1905; Lord Privy Seal 1915–1916; member of the War Cabinet 1916–1918; Foreign Secretary 1919–1824; Lord President of the Council 1924–1925; cr. Baron Curzon 1898; cr. Marquess Curzon of Kedleston 1921.

[26] George Nicoll Barnes (1859–1940): trades unionist; ILP candidate for Rochdale 1895; Lab. MP for Glasgow Blackfriars 1906–1918; left the Labour Party 1918 and re-elected as MP for Glasgow Gorbals against an official Lab. candidate; Minister of Pensions 1916–1917; member of the War Cabinet 1917–1918 and minister without portfolio 1917–1920; Companion of Honour 1920.

13 June

An aeroplane attack on London this morning. We are startled in the Garden Suburb by loud explosions and by the sound of shells bursting in the air and we all run out into Horse Guards Parade to see what is going on. Nothing to be seen, but plenty more noise.

We hear later that many people have been killed and wounded in the City and in the East End – about 100 killed and over 400 wounded. Many children among the victims.

6 July

Long Conference at Downing Street today about the place of meeting of the Irish Convention. The College of Surgeons has been offered and the Provost [Dr. Mahaffy] has offered the Regent House in T.C.D. and twelve other rooms for Committees. I press hard for T.C.D. on the ground of its being obviously the one right place in Dublin and of its being strategically better in every way than the College of Surgeons if, as is apprehended, there should be Sinn Fein demonstrations against the Convention. [...]

A full and very interesting discussion. [...]

After the debate today Ll.-G. announces that the Govt. hopes the Convention will meet on the 25th. They are to choose their own Chairman, Duke acting in that capacity pro tem.

17 July

The Prime Minister sends down a message to me after 7 this evening to say he wants facts and figures about the shipping position – construction, purchases, submarine losses etc. – for a secret conference with journalists he is to hold tomorrow. It is a tough job, for amongst all their voluminous returns and memoranda, the Shipping Controller's people have never given us a clear account of the actual position at any time.

I work at Downing Street until 9.30 or so and then go home. A late and hasty dinner and then at work on the papers I have brought with me until 2 in the morning. For some of these documents, by the way, the Germans would give their ears!

18 July

To Downing Street early to have my Memorandum typewritten. I take it to Mr. Anderson,[27] Secretary of the Ministry of Shipping, who much to my relief and surprise declares my calculations to be accurate. Ll.-G. meets the journalists in the Cabinet room. I cannot be present for I have to attend a Conference on meat and wheat prices in Lord Milner's room at the offices of the War Cabinet, 2 Whitehall Gardens. A spirited tussle between Rhondda,[28] the Food Controller, who is out for beating down farmers' prices and Prothero,[29] President of the Bd. of Agriculture, who puts up a good fight for the agricultural interest.

16 August

March through town today of the first contingent of American soldiers. They are a body of strapping fine men – not yet very well-drilled but the best sort of material. It is strange how different they are from our own ruddy-cheeked types. Are the solemn dryasdusts right in assuming that it takes so many eras in which to change and develop an animal or human type? These Yanks in two or three hundred years have departed ever so far from the original English breed. They are tall, thin and sallow and at least as foreign in appearance as any of the European soldiers of the Continent.

They have a splendid reception, and the Union Jack and Stars & Stripes fly from the Victoria Tower at Westminster.

16 August

Such a turmoil at No. 10 today. The P.M. is to make a general statement on the War position today (on the motion for the Adjournment for the Summer holidays) and the garden suburb is all bustle and activity getting together facts and figures for his speech. My job is to present a

---

[27] John Anderson (1882–1958): civil servant; Governor of Bengal 1932–1937; National MP for the Scottish Universities 1938–1950; Lord Privy Seal 1938–1939; Home Secretary 1939–1940; Lord President of the Council 1940–1943; Chancellor of the Exchequer 1943–1945; cr. Viscount Waverley 1952.

[28] David Alfred Thomas (1856–1918): industrialist; Lib. MP for Merthyr 1888–1910; President of the Local Government Board 1916–1917; Minister of Food Control 1917–1918; Cardiff 1910; cr. Baron Rhondda 1916; cr. Viscount Rhondda 1918.

[29] Rowland Edmund Prothero (1851–1937): Unionist candidate for Biggleswade 1907; Unionist MP for Oxford University 1914–1919; President of the Board of Agriculture 1916–1919; cr. Baron Ernle 1919.

synoptic view of the shipping position and submarine losses. I take my Memoranda up to the great little man whom I find in one of the upper sitting-rooms stretched full length on a sofa surrounded by heaps of papers. His hair is longer than ever and strews wildly over the pillow. My view is that the submarine situation, black as it is, is nevertheless not so black as by some it is painted and I set out losses against gains (by new construction, purchase abroad etc.) in proof.

As always happens, he asks for the very data that I have not provided and I am told off to telephone to the Controller of the Navy and the Ministry of Shipping to make good the deficiencies in my more than ample details.

My Fish Food Committee meets in the afternoon and I miss the P.M.'s speech in the House. I get there in time to hear Asquith following him in full-rounded, sonorous sentences.

13 September

I lunch with Harold (Rothermere) at the Ritz. He has just received a cablegram from Alfred asking him to take his place at the head of the British War Commission in America and has said Yes.

1 October

The Prime Minister comes down to the Garden Suburb this afternoon and carries Philip Kerr and myself off for a walk round the parks. We make in the direction of Knightsbridge – Ll.-G. with short quick vigorous steps – and take tea in a restaurant there. Ll.-G. speaks to the policeman outside St George's Hospital and coming back stops to admire a pretty baby in its mother's arms. He is full of conversation about the air-raids, food supplies, the submarine position and matters generally connected with the War. He refers to the hatred he inspires still in some sections of the Press and wonders what there is in him to excite such rancour. He is as always entirely unaffected and simple. He lets Kerr and myself say exactly what we like to him.

2 October

Yet another glorious Autumn day. A little past one o'clock P.M. the warning of an air raid is given and when the guns begin to go off the population of 10 Downing Street migrates to the vaults of the

Foreign Office – Ll.-G. and Lord Milner, as I hear, among them. The Garden Suburb, all compact as it is of lath and plaster and other flimsy materials, is quickly deserted but Profr. Adams and I are content with the morning room at No. 10. The walls of the old house are very thick and it would need a direct hit on the roof to do it much harm. When the 'All Clear' signal comes along we all repair to lunch at our various resorts. [. . .]

Before getting to Downing Street this morning I call on Harold (Rothermere) at the Ritz Hotel. He tells me that the supply of Army clothing is becoming difficult owing to the panic-stricken rush of the foreign Jew tailors from the East End of London. They are swarming into Brighton and the country towns within 50 miles of town.

3 October

Ll.-G. comes down into the Garden Suburb today. He is full of a scheme for publishing a Record of what his Govt. and the various departments have done. Such a Record is usually prepared by the Chief Whip's department and serves as a handbook for speakers and for other purposes of reference. But in this case the Record is intended to prove to the people what great efforts have been made to solve the bigger problems of the War – Food Supply, Munitions, the Submarine menace etc. etc.

4 October

I am invited to the Cabinet Council this morning and Ll.-G. asks me to explain the situation in regard to insurance against the damage caused by air raids. There is a strong outside Committee, of which the chief spokesman is the Ld. Mayor of London, which advocates free Govt. indemnity in all cases and up to any amount, and they have been pressing Ll.-G. to adopt their view. The question has hung fire for months pending a decision on this point. Today the Cabinet decides to grant free indemnity up to £500. The larger risks are to be insured against under the existing Govt. insurance scheme. (War Cabinet Ministers present on this occasion are Ll.-G., Lord Milner, Lord Curzon, Sir E. Carson and Mr. Barnes, with Mr. Balfour, the War Cabinet Secretaries, Stanley Baldwin, Financial Secy., and myself).

In the late afternoon Ll.-G. sends down for me and takes me out for a run to Richmond Park. We are set down at one gate and walk briskly across the Park to meet the car at another. Ll.-G.'s detective follows us at a respectful distance. We discuss the War situation – Haig's fine advance before Ypres this morning, the satisfactory improvement in food, shipping etc., Horace Plunkett's skilful management of the Irish Convention, and a dozen other matters. Ll.-G. refers to Alfred's desire to return from America and to be succeeded by Harold. He is a good deal afraid that the Americans may jib at this proposal – to the headship of the Mission being treated as a sort of family affair.

The conversation turns on Mr. Asquith and the other eminent occupants of the Opposition Front Bench. Ll.-G. tells me again that Asquith had decided to work with him in the new Govt. and had been persuaded out of this course by some of his political friends and against the advice of other friends, including Bonham-Carter, his son-in-law. We agree that Asquith would have made a superb Ld. Chancellor, the best perhaps for a hundred years; or the head of a College.

Of McKenna's conduct of the Welsh Bill in the H. of C. Ll.G. said that he treated the church and its temporalities as if he were winding up a bankrupt business concern. A good man for figures but strangely incompetent in dealing with a great human problem.

We talked about Simon and Ll.-G. asked me if I had ever heard of Balfour's description of him: 'A very big man on a small occasion, and a very small man on a big occasion.'[. . .] People may say what they like against Ll.-G. but I don't know where you will find a pleasanter companion for an afternoon' s walk.

5 October

Sir Horace Plunkett over from Ireland, full of news of the Irish Convention. All had been going finely with it but the unfortunate affair of the Sinn Feiner, Thomas Ashe,[30] had clouded its prospects. I asked him who were the outstanding figures in the Convention. John Redmond, he said, the Primate (Crozier),[31] and 'A E' (Russell),[32] while Stephen Gwynn and some others had done well. The Provost [Mahaffy] with his jokes and irresponsible speeches was the 'rogue elephant' of the Convention, serving a most useful purpose when

---

[30] Thomas Ashe (Tomás Aghas) (1885–1917): schoolteacher; sentenced to death for his role in the rebellion of 1916 but reprieved and subsequently released; imprisoned once more in August 1917 on a charge of sedition and died on 25 September after being forcibly fed following a hunger strike.

[31] John Baptist Crozier (1853–1920): Archbishop of Armagh of the Church of Ireland and Primate of All Ireland 1911–1920.

[32] George William Russell (1867–1935): poet and writer, who used the pseudonym Æ; author of, inter alia, *Ireland, Agriculture and the War* (n.p.: 1915) and a leaflet, *Talks with an Irish Farmer* (1916).

things were getting too serious. He spoke very highly of a Methodist Nationalist from County Louth (I think) and thought well of Donoughmore.[33] Midleton (Brodrick)[34] he said, was hopelessly narrow-minded, and Mayo absurd.

Later in the day, in conversation with Adams, Plunkett said that Duke would have to go and that I was the right man to succeed him and that he was going to tell Ll.-G. so! I call this a high compliment from one who is perhaps the first Irishman of our time.

8 October

Downing Street. Horace Plunkett in and out all the morning. He thinks there are evidences of a split in the Sinn Fein forces – a MacNeill[35] group and a De Valera[36] group.

13 October

To Downing Street. I want to see Ll.-G. about an important matter connected with the Construction of merchant ships. My only chance is to tack myself on to him as he drives to his dentist's (in Stratford Place), which I do accordingly. Poor little man! Who else, making for his dentist's, would tolerate the intrusion of one of his Secretaries full of some topic, almost as painful as his toothache?

---

[33] Richard Walter John Hely-Hutchinson (1875–1948): Conservative peer and Southern Unionist; Under-Secretary of State for War 1903–1905; succ. as 6th Earl of Donoughmore 1900.
[34] William St John Fremantle Brodrick (1856–1942): Con. MP for West Surrey 1880–1885; Con. MP for Guildford 1885–1906; Financial Secretary to the War Office 1886–1892; Under-Secretary of State for War 1895–1898; Under-Secretary of State for Foreign Affairs 1898–1900; Secretary of State for War 1900–1903; Secretary of State for India 1903–1905; leading Southern Unionist; succ. as 9th Viscount Midleton 1907; cr. first Earl of Midleton 1920.
[35] Eoin (John) MacNeill (1867–1945): scholar of Irish History; editor of the *Irish Volunteer* 1914–1916; Sinn Féin MP for Londonderry City 1918–1922 and also for the National University of Ireland 1918–1921 but did not take his seat; supporter of the Anglo-Irish treaty; Free State Minister of Education 1922–1925.
[36] Eamon de Valera (1882–1975): sentenced to death for his role in the rebellion of 1916 but reprieved and subsequently released; Sinn Féin MP for East Clare 1917–1922 (but did not take his seat); leading opponent of the Anglo-Irish Treaty of 1921; Taoiseach 1932–1948, 1951–1959; President of Éire 1959–1973.

25 October

Horace Plunkett in to see us at the Garden Suburb. The Irish Convention has passed through troubled waters of late but the good ship is still afloat. A Sub-Committee (of seven, I think) has been charged with the delicate task of formulating a definite plan and is meeting now in London. The rest of the Grand Committee continues at work in Dublin. Meanwhile De Valera, the leader of republican Sinn Fein, is making exceedingly provocative speeches in Ireland. His object is apparently to precipitate a crisis and at all hazards to damage the prospects of the Convention.

2 November

All day at the Garden Suburb. Northcliffe is leaving America by the 'St. Paul' tomorrow and I am anxious to hear what steps are being taken adequately to protect his ship. Ll.-G. is concerned about this and urgent messages go to the Admiralty enjoining on them the necessity for fully adequate measures. If the Germans can drown him or take him prisoner in a submarine it will be no end of a score for them.

9 November

A week of strenuous work in the Garden Suburb on the Government 'Record'.
The news is thoroughly bad. Russia is in the midst of a fresh revolutionary convulsion and the Italians are stampeding down into the Venetian plain before the victorious Germans and Austrians. The P.M. is in Italy with Sir Wm. Robertson, General Foch[37] and Cadorna.[38]

15 November

Alfred telephones to me from the office of the British War Mission to the U.S.A. 29 Abingdon Street to read to me his letter to the Prime

---

[37] Ferdinand Foch (1851–1929): French Army officer; Generalissimo of the Allied Armies 1918; Marshal of France 1918.
[38] Luigi Cadorna (1850–1928): Chief of Staff of the Italian Army 1914–1917; Italian representative to the Allied Supreme War Council 1917–1919; Field Marshal 1924.

Minister declining the great office of first Minister of the Air – ranking with a Secretaryship of State.

Lloyd-George must be tired of the Harmsworth family. Since he became Prime Minister nearly a year ago Alfred has declined the Air Ministry, Harold both the First Commissionership and the Ministry of Food and I the joint Chief Whipship of the Coalition.

20 November

During this week we have from Horace Plunkett a series of rather excitable and urgent messages about the Irish Convention. Briefly, the knottiest point of all has been reached i.e., whether or not the Irish Parliament shall have full fiscal autonomy. The Nationalists say 'Yes': the Ulstermen say 'No'. *I* say, that if the Ulstermen will concede the setting-up of any sort of Parliament *for all Ireland* nine points in ten have been gained and that other questions can safely be left to the future. The Nationalists seem unduly nervous of the Sinn Feiners who are clamouring for an independent, a Republican constitution – and the Nationalists are forgetting that a Constitution is a living organism capable of any degree of development. No one maintains that we are framing a cast-iron Constitution like that of the U.S.A.

23 November

J.T. Davies,[39] one of the P.M.'s private Secretaries, comes down to the Garden House today to tell us that Harold has accepted the Ministry of the Air.

1 December

A telegram from Harold to Mother to say that Vyv's wounds though serious enough are not dangerous.[40]

---

[39] John Thomas Davies (1881–1938): private secretary to Lloyd George 1912–1922; knighted 1917.
[40] Rothermere had been informed that morning that his eldest son, Vyvyan, had been wounded. He had also been injured on two previous occasions.

5 December

Plunkett, Dr. Bernard and other Conventionists are over in London seeing the P.M. The Irish Convention is at the very crisis of its fate. (1) The Redmondites demand a large measure of H. Rule for all Ireland with control of Customs and treaty-making powers. (2) The Southern Unionists agree in the main but refuse Customs and the treaty-making powers. (3) The Ulstermen 'lie low and say nuffin'. The object of the Southern Unionists with Plunkett at their head is to get the P.M. and the War Cabinet to bring (1) and (2) to terms. E. Carson, a War Cabinet Minister, is perhaps the key of the situation or it may be W.M. Murphy, the formidable proprietor of the *Irish Independent* and of the Dublin trams etc.

Meanwhile the 'Representation of the People Bill' is in the Commons and the question arises of the redistribution of Irish seats. Tim Healy makes a coarse attack on T.C.D. and I rejoin in a heated little speech which is well thought of.

7 December

Dr. Bernard (Archbishop) and H. Plunkett in and out of the Garden Suburb all day. Bernard and Lord Midleton are the most influential of the Southern Unionists. B. is beautifully clear-minded as usual – H.P. a bit woolly and undecided. Adams and I go over the whole situation with them.

18 December

An early evening air raid. I retire with the others from the garden building at Downing Street and make for the H. of C. When the guns begin to go off Mr. Whitley[41] from the Chair announces that at the request of the authorities of the House he suspends the sitting during the raid and that the division bells will be rung when the sitting is resumed. Some few murmurs at this but the general feeling is that we can't expect the public to obey police directions to take cover during raids if we don't do it ourselves. Our glass roof too is not much of a protection! So we troop off to the Smoking rooms, libraries etc. and

---

[41] John Henry Whitley (1866–1935): Lib. MP for Halifax 1900–1928; Deputy Speaker of the House of Commons 1911–1921; Speaker 1921–1928; Chairman of the BBC 1930–1935.

to the passage downstairs leading to the Harcourt room. This latter is said to be the safest place in the whole building.

19 December

No report in the papers today of our taking cover in the House yesterday. This thought to be a serious blunder. It looks as if we were ashamed of our caution!

20 December

House adjourned. Ll.-G. makes an important statement on the present position. Astor is engaged elsewhere so I act for the nonce as Parliamentary Secretary, sitting behind Ll.G. with his red box full of extra notes and memoranda. He does not ask for any of them.

Afterwards in his room I tell him that Jos Wedgwood[42] is going for Haig, F.M., hot and strong. Ll.-G. by no means sorry to hear it. We discuss the merits of other Generals – Monro,[43] in India, especially. Ll.-G. says he is too delicate – suffers from lungs or throat or something. Then J.H. Thomas,[44] the Labour man, bursts in and no more conversation is possible.

---

[42] Josiah Clement Wedgwood (1872–1943): Lib. (from 1919 Lab) MP for Newcastle-under-Lyme 1906–1942; Chancellor of the Duchy of Lancaster 1924; cr. 1st Baron Wedgwood 1942.
[43] Charles Carmichael Monro (1860–1929): army officer; C.-in-C., India, 1916–1920; Governor of Gibraltar 1923–1928; knighted 1915; cr. baronet 1921.
[44] James Henry Thomas (1874–1949): Lab. MP for Derby 1910–18 36; General Secretary of the National Union of Railwaymen 1916–1831; Colonial Secretary 1924, 1935–186; Lord Privy Seal 1929–1831; Dominions Secretary 1931–1935; resigned from the government and the Commons after he was found to have disclosed Budget secrets to two friends.

1918

18 January

Sir Horace Plunkett in and out of Downing Street all day. The situation in the Convention is most critical. The question turns on whether or not the proposed Irish Parliament is to control Customs. The Southern Unionists are in agreement with the Nationalists except on this point. If Customs are reserved to Impl. Parliament the S. Unionists will support a H R Constitution on the lines of Lord Midleton's resolution now before the Convention. The Nationalists while they desire that Customs should belong to the Irish Parliament are prepared to waive the claim if they hear from the War Cabinet that in the event of their making this concession the War Cabinet will pledge themselves definitely to give effect immediately by legislation to the 'Midleton Compromise'. The fateful Division is to be taken in the Convention on Thursday or Friday next. Sir Horace has come over in the hope of securing the desired Cabinet pledge.

(The Ulster men in the Convention meantime maintain their accustomed non possumus attitude – making no secret, as Sir H.P. assures us, of their delight at the turn things are taking.)

All day long (and on Saturday, the 19th, too) we argue the knotty question. The view of the Garden Suburb is that it would be wrong and unwise of the Govt. to pledge themselves to any group or groups in the Convention. By so doing, they would, we think, trespass on the independence of the Convention and expose themselves to Ulster charges of having sold them behind their backs. The Ulstermen would rejoice at any excuse for blaming the possible break-down of the Convention on the Govt.

Our suggestion is that the P.M. should write to Sir H.P. inviting the leaders of the Convention to come over to confer with the Cabinet thus avoiding a confused and embarrassing Division. So, too, an opportunity would be given to the Cabinet to bring pressure on all parties *meeting together* and to announce the Govt.'s intentions.

Sir H.P. is in a very poor state of health and shows signs of being overwrought. He returns to Ireland Saturday evening.

[Horace Plunkett was, I think, the best of all friends of Ireland in modern times. He was mainly responsible for establishing Agricultl.

Co-Operation on Danish lines in Ireland, with great advantage especially to dairy farming.]

23 January

Mr. Ebenezer Howard to see me this evening. He is full of a great scheme for a large number of Garden Cities to be built during the Reconstruction period after the War. He wants me to be Chairman or at least a member of a new propagandist Committee he proposes to set up. [...]
Resignation of Sir Edward Carson.

24 January

At Downing Street we await with anxious interest news from the Convention. Are they taking the fateful decision or will they accept the P.M.'s suggestion and come over to confer with the War Cabinet before proceeding further?
Following morning we learn that the Convention have decided to accept P.M.'s invitation and that the Division is therefore postponed *sine die*.

7 February

Delegation from the Irish Convention in town. Horace Plunkett (with Captain Shaw,[1] one of the Secretaries of the Convention) in and out of the garden building all day long.
H.P. diffuse as ever and despondent about the Convention's chances. What with the exorbitant demands (Fiscal autonomy, the chief of them) of the Nationalists and the stiff obduracy of the Northerners he is out of patience with them all. Bernard with a new archiepiscopal hat is a frequent visitor. Whenever I look into Adams' room I find him cheek by jowl with Conventionists – now it is Waugh,[2] the Labour man, and again it is Wee Joe Devlin and the formidable Bishop of Raphoe,[3] who

---

[1] Richard James Herbert Shaw (1885–1946): served in the army during the First World War; Assistant Secretary to the Irish Convention 1917; later worked for *The Times*.
[2] Robert Waugh: of the Amalgamated Society of Carpenters and Joiners; representative of the building trades on the Irish Convention.
[3] Patrick Joseph O'Donnell (1856–1927): Roman Catholic Bishop of Raphoe 1888–1922; coadjutor Archbishop of Armagh 1922–1924; Cardinal 1925.

is the head and front of the fiscal autonomists. Anon Midleton favours us with his presence, or Desart, or John Redmond.

All this time, too, we are busy with the 'Government Record' for 1917 – a State document giving an account of the Lloyd-George Govt.'s stewardship during its first year of office. It is a teasing compilation. Many of the chapters have to be written in several different departments and the proof sheets must be revised again and again by the same departments. When we seem to be getting near the end of our task Ll.-G. rejects the admirable Introduction prepared by Adams and the task has to be taken in hand by Philip Kerr, and the Ministry of Food insist, almost at the eleventh hour, on writing their own chapter again! I am sub-editor, 'reader', foreman and printer's devil all in one.

9 February

Very bad news tonight of Vyvyan [Rothermere's eldest boy] who has been lying ill of his wounds these many weeks at the Lady Northcliffe Hospital. His wounds have been septic all along and now his condition is very serious.

12 February

My dear nephew Vyvyan died this day – one of the finest spirits that has fallen in this horrible War. I did not know until Saturday how seriously ill he was.

To see poor Harold.

15 February

Vyvyan's funeral – a terrible thing.

25 February

Today, I think, or-tomorrow Horace Plunkett and the last of the Conventionists go back to Ireland. They have been with us for *weeks*! There has been no room in the basement of No. 10 or in the Garden Suburb where some members of the delegation from the Convention have not been found. Waldorf Astor's little vaulted room is normally, I believe, a butler's pantry. Here, on several occasions, I have found H.P. and Capt. Shaw engaged in earnest colloquy, At other times, or at the same time indeed, the Bp. of Raphoe has been secreted with Adams in his room or Stephen Gwynn has been located temporarily in mine. Now and again Adams has been driven to 'sporting his oak' when engaged in conference with black Northerners or milder Southern Unionists. I think that well-nigh every delegate member of the Convention has been in and out of the Garden Suburb during the last few weeks. H. Plunkett, voluble and seemingly inconstant, has almost lived with us.

Meanwhile the duty of convoying the War Cabinet Record through the Press has fallen more and more on my hands.

5 March

Adams reopens with me the question of proposed changes in the Govt. of Ireland. It is Decies (or Londonderry) for the Lord Lieutenancy. What about the Chief Secretaryship? Adams has mentioned my name and so has H Plunkett. P.M. afraid of having his Govt. described as a 'Harmsworth Govt.' with Alfred at the American Mission and Harold at the Air Ministry.

[I was never at any time offered this appointment. C.H. 31 XII 1937]

6 March

Death of John Redmond this morning after an operation.

H. Plunkett wires from the Convention to say that the event has had a profound effect on that body.

8 March

Requiem Mass in Westminster Cathedral for John Redmond. A splendid ceremony with much impressive if somewhat monotonous music. Cardinal Bourne[4] officiating, now in scarlet biretta and purple vestments with a long train and later in a tall white mitre and a black

---

[4]Francis Alphonsus Bourne (1861–1935): Roman Catholic Archbishop of Westminster 1903–1935; Cardinal 1911.

and gold vestment. The coffin covered with a pall and an Irish flag at the foot of the chancel steps.

The Prime Minister, Bonar Law and Carson present with a great company of members of both Houses.

14 March

Spring is with is indeed but there is no corresponding revival of spirit among is in the Garden Suburb. In the double-windowed Cabinet room above the Prime Minister is in daily conference, cheek by jowl, with M. Clemenceau,[5] the French Prime Minister, and the immediate affairs of the Allies are subjects of constant and eager debate. Meanwhile, the cause of the Allies goes heavily. The Germans are in or before Odessa and there is rumour of the Congregation against us on the Western front of an almost unlimited number of German divisions.

21 March

The Germans begin today their great offensive on a front of about 55 miles. News this evening that they have taken our first line trenches over perhaps a third of this front.

26 March

This appears to be a retrospective, post-war entry, but it is not clear exactly when it was made.
Downing Street.
One day about this time I was leaving No. 10 by the garden gate when I met the Prime Minister coming in with Philip Kerr. He had been to the War Office to discuss there the latest phases of our disastrous retreat. He was pinched and very white and merely shook his grey locks at me when I held the door for him and said 'Terrible times, sir.' He replied, 'Terrible times! Yes, but we shall pull through all right.'

---

[5] Georges Benjamin Clemenceau (1841–1929): Prime Minister of France 1906–1909, 1917–1920.

This was the only occasion during the War when I saw Ll.-G go white with apprehension. Most other times he, with his high confident spirit, was keeping his colleagues from 'cold feet'.

29 March

Downing Street all day. The terrible battle for Amiens, and the problems of Ireland, occupy our thoughts. In regard to Ireland the question is whether to apply Conscription and, if so, whether before or simultaneously with the introduction of legislation for 'settling' Ireland on the lines to be announced as recommended by the Convention.

30 March

A brief talk with the Prime Minister about applying Conscription to Ireland. [. . .]

The P.M. is for taking the plunge out of hand: we, in the Garden Suburb, are for Home Rule first or at least simultaneously with Conscription preferably with an appeal for voluntary enlistment before stronger measures are applied.

10 April

To town and Downing Street. Not a cheerful face to be seen anywhere. In the House of Commons there is the utmost gloom. Men's heads are bowed and the lines on every face seem to have sensibly deepened. Such weeks as we have passed through! There is not merely anxiety: there is stupefaction and bewilderment at the spectacle of the hurried and confused retreat of our glorious Army – just as if they were so many Italians or Roumanians.

Of angry criticism or recrimination there is not much on the surface.

15 April

With Lloyd-George in his car to the H. of C. The little man shows unmistakable signs of wear and tear. I mention to him Northcliffe's desire for a firm assurance that, if he supports Home Rule with all vigour in his newspapers, he can rely on Ll.-G. going through with it to a finish. Ll.-G. most positive on the point, saying that he will resign if he cannot have his way in this matter.

18 April

Austen Chamberlain becomes this week a member of the War Cabinet, hugely to Northcliffe's disgust.

19 April

Downing Street. Horace Plunkett is in and out constantly and deeply distressed about the Irish situation. Nationalist Ireland – Dillonites, O'Brienites and Sinn Feiners – is in revolt against Conscription and on all hands we hear that so great is their resentment that no interest whatever is being taken in the forthcoming Home Rule proposals. The hierarchy and the priests of the Roman Church are solid against Conscription, too. A pretty kettle of fish!

25 April

Harold resigns from the Air Ministry. I am sitting in the House when Bonar Law makes the announcement in reply to a question. It is the first I have heard of it. I hurry to Downing Street to ascertain the facts of the case and find that Harold has sent in his resignation (dated today) and that it has been accepted. (I have not seen Harold for some weeks and do not know what reasons, if any, other than those given in his letter to Ll.-G. are influencing him.) I go to the Savoy Hotel where he is now staying but cannot find him there or obtain any particulars of his movements.

9 May

Asquith's vote of censure on the Government, arising from Genl. Maurice's[6] letter to the Press alleging that the recent statements of Lloyd-George and B. Law in regard to the state of the War are

---

[6] Frederick Barton Maurice (1871–1951): army officer; Director of Military Operations at the War Office 1915–1918; knighted 1918.

'incorrect'. Ll.-G. in first-rate fighting trim, reduces the Opposition to speechlessness.

This is the first full-dress attack on and vote against a Government since the War began on August 4th 1914. One unhappy result may be the definite splitting of the Liberal party. In effect, however, the split has been a fact for a long time past not on any question of fundamental policy but because so many of the men who surround Asquith loathe Ll.-G. with a deadly loathing.

22 May [7]

It is now exactly a year since I became a member of the Prime Minister's Secretariat – waggishly known as the 'Garden Suburb' from the fact that the temporary building that houses us is built in the garden of 10 Downing Street. [...] This is a lath & plaster erection exactly similar on a small one-storeyed scale to those now to be seen in every open space in this Whitehall district. Horse Guards Parade has several such & the pleasant old garden at the back of the Board of Trade is full of them: so also is a great part of the dried-up bed of the lake in St. James's Park where the Ministry of Shipping is in habitation.

What is our function? I find it very difficult to explain: 'Helping Lloyd-George' is the simplest definition: the taking off his shoulders of as much detail work as our several qualities and our strict constitutional limitations permit. [...]

In some quarters outside the Secretariat (which is personal to the P.M. & quite distinct from the War Cabinet Secretariat) is regarded as a dangerous constitutional innovation. Our ministerial heads deplore the supercession of the former omnibus cabinets of twenty members & more by the War Cabinet of five or six supported by mysterious secretariats. True enough we often serve as liaison officers between ministers and ministries at loggerheads but it is an entire mistake to suppose that there is less contact between War cabinet ministers & ministers outside the War cabinet than obtained under the former regime. Departmental ministers are summoned always to Cabinet Councils when affairs relating to their departments are to be discussed. This means that the heads of the war-like Offices – War Office, Admiralty, Foreign Office, Food Control, National Service – are more frequently in consultation with the heads of the Govt than they were

---

[7] This is one of the longest entries in the diary, and for reasons of space it is not possible to include all of it. CBH appears to have considered it to be of some sensitivity, as he wrote it in a volume separate from that which contained the other entries for 1918.

or were likely to be under the old dispensation. We have much to do with the latter departments & controls – the dozen & one new minor offices that have sprung up to meet wartime emergencies. Sometimes, as in the case of Belgian Relief, there is no department ultimately responsible but control is scattered among several authorities – in this instance the ministry of Shipping, the Admiralty, the Wheat Executive, the Commission for Relief in Belgium & perhaps two or three others. (I have spent the last few tropical days trying to co-ordinate these various activities. My simple suggestion that the whole matter should be referred to a War cabinet minister has not yet been adopted by Ll.-G. [. . .]

On the few occasions that I have been present at Cabinet the Wizard has ruled the roost with no appearance of challenge from any quarter. When, too, he has been absent in France or elsewhere it has been interesting to observe from the Cabinet ministers how many decisions have been deferred 'until the Prime Minister returns'. He is in truth the life & soul of the party in no merely conventional meaning of the expression. His vivid personality prevails in the Cabinet room as in the world outside.

An easier chief to work with in some respects it would be difficult to find. He is wholly unaffected & unspoilt by enormous success. I knew him slightly in the dark days of the Boer War when he was certainly the most unpopular man in England. I see no change in his manner now when he is, I suppose, the most popular man in the whole great Alliance. I have often spoken to him more directly than I dare to my brother N. &, whether he has agreed with me or not, he has never resented anything I have said. The experience of Adams & of the other members of the Secretariat has been the same.

[. . .]

My experience in the Secretariat has been of great service to me in preparing minutes and memoranda. Ll.-G. is notoriously impatient of long-windedness: indeed I have often wondered if he ever reads a long memorandum through. In writing a minute for him I always put the salient facts on the first page, advising him that he will find fuller details in the longer memo if he desires to consult it. One has to be most careful in presenting figures to Ll.-G. he is no more to be trusted with them than a lady-secretary. Sometimes I have doubted whether he knows the difference between 100,000 & 1,000,000 as they are written down, or realizes that an estimate is not the same thing as an accomplished reality. More than once in debate he has been in danger of a charge of positive untruthfulness because of his vagueness about figures & when I have myself provided him with statistics for a speech in the House I have been on tenterhooks as I have watched his Celtic imagination playing on them & developing them. Matchless in his handling of broad situations & unique in his darting aim at the very heart of a problem he is *[illegible word: ever?]* intolerant of details & a decimal point or a comma in a big figure seems to have no meaning to him. The House is fully aware of this weakness of his & follows him with ever increasing nervousness when he plunges into arithmetical calculations.

[...]

We are permitted to see something of the P.M.'s domestic life. I have heard him talking Welsh to Mrs. Ll.-G over the banister at No. 10 & I have dined with him and his family at the end of a big table in the great oak-panelled dining-room. On one such occasion there were present Ll.-G himself, Mrs. Ll.-G, one of their sons with his pretty new wife & J.T. Davies. It was at one of the most critical moments of the War & the Wizard had a dozen grave anxieties on his mind. These for the moment he had shaken off, & he was full of gaiety & fun. He even broke into a stave of a Welsh folk-song as he moved briskly around the table helping himself & them from the sideboard. On another such occasion there was much merriment over a big store jar of whisky that some ardent admirer had sent him. He was not to be satisfied until we had all tasted it & given our opinion of it.

Or perhaps we are bidden to accompany him on his walks in town or in the country. A messenger comes down saying 'The Prime Minister wants you to go for a walk with him, Sir.' He walks quickly & sturdily with one shoulder down & is of course recognized by everybody. One afternoon we strode off through St. James's park & the Green park to Knightsbridge where eventually we took refuge in a tea shop. Needless to say, every eye was glued on him from the time we entered until we departed. I have, too, a full note of a tramp with him in Richmond Park.

He is an exceedingly pleasant companion – not a conversationist as let one say Lord Rosebery, Mr. Asquith and Mr. Birrell are, but a bright and cheerful talker. A Boswell would be hard put to it to fill a note-book with Lloyd-Georgian obiter dicta of any permanent value. He loves best to talk about party politics & party personalities. No man of our time has more intensely or more successfully devoted the powers of his mind to the problems of the first magnitude to Ll.-G's heart. Every public man of whom I know anything has had an interest secondary to that of the high offices of state that have absorbed the best part of his energies. Did not Lord Rosebery in literature & Balfour in metaphysics & magic. Ll.-G's life-work is high-politics; his hobby or recreation political chit-chat & political manipulation. I know of no other absorbing interests that he gives his mind to.

3 May

Leicester's baronetcy announced today in the Birthday honours.

25 May

Lunch with the Belgian Minister at Claridges. Genl. Smuts[8] there, Sir John Field Beale,[9] Chairman of the Wheat Commission, and other Belgian Relief people.
Debate on the situation in Ireland. The Conscription threat has convulsed the country and the H. Rule Committee of the Cabinet has been making no progress.
Much thin-ice skating on the part of Ll.-G. and Shortt [Chief Secy. for Ireland], and a great speech by Carson. Later on, during the dinner-hour indeed, I have a chance and say a few words. House so thin that a count is called in the midst of my remarks – a disconcerting incident! Mem – don't speak during the dinner-hour.

4 July

The Fourth of July is celebrated with much enthusiasm in London. The Union Jack and Stars and Stripes flown side by side from the Victoria Tower and from other buildings. A great meeting in the Central Hall, Westminster: speeches by Lord Bryce,[10] Winston, Admiral Sims[11] (US Navy) and General Biddle[12] (U.S. Army).

---

[8] Jan Christiaan Smuts (1870–1950): General in the Boer Army during the Second Boer War; Lieutenant-General in the British Army during the First World War; member of the British War Cabinet 1917–1918; Prime Minister of South Africa 1919–1924, 1939–1948; British Field Marshal 1941.

[9] John Field Beale (c.1874–1935): businessman and wartime civil servant; knighted 1918.

[10] James Bryce (1838–1922): Regius Professor of Civil law at Oxford University 1870–1893; author of *The American Commonwealth* (London: Macmillan, 1888); Lib. candidate for Wick Burghs 1874; Lib. MP for Tower Hamlets 1880–1885; Aberdeen South 1885–1907; Chancellor of the Duchy of Lancaster 1892–1894; President of the Board of Trade 1894–1895; Chief Secretary for Ireland 1905–1907; Ambassador to the United States 1907–1913; cr. Viscount Bryce 1914.

[11] William Sowden Sims (1858–1936): commander of US naval forces operating in European waters during America's participation in the First World War.

[12] John Biddle (1859–1936): commanded the US army forces in Great Britain 1918–1919.

23 July

Lord Mayor's lunch to Mr. Hoover,[13] the American Food Controller, at the Mansion House.

[One of my duties at Downing Street was to act as liaison officer between Hoover's Relief organization and the British Govt. Hoover had a London Headquarters with which I had to be in constant touch and his London representative Mr. Poland sometimes kept me very busy. He was always clamouring for British ships to convey the food supplies to Belgium and I had to try to wangle these out of the Shipping Controller. The task became more and more difficult as the Germans sank more and more of our ships. (C.H. August 1927)]

25 July

Conference about Belgian Relief with General Smuts in his rooms at the Savoy Hotel. Mr. Hoover present. Before America came into the War he was in charge of relief in Belgium and he still takes an intense interest in the problem.

Dinner by our Food Ministry to Hoover at the Carlton Hotel. Admirable speech by Ll.-G. based to some extent on notes prepared by me.

31 July

Belgian Relief. A Conference on extra supplies of rice to Rotterdam.

The rest of the day I am busy preparing notes for Ll.-G.'s address to the Manufacturers who are coming tomorrow to ask him about the Govt.'s economic policy after the War.

3 August
Henley.

Anniversary services to celebrate our entry into the great War. [...] Very good news today of Foch's great offensive on the Soissons-Rheims line.

---

[13] Herbert Clark Hoover (1874–1964): organised famine relief in Europe during and after the First World War; US President 1929–1933.

15 August

The MS of Max Pemberton's[14] life of Northcliffe is sent down for my correction. Most of it sad rubbish, I fear, and much of it absurdly inaccurate. I should like to 'blue-pencil' the whole narrative.[15]

16 August

To town to attend Alfred's luncheon to the Dominion and foreign Press representatives now in England, at the *Times* office. Printing House Square is filled by a great marquee and there are about 150 guests including the Prime Ministers of Canada, Australia and N. Zealand (Borden,[16] Hughes and Ward[17]), Lord Reading, the Sheriffs in their robes and chains, and other notabilities. A most interesting occasion and Alfred makes a fine strong War speech.

I look in at Downing Street and return to Henley by the 6.10 train.

3 September

Ll.-G. sends for me to draft a reply to a telegram about arms in Ireland which has been received from Shortt, Chief Secretary. I find Ll.-G. in Bonar Law's study at No. 11 – he puffing away at a cigar and Bonar at his inseparable pipe, and the floor littered with papers.

Shortt and French are about to invite the Irish people to make a voluntary delivery of arms to the military authorities.

4 September

Pretty slack times in the Garden Suburb: it is very generally so when Parliament is not sitting and the War is going well with us. Our anxieties of last year have been largely relieved – food, labour unrest and the submarine menace. Ship-building is still very backward in

---

[14]Max Pemberton (1863–1950): journalist and author; director of Northcliffe Newspapers, knighted 1928.

[15]Pemberton subsequently abandoned the project, but revived it after Northcliffe's death: see Max Pemberton, *Lord Northcliffe: A Memoir* (London: Hodder & Stoughton, 1922).

[16]Robert Laird Borden (1854–1937): Prime Minister of Canada 1911–1920; knighted 1914.

[17]Joseph George Ward (1856–1930): Prime Minister of New Zealand 1906–1912, 1928–1930, cr. baronet 1911. CBH was mistaken: Ward was Deputy Prime Minister rather than Prime Minister at the time of this entry.

spite of the appointment of Lord Pirrie – but Ll.-G. has only at intervals had his mind fully on the subject and our best efforts to goad him to activity have only been partly successful. It is odd that the best 'galvaniser' of our time (except Northcliffe) should have been so slack in this respect. Well for us that the submarine danger should have been so far mastered by the Admiralty and by the splendidly efficient management of tonnage by Maclay,[18] the Shipping Controller. Otherwise – !

5 September

Weather bad, with deluges of rain, but the best of news from the Front where the Allies are driving the Huns back to the line from which they advanced on March 21st.

12 September

Ll.-G. today to Manchester to receive the Freedom: tomorrow to Salford and on Saturday to Preston and Blackpool for the same purpose.

I am left alone in my glory in the Garden Suburb, Adams and Kerr being on holiday. Some Belgian Relief matters to deal with and the supply of wool to go into with the Ministry of Shipping and Andrew Weir,[19] Surveyor-General of Supply, War Office.

13 September

The Prime Minister has an attack of influenza with a sore throat and is obliged to abandon the rest of his Lancashire tour.

14 September

In to town by early train – then to Downing Street to see if anything is doing there – and then to Luton for the Allotment Holders' Show.

---

[18] Joseph Paton Maclay (1857–1951): ship-owner; Minister of Shipping 1916–1921; cr. baronet 1914; cr. Baron Maclay 1922.

[19] Andrew Weir (1865–1955): shipowner; Surveyor-General of Supply 1917–1919; Minister of Munitions 1919–1921; cr. Baron Inverforth 1919.

Mr. Prothero, President of the Bd. of Agriculture & Fisheries, also present. Lunch (and champagne!) in the Mayor's (Dillingham's) [20] parlour. Then to the Park where the fruit and vegetable show is exhibited in a marquee: wonderful potatoes, cauliflowers, carrots and all kinds of late vegetables – I don't believe the whole farming world combined could beat the Luton allotment-holders in vegetables. Prothero and I address a small damp crowd from the band-stand. Then I go to have high tea with Mr. Edwin Oakley and, at last, home to Montagu Square (another high tea) and then out again to Henley. Such a day!

Before the War there were at Luton 125 acres under allotments and 1,000 holders: now there are 278 acres and 2744 holders.

16 September

Ll.-G. still confined to his bed at the Manchester Town Hall – chafing like a caged lion, I hear.

Austrian Govt. issues its invitation to the belligerents for a preliminary discussion about Peace terms.

17 September

Sir Horace Plunkett, just back from a visit to France, in and out of the Garden Suburb all day. He is now to a large extent in charge of Irish propaganda – or rather of 'War aims' in Ireland – and has a scheme for enlisting Irish women for auxiliary service with the American army in France. He expects good results on Irish opinion from this.

18 September

Ll.-G. now convalescent but still at Manchester.

19 September

Downing Street all day. I have been busy the last two days getting information for Ll.-G. about the demand that is being made in Labour

---

[20] Charles Dillingham (*c*.1860–1925): hat manufacturer; Mayor of Luton 1917–1918.

circles for a general increase of pay in the Navy and Army. Interviews with Dr. Macnamara (Admiralty) H.W. Forster (War Office) and Col. Leslie Wilson[21] (War Cabinet Secretariat).

10 October

Today appears in the papers President Wilson's reply to the German request that he should propose an armistice to the Allies. Wilson asks for a clearer statement as to what the Germans mean.

13 October

Downing Street – the only time I have ever been there on a Sunday. In today's papers is the German reply to Wilson accepting or seeming to accept all his conditions. The anxious point is, however, that if the armistice is granted *before* the Germans have given solid proof of their bona fides they may never give it. Clearly, once the War ceased it would be impossible to revive it, no matter how much the Huns defaulted.

It appears that Wilson did not consult the Allies before answering the Germans.

The principal Ministers – or some of them – Bonar Law, Milner, Mr. A.J. Balfour and Lord R. Cecil, are with Ll.-G. at his country home and there is talk of Ll.-G. and others going over to Paris tomorrow to see Clemenceau and Foch.

Northcliffe comes up from Broadstairs and I go to him at the *Times* Office. The peace situation troubles him but he thinks things will be all right in the end. I dine with him at the *Times* Office with Sir Campbell Stuart[22] his principal Secretary.

---

[21] Leslie Orme Wilson (1876–1955): army officer; Con. candidate for Poplar Jan. 1910; Reading Dec. 1910; Con. MP for Reading 1913–1922; Con. candidate for St. George's, Westminster 1922; Con. MP for South Portsmouth 1922–1923; Parliamentary Assistant Secretary to the War Cabinet 1918–1919; Parliamentary Secretary to the Ministry of Shipping 1919–1921; Parliamentary Secretary to the Treasury and Unionist Chief Whip 1921–1922; Government Chief Whip 1922–1923; Governor of Bombay 1923–1928; Governor of Queensland 1932–1946; knighted 1923.

[22] Campbell Arthur Stuart (1885–1972): born in Canada; military secretary to Northcliffe's 1917 mission to America; became a key figure in Northcliffe's newspaper empire; knighted 1918.

23 October

On one of these days the P.M. desires me to enquire into the causes of Miss Douglas-Pennant's dismissal from the W.R.A.F.

29 October

These are wonderful days. The central alliance is crumbling in every direction. Events succeed one another breathlessly and it is impossible to record them.

3 November

The newspapers today record the setting up of four new Republics:

Hungary

Bohemia

Bulgaria (where Ferdy's[23] successor Boris[24] has abdicated after a reign of 29 days)

(?) Austro-Germany

Bosnia and Herzgovinia have elected to join Servia; Croatia and Slavonia are thought to be going the same way; and Fiume is said to have declared for union with Italy.

Meanwhile Turkey is clean out of the War and at Versailles the Allies are settling the terms of armistice for Germany. Northcliffe, fearful lest the jellyfish (as he calls our statesmen) should treat the Germans too tenderly, has gone to Paris to administer ginger if it should be necessary.

What wonderful days & the most wonderful thing is that the English people are as undemonstrative in these weeks of triumph as they were in all the four years of disappointment, disaster and apparent failure.

---

[23] Ferdinand Maximilian Karl Leopold Maria of Saxe-Coburg and Gotha-Koháry (1861–1948): Prince Regnant of Bulgaria 1887–1908; proclaimed himself Tsar and ruled as Ferdinand I until his abdication in 1918.

[24] Boris III 'The Unifier' (1894–1943). Although his abdication was reported in *The Times* of 4 November 1918, he in fact reigned until his death.

6 November

Lines and lines of German guns in the Mall two deep in some places. Many of them have been painted all sorts of colours for camouflage purposes.

Prime Minister announces in the House today the terms of the armistice granted to Austria–Hungary and arranged at Versailles. [...]

I have seen infinitely greater excitement in the House when the Opposition have run the Govt. of the day close in the Division lobbies.

11 November

My dinner at Dr. Johnson's House to thirteen American editors. [...]
THE ARMISTICE WAS SIGNED AT 5 a.m. TODAY – TODAY CEASE FIRE ORDERED AT 11 a.m.
Big Ben illuminated tonight for the first time for four years.

13 November
Visitors' Chateau, G.H.Q.

The armistice was signed on Monday and the War is, I suppose, over. I could have wished to come here before the last shot had been fired but long pre-arranged plans bring me here at this time and I am content.

Of the Parliamentary party there are with me Jimmy Rowlands,[25] Sir Bevill Stanier, G.W. Currie,[26] and C. Thomas-Stanford.[27] [...]

Customs formalities are merely perfunctory and we are soon on the road in 3 or 4 motor cars. The streets of Boulogne are full of British and British Colonial soldiers. Then a drive in perfect moonlight of – what? – 35 or 40 miles to the visitors' chateau at Tramecourt.

---

[25] James Rowlands (d. 1920 at age 69): Lib. MP for East Finsbury 1886–1895; Lib. (then Coalition Lib) MP for Dartford 1906–1910, 1910–1920.

[26] George Welsh Currie (1870–1950): Unionist MP for Leith 1914–1918; later joined the Labour Party.

[27] Charles Thomas-Stanford (1858–1932): Unionist MP for Brighton 1914–1922; cr. baronet 1929.

14 November

About 9 o'clock we leave the chateau in two motor-cars[...] It is many miles before we come on any signs of the war and then there are trenches and barbed wire in the fields. Aire is our first town and there a good deal of damage has been done as a shattered church and many houses in ruins testify, but it is not until we reach Bailleul that we find absolute desolation. There are few if any buildings in the town that are not tangled heaps of brick, woodwork and twisted iron. Some streets were, as one of our party suggested, more like streets in excavated Pompeii than anything else imaginable.

After Bailleul, Poperinghe which has come off pretty well. There are many damaged houses but restoration in Poperinghe should not prove a very difficult matter.

Then Ypres! Ypres and the Ypres salient have been in all our minds for four years and surely in the history of the world no town of equal size – except Bailleul – has witnessed so complete a destruction or has entailed so much loss and heroic suffering. In Ypres it is only buildings of great bulk and solidity – the Cloth Hall, the Cathedral and the Hospital – that still rear a few high pinnacles above the surrounding desolation. Here and there one recognises the shape of a fine gothic arch or other feature; but there is scarcely a square foot of the still standing ruins that has not been shaled off as if by fire. Four years have done as much for Ypres as four centuries of slow decay might have done. Not Milton even imagined anything so hellish.

16 November

To-day our journey is over monotonous roads to Arras and Cambria. The other side of Arras we come on the British Expeditionary Force in being. There are camps and billets (full of men) and dumps everywhere, and everywhere the British and Colonial soldier is lord of all he surveys. On the roads are troops and artillery trains, sometimes with great guns painted green and yellow and black and drawn by 'caterpillars' that wake the dead with their shattering noises. There are A.S.C., R.E., and Hospital trains too and the whole region is alive with military activity. Here and there by the roadside are aerodromes, barbed wire cages for prisoners of war, and stacks of live shells. The fields are pitted with shell-holes, and in many places the trees have been torn and riven by shells. The retreating Hun blew up the road at intervals, and everywhere today we cross R.E. bridges that have been hastily built to replace those mined by the foe. [...]

(We members of Parliament learnt yesterday that a General Election has been announced and that we shall be required to begin work early in next week. Well for us that we have snatched this intensely interesting little holiday in advance!)

23 November

I am adopted Liberal-Coalition Candidate for S. Beds.

25 November

To Downing Street in the morning.
In the afternoon to Luton to begin the campaign of 1918.

26 November

Indoors most of the day writing my Address to the Electors and preparing notes for speeches.

28 November

I have a bad cold coming on and stay in until the evening when at 8 o'clock I address a meeting in the Tory Club (Chairman, Mr. Hugh Cumberland).[28]
A novel experience for me.

29 November

Today first meeting of our joint Liberal & Unionist Associations to set up various Election Committees.
I address a meeting of women Electors in the Town Hall.

---

[28] Hugh Cumberland (d. 1950 at age 92): auctioneer, surveyor, and Justice of the Peace.

30 November

A message early this morning from Downing Street saying that the P.M. wants to see me urgently.
 Ll.-G. discusses with me the reasons for Northcliffe's unfriendly attitude to him and his Govt. I tell him that I have not seen N. for many weeks and can only surmise that the reasons are (1) the fact of Ll.-G.'s not having asked him to go to the Peace Conference and (2) the lack of any statement from Ll.-G. about the personnel of his Govt. in the new parliament.
 Ll.-G. low-spirited, I think, about the Election. He seems to wish he had not embarked on it and had left the work of Reconstruction to other hands. He paces up and down the Cabinet room more agitated in his manner than I have seen him during the War save on one or two very critical occasions.
 After dinner I ring up N. who is at Elmwood giving him hints on the situation and asking if there is any use in my coming down to Broadstairs to talk things over with him. 'Not the slightest' he says. He tells me to remind Ll.-G. of a conversation between them in Paris when N. urged him to cut adrift from his embarrassing high Tory alliances and to go to the country 'as Ll.-G.' As it is, N. says, Ll.-G. will be tied hand and foot to the Junkers of the Tory 'old gang' party.

1 December

Downing Street in the morning. A council of the Allies in the Cabinet Room. I see Foch – a very smart soldierly little figure – Clemenceau, Sonnino[29] and others as they leave.
 As I have to leave early in the afternoon for Luton I dictate a letter to Ll.-G. recording my conversation with N.

4 December

Nomination day. Mr. George Warren, Mr. Harry Arnold,[30] Cotchin and I attend at the Town Hall and hand in nomination papers and

---

[29]Sidney Costantino Sonnino (1847–1922): Prime Minister of Italy 1906, 1909–1910; Foreign Minister 1914–1919.
[30]Harry Arnold (b. c.1864): timber merchant; Mayor of Luton 1920–1921; Lib. candidate for Luton 1922.

cheque for £150. I meet my opponent Mr. Willet Ball[31] in the street and shake hands with him. We sympathize with one another over the fatigues of the Election.

5 December

At night meetings at Houghton Regis and Dunstable, the latter much interrupted by some young Scotch hecklers from Luton.

7 December

At 3 o'clock to attend the opening of the Ivy Leaf Club for Discharged Sailors & Soldiers.

9 December

Works meeting at Kents – consisting chiefly of munitions girls (Kents have been making fuses for shells).

Busy all day and evening meetings at: Streatley & Sundon.

At Sundon there are lime-workers and my impression is that the village has gone over body and bones to Labour.

10 December

Fine dinner-hour meeting at the Vauxhall Works and after that a big women's meeting at the Town Hall, Dunstable.

On my return to Luton a deputation of women teachers and then a visit from my opponent Mr. Willet Ball and his agent Mr. Madley.[32] They come to complain that our canvassers at Leagrave are saying that Ball neglects his children and is an Atheist. I promise to do everything I can to scotch these libels and I expressly repudiate them at our evening meetings at: Stopsley & Barton (the best village meeting we have had.)

---

[31] Willet Ball (b. c.1874): journalist; editor of *Railway Review* 1917–1922; Lab. candidate for Luton 1922 and 1923.
[32] Unidentified.

12 December

I reserve myself today for the great meeting at the Assembly rooms. [...]
Before the meeting tonight a soldier from Biscot Camp comes to me to voice the grievances of the old Service men at the camp: pay, food, Christmas leave and unnecessary and severe elementary drills. They had intended to 'demonstrate' at our meeting but I tell them I will look into the questions in the morning. I beg them to preserve strict discipline.
A fine meeting with hosts of questions.

13 December

After lunch to Biscot Camp to see the Commandant, Col. de la Motte,[33] about the soldiers' grievances. He receives me kindly, takes notes and promises to make immediate enquiries.

14 December

Polling Day. We drive round the Constituency – Em, Daff, Cotchin, Earle and I. Our car is decorated with the flags of U.S.A., France and the Union Jack, the old Liberal, colours, primrose and Cambridge blue, forming a background. We lunch happily at the Sugar Loaf, Dunstable, the hostess and maids all wearing Liberal colours. Very few signs of buzz or enthusiasm at this Election. Our Liberal people understand a straight fight between Liberal and Tory but this Coalition business puzzles and disconcerts them. The villages seem staunch in spite of Willet Ball's desperate efforts to capture them and everywhere we hear that the women are polling well – in some places much better than the men. The northern belt of S. Beds having been thrown into the newly-formed Mid Division, our round is a short one and we are back in Luton at tea-time.
Needless to say there is the usual crop of eleventh-hour rumours – that the Labour men are backing themselves 10 to 1 to win, and the rest. On all hands it is agreed that the Poll is a moderate one.
Cotchin's estimate is that about 20,000 or 21,000 votes will be polled and that we shall have a majority of 5,000. Frank[34] says nothing about

---
[33] Unidentified.
[34] Frank Henry Parsons (b. c.1883): worked for the Luton Liberal Association.

the poll but gives us a majority of 3,500. The Mayor gives us a 2 to 1 majority.

One reason why the Election is so quiet is that the count is not to take place until this day fortnight. So that the soldiers and sailors on Service may be able to return their voting papers.

A message from the soldiers at Biscot camp saying that certain concessions have been made, and thanking me.

16 December

To have my hair cut at Douglas's in Bond Street and then to Downing Street. I see Ll.-G. for a few minutes. He asks how I have been getting on and inveighs against the attitude during the Election of the 'Northcliffe press'. (Alfred has been doing his best to queer the Coalition pitch – largely because of his belief that Ll.-G. is more than ever under the thumb of his enemies, the Tory 'Old Gang' – and has been successful, I think, in muddling the issue and taking the fizz out of the Coalition appeal.)

26 December

We see President Wilson, on his way from Charing X to Buckingham Palace, from Mr. Roper's[35] flat 90 Piccadilly. The President drives in the first carriage with the King and the Duke of Connaught. He is the guest of honour of course and. takes the salutations of the crowd with wide sweeps of his brand new tall hat – smiling largely the whiles all over his keen intellectual spectacled face. A fine reception and a fine, sunny, misty London winter's day. Overhead some aeroplanes perform all sorts of evolutions.

27 December

With Em and the children to the Counting of the votes. It is a dull damp day and the count after a fortnight's interval since the Poll is a spiritless affair. It is held in the council chamber at the Town Hall. Em and the children are admitted (quite irregularly, I think) to the council chamber and sit on the dais. At the other end of the horse-shoe table are Willet Ball and two or three of his principal supporters. We

[35] Possibly E.W. Roper.

talk together in friendly fashion during the 3 or 4 hours of the count which discloses pretty early in the proceedings that I am in. Half way through I receive an urgent message from the Mayor's parlour where I find Mr. Impey[36] and others smoking cigars and speculating on the size of the majority. The Town Clerk, too, asks me to his room where he produces a very welcome glass of port. He sends coffee and biscuits in to Em who won't leave the counting-room.

The result is announced about 3.30 [. . .] and Willet Ball and I make short speeches to a huge crowd outside the Town Hall. [37] After a visit to the Liberal Club where I make another speech we go to Cotchin's for a sort of meat tea and then back to town.

News comes along during the day of sensational defeats of leading Asquithians and pacifist Labour men.

30 December

To Downing Street in the morning where the utmost cheerfulness prevails. Long talk with Adams and Philip Kerr about the future of the Secretariat. Adams is going back to his work at Oxford and I have made up my mind to leave whether I get office or no. It is agreed that the Prime Minister ought to have a department of his own and it is understood that Ll.-G. is in favour of continuing the present one.

---

[36] Henry Impey (b. *c*.1865): Mayor of Luton 1918–1919.
[37] Election result: Cecil Harmsworth (Coalition Liberal) 15,501; Willet Ball (Labour) 5,964. Coalition majority 7,557.

1919

7 January
Henley

Round the town in the morning and a walk with Daff and Bud in Mr. Mackenzie's deer park after lunch. Arrived home I find a telegram from Em saying that Harold considers it imperative I should be 'on hand' in London while Ll.G. is reconstructing his Ministry. Much to the disgust of the happy little Henley party I resolve to catch the 6.40. Gol says: 'Why didn't you let Willet Ball win?'

8 January

To breakfast with Harold (Rothermere) at Savoy Court. He is sure that Ll.-G. is going to offer me 'something good' in his Ministry. He is to see Ll.-G. at Downing Street this evening and will press the point.

I spend most of the day in the Garden Suburb writing letters. Ll.-G. does *not* send downstairs for me and I am not going to besiege him the Cabinet room.

9 January

A letter from the P.M. offering me the post of Under-Secretary of State for Foreign Affairs in his new Ministry. I write immediately accepting the offer.

14 January

Foreign Office. If I wanted responsibility surely I have found it here! With Mr. Balfour and half the F.O. staff away at the Peace Conference in Paris and Lord (Curzon (Ld. President of the Council) coming in only 1 or 2 hours a day I have all I can do to keep going.

17 January

Meeting at Board of Trade to consider the whole question of the Blockade. Board of Trade want to smash the Blockade: we <u>insist</u> on its maintenance as an effective weapon during the Armistice period.

22 January

With red boxes full of F.O. telegrams and other papers following me to Montagu Sq. every evening I have little or no chance of writing up my Diary.

28 January

Allied Blockade Committee. The chief question this morning is whether we shall recommend the Paris Committee – it being not clear whether we have the power or they – to lift the Blockade as far as it affects Serbia and Roumania. We agree unanimously to make this recommendation and to press it urgently on Paris.

31 January

A message today from the P.M. saying that he wants me in Paris and that I am to bring with me such advisers on the Blockade as I think necessary.

1 February

We arrive in Paris about 10.30 and proceed direct to the Hotel Majestic where most of the British and Colonial peace-makers are installed. The great lounge of the Hotel is full of people I know the first to greet me being Lord Robert Cecil (my predecessor in office) and Edwin Montagu, the S. of S. for India.

2 February

About noon I call round at the Villa (the late Lord Michelham's)[1] which the P.M. occupies. I find him and Mrs. Ll.-G. and Megan in J.T. Davies' room, they having just returned from church. Ll.-G. greets me warmly and invites me to join his party for a drive and walk in the Bois. He is exceedingly fond of his pretty little Megan whose hand he clasps as we drive along. We alight in one of the quieter drives in the Bois which are looking delightful with three or four inches of snow on the ground. The paths are very slippery and the P.M. narrowly misses several croppers as we walk gingerly along. He is lively and interested in everything – except the Blockade which I vainly endeavour to press on his attention. I know him too well to pester him. When his mind is not on a subject there is no use talking to him about it. My difficulty is that he summoned me to Paris to consult with him about the Blockade, and this may be my one chance of broaching the subject! But there it is. He talks about Asquith, the present condition of the Liberal Party, Northcliffe, his love for France, the astonishing quantity of mistletoe in the trees of France ('But France is a Druidical country, you see', he explains), Free Trade ('I don't care a d–n for Free Trade'), and much else. I like the little man more and more and am pleased when English Tommies in the Bois salute him and French bourgeois take off their hats. He seems to be universally known.

At lunch today I join Mr. Balfour's party at the Majestic. He, Sir Wm. Tyrrell,[2] Eric Drummond[3] and Lord Eustace Percy[4] have been playing tennis and A.J.B. has the glow of health and exercise about him. It is my first meeting with him since I became his junior at the FO. He tells me he doesn't know and never did know anything about the Blockade. His conversation is light and discursive – gossip mainly about the celebrities at the Peace Conference – his manner exquisitely graceful and refined. He is treated with a sort of filial affectionate deference by the younger men with him.

[1] Herbert Stern (1851–1919): merchant banker; cr. Baron Michelham 1905; knighted 1912.
[2] William George Tyrell (1866–1947): civil servant; attached to the British delegation to the Paris Peace Conference with the rank of Minister-Plenipotentiary; Ambassador to France 1928–1934; knighted 1913; cr. Baron Tyrrell 1929.
[3] James Eric Drummond (1876–1951): civil servant; Secretary-General of the League of Nations 1919–1933; Ambassador to Italy 1933–1939; succ. as 7th Earl of Perth 1937.
[4] Eustace Sutherland Campbell Percy (1887–1958): civil servant, politician and educationalist; Con. candidate Kingston upon Hull 1919; MP for Hastings 1921–1937; Parliamentary Secretary to the Board of Education 1923; Parliamentary Secretary to the Board of Health 1923–1924; President of the Board of Education 1924–1929; Minister without Portfolio 1935–1936; Rector of King's College, Newcastle 1937–1952; cr. Baron Percy of Newcastle 1953.

Dancing this evening in the ballroom. It is a bright scene – the pretty girl secretaries and the many young naval and military officers enjoying themselves to the utmost. This is a regular and attractive feature of our evenings here. I asked the P.M. this morning if he ever joined in these revels. He said no but that he was more than adequately represented by Megan who is indeed having the time of her life.

[Later: It is incredible but a fact that I don't know to this day what Ll.-G. fetched me over to Paris for! I had one or two chances of brief conversation with him before I returned to London but not a word would he say about the Blockade. I knew what I wanted in this connection and this was that somebody of high political rank should be appointed to represent our Blockade interests in Paris, and before I returned I left a note for Ll.-G. suggesting that he should invite Lord Robert Cecil to act for us. He did so and Lord Robert consented. C.H. 19th Jany. 1934.]

20 February
[London]

These last days there has been a fine crop of Foreign Office questions in the H. of C. One of my difficulties has been that as Minister of Blockade I have had since my appointment to the F.O. but little time to devote to 'foreign affairs'. All goes well nevertheless.

17 March
Paris. Hotel Majestic.

This morning a meeting of the Supreme Economic Council, on which I am one of the Allied delegates as representing our Blockade interests. M. Clementel[5] in the chair and present also Lord R. Cecil, Mr. Hoover (U.S.A.), M. Seydoux[6] (France), Mr. Vance McCormick[7] (U.S.A.), Mr. Crespi[8] (Italian Food Controller), Mr. Baruch[9] (U.S.A.),

---

[5] Étienne Clémentel (1864–1936): French Minister of Commerce 1915–1919.
[6] Jacques Seydoux (1870–1929): diplomat.
[7] Vance Criswell McCormick (1872–1946): chairman of the Democratic National Committee, 1916–1819; chairman of the American delegation to the Paris Peace Conference.
[8] Silvio Benigno Crespi (1868–1944): Italian industrialist and politician; Minister of Food 1918–1919.
[9] Bernard Mannes Baruch (1870–1965): financier and presidential adviser.

Signor Attolico[10] (Italy), Sir H. Llewellyn Smith[11] (Board of Trade), Mr. Keynes[12] (Treasury), Sir Wm. Mitchell-Thomson, M.P. (my deputy at ordinary times), Admiral Hope,[13] Capt. Hardy, R.N.,[14] and a dozen or two more. We decide formally to raise the Blockade on the late Austro-Hungarian Empire, subject to the approval of the Supreme War Council. Coal for Italy and raw materials for Germany are among the other subjects raised. In regard to Austro-Hungary the Americans are in favour of allowing all imports to leak through into Germany. I resist this and the Council upholds me. I urge the shortness of the time before the Blockade is likely to be raised and the foolishness of scrapping our most powerful weapon against the Germans just before the conclusion of the treaty of Peace. Bob Cecil patters French briskly with Clementel and is a strange figure as he sits low down on his shoulders in one of the beautiful tapestried chairs of the Conference room. He is an admirable spokesman – taking a strong lead when necessary and exercising remarkable influence over the mixed and somewhat refractory gathering.

16 April

Ll.-G.'s speech in the House on Peace Conference matters. He makes a furious attack on Northcliffe. I in some doubt whether I should not resign from his Ministry. I discuss the matter with Ll.-G.'s private Parliamentary Secy., Sir Wm. Sutherland,[15] who strongly dissuades me from taking such a step.

I speak on some F.O. points that have arisen during the debate.

[Later: I was sitting on the Treasury bench at the time. My first impulse was to protest there and then – a second thought was to do so when later in the day I had to speak myself. But why should I sacrifice my career in the midst of a Donnybrook row between N. and Ll.-G.?

---

[10] Bernardo Attolico (1880–1942): diplomat.

[11] Hubert Llewellyn Smith (1864–1945): civil servant; Permanent Secretary of the Board of Trade (1907–1919); Chief Economic Adviser to the Government 1919–1927; knighted 1908.

[12] John Maynard Keynes (1883–1946): economist; resigned from the Treasury and published his highly critical *The Economic Consequences of the Peace* (London: Macmillan, 1919); cr. Baron Keynes 1942.

[13] George Price Webley Hope (1869–1959): naval officer; Deputy First Sea Lord 1918; knighted 1919.

[14] Charles T. Hardy: naval officer; Assistant Director of the Admiralty Trade Division during the First World War.

[15] William Sutherland (1880–1949): civil servant and politician; private secretary to Lloyd George 1915–1919; Coalition (then National) Lib. MP for Argyllshire 1918–1924; Lord of the Treasury 1920–1922; Chancellor of the Duchy of Lancaster 1922; knighted 1919.

Both were controversial bruisers, given to very rough blows on the one side and the other and exceedingly well able to look after themselves. As to the merits of their dispute, if I remember, I was out of sympathy with both of them. N. was opposed to my resigning. C.H. 29th Jany. 1934.]

17 April

War Cabinet meeting this morning to discuss the Censorship. I attend as acting Minister of Blockade. Bonar Law in the Chair – Ll.-G. having returned this morning to Paris.

15 May

F.O. vote in the H. of C.: chief subject Egypt. Other matters raised are the Blockade, Spitzbergen and the vacant embassy at Washington. I am on the bench all the afternoon and evening with only a few moments off for a sandwich or two and a whisky and soda.

30 May

Anniversary Dinner tonight of the Printers' Pension Corporation – Waldorf Astor presiding. The Prince of Wales[16] is the guest of the evening. He is surely the most attractive Prince we have had for centuries – small, very fair and quite boyish in spite of his twenty-five years. I see him furtively peeping at his notes during the dinner and too much absorbed for conversation. When his time comes he makes just the nervous little speech that goes down best with an English audience, without a trace of the guttural accent that his father has and that was so much more strongly marked in the case of Edward VII. To one who has been many times through the same ordeal it was pleasant to see H.R.H. nervously fingering the lapels of his coat and shifting wineglasses about on the table during his speech. Such a good-looking lad, too with pink cheeks and wide-open English eyes.

---

[16] 1894–1972; reigned as Edward VIII from January to December 1936; abdicated and was created Duke of Windsor.

6 June

Adjournment of the House for the Whitsuntide recess. Two questions concerning me – Egypt and Miss Douglas-Pennant – are threatened but I wait all day and nothing happens. I suspect that the Members interested in these matters are catching early trains for long Whitsuntide week-ends.

18 June

Alfred undergoes (very successfully) today an operation to his throat.

20 June

Lunch today at the Savoy to Alcock[17] and Brown[18] the winners of the *Daily Mail* £10,000 Atlantic flying prize. Winston Churchill presents the prize and announces that the heroes have been created Knights by H.M. They make characteristically modest and inarticulate speeches.
Many friendly references at the lunch to Alfred and his illness.

21 June
Henley.

Lovely day. I work at F.O. papers and loaf enjoyably.
A messenger from the F.O. with an urgent paper about the printing of the Treaty of Peace.

27 June

Victory Loan meeting in the Town Hall, Luton. Small gathering.

28 June

Today the Germans signed the Peace at Versailles.

---

[17] John William Alcock (1892–1919): aviator; knighted 1919; killed in an air crash.
[18] Arthur Whitten Brown (1886–1948): aviator and engineer; knighted 1919.

29 June

I ought to be at Church thank-offering for the Peace. Instead I spend the morning disposing of an accumulation of F.O. papers.

11 July

Harmsworth and his wife attended the Garden Party at Buckingham Palace. It is a glorious hot day and the beautiful lawns of the Palace garden are bright with a fashionable throng. The King and Queen with Princess Mary[19] (a bonnie girl with a fine colour and pretty fair hair) move about amidst the throng talking to people they know and receiving the presentations of debutantes.

[...] Later, I am specially presented to the King who remarks on the number of questions I am asked in the House – 'very dangerous some of them are, too,' he says. H.M. disapproves strongly in his rapid guttural way of attempts to carry on the business of diplomacy in the open. 'You might as well show your cards at Bridge and expect to succeed,' he says.

H.M. is very easy and gracious in his manner and not in the least formidable.

(The lake in the Palace garden is still dried up – having been drained during the War to avoid observation by German aeroplanes.)

19 July

Peace Celebration Day.

We have four tickets to view the great procession from the Members of Parliament stand on the south side of the Mall. The party consists of Em, Dora, Daff and myself. It is a fine position and we see everything perfectly. A splendid reception for Pershing,[20] the American General, and positively rapturous ones for Foch, Haig, Beatty[21] – and the tanks (four growling pachyderms under surprisingly easy and skilful management). Foch is a grand little figure with his baton and his set determined features and heavy moustache. The French soldiers and

---

[19] Victoria Alexandra Alice Mary (1897–1965): the third child and only daughter of George V and Queen Mary; cr. Princess Royal 1932.
[20] John Joseph Pershing (1860–1948): US Army officer; led the American Expeditionary Forces during the First World War.
[21] David Beatty (1871–1936): naval officer; Commander-in-Chief of the Grand Fleet 1916–19; First Sea Lord 1919–27; knighted 1914; cr. Earl Beatty 1919.

sailors and our own get the biggest and most spontaneous cheers – those for the Italians and Greeks being, as is only meet, much less general.

I am most affected by the contingents from the British fighting regiments – by the plain unconquerable men from Norfolk and Kent, Devon and Bedfordshire. [. . .]

About 2.30 when I have been in bed some time Em comes to tell me they are telephoning from Luton to say that the Peace celebrations there have ended in a serious outbreak, that the police are overpowered and the Town Hall in flames! I slip down in my dressing gown and hear the tragic story in the weary tones of Mr. Smith,[22] the Town Clerk. It is a somewhat confused narrative. Of the denouement, however, there is no doubt and I am entreated to use my influence with Scotland Yard to get some hundreds of policemen sent down to Luton or with the War Office for soldiers. Scotland Yard say they can't send men down without the expressed sanction of the Secretary of State. The W.O. say that they will put the matter in the hands of the Director of Personal Services. And so after much fatiguing telephoning – with an assurance to the Town Clerk – to bed again.

20 July

At 7 a.m. on the telephone again to Luton to find that some hundreds of soldiers are immediately expected. The Town Hall is in ruins, some few shops have been looted but the situation generally is in hand.

I run to Luton in the car and see the Chief Constable and Mr. Thomas Keens.[23] They pour out their troubles to me. 700 or 800 soldiers are in the town.

It is decided that my visit to Luton had best not be made known: it might be thought that I had come to take part in the proceedings and undesirable crowds might assemble.

Cause of the riot obscure. It began apparently in fairly good humour and fast degenerated into Bolshevism.

To town more dead than alive.

---

[22] Unidentified.
[23] Thomas Keens (1870–1953): accountant; Luton Alderman; Lib. MP for Aylesbury 1923–1924.

19 August

House rises for the Summer holiday.
Harold (Rothermere) lunches with Lloyd-George at the H. of Commons. I join them for coffee and cigars. Harold urges Ll.-G. to break with the reactionary members of the Coalition and much amuses him by offering him 2,000 guineas for an article in the *Sunday Pictorial*. Ll.-G. in a reckless mood today. He talks 'going for' Northcliffe again – N. having been going for him vigorously in his Press of late.
The P.M. is just now much taken with the possibilities of waterpower as a substitute for the coal that the miners seem less and less inclined to deliver. My view is that he and Harold exaggerate the resources of the U.K. in this direction.

5 September

Mr. Hoover, the U.S. Food Controller, passes through London on his way back to America – and to his home in California – after his labours in relieving the distress of Europe. At shortest notice I entertain him at dinner at the Carlton Hotel and with him Rt. Hon. J.H. Thomas, the railwaymen's leader, Lord Crawford,[24] McCurdy, M.P.,[25] Parly. Secy. to the Ministry of Food, Sir John Tilley,[26] and Sir Wm. Goode.[27] It is the best I can do on the spur of the moment and we have a very interesting evening together. Hoover, who lacks altogether the volubility of the average American, thaws completely and tells us many interesting things about conditions in Poland and other places in central Europe he has recently visited.
[Late in the Season as it was Hoover was strangely neglected by the Court and the Govt. and I was given to understand that he resented this neglect. If he had been Crown Prince of Montenegro he

---

[24]Lindsay, David Alexander Edward, (1871–1940): Con. MP for Chorley 1895–1913; President of the Board of Agriculture 1916; Lord Privy Seal 1916–1919; Chancellor of the Duchy of Lancaster 1919–1921; First Commissioner of Works in 1921–1922 (and additionally Minister of Transport in 1922); succ. as 27th Earl of Crawford and 10th Earl of Balcarres 1913.

[25]Charles Albert McCurdy (1870–1941): Lib. (then Coalition/Nat Lib) MP for Northampton 1906–1923; Parliamentary Secretary to the Ministry of Food Control 1919–1920; Minister of Food Control 1920–1921; Parliamentary Secretary to the Treasury (Chief Whip): 1921–1922.

[26]John Anthony Cecil Tilley (1869–1952): civil servant; ambassador to Japan 1926–1931; knighted 1919.

[27]William Athelstane Meredith Goode (1877–1944): journalist and civil servant; British Director of Relief in Europe 1919–1920; knighted 1918.

would have been made much of. My little dinner-party was the only recognition he received and I had this grateful note from him: –
> Ritz Hotel
> Sept. 6.
> Dear Mr. Harmsworth
> Just a line to thank you again for a delightful and profitable dinner. Please call on me if I can be of any help on our side.
> Yours faithfully,
> HERBERT HOOVER

(C.H. July 1936)]

18 September

To town, alas, to make ready for my visit with the Supreme Economic Council to Brussels.

**20 September
Brussels.**

At 10 o'clock we meet at the Palace des Academies. M. Jaspar,[28] Belgian Minister is in the Chair. The principal French delegates are M. Clementel (Minister of Commerce) and M. Loucheur[29] (M. of Reconstitution). The Italians are unknown to me and the Americans are absent.

The chief questions discussed are (1) the German demands for food and raw materials (2) the differential rates for coal charged by us to our own people and to our Allies respectively. J. Loucheur raises the latter question in a speech of much moderation but with obviously serious intent. (1) is referred back to the Consultative Food Committee and the Raw Materials Committee for reconsideration and (2) is to be brought to the notice of H.M.G. at home. [. . .]

There are no signs of the War at Brussels but rather of bustle and even of prosperity!

We end the day by dining at the Palace with the King. A brilliant affair.

---

[28] Henri Jaspar (1870–1939): Belgian lawyer and politician; Minister of Economic Affairs 1918–1920; Prime Minister 1926–1931.
[29] Louis Loucheur (1872–1931): French industrialist and politician; Minister of Industrial Reconstruction 1918–1920.

8 October

We entertain the Emir Feisal[30] at Montagu Square with Haddad Pasha,[31] his interpreter. [...] Feisal (of middle height with a close black beard and moustache and no darker in colour than an Italian) comes in his flowing Arab robes, white and gold, and corded headdress. He speaks only Arabic and a little broken French. Haddad Pasha is in a khaki uniform of some sort and likes to be described as His Excellency. I leave Feisal to cultivate Wickham Steed,[32] all-powerful editor of *The Times* and avoid (easily) too much conversation with him. My position at the F.O. renders it very undesirable for me to come into too close touch with the Emir. Indeed I tremble to think what would be thought and said at the Quai D'Orsay if it were known that I was entertaining Feisal at my private house.

11 November

Armistice Day. On this day last year the Armistice was signed. H.M. the King issued two or – three days ago an order enjoining on all, his faithful subjects the duty of celebrating the great event by abstaining from all work for two minutes at 11 o'clock – this morning. In London, maroons were fired and I, walking to the Foreign Office, had nearly reached at that moment the Horse Guards Parade entrance to the office. As I stood with my hat off during the two minutes I saw that every man woman and child within sight had come to a standstill and so with vehicles of all kinds. An impressive and affecting sight.

19 November
Meeting of the Supreme Economic Council in ROME.

Accompanied by Mr. Howe[33] of the F.O. (attached to me for this trip on account of his knowledge of Italian) I leave Charing X at 8 o'clock this morning for Paris and Rome.

---

[30] Faisal bin Hussein bin Ali al-Hashimi (1885–1933): a key figure in the wartime Arab Revolt against Ottoman rule; reigned as Feisal I of Iraq from 1921.

[31] Gabriel Haddad Pasha (d. 1923): a Syrian who served in the British administration in Cairo and Jerusalem during the First World War and who later became Faisal's representative in London.

[32] Henry Wickham Steed (1871–1956): editor of *The Times* 1919–1922.

[33] Possibly Robert George Howe (d. 1981 at age 87): diplomat; Governor-General of the Sudan 1947–1955; knighted 1947.

Paris about 6 o'clock. We have 3 hours to wait before our special train leaves the P.L.M. station. Howe and I make for the Hotel Majestic where we dine. The Majestic is no longer exclusively in British Govt. hands and is shorn of much of the glory of the early Peace Conference days: the lounge is no longer thronged with the statesmen of all Allied Countries and I miss the Colonial Premiers and turbaned Indian magnificoes. There are still a few 'peace girls' (young ladies engaged in the Secretariat work of the British Peace Delegation) and a handful of F.O. and other officials. The only Minister I see is Sir E. Pollock,[34] Solr. Genl., who is over here in connection with the arrangements for the trial of the Kaiser.

We telephone to Sir Eyre Crowe[35] at the Astoria and learn that the Bulgarian Treaty is certainly to be signed on the 27th.

21 November

At the station in Rome we have a fine reception. We are met at the entrance of what is, I suppose, the royal waiting-room by a group of Ministers and officers. [. . .]

Our first engagement is at the Prime Minister's official house, the Palazzo Braschi. Signor Nitti[36] is a stout little fellow with a big round head, a crop of short white hair and a humorous eye. He receives us in the Cabinet room – an apartment with red brocade on the walls, indifferent portraits of the King and Queen and cane-bottomed chairs round a table. Signor Nitti speaks no English but my old Brussels friend Senator Maggiorino Ferraris[37] helps me out with him. It is clear that the conversation with me is intended to make a certain impression: to persuade me, and through me, H.M. Govt. that if the Entente Powers and particularly H.M.G. will exercise their influence they can induce the Jugo-Slavs to recognize Italy's claim to Fiume and so rescue them from the awkward fix in which D'Annunzio's[38] raid has put them. The

---

[34] Ernest Murray Pollock (1861–1936): called to the Bar 1885; KC 1905; Con. candidate for Spalding 1900 and 1906; MP for Warwick and Leamington 1910–1923; Solicitor General 1919–1922; Attorney General 1922; Master of the Rolls 1923–1935; knighted 1917; cr. baronet 1922; cr. Baron Hanbury 1926.

[35] Eyre Alexander Barby Wichart Crowe (1864–1925): civil servant; Permanent Secretary to the Foreign Office 1920–1925; knighted 1911.

[36] Francesco Saverio Vincenzo de Paola Nitti (1868–1953): Prime Minister of Italy 1919–1920.

[37] Maggiorino Ferraris (1856–1929): Italian journalist and politician.

[38] Gabriele d'Annunzio (1863–1938): Italian writer and military adventurer; in 1919–1920 he headed a short-lived independent state in the Italian-majority city of Fiume (today known as Rijeka, in Croatia).

point is developed at some length, I listening with polite attention and making a mental note for Lord Curzon. Senator Ferraris who is with us a good deal during our visit returns again and again to the question. The afternoon is spent in conference at the Academia dei Lincei, a fine palace with an indifferent collection of pictures and some Roman busts. Our deliberations are prolonged and at the end of this our first session in Rome there is not much more than enough time to get back to the Hotel to dress for the banquet to be given to the Council at the Chigi Palace by Signor D. Ferraris.[39]

22 November

Early this morning to the A. dei Lincei to resume our deliberations. These inter-Allied gatherings are useful and even necessary but their proceedings are infinitely tedious. French is the language generally spoken but every speech must be interpreted and the ear is at a stretch all the time to understand what is being said amidst the murmurs of a numerous assembly and the rustling of papers. Every now and then the secretarial staff shower down on us typewritten slips with new points for discussion or revised forms of resolutions. Our interpreter is very good but his voice is weak and it is only those French speakers who enunciate clearly that I am able to follow with any comfort. So the hours go by and we are not to be blamed if sometimes we gaze wistfully out of the windows of the Conference room towards the Borghese Palace bathed in glorious sunshine.

26 November

It is a wet smeary day and Paris looks anything but her best when we arrive there about 2.30 o'clock.

27 November

Up early and dressed in my best for the signing of the Treaty of Neuilly – I having been appointed a plenipotentiary for the purpose. Now am I rewarded for lugging my tall hat all across Europe. I find that the High Commissioners are all similarly equipped. At 10 precisely we set

---

[39] Dante Ferraris (1868–1931), industrialist and politician.

off from the Majestic in Peace Conference cars – Sir G. Perley,[40] Howe and I together.

At the Hotel de Ville at Neuilly there is a crowd and a guard of honour of poilus in their grey blue uniforms and blue war helmets. There is upstairs a large salon with brightly-coloured frescoes on the walls and great crystal chandeliers. Here is set a horseshoe table with a named place for each plenipotentiary, a blotting-pad, inkpot, paper-knife and a brand new pen. On a smaller table between the ends of the horseshoe are the Treaty with red seals and ribbons and the Protocols. M. Clemenceau presides in grey suede gloves and has Mr. Polk[41] the principal American delegate on his right and me on his left with Sir E. Crowe next me and then the High Commissioners in order of precedence. We sign in alphabetical order of States – America first, Great Britain next and so on.

I have an opportunity of a little talk with the 'Tiger' as Clemenceau is affectionately called. He is easily recognised by the many photographs and caricatures of him that one has seen. His round head with its fringe of white hair, his great white moustache and plain humorous features must be known all over the world. His manner is astonishingly vigorous for his years (78, I think) and he is full of lively talk in excellent idiomatic English. I asked him what they would do with the original Treaty documents. 'Burn them I should think' he replies with a laugh. 'Probably the best thing they could do with them – seeing that so many of the signatories are breaking them already.' In answer to a further enquiry why the several treaties are being signed in different places – Versailles, St. Germain-en-Laye, Neuilly – he says it is in order they may be conveniently known in history by different names: The Treaty of Versailles, the Treaty of Neuilly etc. He refers with some admiration to M. Stambulinski,[42] the burly Bulgarian plenipotentiary. He says that Stambulinski was always strongly pro-Ally, that he was kept in prison for 3 years by Ferdinand and that he took the precaution before leaving Bulgaria for Paris of shutting up his opponents who might otherwise have been troublesome during his absence.

M. Clemenceau's method of conducting the proceedings is almost too businesslike. When all the delegates are seated in their places, 'Messieurs,' he says with a rap on the table of his paper-knife, 'La séance est ouverte.' When all have signed he shouts 'Messieurs, la

---

[40] George Halsey Perley (1857–1938): Canadian politician; High Commissioner in London 1917–1822; knighted 1915.
[41] Frank Lyon Polk (1871–1943): lawyer and State Department official.
[42] Aleksandar Stamboliyski (1879–1923): Prime Minister of Bulgaria 1919–1923, then ousted in a coup and killed.

séance est terminée' and when the general body of spectators has filed out we go out too. I ask him if I may keep my paper-knife as a souvenir and he readily assents explaining that it is not ivory but a composition and perishes if it is wetted. During the session he is a good deal teased by people bringing up their agenda papers for him to autograph.

There is a great cheer front the crowd outside when the Tiger emerges from the Hotel de Ville. [...]

Conversation this evening with General Mance[43] and Haddad Pasha, Feisal's interpreter and confidant. Feisal is still in Paris. Haddad says he has patched up a fairly satisfactory arrangement with the French.

1 December

The Viscountess Astor, M.P.,[44] introduced in the H. of C. by the P.M. and Mr. Balfour. House packed and flushed with excitement and curiosity. The new Member in her neat dark frock and toque (is it?) carries it off very well but her sponsors, as somebody says, are as nervous as boys at their first dance. One controversy is settled right off – 'Our Nancy' bows and does not curtsey to the Chair.

2 December

Esmond comes in today. His introducers are Macquisten[45] and Colonel Wheler.[46] I am not clear why neither Leicester nor I have been asked to accompany him. He makes the best of impressions with his great height, good looks and splendid youth. He is the youngest M.P. by two or three years.

---

[43] Harry Osborne Mance (1875–1966): soldier and transport expert; transportation adviser to the British delegation at the Paris peace conference 1919; knighted 1929.

[44] Nancy Witcher Astor, née Langhorne (1879–1964): m. Robert Gould Shaw (1871–1930), 1897 and divorced 1901; m. Waldorf Astor 1906. When he succeeded to his father's viscountcy in 1919; she succeeded him as Con. MP for Plymouth Sutton in 1919 and served until 1945.

[45] Frederick Alexander Macquisten (1870–1940): solicitor; called to the Bar 1919; Scottish KC 1919; English KC 1932; Unionist candidate for Leith Burghs Dec. 1910, Leith Burghs 1912; MP Glasgow Springburn 1918–1922, Argyllshire 1924–1940.

[46] Granville Charles Hastings Wheler (1872–1927): called to the Bar 1898; Unionist candidate Osgoldcross 1906, Colne Valley 1907; MP for Faversham 1910–1927; cr. baronet 1925.

9 December

With Lewis Haslam,[47] the 'worthy member', to Newport to speak at a mass meeting in support of the Coalition Govt. A large gathering in the Central Hall including a number of extreme Labourists who, skilfully disposed at strategic points in the galleries and on the floor of the building, proceed to exhibit their devotion to free institutions by denying to Haslam and myself the right to make ourselves heard. Such a babel of voices I have never heard at a public meeting: voices, some of them, as powerful as those of the big Bobbies who shout for members' motors in Palace Yard. It is only in the rarest intervals that we are able to get in an audible word edgewise. I keep going for about ¾ of an hour. One remark of mine – overheard above the storm – that my opponents seemed to possess greater lung power than reasoning power arouses intense indignation. A lady in the gallery asks me to withdraw in the interests of peace and I immediately comply but the hurricane rages to the end.

The meeting concludes with the singing of the 'Red Flag' by the dissentients.

10 December

To town and direct to the F.O. to look over my Questions for the day.

Housing Bill in Committee and after that the Report stage of Miscellaneous F.O. Votes.

But unhappily the Housing Bill takes up the whole day and all the night I must be on hand to speak on our Vote if any point is raised. Supper – eggs and bacon and Guinness in a tankard at about 3 a.m. – Six o'clock the Housing Bill ends and the F.O. Vote, with others, goes through without challenge in the twinkling of an eye. All my devotion for nothing!

11 December

To the F.O. a good deal jaded. Afterwards the H. of C. where Auckland Geddes[48] introduces the Coal Bill. Labour people say they don't want

---

[47] Lewis Haslam (1856–1922): businessman and politician; Lib. MP Monmouth 1906–1918; Co. Lib. MP Newport (Monmouth) 1918–1922.
[48] Auckland Campbell Geddes (1879–1954): businessman and politician; Unionist MP for Basingstoke 1917–1920; Minister of National Service 1917–1918; President of the Local

it and, as it is obvious that nobody else does, B. Law moves the adjournment of the debate.

26 December

Busy most of the day at the F.O. in connection with the question of our prisoners in Soviet Russia. A long Conference with Mr. O'Grady[49] just home for a few days from Copenhagen.

[This was one of my most anxious and difficult jobs at the F.O. After the Counter-revolutionary movement in Russia, in which we assisted the White Armies with men, munitions and stores, there was a number of British officers and men in the hands of the Bolshevist Govt., with a larger number of British civilians of both sexes. The question was how to get them out of Russia. The stories of Bolshevist atrocities had filled the public and the Rouse with alarm and there was no knowing what might happen to these People at any time. Incidentally, we were on the worst of diplomatic terms with the Soviet Govt.

Negociations were begun and after prolonged talk on both sides the Soviet Govt. agreed to a meeting at Copenhagen. They appointed M. Litvinoff as their representative and we chose Mr. James O'Grady, Labour M.P. for S.E. Leeds – a Labour man rather than a trained diplomat as being likely to have more of 'a way with him' in the peculiar circumstances than a Foreign Office young gentleman with the prejudices of Eton and Oxford.

The discussions at Copenhagen went on for months. At some moments we seemed to be on the very point of success, at others the prospect clouded over, and once at least negociations were suspended. In the end O'Grady pulled it off. A thousand or so British subjects returned happily to these shores – some of them, strangely enough, unable to speak their native English, many of them without money or friends. They cost us a pretty penny before eventually they were absorbed in our population.

What made our job at the F.O. all the more difficult was the intense dislike of the S. of S. to the whole transaction. Lord Curzon could not bring himself to have anything to do with the Bolshies. He left the whole of this business in my hands and those of the

---

Government Board 1918–1919; President of the Board of Trade 1919–1920; Ambassador to the USA 1920–1923; knighted 1917; cr. Baron Geddes 1942.

[49] James O'Grady (1866–1934): trades unionist and politician; Lab. MP Leeds East 1906–1918, Leeds South-East 1918–1924; Governor of Tasmania 1924–1930; Governor of the Falkland Islands 1931–1933; knighted 1924.

permanent officials, and when O'Grady had completed his job would not hear of his being recommended for an Honour of any kind.

O'Grady was subsequently Governor of Tasmania and, as I have heard, the most popular they ever had there.

C.H. 29.1.1934.]

1920

Harmsworth had an operation on 17 January and spent several weeks recuperating.

5 March

To see Harold (Rothermere) at Savoy Court. He tells me that Lloyd-George is gravely uneasy about the way the bye-elections are going and is angling for his support in the Press. Broad hints have been thrown out by a trusted emissary of Ll.-G.'s that Harold can have the Colonial Secretaryship if he likes. He is to see Ll.-G. on Monday.

Afterwards to the F.O. where my unwelcome task is to inform O'Grady that he is not to return to Copenhagen to resume negociations with Litvinoff. Lord Curzon is persuaded that Litvinoff has enmeshed O'Grady and that there is serious danger in a continuance of their relations. O'Grady accepts the decision loyally and more cheerfully than I expected.

25 March

Lunch in honour of Auckland Geddes at 10 Downing Street. Ll.-G. in high spirits. He confirms the truth of a story about himself and Charles Masterman that I have heard before. Charles M. is a high Church Liberal of a somewhat oleaginous type. In the midst of one of Ll.-G.'s tearing and raging Radical campaigns the two met in one of the Lobbies of the House:

'Hallo, demagogue!' says Masterman.
'Hallo, acolyte!' retorts Ll.-G. He tells the story with great delight today.

3rd Reading Consolidated Fund Bill today. Full dress debate on Foreign Affairs led off by Mr. Asquith followed by Clynes[1] and Ll.-G. I wind up on the debate about 9 o'clock.

31 March

Second Reading of Home Rule Bill. Fine dramatic speech by Carson in which he promises that Ulster will do her best to make her Parliament a success.

13 April

Harmsworth was staying with his children at the Haven Hotel, Sandbanks, Poole.

A message from the F.O. saying that Bonar Law (who is acting as Prime Minister in Ll.-G.'s absence at San Remo for, let us hope, the concluding stages of the Turkish etc. Peace Treaties) expects me to introduce the Austrian and Bulgarian Peace Treaties Bill in the H. of C. tomorrow. As my practice is, when important business relating to foreign affairs is before the House, I have made already considerable preparations and have a pretty full brief with me but I have to spend a good part of the day getting my notes into shape.

14 April

By early train and then straight to the F.O.
In the H. of C. immediately after Questions I move the Second Reading of the Treaties Bill. Mr. Asquith follows and is complimentary.

30 April

Em and I to the Opening of the Royal Academy – the function of the year that above all others we like going to together.

---

[1] John Robert Clynes (1869–1949): trades unionist and politician; Lab. MP Manchester North-East 1906–1918; Manchester Platting 1918–1931, 1935–1945; Chairman of the Parliamentary Labour Party 1921–1922.

It is what you might call an Orpen[2] year, with his fine portraits and Peace Conference pictures. In the latter are life-like portraits of Clemenceau with his famous grey gloves and in one of them a beautiful caricature of Lloyd-George with a great mane of grey hair: Balfour and Bonar Law not so convincing. The scenes depicted are precisely like the one I witnessed at Neuilly.

5 May

Alfred (Northcliffe) comes for me this morning and we drive out to Totteridge. He is better in health than I have seen him for many a day and is full of interesting chat about his recent travels in Spain and Morocco.

11 May

This evening a Coalition Liberal meeting in the Lower Central Hall, Westminster. Rousing speeches by Gordon Hewart,[3] Macnamara, Addison, McCurdy and Kellaway.

31 May

Momentous meeting in the Cabinet room at 10 Downing Street: P.M., Bonar Law, Curzon, Sir Robt. Horne,[4] C.B.H., E.F. Wise,[5] and Krassin[6] and Klishko,[7] two of the Bolshevist emissaries who are to treat

---

[2] William Newenham Montague Orpen (1878–1931): artist; knighted 1918; later painted CBH's portrait.
[3] Gordon Hewart (1870–1943): called to the Bar 1902; KC 1912; Lib. (then Coalition Lib) MP for Leicester (East Leicester from 1918) 1913–1922; Solicitor General 1916–1919; Attorney General 1919–1922; Lord Chief Justice 1922–1940; knighted 1916; cr. Baron Hewart 1922.
[4] Robert Stevenson Horne (1871–1940): called to the Scottish Bar 1896; KC 1910; wartime civil servant; Con. candidate for Stirlingshire in both general elections of 1910; MP for Hillhead 1918–1937; Minister of Labour 1919–1920; President of the Board of Trade 1920–1921; Chancellor of the Exchequer 1921–1922; knighted 1918; cr. Viscount Horne 1937.
[5] Edward Frank Wise (1885–1933): civil servant and left-wing intellectual; Lab. candidate for Bradford North 1924; MP for Leicester East 1929–1931.
[6] Leonid Borisovich Krasin (1870–1926): Soviet politician; People's Commissar for Foreign Trade 1920–1924.
[7] Nicolas Klishko (1880–c.1937): secretary to the Russian trade delegation to Britain in 1920.

for the resumption of trade and perhaps for a settlement of all our quarrels with Russia. Krassin states his case clearly in Russian and is interpreted on his own behalf by Klishko and for us by Mr. Peters.

3 June

Conference – virtually a Cabinet Meeting – in Bonar Law's room behind the Speaker's Chair on Krassin. P.M. presides.

16 June

This week I see a good deal of Dr. Nansen[8] who has been charged by the League of Nations with the difficult task of getting Austrian and Hungarian prisoners out of Russia and Russian prisoners out of Germany: one of the big and anxious after-the-war jobs. Shipping is wanted of course and when people need shipping they come to H.M.G. Nansen wants me to use influence with the Ministry of Shipping.

The L. of Nations, if they had ransacked Europe, couldn't have found as good an agent as Nansen. He is still a 'super-man' despite his thin grey hair, and is as wise as he is brave and modest. I notice particularly his fine blue eyes. He has a nearly complete knowledge of English but speaks with a strong foreign accent.

12 August

The House adjourns until Monday. The situation is this:

For a long time past we (that is H.M.G.) have been trying to come to some sort of terms with Bolshevik Russia. Mr. Krassin has been for many weeks in London conferring with the Supreme Economic Council with a view to the resumption of trade relations and latterly he has been joined by Mr. Kameneff[9] who has pretty full powers to treat for peace. These proceedings have been looked at askance by

---

[8] Fridtjof Nansen (1861–1930): Norwegian explorer, scientist and diplomat; League of Nations High Commissioner for Refugees 1921–1930; winner of the Nobel Peace Prize 1922.

[9] Lev Borisovich Kamenev (1883–1936): leading Soviet politician; executed following a show trial.

the French who are not willing to have anything whatever to do with the Bolsheviks.

Meanwhile, the rash forward movement of the Poles against the Bolsheviks has resulted in disaster and the Red Armies are at this moment advancing on Warsaw. It was agreed at the Anglo-French Conference at Lympne to advise the Poles to make peace with the Bolsheviks on honourable terms but a difference has arisen between us and the French as to what these terms should be. The French have now taken the bit between their teeth and suddenly recognized Genl. Wrangel[10] leader of the last remaining Russian counter-revolutionary force and to accredit *[sic]* a High Commissioner.

The situation is, to say the least, highly strained and it is considered prudent that Parliament should meet again on Monday in the hope that by then we shall have had reassuring news from Minsk where Poles and Russians are meeting to discuss terms.

16 August

House rises soon after dinner. Nothing much new is reported of the Polish situation and the adjournment is agreed to subject to a rider that it may be summoned by Mr. Speaker in consultation with the Govt if necessary.

7 September

Extract from the Morning Post, 7 September, included in diary:

While every effort is being made by the Government to secure a just settlement of the crisis which has arisen in consequence of the miners' demands, steps are being taken to ascertain what will be the position in the country in the event of the threatened strike taking place.

We are informed in this connection that a number of the Civil Commissioners have this week commenced a tour of inspection of various areas for the purpose of reporting to the Government on the situation which would then arise, and as to the measures to be taken to reduce the inevitable loss and suffering to the general community [...] Mr. Cecil Harmsworth, M.P., Parliamentary Under-Secretary for Foreign Affairs, is in the Eastern Counties.

---

[10] Baron Pyotr Nikolayevich Wrangel (1878–1928): commander of the anti-Bolshevik forces in Southern Russia during the latter stages of the civil war.

[The Government's Anti-Strike Organization.

The statement in the *Morning Post* [...] gives a very colourless impression of a remarkable organization. It was in fact a fully matured plan for safeguarding public interests – in the case of a serious Strike affecting the welfare of the general community, and I have no doubt that it is still in being. It had regard to Strikes relating to essential services – food supplies, transport, fuel, communications and the like.

We Commissioners were not sent down in times of emergency to our several districts to make enquiries only and to report. We went there to take charge of the organization in our districts, to travel about and satisfy ourselves that the system was in working order, and to assume, if need be, far-reaching powers and responsibilities. It was for this reason that junior members of the Govt., responsible to the Govt., were told off to act as Commissioners.

My own district comprised the Counties of Cambridge, Bedford, Huntingdon, Suffolk and Norfolk, with Cambridge as headquarters. I acted twice as Commissioner, both Strikes ending however before I was called upon to exercise any of the plenary functions assigned to me. My Diaries give no account of my more serious activities on these occasions, I being afraid of their falling into the wrong hands.

When Howard-Smith[11] and I arrived at the Bull, Cambridge, on the 7th Septr. there was a message for me asking me to call without delay at a suburban address where I found Brig.-General? *[sic]* sitting in the midst of a veritable spider's web of organization. The walls of his official rooms were covered with great maps of his (and my) district, showing where supplies of food, fuel and other necessaries existed and the services – water-works, gas and electric works, sewage fans, hospitals – that were to have the first call on the available supplies of coal and in the case of hospitals of coal and flour. The Brigadier (who had distinguished himself in the A.S.C. during the War) had files and reports of all kinds relating to the 5 Counties.

It was possible to gather from his maps and records, almost at a glance, what our resources would be in the event of the Strike dislocating the railway services. We had, too, details of the available motor transport in the different areas and I had power to commandeer every motor vehicle in the 5 Counties.

When I travelled round my province my time was very little occupied with sight-seeing (as might be inferred from my Diary) but in Conference with Mayors of Boroughs, Chairmen of Councils and local govt. officials of all kinds. One day I invaded the town hall of Luton, to

---

[11] Charles Howard-Smith (1888–1942): civil servant; private secretary to CBH 1920–1922; British Minister in Denmark 1939–1940; British Minister in Iceland 1940–1942.

find the Mayor and excellent Mr. Smith, the Town Clerk, cheerfully prepared, as far as Luton was concerned, for any emergency.

I was a little disappointed when the two Strikes that threatened during my reign as Commissioner ended in smoke. I have never had any other chance of playing the autocrat!

The worst of it was that I could only enjoy these country jaunts 'with a trembling'. My F.O. red boxes were piling up against me all the time.

C.H. 28th Jany, 1934.]

Harmsworth returned to London on 15 September.

22 October

The strike situation serious today. C. Howard-Smith [My F.O. Secy.] and I by road to Cambridge where we are to 'stand by' pending developments.

24 October

A telegram from town saying that we may return.

28 October

Announcement by Sir Robert Horne in the House today that the Strike has been settled subject to a further ballot of the miners.

I have a talk with Ll.-G. in his room behind the Speaker's Chair. I find him with Lady Astor and his pretty daughter Megan – the apple of his eye. He stretches himself luxuriously in a deep armchair after the almost endless fatigues of the Strike negotiations and puffs away at a big cigar. His hair hasn't been cut for weeks and his face is a little pallid but his wonderful eyes are as keen and bright as ever.

When he was expected back from the Spa Conference and I had to go off to the Eastern Counties (early in Septr.) in connection with the threatened Strike of the miners I left a letter for him in which I urged strongly that Terence McSwiney,[12] the Lord Mayor of Cork,

---

[12] Terence James MacSwiney (1879–1920): Sinn Féin MP Mid-Cork 1918–1920 but did not take his seat; Lord Mayor of Cork and commandant of the Cork brigade of the

should not be allowed to starve himself to death in Brixton Gaol. I said I felt it my duty as one of his Ministers to let him know that I dissented altogether from the Govt. policy in this case. McSwiney had not been convicted of murder or of incitement to murder and was in fact a political prisoner: I feared the worst results in Ireland if he was permitted to die. Why make the Irish the gift of another 'martyr'? Why not release McSwiney under the so-called 'Cat & Mouse' Act?[13] Well, McSwiney had died and on this very day his body was being taken in procession from Brixton to Euston on its way to Cork. I thought that as a dissentient from an important point of his policy I ought to see the P.M. and place myself unreservedly in his hands.

Ll.-G. listened to my story with sympathy and treated me with every kindness. He had read my letter but had not replied to it because, as I knew, he was a bad hand at writing letters. He had welcomed my representations [and] was always glad to receive the opinions of his Ministers on points of policy. How otherwise was he to know what was in their minds? I had acted quite correctly and he hoped I would always treat him with the same confidence.

I thanked him warmly and withdrew. I had looked forward to the interview with some discomfort and left him in a more cheerful frame of mind than when I broke in on him and drove Lady Astor and Megan from his room.

26 November

The memorial service in Westminster Abbey to six of the officers murdered in Dublin on Sunday last by the Sinn Feiners. The coffins are carried into the Choir one after the other by soldiers or policemen of the various services to which they belonged – the troops marching with slow heavy step and with their reversed arms held behind their backs. It is the most affecting and terrible public ceremony I have ever witnessed.

IRA1920; imprisoned for sedition August 1920 and died as a result of his hunger strike on 25 October.

[13] i.e. the Prisoners (Temporary Discharge for Ill Health) Act 1913, which had been used to free suffragettes who were on hunger strike until such time as they recovered physically.

29 November

The rumours that the Sinn Feiners are transferring their attentions to England and have criminal designs on the Houses of Parliament result in the closing of both Houses to visitors. We have policemen in uniform and plain clothes everywhere and visitors can get no nearer to us than St. Stephen's Hall.

Again, all the approaches to Downing Street are barricaded.

News in the papers this morning that the Sinn Feiners have set fire to 15 warehouses in Liverpool.

Strange that these things should be going on at a time when the Lords are discussing the most generous measure of Home Rule ever presented to Parliament!

1921

28 January

A long talk with Harold (Rothermere) today. He has been seeing a good deal of Ll.-George lately and has been offered and has refused the post of First Lord of the Admiralty from which Walter Long is retiring.

15 February

Opening of Parliament by the King.
I hear the King read his Speech in the House of Lords. He wears his crown and purple robes lined with ermine: the Queen a splendid tiara and flaming jewels on her breast. The P. of Wales is almost lost in his robes as he takes his place in his little chair to the right of H.M.

25 February

On First Commissioner's Supplementary estimate today we can do no better than 88 to 78. Some of our supporters would certainly have voted against us if they had not suspected that the Govt. was in difficulties. The portents are ominous at this so early stage in a new Session. But where is the Govt.'s large majority?

17 March

First dinner of the 1920 Club. [...]
A sparkling speech by Ll.-G.
Today, announcement is made by Ll.-G. in the House that Bonar Law is seriously ill and has been ordered by the doctors to rest for some months. The news is wholly unexpected and fills the House with genuine regrets. We have all come, Liberals as much as Tories, to feel

a warm liking for the unassuming Chief who has led the House for so long.

18 March

To Luton this evening to speak, with Lord Hugh Cecil, at a League of Nations Union meeting.

21 March

Austen Chamberlain elected by the Tories leader in the H. of Commons of their Wing of the Coalition.

In early April Harmsworth took a fishing holiday at the Three Cocks Hotel, in the Wye Valley.

4 April

It is in Butler's Catch and about 5.30 in the evening that I hook a great fish. When he leaps at the end of my line I think of a thirty pounder at least and his dogged struggle of 25 minutes suggests unusual size and weight. I bring him alongside at last [. . .] The fish weighs in fact 18 pounds.

5 April

The Coal Strike is on and there is likelihood of the railwaymen and transport workers coming out in sympathy. I must cut my little holiday short.
 [Later: –
 I blush even now when I remember that I took French leave from the F.O. and the House, when I went to fish the Wye at Three Cocks. By an inadvertence which I cannot explain I made no arrangement for the answers to my F.O. Questions and other F.O. business in the House. Some important Questions were in fact asked and there was surprise and some little impatience when they were answered by junior Ministers with, necessarily, no more information than that contained in the written answers. 'Where is the Under-Secy?' was the cry.

Exculpating myself afterwards to my Chief, Curzon of Kedleston, he was delighted with my story of the jolly 18 pounder. But there was a hint in his eye that this sort of thing ought not to occur again. And it didn't.
C.H. (July 1936)]

20 April

I introduce the Hungary Peace Treaty Bill in the H. of Commons.

27 April

Mr. Whitley elected Speaker nem. con., the proposed Opposition candidature of Sir Frederick Banbury having been withdrawn.

What an unnerving place the H. of Commons is. Here is Whitley, who has been Chairman of Ways & Means for 10 years, going white as a sheet when he is conducted to the Chair which he has so often occupied in a deputy capacity, by Mildmay[1] and Arthur Henderson. In its moments of ceremony the House is very grand indeed.

1 May

Today the *Daily Mail* celebrates its 25th birthday by a Luncheon party at Olympia. It is an immense gathering, some 7,000 invitations having been issued to members of the staff of all grades, and their womenfolk, the whole affair being superbly organized by J. Lyons & Co.

Alfred shakes hands with the guests who pass by him in an almost endless queue. Dear Mother and Mary Northcliffe come in just before lunch begins at 1 o'clock and are received with great cheering and the waving of little flags. The 'Stentorphone' arrangements made to enable Alfred to address the multitude are not very successful and even the City toast-master with his huge voice and a megaphone is not, I think, very widely heard.

As soon as lunch begins the people pull the Christmas crackers they find in their places and many of them don the gaily-coloured paper caps and so add to the brightness of a wonderful scene. The lunch

---

[1] Francis Bingham Mildmay (1861–1947): Lib. (then Unionist) MP for Totnes 1885–1922; cr. Baron Mildmay 1922.

itself is cold and is as good in quality and as well-served as in a first-rate restaurant.

And this concourse represented only a part of the huge body of workers that Alfred's genius has brought into co-operation! Afterwards Daff, Bud and I to Poynters where we find dear Mother none the worse for her fatiguing and affecting ordeal.

26 May

Breakfast at Lord Derby's in Stratford Place 'to meet the P.M.' Ll.-G., who must have the constitution of an internal combustion engine, bright and gay and smoking a long cigar immediately after breakfast. The talk is about Silesia, the coal strike and the coming visit of the Dominion Prime Ministers. About 25 sturdy Coalitionists present. But defend me from such unseasonable entertainments.

[Later: It was Ll.-G. who started (? revived) these horrible political breakfasts. He has the digestion of an ostrich, sleeps always like a top and is as gay in the earliest hours as the gayest of us at lunch time. Two or three of them were quite enough for me. C.H. 27th Jany. 1934.]

This evening we give a dinner-party at the H. of C. [...]

The Hamar Greenwoods pretty cheerful in spite of the desperate news from Ireland this morning. The rebels have burned down the Custom House, the most beautiful building in Ireland. Lady Greenwood tells me of an exciting experience at Chequers. Some of the house-party including the P.M. were out walking in the grounds – the P.M. and another ahead of the others and the private detectives as usual in sight. When the P.M. came to a summer house he found Sinn Fein inscriptions in chalk in the walk – 'Up the rebels!' 'Up the I.R.A.!' and the like. Four men were seen making off in the grounds. They were subsequently caught and taken to Aylesbury Gaol. Three were released next day and one, who confessed to being Irish, was detained. So the matter stands at present.

24 June

Dinner this evening 'to welcome the Dominion Prime Ministers' in the Royal Gallery of the H. of Lords. The function is ruined by the prolixity of Mr. Meighen[2] (Canada) [Mr. Meighen's name is pronounced

---

[2] Arthur Meighen (1874–1960): Prime Minister of Canada 1920–1921, 1926.

Mee-han.] Mr. Hughes (Australia) and Mr. Massey (N.Z.)[3] 'F.E.', the Lord Chancellor, in the Chair but not equal to his best as an orator. Mr. Speaker, short and plain. Sir Thomas Smartt[4] speaks and speaks briefly and well for S.A. in place of General Smuts. The honours of the evening rest with the Hon. V.S. Srinivasa Sastri,[5] who, in a turban, represents the Indian, the youngest of Imperial parliaments. He is dignified, measured and witty and above everything on a tropical night and at a late hour, BRIEF.

14 July

The P.M. is engaged in his momentous talks with De Valera. It is curious to observe at the Whitehall end of Downing Street a crowd of Irish people with green, yellow and white Sinn Fein flags. So intolerant a people are we!

Dinner at the Hotel Cecil to McCurdy the Chief Liberal Whip of the Coalition. P.M. arrives very late after his Conference with De Valera and is enthusiastically received.

16 July

To town this morning to see Alfred off at Waterloo on his tour round the World. A large gathering from *The Times, Daily Mail* and the other newspapers – including some of the workpeople and their wives and children.

18 July

I attend meeting at the Colonial Office of a Committee of the Imperial Conference to consider the retention of British nationality by British people in foreign countries – the S. American states, Japan, etc., etc. Winston in the Chair and present also Hughes of Australia, Massey of N.Z., Sir T. Smartt of S.A., somebody from Canada, an Indian delegate, Shortt (Home Secy.) and others. We dispose of our particular business in about three and a half minutes. Hughes, who is exceedingly

---

[3]William Ferguson Massey (1856–1925): Prime Minister of New Zealand 1912–1925.
[4]Thomas William Smartt (1858–1929): South African politician.
[5]Valangiman Sankaranarayana Srinivasa Sastri (1869–1946): politician; represented India at the 1921 Imperial Conference in London.

deaf, carries about with him a small black box that you might mistake for a camera. He puts this on the table in front of him, opens the lid and adjusts a receiver to his ear. Seems then to hear pretty well but doesn't need to hear much for he talks himself most of the time in a hard metallic voice. Even Winston can't always get in a word.

19 August

The House adjourns at long last. It had been intended to prorogue but the state of the negotiations with De Valera is such that it has been thought best to keep the Session in being.

The most wearisome and thankless parliamentary year in my experience!

12 October

Opening of the Anglo-Swedish Chamber of Commerce, Trinity Square. At the subsequent luncheon I sit by the Crown Prince of Sweden[6] – a tall man of about 30 years of age, speaking perfect English and with a most modest, approachable manner.

He asks me about Northcliffe and his travels. Among other things he discusses with me is the future of Lithuania, Latvia and Esthonia. We agree that, historically speaking, they are little likely to continue to exist without the good favour of Russia.

To the annual Dinner of the Pembroke College Oxford Johnson Society at Dr. Johnson's House. A humorous speech by Dr. Inge,[7] Dean of St. Paul's, who is known in the London Press as 'the Gloomy Dean', as indeed he is the most dreary looking man of our time.

21 October

The Provost of T.C.D. dines with Bud and me at Montagu Square.

Bernard is more gloomy about the state of Ireland than I have ever known him. He tells me of the enforced money levies of the Sinn Feiners on helpless citizens – even (and I have heard it before) on notable loyalists. It is rumoured, he says, that conscription is being

---

[6] Oscar Fredrik Wilhelm Olaf Gustaf Adolf (1882–1973): reigned as Gustav VI Adolf from 1950.
[7] William Ralph Inge (1860–1954): Dean of St. Paul's 1911–1934; knighted 1930.

enforced and he is apprehensive lest it should be imposed also on the College boys.

1 November

Em and Daff return from Ireland this evening. They are full of amusing stories of their adventures in Dublin. The truce (established during the period of the negotiations between H.M.G. and the Sinn Feiners) is in force in Ireland and people breathe more freely there though they do not yet speak freely in public places.

2 November

Annual Dinner of the Printers Pension Corporation. Early this morning, Mr. Mortimer, the excellent Secretary, telephones to say that the Ld. Chancellor (Birkenhead) who was to have replied for 'His Majesty's Govt.' will be prevented by the Irish negotiations, in which he is taking a leading part. Will I oblige in his place? What else can I do?

An anxious day piecing together my notes for tonight's speech amidst many distractions. The humour of it is that I had originally consented to attend the Dinner on the express understanding that I was to say nothing and to enjoy myself listening to 'F.E.'

A boiling hot company of some 600 people at the Connaught Rooms. Who can make an after-dinner speech to such a multitude? And in a hall of such abominable acoustics?

11 November

Remembrance Day and this year Flanders 'Poppy Day' because of Lord Haig's emblem for the fund he is raising. At 11 o'clock the maroons sound and all the activities of life cease in London and generally throughout the country. At the end of our Square men stand with their hats off and such few vehicles as there are, are stationary.

I go down to Bedford to the unveiling (by S.H. Whitbread, Ld. Lt.) of the memorial to the Bedfordshire Regiment. It is a handsome small domed structure with an obelisk.

17 November

Maurice Burton takes Em and me in his beautiful touring Rolls-Royce all the way to Leicester to see, at Hamshaw's, a Vauxhall car we noticed at the recent Motor Show in London. The Vauxhall is an elegant Limousine (a closed car well-suited to town work) but there is little head room and a poorish look-out and I am disposed to turn it down. I must have a Vauxhall because (1) they are made in my Constituency (at Luton) and (2) there is much unemployment in the Vauxhall works.

23 November

Coalition Meeting at Barking. Captain Martin[8] the local Member in the Chair. Trouble is expected because of the present very severe unemployment and of the growth of a small but intolerant Communist party in the E. end of London.
However, all goes well.

14 December

Special Session of Parliament opens today to ratify the agreement with Sinn Fein Ireland. The King and Queen (and Princess Mary) in State.
By a curious oversight the King omits to end his speech with the customary invocation of Almighty God to bless our labours. Shortt, the Home Secy., tells me at lunch that the omission had passed wholly unnoted by himself and by all others responsible for H.M.'s Speech. Later, the Speaker in addressing the H. of C., repairs the omission.

15 December

Debate on Ireland in full swing in both Houses today.

---

[8] Albert Edward Martin (1876–1936): Coalition/Nat Lib. MP for Romford 1918–1923; joined the Conservative Party in 1923.

Em and I dine with the Swiss Minister and Madame Paravicini.[9] Also present Herr Sthamer,[10] the German Ambassador and his wife, an American lady – the first German we have met since the War. We look forward with apprehension to meeting them but they prove to be quite decent people.

Strange that M. Paravicini, a trained diplomatist, should have sent word to the F.O. today advising me that the Germans were to be present at his dinner-party so that I may have a chance of excusing myself if I so desire! But how could I, whatever my feelings might be?

Of course, Herr Sthamer has been several times to the F.O. to see Curzon. But I have not hitherto met him.

16 December

Ratification of the Irish Treaty carried in the H. of C. today by 401 to 58 and in the H. of L. by something like 3 to 1.

Great speech in the Lords by 'F.E.' (Ld. Chancellor) of which I am able to stay to hear only the opening sentences. Their Lordships muster in, for them, good strength. 'F.E.' follows Lord Salisbury, a political lightweight, and the only Salisbury who is totally devoid of grey matter. It is a strange reflection on the H. of L. as at present constituted that so silly a fellow should ever figure so importantly there.

19 December

Parliament prorogued. In Dublin the Dail Eireann is engaged in discussing the terms of the Treaty. [. . .]

Lord Curzon asks me to go to Geneva as Government representative on the Council of the L. of Nations at the meeting to be held in January. I gladly assent.

---

[9] Charles Rudolf Paravicini (1872–1947): Swiss Minister in London 1920–1939; m. Lilian de Watteville 1910.
[10] Gustav Friedrich Carl Johann Sthamer (1856–1931): German Ambassador to London 1920–1930.

1922

2 January

At the F.O. all the morning and afternoon going over the Agenda for the forthcoming Session of the League of Nations at Geneva. At 6 o'clock to 1 Carlton House Terrace to see Lord Curzon and to discuss with him any points of policy arising out of the Agenda. Lord C. is off to Cannes tomorrow to attend the Inter-Allied Conference that is to discuss the question of German reparations, trade with Russia, etc.

9 January
Geneva.

First we visit Sir Eric Drummond at the Palace of the League of Nations – formerly an hotel – seemingly well adapted to its present purpose. English type-writing girls everywhere. We talk over the Agenda and return to dejeuner at the Bellevue. [. . .]

Everybody and everything in Geneva looks prosperous. The Swiss are a wise folk who look on and make money in hatfuls while other people are fighting.

We are not to begin our L. of Nations work until tomorrow afternoon because M. Hanotaux,[1] the French delegate, has not yet arrived; The Marquis Imperiali,[2] the Italian delegate, whom we meet in a book-shop (one of several very good ones), hopes we shall get through our business quickly as he wants to be back soon in Rome.

10 January

After lunch to the Palace of the L. of Nations where we dispose very quickly of some smaller matters. Our president is M. Hymans, the Belgian representative, a delightfully vivacious personality.

---

[1] Albert Auguste Gabriel Hanotaux (1853–1944): politician and diplomat.
[2] Guglielmo Imperiali di Francavilla (1858–1944): politician and diplomat; Ambassador to London 1910–1920.

M. Hanotaux looks more like a Yorkshireman than a Frenchman and the Marquis Imperiali, formerly Italian ambassador in London, with an eyeglass, is as courtly and mannered as ever. Viscount Ishii, representing Japan, is small and grizzled and self-contained while Mr. Tang Tsai-Fou, the Chinese, is unobtrusive and of clerical aspect. Senor Quinones de Leon (Spain) is short and round and Mr. da Cunha (Brazil) is smart and fancies himself as a wit. M. Hanotaux understands very little English and I as little of the spoken French so that the admirably efficient interpreters are kept briskly going. Business except on really important occasions proceeds informally and there are private conferences at which agreement is sought, and so far successfully.

12 January

A very full day. The chief questions are those relating to Danzig (administered by the L. of Nations under Genl. Haking[3] as High Commissioner) and to the serious dispute between Poland and Lithuania.

After dinner, the Saar Valley people come to see me – 4 Germans not distinguishable from a similar deputation from Luton. They have many complaints to make about the way they are governed by the Commission of which M. Rault, a Frenchman, is president. In the end I tell them that my Constituents make more serious complaints against our own govt. When they explain to me that so bad is the govt. that the Post Office is carried on at a loss I point to the fact that the same thing is happening with us at home at this moment. They retire full of good humour and with expressions of gratitude etc.

13 January

Full day's work at the Palace of Nations. The translation of every important speech into English (or French) lengthens our proceedings tediously at times but M. Hymans[4] is an admirably brisk chairman and gets things done with only such delay as is unavoidable.

After dinner tonight the Polish representative attached to the L. of Nations comes along and gives us an account of the obstructive

---

[3] Sir Richard Cyril Byrne Haking (1862–1945): army officer, High Commissioner of the League of Nations in Danzig (1921–1923); CB 1910, KCB 1916, KCMG 1918, GBE 1921.

[4] Paul Louis Adrien Henri Hymans (1865–1941): Belgian politician; President of the League of Nations 1920–1921, 1932–1933.

methods of the Free State of Danzig which is, he says, Poland's only port.

14 January

Business begins at 9.30 this morning. [...]
The chief subjects are the provisions for Minorities made by Esthonia, Lithuania and Latvia and 'publicity' in connection with the meetings and proceedings of the League. The Session ends about teatime. Next meeting of the Council is to be on April 25th.
The principal delegates dine with the Drummonds at their villa. Lady D. tells me of the exceedingly high prices prevailing in Switzerland. When she first came here she paid 95 (gold) francs for a leg of mutton and £15 a ton for coal. Members of the Secretariat trip over the frontier into France to make purchases. They have there the advantage of the low exchange and enjoy diplomatic privileges, avoid Customs duties.

Harmsworth returned to London on 16 January.

20 January

Coalition Liberal reception at Devonshire House. A dreadful crush – everybody outside trying to get in and everybody inside trying to get out. Ll.-G. supposed to be somewhere receiving the company but we don't see him.
The last function, I suppose, that will take place in this grand old house. All the furniture has gone and little of its former splendour remains but the gilded ceilings.

21 January

Great Co-Lib. meeting at the Central Hall, Westminster. Ll.-G. in a long speech not quite at his best but still very good.

22 January

After tea I read to the family the latest installments of Northcliffe's Round the World Diary in which he deals with his adventures in Japan.

31 January

In the evening we all to a meeting at the Queen's Hall where Dr. Nansen lectures on the dreadful famine in Russia.

1 February

I call on Dr. Nansen at the Hyde Park Hotel and tell him quite plainly that I think he is striking a jarring note in his addresses on the Russian famine. He seemed last night to contrast the activities of the Soviet Govt. with ours and those of the other Allies – to our disadvantage. We were blamed indeed for the so-called Blockade (long since removed), for our assistance to the counter-revolutionaries and for the small measure of our actual contributions to the relief of the famine. The main causes of the famine were in my opinion (1) the drought, (2) the breakdown, due to Soviet interference, in all the machinery of marketing, distribution and transport and (3) the requisitions by the Soviet Govt. on the producers of food in Russia. The Russian cultivator, restrained on by the Soviet authorities for food for Moscow, Petrograd and for their Red Armies, had restricted cultivation to his own immediate needs.

I advised Dr. Nansen, moreover, that the Soviet Govt. was desperately unpopular in this country, on account partly of its subversive policy and because it was regarded as having let us down badly in the War.

Nansen takes all this in the best part and we part the best of friends.

[All of which now reads presumptuously, but I was then U.S. of S. for Foreign Affairs, and had been *pressed* to give Nansen's appeals some sort of official sanction by attending them and Nansen said many things that I could not lend my ears to, officially. A very splendid person he was. (C.H. 2nd Febry. 1934.)]

6 February

This evening the Prime Minister's Ministerial dinner at 10 Downing Street. The little man in excellent health and spirits. He is hugely amused when Hamar Greenwood turns up in his full dress coat with his levee trousers. Hamar takes the shine out of us all.

Afterwards with Em to a reception given by Lord and Lady Farquhar[5] in Grosvenor Square. A gay Coalition gathering.

17 February

Mr. Speaker's Ministerial dinner – the first since before the War. A very splendid affair. We are all in our 'glad rags' and are a gay crowd.
I have a long talk with Mr. Balfour and Mr. Speaker Whitley. Mr. Balfour, fresh from his triumphs at Washington, is in the uniform of an Elder Brother of Trinity House, his epaulettes and big sword sorting oddly with his slender philosophic figure. The conversation turns on the means of exercise adopted by the two eminent men. Mr. B. plays tennis and golf. The Speaker plays racquets with somebody in Westminster who has a court. He does everything he can in his spare moments to shake off the lethal atmosphere of the H. of Commons and is making a sort of roof garden where he can get, the western breezes and the western sun. [. . .]
The Prime Minister is in high spirits and is full of fun about a portrait of Trevor[6] whom he describes as the only Welsh (? Cornish) Speaker – a deuced ugly fellow with a cock eye. 'How difficult it must have been,' says Ll.-G. 'for Members to "catch the Speaker's eye" in Trevor's time.'

26 February

Em, Daff, Bud and I to Victoria to greet Northcliffe on his return from his journey round the World.

---

[5]Horace Brand Farquhar (1844–1923): financier and royal official; Lib. Unionist MP for Marylebone 1895–1898; sacked as Conservative Party Treasurer 1923 after a financial dispute; cr. baronet 1892; cr. Baron Farquhar 1898; cr. Viscount Farquhar 1917; cr. Earl Farquhar 1922; m. 1895 Emilie Scott, née Packe (d. 1922): the widow of Sir Edward H. Scott.

[6]John Trevor (c.1637–1717): served as Speaker of the House of Commons 1685–1687, 1690–1695, but was expelled for corruption; knighted 1671. Lloyd George was correct to describe him as Welsh rather than Cornish.

28 February

Princess Mary's marriage to Lord Lascelles.[7] Em and I have splendid seats in the nave of Westminster Abbey. A gracious and beautiful ceremony – the Princess very sweet in a wonderful dress of silver and white.

There are gleams of sunshine all the morning and enthusiastic crowds of sightseers throng the streets. (The children have places at Henry Maurice's office in Parliament Street.)

17 March

I [...] take Em and Daff to the Lord Chancellor's reception at the House of Lords. F.E. is resplendent in full-bottomed wig, lace ruffles, and his gown of state. He greets us cordially, saying to me: 'Thank God, my dear Cecil, we have still one member of your family with us!' A brilliant crowd, including the Duke of York.

26 May

Earl of Balfour comes to the F.O. to take the place temporarily of Lord Curzon who has been and is seriously ill.

Lord Balfour was S. of S. when I was appointed Under S. of S. He greets me warmly and we discuss one or two of the outstanding problems in foreign affairs. He explains that he had formerly bargained with the Govt. that he was never again to occupy a Cabinet place with heavy departmental duties and describes himself as extremely rusty in the affairs of the F.O. He has seen no F.O. telegrams, except those relating to Washington and Geneva for many months.

Everybody talks about Lord Balfour's 'charm' and popular opinion is right. No more perfect gentleman has been seen in our time – I observe during our conversation his frequent recourse to the little gold-topped vinaigrette that he always carries with him and uses like Cardinal Wolsey's orange.

---

[7] Henry George Charles Lascelles (1882–1947): Con. candidate for Keighley 1913; served in the army during the First World War; knighted 1922; succ. as 6th Earl of Harewood 1929.

1 June

Winston makes today the eagerly anticipated statement about Ireland where latterly things have been going from bad to worse. There are many murders in Belfast and in the South the irregulars who follow de Valera have been defying the Free State Govt. Michael Collins[8] and Arthur Griffith[9] occupy places in the Distinguished Strangers Gallery. Collins, a strongly-built young man with rough black hair, is greatly amused by our proceedings and laughs much at some preliminary talk about the order of business. Griffith is a quiet sedate elderly man with gold-rimmed glasses.

10 June

News of Alfred's serious illness.

18 June

Alfred and party, with Leicester, return from Evian les Bains. His illness causing us all intense anxiety.

22 June

At question time today the rumour runs along the Treasury Bench that F.M. Sir Henry Wilson[10] has been foully murdered. The bad news spreads to the rest of the House and all is tension and excitement until the ordinary questions are over.

Sir Henry Wilson had been a member for only a few months but he had already made his mark in the House, and a very high mark too. I thought his maiden speech among the first two or three I have heard perfectly expressed in a beautiful voice that was easily heard in

---

[8] Michael Collins (1890–1922): Irish revolutionary and political-military mastermind who took a leading role in the negotiation of the Anglo-Irish Treaty of 1921.

[9] Arthur Griffith (1871–1922): Irish nationalist and journalist; founder of Sinn Féin; led the Irish side in the 1921 treaty negotiations.

[10] Henry Hughes Wilson, Bt (1864–1922): army officer; Chief of the Imperial General Staff 1918–1922; Field Marshal 1919; MP for North Down 1922; cr. baronet 1919; an uncompromising opponent of negotiations with the Irish, he was murdered by republican gunmen, who were caught and hanged.

every part of the House. It was altogether unlike the rugged staccato speech of the usual bluff soldier-man.

23 June

To Poynters to see Mother. She very anxious about Alfred.

1 August

[The many blank days this Diary were days of extreme anxiety for the family and for me days of exceptional strain, I had my Foreign Office and H. of C. work all the time, with very frequent attendance at night and in other spare intervals at Carlton Gardens, Leicester taking turn and turn about and Georgie during the last phase of Alfred's illness. C.H.]

3 August

A conference at 10 Downing Street (the P.M., Lord Balfour, Lindley,[11] Sir E. Grigg,[12] R.G. Vansittart[13] and myself) to discuss what the P.M. is to say in his Speech today on the Turko-Greek situation. Lord Balfour leaves today his temporary post as S. of S. for Foreign Affairs and I tell him how sorry I am he is going. He dwells very kindly on our happy relations at the F.O.

Lord Curzon is returning from his cure in France.

[Following my established (and perhaps unfortunate) practice I kept no further record at the time of this important occasion. Ll.-G. ran over with us the notes of his speech which was all anti-Turk and pro-Greek. I asked whether it was right and wise of us to encourage the Greeks in their ambitious policy in respect of Smyrna and Asia Minor

[11] Francis Oswald Lindley (1872–1950): diplomat; Ambassador to Portugal 1929–1931; Ambassador to Japan 1931–1934; knighted 1926.

[12] Edward William Macleay Grigg (1879–1955): journalist prior to 1914; served in the army during the First World War; private secretary to Lloyd George 1920–1922; Nat Lib. MP for Oldham 1922–1925; Nat Con. MP for Altrincham 1933–1935; Governor of Kenya 1925–1930; Parliamentary Secretary to the Ministry of Information 1939–1940; Financial Secretary at the War Office 1940; Joint Parliamentary Under-Secretary at the War Office 1940–1942; Minister Resident in the Middle East 1944–1945; knighted 1928; cr. Baron Altrincham 1945.

[13] Robert Gilbert Vansittart (1881–1957): diplomat and Foreign Office official, later notorious for his anti-German views; knighted 1929; cr. Baron Vansittart 1941.

generally unless we were ready to assist them with men and arms. Ll.-G. had the bit between his teeth and nothing would stop him. The speech was fatal to him and to his Government. (C.H. Oct. 1936)]

5 August

Alfred very, very ill today after his eight weeks dreadful illness. I stay the night at Carlton Gardens.

14 August

My dear brother Alfred died today at 12 minutes past 10 o'clock in the morning at 1 Carlton Gardens. Vyvyan and I with him at the end.

17 August

Alfred's funeral at Finchley. [After the Service in Westminster Abbey.]

8 September

After lunch I drive in Harold's car from Hemsted to Clayton – a pleasant drive indeed through hop-fields and orchards and snug old villages wholly unknown to me. At Southdown Lodge I find dear Mother in the best of health, bearing her great bereavement with sweet fortitude. 'It is the Lord's will,' she says again and again, and marvels that she should be so well in health and so resigned. She has the confident faith – a reasoned faith, too – that is so rare in these days and nourishes her wonderful mind on religious food that weaker spirits have rejected, to their own immeasurable loss.

19 September

I see by this morning's papers that my Chief, Lord Curzon, is going today to Paris to discuss the Turko-Greek crisis with the French Prime Minister, M. Poincaré. Needs must therefore that I go back to town instead of proceeding to Totland Bay.

5 October
Totland.

The last few days have been uneventful. [. . .] One day we went trout fishing and caught some three dozen. Our pursuit on other occasions of the nobler bass has been unavailing. When it has rained I have busied myself with F.O. pouches.

Today I write to Frank Parsons telling him it is not my intention to stand for Parliament at the next Election. This is a big decision but I have given much thought to it and Em agrees. The children are even delighted.

17 October

To Luton (with Em and Daff) to see some members of my Executive Committee to whom I re-affirm my intention not to stand at the forthcoming Election.

Then to a Bazaar at the Assembly rooms in aid of the Welfare of the Blind Committee. I stay only a few minutes and, leaving Em and Daff behind, hasten back to town to Downing Street to the P.M.'s meeting of Liberal Ministers. We gather in the Cabinet room and Ll.-G. discusses fully and frankly with us all the ins and outs of the tangled political situation. I tell him I hope that the Tories will break with the Coalition and set him at liberty to rally and lead the Liberal and progressive elements in the country.

18 October

The papers are full today of chat about the crisis. The situation is briefly like this: Austen Chamberlain, Lord Balfour, Lord Birkenhead and other Tory leaders are all for continuing the Coalition under Ll.-G.'s leadership, partly out of loyalty to him and partly because they dread the return to party warfare.

They think, moreover, as I understand their views, that there is still urgent need for what may be called a national govt. and that a split between Tories and Liberals will involve the risk of a Labour Govt. Meanwhile the general sense of their own party and of the country is against them. The majority of Tories believe that they can win the forthcoming Election off their own bats and are anyhow tired to death of coalition with all its compromises. (Liberals too are generally weary of coalition.)

There is to be a meeting of the Tory M.P.s at the Carlton Club tomorrow. What will happen, and what will Austen and his friends do if they are voted down?

19 October

At the Carlton Club this afternoon Austen Chamberlain and his group are defeated by 186 votes to 87.

As I am sitting in my room at the F.O. this afternoon a message comes from No. 10 saying that the P.M. will meet his Liberal colleagues there at 5 o'clock. He comes to us directly from audience with the King to whom he has handed his resignation, advising H.M. to send for Bonar Law. Ll.-G. is quiet but remarkably cheerful and he breaks into merry laughter more than once during the long discussion that ensues. What is to be done now? What is he to say at the meeting, already arranged, at Leeds on Saturday? Is he to survey the new situation only and to defend the past policy of the Coalition or is he to go further and sketch the outlines of a programme? He invited suggestions. What, again, are to be his relations to A. Chamberlain and the other Tory chiefs who remain loyal to him and to the Coalition idea? After his opening statement Ll.-G. listens while we others do most of the talking. [My own contribution was that after the un-avoidable Leeds meeting he should go into retirement for a long spell & only emerge as a national statesman on a national occasion.] It is the Leeds speech that bothers him more, he says, than the crisis itself and his own resignation. Somebody suggests that the Leeds meeting should be cancelled but this is generally scouted. It is obviously a great advantage for Ll.-G. to open the political campaign.

He reads us a long letter written by him in February last (I think) offering to resign and to assist a Tory Govt. provided that the Irish treaty is maintained, that a policy of peace is pursued and that there is no reactionary legislation. He was begged at the time by all his colleagues to carry on.

At the end of the Conference he thanks us all warmly for our assistance during the last 4 years.

One of Ll.-G.'s bright sallies today was about Winston who is in bed after an operation for appendicitis – but 'busily drafting political programmes,' said Ll.-G. Much laughter.

20 October

A formal letter from Ll.-G. today:
  My dear Parliamentary Under Secretary
  I write to inform you that I have tendered my resignation and that of the Government to the King this afternoon. I understand that His Majesty will he graciously pleased to accept these resignations as soon as he is assured that an alternative government can be formed.
  I should like to take this opportunity of thanking you for your valuable services during your tenure of office under my premiership.
  Ever sincerely
  D. Lloyd George.
  The signature affects to be Ll.-G.'s but it is pretty certainly the work of his principal secretary J.T. Davies who *almost invariably* performs this function for Ll.-G. I have often seen him doing it when I was at No. 10 and very good he was at it too. I wonder in how many collections of autographs the handiwork of 'J.T.' is treasured! Ll.-G.'s own autograph signature I have rarely seen – not more than two or three times for certain [one of them in Em's Birthday Book]. He writes a slow difficult crabbed fist and never, so far as I have observed, at any length. A few words arranged in rough columns on a couple of long envelopes suffice him for his biggest speeches in the H. of Commons.

24 October

My last official engagement today when I take the Chair at Lancaster House at the Govt. Dinner to the International Commission for Air Navigation in place of Freddie Guest, S. of S. for the Air. He, as I explain to the distinguished gathering, has been swept away in the political gales.

26 October

Em and I to the Wesleyan East Ham Mission where I take the Chair at a great meeting (or service). In addition to my eloquent friend, the Rev. Moffat Gautrey, two or three other remarkably able ministers take part in the proceedings.

27 October

I have been busy these last two or three days bidding farewell to my friends at the F.O. – to Lord Curzon who is positively warm in his appreciation of my services; to Crowe, Tyrell, Lindsay,[14] Montgomery,[15] Murray[16] and many others. I think they are all sorry to part with me.

1 November

Very busy these days correcting the final proofs of 'Holiday Verses and Others' and preparing for publication Alfred's Diary of the World Tour.[17] I am becoming quite a literary character!

3 November

At this Election Leicester has against him another Liberal, Sir Archibald Sinclair,[18] a great friend of Winston Churchill. Leicester wires to me (from Wick) begging me to see Winston and to get him to secure the withdrawal of Sinclair, on the understanding that if he does so L. will leave the field open to him at the next Election.

Winston, who is recovering from a severe operation for appendicitis, readily consents to see me and I find him in bed at 2, Sussex Square. He greets me in very friendly fashion, but regrets that he cannot intervene. He has sent Sinclair a letter of recommendation, which has already been widely circulated in the Constituency (Caithness & Sutherland).

Winston congratulates me warmly on my work for the F.O. in the H. of Commons and says that I never once let the Govt. down in all

---

[14] Ronald Charles Lindsay (1877–1945): Foreign Office official and diplomat; Ambassador to Turkey 1925–1926; Ambassador to Germany 1926–1930; Ambassador to the USA 1930–1939; knighted 1925.

[15] Charles Hubert Montgomery (1876–1942): Foreign Office official and diplomat; Minister to the Netherlands 1933–1938; knighted 1927.

[16] John Murray (d. 1937 at age 53): Foreign Office official and diplomat; Minister to Mexico 1935–1937.

[17] Cecil Harmsworth and Desmond Harmsworth, *Holiday Verses and Others* (Dublin: Cuala Press, 1922); Lord Northcliffe, *My Journey Round the World*.

[18] Archibald Henry Macdonald Sinclair (1890–1970): served in the army during the First World War; Nat. Lib./Lib. MP for Caithness and Sutherland 1922–1945 and Lib. candidate in 1950; Leader of the Liberal Party 1935–1945; Secretary of State for Air 1940–1945; cr. Viscount Thurso 1952.

my four years as Under-Secretary. He is sorry I am giving up active political life.

For himself, he is determined to take part in his own election at Dundee before the fight is over. I urge him to be prudent and not to take any risks.

On 13 November Harmsworth set off with his brother St. John for a holiday in Vergèze, France.

17 November

A telegram from Earle to say that the Conservative candidate for Luton, Sir J.P. Hewett, has won by over 3,000 votes in the triangular contest. It is what I always expected in such circumstances. Luton has never been anything but Liberal before:

Sir J.P. Hewett[19] (C.) 13,501
Mr. H. Arnold (L.) 10,137
Mr. P Alden[20] (Lab.) 7,107

---

[19] John Prescott Hewett (1854–1941): Indian administrator; Lieutenant-Governor of the United Provinces 1907–1912; Unionist MP for Luton 1922–1923; knighted 1907.

[20] Percy Alden (1865–1944): expert on social, economic and labour questions; Lib. MP for Tottenham 1906–1918; Lab. MP for Tottenham South 1923–1924; knighted 1933; killed by a bomb during the German V-weapons campaign.

even
INDEX

1920 Club 319

Academia dei Lincei 302
The Academy 7
Adam, William 55
Adams, William George 248, 249, 251, 257, 260, 265, 266, 271, 276, 287
Addison, Christopher 24, 241, 246, 247, 251, 311
Admiralty 168, 169, 176, 187, 211, 228, 245, 250, 258, 270, 271, 276, 278, 319
Adshead, Stanley 109
'Æ', George William Russell 256
Africa 239
agricultural co-operation 263–264
Agricultural Education Conference (1912) 125, 126
Agricultural Organisation Society (AOS) 141n, 149, 161
air raids 17, 23, 173, 176, 186, 187, 188, 197, 201, 252, 254, 260; development of insurance against air raids 17, 255
Aitken, William Maxwell (Sir Max Aitken), Lord Beaverbrook 187
Alexandra Day 123
Alexandrovich, Grand Duke Michael 196, 242
Alcock, Sir John, aviator 295
Alden, Percy 343
Aldwych Club 230
Allsopp, Frederick 116
Alton, Ernest 221
Amalgamated Press Ltd. 30, 63, 72, 103, 124, 130, 155
Amalgamated Society of Co-operative Employees 200
Amalgamated Society of Carpenters and Joiners 264n
Amalgamated Society of Railway Servants (ASRS) 51
American (US) army 253, 277
Amery, Leopold (Leo or L.S.) 69, 105
Anderson, John 253
Angell, Norman, or Ralph Lane 60

Anglo-Irish relations 5, 223, 327, 336
Anglo-Irish Treaty (1921) 327, 340
Anglo-Newfoundland Development Coy 152
Anglo-Soviet relations 18, 306, 311, 312, 333; British prisoners in Soviet Russia 306
Anglo-Swedish Chamber of Commerce 324
Anderson, Sir Kenneth 141, 149
Anderson, Robert 105
d'Annunzio, Gabriele 301
Answers 5
appeasement, policy of 21
Ardagh, Arthur 105
Armistice Day (1919) 300
Army Vote 146
Arnold, Harry 283, 343
Artists (8th London) Rifles 171
Artists (28th London) Battalion 172
Ashe, Thomas (Tomás Aghas) 256
Ashton, Thomas Gair 12, 82, 119
Asquith, Anthony 210
Asquith Coalition Government 184, 185, 188, 209, 218, 229, 235; Cabinet crisis 197, 206, 214, 215, 228, 234
Asquith, Emma Alice Margaret (Margot), née Tennant, Asquith's 2nd wife 74, 155, 192, 210
Asquith, Helen Violet (Lady Violet Bonham Carter) 135
Asquith, Herbert Henry 1, 10, 15–16, 22, 35, 45–46, 88, 90–93, 95, 112, 113, 114, 115, 116, 118, 121, 123, 134–135, 139, 140, 155, 157, 160, 161, 162, 163, 164, 169, 170, 172, 178, 179, 183, 185, 188, 190, 193, 196, 197, 199, 201, 204, 206, 207, 210, 214, 215, 216, 217, 220, 221, 222, 224, 227, 228, 235, 236, 237, 238, 241, 254, 256, 269, 270, 272, 291, 310; Asquithians 287; resignation as prime minister (PM) 16, 236; speeches 41, 46, 112, 121, 139, 241, 242

344 INDEX

Ashton, Eva James, Lady 119
Associated Newspapers Ltd. 5–6
Astley, Henry J. Delaval, aviator 81
Astor, Nancy, Viscountess, MP 304, 315, 316
Astor, Waldorf, 2nd Viscount 249, 251, 261, 266, 294, 304
At the War, Lord Northcliffe (1916) 238
Atkinson, Edward 131, 132, 135, 136, 138, 139
Atkinson, John 40
Attolico, Bernardo 293
Austria-Hungary 15, 280, 293; Austria 163, 277, 310, 312; Hungary 279, 312
Australia 275, 323
Australasia 23, 154, 156

Baden-Powell, Robert 104
Baker, Constance 65, 77, 94
Baker, Harold 113, 179, 190
Baldwin, Stanley 89, 255
Balfour, Arthur James 36, 42, 46, 80, 81, 88, 91–92, 94, 159, 160, 190, 203, 211, 220, 227, 234, 255, 256, 272, 278, 289, 291, 304, 311, 334, 335, 337, 339
Balfour, Gerald 80
Balkans 240
Ball, Willet 18, 284, 285, 286, 287, 289
Banbury, Sir Frederick 218, 321
Bank of Ireland 224
Barclay, Thomas 66
Bark, Pyotr Lvovich 199
Barker, Harley Granville 134
Barker, John 149
Barker, Lillah 134
Barking 326
Barnes, George Nicoll 251, 255
Barran, John 224
Baruch, Bernard Mannes 292
Batchelor, Gaius 151
Bath 183
Bathurst, Charles 166
Beakbane, Henry 55
Beale, Sir John Field 273
Beatty, Admiral Sir David 296
Beauchamp, Lady 65–66, 147
Beauchamp, William Lygon, 7th Earl 48, 65–66, 71, 147, 153
Beaverbrook, William Maxwell Aitken, Lord 187
Beck, Cecil 40
Bedford 96, 314
Bedfordshire 297

Beeton, Henry 108
Belbroughton 53
Belfast 97–98, 336
Belgium 148, 149, 164, 165, 167, 168, 230, 239, 271, 273, 274
Bellhouse, Gerald 193
Benckendorff, Count Alexander Konstantinovich 227
Beresford, Admiral Lord Charles 226, 227
Bernard, John Henry 4, 22, 62, 222, 225, 229, 260, 264, 324
Bernard, Maude Nannie 62, 229
Betham, Ernest Burton 168
Bethmann-Hollweg, Theobold von 239
Biddle, General John, US Army 273
Birchenough, William 233
Birkenhead, Lord, *see* F.E. Smith
Birmingham 6, 8, 184
Birrell, Augustine 40, 137, 161, 201, 217, 272
Blackpool 276
blockade 290, 291, 292, 293, 294, 333
Board of Agriculture and Fisheries 13, 97, 104, 108, 114, 123, 128, 130, 141, 142, 148, 165, 166, 187, 211, 253, 277
Board of Education 191, 202
Board of Trade 15, 165, 166, 167, 168, 169, 170, 174, 175, 176, 177, 178, 179, 209, 210, 211, 227, 237, 270, 290; requisitioning of the railways 169
Bohemia 279
Boland, John 89
Bonar Law, Andrew 127, 160, 162, 172, 187, 188, 190, 220, 227, 229, 230, 235, 236, 237, 238, 241, 242, 245, 248, 251, 267, 269, 275, 278, 294, 306, 310, 311, 319, 320, 340
Bonham Carter, Maurice 134, 256
Booth, Frederick Handel 110
Boraston, John 192
Borden, Sir Robert, Canadian PM 275
Borghese Palace 302
Boris III, Tsar of Bulgaria 279
Bosnia 279
Bostock, Samuel 141, 149
Boulogne 61, 280
Bourne, Francis, Cardinal 266
Bournemouth 63–64
Bowerman, Charles 89
Boy Scouts 104
Boyle, Alan, aviator 64
Brace, William 15, 141, 186, 187, 209
Bradbury, Sir John 189, 199, 205, 229
Bradley Green 54

INDEX   345

Brazil 330
Brighton 73; West House, Brighton 45
Bristol 61
British Army 157, 230, 268, 278, 297, 325
British Communist Party 326
British Expeditionary Force (BEF) 167, 168, 169, 281
British Union of Fascists (BUF) 20
Brixham 133-134
Brockbank, J.W.K. 54
Brocket, Lord 21
Brookes, Clifford 111, 69
Brooks, Collin 20-21
Brown, Sir Arthur Whitten, aviator 295
Bruce, William
Bruce-Joy, Albert 72
Brussels 299
Bryce, James (Lord Bryce) 273
Buckingham Palace 125, 160, 162, 163, 165, 197, 236, 247, 286, 296
Buckmaster, Stanley Owen 31, 68, 185, 186, 199
Budget (1909) 10-11, 22, 30-31, 33, 34-35, 36-39, 44, 46, 74; (1912) 116; (1914) 163; (Autumn 1915) 194, 195, 196, 197, 198; (1916) 213; (1917) 248
Budleigh Salterton 132
Bulgaria 193, 279, 301, 303, 310
Bulwer-Lytton, Victor (Lord Lytton) 119, 120
Bund, John William Willis 57
Burr, Alfred 73
Burns, John 15, 34, 35, 38-39, 46, 88, 90, 114, 165, 167, 206
Burton, Maurice 326
Burton, Percy Basil Harmsworth (Basil) 144, 160
Burton, Percy Collinwood 144n
Butt, Alfred 248n
Buxton, Sidney 89
by-elections: North-East Lanarkshire (1901) 6-7; Peckham (1908) 41; South Bedfordshire (1911) 12-13, 82, 84-87
Byles, Sir William Pollard 89

Caithness & Sunderland 343
California 298
Camberwell 137
Cambon, Paul 227
Cambridge 314, 315
Campbell, James Henry Mussen 137, 188, 189
Campbell-Bannerman, Henry 9-10, 46

Canada 275, 323
Cap Martin, La Dragonnière 142, 143
Cardona, Luigi 258
Carlisle, Margaret Montgomery 220
Carr-Gomm, Hubert 45, 70, 73, 128
Carruthers, Lt Col. Andrew 126
Carruthers, Emily 126
Carson, Edward Henry 78, 143, 156, 158, 159, 161, 162, 188, 189, 201, 202, 215, 216, 217, 218, 229, 231, 232, 235, 250, 251, 255, 260, 264, 267, 273, 310; Carsonites 233
Castlemaine, Albert Edward, 5th Baron 221n
Castlemaine, Lady (Annie Evelyn, née Barrington) 221
Castleton, Newport 175
'Cat and Mouse Act' 316
Central Land & Housing Council 153
Chaddesley Corbett 43, 53
Chalmers, Robert 224, 232
Chamberlain, (Arthur) Neville 17, 171, 241, 340; Director General of National Service 17
Chamberlain, Joseph 6, 9, 160, 171
Chamberlain, Joseph Austen 66, 171, 269, 320, 339, 340
Cheney, E.J. 122
Chester 35, 36, 40
China 330
Chisholm, Hugh 191
Churchill, Winston 20, 35, 70, 81, 88, 114, 127, 145, 157, 158, 184, 185, 199, 211, 218, 220, 229, 230, 236, 238, 249, 273, 295, 323, 324, 336, 340, 342; speeches 114, 211
Clack, Thomas 152
Clarke, Basil 212
Clarke, Thomas James 217
Clemenceau, Georges 267, 278, 283, 303, 311
Clémentel, Étienne 292, 293
Clent 51
Clerical Employments Committee (1915) 202, 204, 206
Clough, William 89
Clynes, John 310
Coal Bill (1919) 305
coal strikes 113, 320, 322
Cobden, Richard 52
Cobham, Viscount 11; see also Lyttelton, John
Cokayne, Brien 189n

Colebrook, Edward, Lord 156, 192
Colefax, Henry Arthur 80
Colefax, Sybil, née Halsey 80
Collins, Michael 336
Collins, Stephen 89
Collings, Jesse 228
Colonial Conference 81
Commons & Footpath Preservation Society 109
Copenhagen 306, 309
Congested Districts Board 107
conscription 214, 217, 230, 268, 269, 273; Compulsory Service 196, 197, 206, 207, 217
Conservative and Unionist Party 9–10, 18–21, 35, 37, 41, 44, 53, 54, 65, 72, 78, 87, 89, 91–93, 127, 132, 146, 154, 155, 157, 158, 159, 162, 163, 165, 171, 185, 190, 218, 225, 226, 229, 238, 257, 283, 285, 286, 319, 320, 326, 334, 339, 340, 343
Consolidated Fund Bill (1920) 310
Constantinople 239
constitutional crisis 2, 45, 88, 91, 93–96, 111
Consultative Food Committee 299
Cookley 48
Cooper, Duff 19
Cork 100–101; University College Cork 101
Cornwall 14, 130, 138, 139, 140, 141
Corbett, John 8
Cory, Sir Clifford 75
Costello Lodge 35, 39
Cotchin, Charles 84, 126, 128, 129, 283, 285, 287
Cottage Committee 152–153
cotton industry 193, 195
Cotton-Joddrell, Sir Edward 149
Country Life 160
County Antrim 161
County Armagh 162
County Down 161
County Londonderry 161
County Tyrone 162
Courtney, Leonard, Lord 103, 151
Cox, Harold 78
Cox, Joseph 86
Cox, Dr Michael 97
Coysh, F. 52
Craig, Herbert 31, 38, 128
Craig, James 162
Craig, Norman, KC 141

Crawford, David Lindsay, 27th Earl of 21, 298
Crawshay-Williams, Alice 100, 129
Crawshay-Williams, Eliot 45n, 100, 129
Crespi, Silvio Benigno 292
Crewe, Robert Crewe-Milnes, Marquess of 170, 199
Croatia 279
Crooks, William 186
Cross, Elihu 166
Crowe, Sir Eyre 301, 303, 342
Crozier, Archbishop John 256
Criminal Law Amendment Bill (1914) 162
'Cryptos' 43n
Culpin, Ernest 23, 75, 107, 154, 156
Cumberland, Hugh 282
Cunha, Gastao da 330
Cunliffe, Walter, Lord 189, 191
Currie, George Welsh 280
Curzon, George 18, 251, 255, 289, 306, 309, 311, 321, 327, 329, 335, 338, 342
Cutnall Green 55

d'Annunzio, Gabriele 301
Dail Eireann 327
Daily Independent 106, 223
Daily Mail 2–3, 6–7, 20, 32, 33, 42, 60, 80, 88, 117, 120, 155, 162, 177, 184, 187, 212, 233, 295, 321, 323
Daily Mirror 155
Dalziel, Davison 32
Dalziel, James 89, 103
Danzig 330, 331
Davidge, William 154n, 156
Davidson, Archbishop Randall 44n
Davies, David 251
Davies, John Thomas 259, 272, 291, 341
Davies, Joseph 251
Dawson, Dr Bertrand 60, 62, 65
de Valera, Eamon, *see* Valera
Deane, Marcella Amelia 29, 106
Delevingne, Malcolm 202, 206
Dent, Joseph Malaby 79
Departmental Committee on Small Holdings 116–117, 120, 124, 129, 134
Departmental Committee on the state of Inshore Fisheries 141, 142, 144, 158
Derby, Edward George Villiers Stanley, 17th Earl of 200, 322
Desart, Hamilton Cuffe, Earl of 229, 230, 265

Devlin, Joseph 97, 98, 264
Devon 14, 130, 133, 139, 140, 141, 297
Devon and Cornwall Enquiry 130, 133, 138, 140
Devon and Cornwall Sea Fisheries Committee 130, 131, 133, 135, 136, 139
Devonport, Hudson Kearley, Viscount 248, 250
Devonshire Club 104
Devonshire House 331–332
Dewar, Arthur 311n
Dewar, Sir John 211
Dewar, Thomas 130
Dickinson, Minnie, née Meade 132
Dickinson, Willoughby Hyett 132
Dillingham, Charles 277
Dillon, John 22, 162, 219, 238, 242; Dillonites 269
Dilke, Sir Charles 7
Disraeli, Benjamin 68
Distinguished Strangers Gallery 216, 336
Distributing tradesmen 183
Dobson, A.T.A. 141
Dobson, Thomas William 85
Dodds, George Elliott 101
Doran, Henry Francis 107
Dougherty, James 218
Douglas-Pennant, Violet Blanche 80n, 279, 295
Downing Street 17, 61, 69, 74, 79, 90, 108, 118, 122–123, 155, 179, 192, 194, 196, 225, 226, 246, 247, 249, 250, 251, 252, 253, 257, 260, 263, 264, 265, 267, 268, 269, 270, 274, 275, 276, 277, 282, 283, 286, 287, 289, 309, 311, 317, 323, 333, 337, 339, 340
Draper, Warwick Herbert 110, 136
Drexel, John Armstrong 64
Drogheda 126
Droitwich 36, 48, 51, 53, 55, 56, 57, 58, 65, 69, 82, 129
Drummond, James Eric 291, 329, 331
Dublin 2, 22, 35, 62, 67, 96, 105, 216, 220, 221, 222, 223, 224, 252, 258, 316, 325, 327; General Post Office 216, 217, 221
Duke, Henry Edward, QC 218, 232, 252, 257
Dumb Friends' League 148
Dunbartonshire 11
Dundee 343
E. India vote 90
Earle, Arthur 52, 58, 151, 188, 285, 343

The Economist 189, 191
education 88
Edward VII, King of Great Britain and Ireland 61, 90, 144
Edward Albert Christian George Andrew Patrick David, Prince of Wales 83, 294, 319
Edwards, Hugh 94, 101
Egypt 294, 295
Eighty Club 67, 68, 96–98, 101
Elibank, Alexander Murray, Master of, 11, 61, 62, 79, 82, 88 91, 108, 117,118, 122, 127, 161, 197, 226
Elliott, George 155
Ellis-Griffith, Ellis 68, 90, 180, 218
Ellis-Griffith, Mary, née Owen 68n
Elwes, Gervase Henry 80
Elwes, Lady Winifrede, née Fielding 80
Entente Cordiale 164
Erskine, Henry David 74
Estonia 324, 331
Evans, Sir Samuel 31, 37, 74
Everard, Sir Nugent Talbot 97
Eversley, George Shaw-Lefevre, Lord 109
Evesham 47
Exeter 130, 131
Exmouth 132
Exportation of Horses Bill (1914) 14–15, 158, 161

Fairfield 54
Faisal I Faisal bin Hussein bin Ali al-Hashimi, Emir 300; King of Iraq 300n
Farquhar, Horace Brand, Viscount 334
Farquhar, Emilie, Viscountess 334n
Fay, Sir Samuel 141
Fenwick, Robert 83n
Ferdinand I (Ferdinand Maximilian Karl Leopold Maria of Saxe-Coburg and Gotha-Kohárý), Tsar of Bulgaria 279, 303
Ferraris, Maggiorino 301
Ferraris, Dante 302
Field, George 126, 151
Fielding, Lady Winefride Mary Elizabeth 80n
Finance Bill (1909) 40, 41, 95, 161
Finlay, Robert Bannatyne 219
Finlay, Thomas A. 105
Finstall 56
First Garden City Ltd., Letchworth 102, 103, 117

348　　　　　　　INDEX

First World War (Great War) 1, 15, 22, 115, 152, 163, 164, 173, 174, 189, 190, 192–193, 196, 197, 199, 200, 202, 204, 205, 206, 209, 212, 222, 227, 234, 246, 253, 254, 256, 265, 267, 268, 269, 270, 274, 275, 276, 277, 278, 279, 280, 283, 296, 333; air raids 23, 173, 176, 186, 187, 188, 197, 201, 252, 254, 260, 272,; Amiens offensive 268; armistice 17, 278, 279, 280; Asquith Coalition, formation of 15, 184; August crisis 164–165, 226–227; 'Battle of the Somme' film 233–234; Belgian refugees 23; blockade 290; bombardment of towns on the east coast of Britain 216; *Britannic*, sinking of 234; declaration of war 15, 165; Dardanelles 194, 202; Derby recruiting scheme 200, 205, 206, 212n; eastern front 195, 196, 226; entry of USA into the war 245; food supplies and food situation 244–245, 248, 249, 250, 251, 254, 255, 256, 275, 277; Gallipoli 193, 231; German propaganda films 177–178; Grey's speech to the House of Commons 164; Labour unrest 275; Lloyd George Coalition, formation of 16; *Lusitania*, sinking of 183; Mesopotamia 231; Minister of Munitions 187, 189; munitions production 212–213, 227, 255, 284; Paris Peace Talks 18 279, 280, 283, 289, 290, 291, 293, 295, 296, 302, 303, 311; retreat of the BEF from Mons 169; Somme offensive 16, 226, 234; substitution of women for men in the workforce 193, 202, 204, 210, 214, 227; submarine warfare 245, 246, 252, 254, 255, 274, 275; recruitment 23, 173, 180, 181, 182, 184, 191, 193, 195, 199, 200, 206; tank development 243; ultimatum to Germany 165; War Loan campaigns 190,191, 192, 193; western front 194, 200, 211, 267, 276; Verdun offensive 211; Ypres offensive 256; Zeppelin attacks 173, 176, 186,187, 188, 197, 199, 201, 216, 252, 260
fiscal reform 112
Fish Food and Motor Loan Committee (1917) 244, 247, 251, 254
Fisher, Admiral John Arbuthnot (Jackie) 202

Fisheries Organisation Society (FOS) 14, 149, 161, 211
fishing industry 14, 130, 131, 135, 139, 141, 244, 245
FitzAlan-Howard, Edmund 192
Fiume 239, 279, 301
Fleetway House 130, 145
Flitwick 144
Foch, Marshal Ferdinand 258, 274, 278, 283, 296
Foot, Isaac 100
foot and mouth, outbreak 126
Forbes, Bernard, *see* Granard
Ford, Henry 131
Foreign Office 19, 168, 255, 270, 289, 290, 292, 293, 294, 295, 296, 300, 301, 305, 306, 309, 310, 315, 320, 327, 329, 335, 337, 339, 340, 342
Forest of Dean Battalion of the Gloucester Regiment 175
Forster, Henry 188
Fotheringham, Revd David 54
Francavilla, Guglielmo di 329, 330
France 164, 230, 239, 246, 248, 271, 285, 291, 313, 337
France, Gerald 137
Franchise Bill (1913) 140; Woman's Franchise Amendment 140
Fraser, Edward 51
Free Trade 9, 11, 159, 198, 291
Free Trade Union 159
Freeman 106
Freeman-Thomas, Freeman, Lord Willingdon 75
French, General Sir John 72, 190, 275
Fremantle, Francis 110
Fremantle, Selwyn 14, 131, 132, 135, 136, 138
Friendly Societies' Medical Alliance 116
Furse, Charles Wellington 80n
Furse, Katherine 80
Furse, Michael Bolton 80

Galway, Mary 97
Garrick Club 219–220
Garvin, James Louis 80
Gascoyne-Cecil, Edgar Algernon Robert (Lord Robert Cecil) 78, 120, 135, 150, 166, 188, 226, 251, 278, 290, 292, 293
Gascoyne-Cecil, Hugh Richard Heathcote (Lord Hugh Cecil) 92, 320

INDEX 349

Gascoyne-Cecil, James Edward Hubert, 4th Marquess of Salisbury 44, 327
Garden Cities movement 22, 79–80, 116–117, 144, 146, 264; Garden Cities Association 75, 76, 79, 107–108, 110, 119, 125, 154, 211; Garden Cities and Town Planning Association 76, 109; Finance & General Committee Garden City Association 108;
'Garden Suburb' 17, 247, 248, 249, 252, 253, 254, 255, 258, 263, 265, 266, 267, 268, 270, 275, 276, 277, 289
Gaunt, Walter 102
Geddes, Sir Auckland 305, 309
general elections: (1900) 12; (1906) 8–9, 53; (January 1910) 10, 12, 49, 58–59; (December 1910) 10, 12, 70, 71; (1918) 18, 282, 283, 284, 285, 286, 287n; (1922) 339, 342, 343
Geneva 18, 327, 329, 335
George V, King of Great Britain and Ireland 111, 124, 144, 155, 160, 162, 163, 174, 197, 210, 214, 236, 237, 247, 286, 295, 296, 299, 300, 301, 319, 326, 340, 341; coronation celebrations 82–83
Germany 15, 21, 163–164, 165, 168, 239, 244, 293, 312, 329; Austro-Germany 279
G.H.Q. 280
Giltrap, John 106
Gladstone, Henry Neville 159
Gladstone, W.E. 6–8, 23, 137, 159
Gladstone, W.G.C. 137, 182
Gladstone, William Henry 137
Glazebrook, Dr Richard Tetley, FRS 42
Goode, Sir William 298
Goodman, Richard 126, 144
Gough, Brigadier-General Hubert 157
Goulding, Edward Alfred 36
Goulding, Sir William 224
Grahame-White, Claude, aviator 63, 81
Granard, Bernard Forbes, 8th Earl 81, 113
Gray, Milner 85, 117, 118, 126
Great Britain 303
Great Mrs Alloway, The 45
Great War, *see* First World War
Greece 145, 193, 337
Greenwood, Adeliza Florence Louise Hamar (Florence Amery) 69
Greenwood, Granville George 89
Greenwood, Hamar 69, 109, 243, 322, 333
Greenwood, Margery, née Spencer 109
Grenfell, Field Marshal Lord 72

Grey, Albert, 4th Earl Grey 115
Grey, Sir Edward 88, 92–93, 113, 115, 119, 128, 162, 164, 185, 195–196, 199
Griffith, Arthur 336
Griffith-Boscawen, Sir Arthur 114
Grigg, Sir Edward 337
Grocers' Federation 183
Guest, Frederick Edward 243, 341
Gulland, John William 185, 187, 191, 192, 196, 237
Gustaf Adolf, Crown Prince of Sweden 324
Guy, Selina 78
Gwynn, John 4
Gwynn, Stephen 145, 256, 266

Hageans, Mary Constance 80
Haig, Field Marshal Sir Douglas 234, 261, 296, 325
Haking, General Sir Richard 330
Haldane, Richard, Lord Chancellor 75, 230
Halsey, Lionel, 4th Sea Lord 240
Hamburg Amerika 167
Hamilton, Lord Claud John 218
Hamilton, Horace 192, 207, 236
Hamilton, Helen 164
Hammersmith 136
Hampshire House 136
Hampstead Garden Suburb 43
Hampton Court 90
Hankey, Maurice 109
Hanotaux, Albert 329, 330
Hansard 52
Harben, Agnes Helen 109, 111
Harben, Henry Devenish 69, 109
Harcourt, Lewis Vernon ('Lulu') 141, 199
Hardie, Keir 7
Hardinge, Lord 223n
Hardy, Capt. Charles, RN 293
Harland & Wolff 97, 220n
Harmsworth, Alfred, see Northcliffe
Harmsworth, Cecil Bisshopp: *character and early life*: background 1–4, 29; early career 5; education 3–4; at Trinity College Dublin 4; marriage 4; influenza 60, 145
 family life 1–6, 45, 46, 48, 49, 59, 94, 103, 104, 105, 106, 107, 113, 119, 127, 129, 132, 133, 134, 137, 154, 164, 168, 169, 175, 176, 177, 187, 238, 286, 289, 310, 335, 339
 and Northcliffe 1, 19, 32, 61, 73, 75, 76, 80, 88, 95, 103, 108, 112, 119, 122, 124,

127, 128, 142, 144, 145, 152, 155, 175, 183, 199, 200, 203, 206, 207, 212, 214, 222, 223, 225, 231, 234, 235, 254, 258–259, 275, 311, 321, 323, 336, 337, 338, 342
overseas trips: Belfast 97–98; Cork 100–101; Dublin 22, 67, 105, 220–225; Galway 98–99; Geneva 18; Killaloe 99–100; Paris 60–61, 290, 291, 292, 300, 301, 302; Rome 300, 301, 302;
pastimes and interests: aviation 23, 42, 63–64, 81, 233, 295; efforts to preserve Dr Johnson's house 2, 22, 73, 77, 79, 185, 201, 280, 324; fishing 18, 20, 23, 122, 124, 186, 320; Garden Cities movement 23; golf 23, 75–76, 80–81, 127, 144, 231, 334; town planning 23
politics: adopted as Liberal-Coalition candidate for Bedfordshire Luton 18, 282; Liberal candidate for Mid-Worcestershire (1899–1900) 6; Liberal candidate for North-East Lanarkshire (1901) 6; Liberal MP for Mid-Worcestershire 8–9, 10–11; Liberal MP for Luton 12–13; Amendment to the National Insurance Bill (1911) 13; speeches in the House of Commons 32, 34, 39, 94, 112, 129, 130, 137, 158, 219, 242, 260; voted against the guillotine in the Home Rule Bill (1912) 13, 128; retirement from Parliament 19–20
political appointments: acted as Lloyd George's Parliamentary secretary 146; Parliamentary private secretary (PPS) for Walter Runciman at the Board of Agriculture and Fisheries 13, 104; chaired committee of inquiry into Devon and Cornwall fisheries 13–14; PPS for Walter Runciman at the Board of Trade 15, 168, 189; Parliamentary Under-Secretary for Home Office 15, 178, 179; Under-Secretary of State for Foreign Affairs in post-war coalition government 18, 289, 333, 343; Minister of Blockade 18, 292, 294; created 1st Baron Harmsworth of Egham 21; presents resignation to McKenna 184; offered position of Coalition Liberal Chief Whip by Lloyd George 16, 246, 259; report on the Decrepit Horse trade for Walter Runciman 148–149
and Rothermere 21, 23, 33, 34, 58, 61, 79, 81, 82, 107, 121, 142, 143, 148, 152, 153, 156, 160, 161, 175, 176, 187, 190, 195, 197, 203, 205, 206, 226, 230, 234, 236, 240, 254, 255, 256, 258–259, 265, 266, 269, 289, 298, 309, 319, 338
views on: appeasement 21; Asquith 22, 46, 92, 112, 114, 139, 155; Nancy Astor 304; John Burns 38–39, 167; Edward Carson 78, 228; Churchill 114, 211, 228, 324; Clemenceau 303–304; Joseph Devlin 97–98; T. W. Dobson, MP 85; Dublin Castle 98; enfranchisement of women 140; First World War 23, 170, 186, 192–193, 196, 229, 234, 265, 268, 279, 280, 281; David Lloyd George 22, 68–69, 140, 254, 256, 268, 271–272, 283, 291, 337; W.G.C. Gladstone 182; Edward Grey 195–196; guillotine resolutions 13, 128, 135, 161; Ebenezer Howard 76–77, 116; Home Rule 7; House of Commons 13, 92, 128, 157–158, 175, 228; William Hughes, Australian PM 212, 323–324; Dr Inge 324; Ireland 22, 98, 216, 224–225; Jews 20–21, 218; John Jellicoe 240; Luton workhouse 151; Charles Masterman 309; mother 338; Nansen 312, 333; parliamentary career 158, 324; role as MP 204–205; role as member of PM's secretariat 271–272; sale of honours 2, 246; suffragettes 113; Swiss population 329; tanks 242; Prince of Wales 294; Henry Wilson 336–337; York 66–67
writing: 'Pleasure and Problem in South Africa' (1908) 1n, 9–10; 'A Plea for a Limitation of Speeches' (1909) 35; 'Parliamentary Letter'(1911) 91–94; *Holiday Verses and Others* (1922) 342; *A Little Fishing Book* (1930) 20, 23; *Immortals at First Hand: Famous People as Seen by their Contemporaries* (London: Desmond Harmsworth, 1933) 20
miscellaneous: Agadir Crisis of 1911 90; coronation celebrations of George V 82–83; funeral of Edward VII 61;

INDEX

offers to re-join the Army 171, 172; rumour that Russian soldiers had passed through Great Britain 171, 172; Scott's disaster at the South Pole 142; *Titanic* 118

Harmsworth, Cecil Desmond Bernard (Bud, son of diarist, later Desmond) 8, 43n, 45, 61, 65, 77, 207, 245, 289, 322, 324, 334

Harmsworth, Charles 3

Harmsworth, Christabel Rose (diarist's sister) 3, 144n, 160

Harmsworth, Daphne Cecil Rosemary (Daff, daughter of diarist) 8, 43n, 61, 65, 77, 106, 129, 186, 199, 211, 221, 222, 233, 285, 289, 296, 322, 325, 334, 335, 339

Harmsworth, Emilie Alberta (wife of diarist) 4, 22, 29, 39, 43, 45, 49, 52, 58, 59, 65, 67, 68, 72, 73, 77, 81, 94, 96, 101, 106, 107, 110, 111, 113, 117, 119, 120, 125, 126, 134, 137, 145, 147, 149, 155–156, 160, 172, 173, 174, 175, 176, 177, 179, 182, 188, 193, 204, 211, 216, 221, 222, 285, 286, 287, 289, 296, 310, 325, 326, 327, 334, 335, 339, 341

Harmsworth, Eric Beauchamp Northcliffe (Gol, son of diarist) 8, 43n, 45, 65, 77, 111, 188, 205–206, 210, 289

Harmsworth, Esmond Cecil 23, 176, 234, 304

Harmsworth, Geraldine Mary (mother of diarist) 2, 3, 7, 38, 49, 61, 62, 110, 119, 127, 156, 160, 175, 179, 199, 200, 206, 231, 259, 321, 322, 337, 338

Harmsworth, Harold Alfred Vyvyan St George (Vyvyan) 23, 195, 206, 234, 259, 265, 338

Harmsworth, Harold Sidney, see Rothermere

Harmsworth, Hildebrand Aubrey 3, 7, 60, 160

Harmsworth, Mary Elizabeth, Viscountess Northcliffe 73n, 108, 113, 212, 265, 321

Harmsworth, Mary Lilian (Lil), Viscountess Rothermere 33, 81, 122, 155

Harmsworth, Robert Leicester (Leicester) 3, 16, 88, 91, 160, 175, 234, 237, 243, 273, 304, 336, 337, 342

Harmsworth, William Albert St John (St John) 3, 20 38, 45, 79, 122n, 160, 176, 200, 204, 207, 342n, 343

Harmsworth, Vere Sidney Tudor 23, 34, 145, 234

Harmsworth, Violet (diarist's sister) 3, 160

Harmsworth, Vyvyan 3, 19

Harmsworth Brothers Ltd. 5

Harmsworth Magazine 5

Harrel, William Vesey 223

Harris, George Montagu 110

Harris, Percy 213

Harrisson, Hilda 220n

Harrisson, Roland 220n

Haslam, Lewis 305

Haversham, Arthur Hayter, Lord 47

Hawkin, Robert Crawford 67

Hayle Harbour 139

Headlam, Cuthbert 23

Healy, Maurice 232n

Healy, Timothy (Tim) 106, 132, 232, 260

Heath, Sir Thomas 228

Heaton, John Henniker 42

Hellyer, Charles 141

Helme, Sir Norval 141

Hely-Hutchinson, Richard, 6th Earl of Donoughmore 257

Hemmerde, Edward George 31, 82

Henderson, Arthur 16, 166, 192, 209n, 321

Henley 29, 63, 70, 72, 76, 94, 116, 127, 142, 146, 147, 164, 169, 170, 229, 275, 277, 289

Henley Regatta 23, 29, 124, 146

Henry, Sir Charles 68, 143

Henry, Lady, née Julia Lewisohn 68n

Herbert, Auberon Thomas (Lord Lucas), *see* Lucas

Herbert, Sir Jesse 82, 192

Herzegovina 279

Hewart, Gordon, KC 311

Hewett, John Prescott 20, 343

Hewitt, Vivian, aviator 81

Hickman, John Owen 87, 173

Hickman, Thomas Edgecumbe 87n

Highcliffe Castle 33, 63–64, 121

Himbleton 54

Hitchin 150

Hobhouse, Charles Edward Henry 218

Hobson, Cyril 52, 59

Hobson, George 48

Hodge, John 239

Holland 148, 149, 164, 244

Holiday Verses and Others, Cecil Bisshopp Harmsworth and Desmond Harmsworth (1922) 342n

Holt, Richard Durning 24

Home Office 15, 178, 179, 180, 181, 182, 183, 184, 185, 186, 187, 193, 199, 200, 202, 203, 204, 205, 206, 209, 210, 218, 219, 241
Home Rule 7, 9, 13, 67, 74, 96, 99, 106, 112, 114, 116, 117, 118, 120, 121, 122, 124, 128, 129, 130, 131, 136, 137, 138, 139, 140, 145, 156, 157, 159, 163, 188, 223, 224, 225, 226, 232, 260, 263, 268, 269, 317
Home Rule Bill (1912) 116, 118, 120, 121, 124, 128, 129, 130, 131, 136, 137, 138, 139, 140, 157, 159, 163, 223
Home Rule Bill (1920) 310, 317
Home Rule Committee 273
Homesgarth 151
Hook 122, 124
Hoover, Herbert 274, 298, 299
Hope, Admiral George 293
Hope, Maximilian 55
Horne, Charles Silvester 87, 89–90
Horne, Sir Robert 311, 315
Horsley, Sir Victor 76
House of Commons 1, 11, 13, 18, 21, 30, 31, 32–33, 35, 37–39, 40–42, 45–47, 69, 74, 78, 82, 83, 88–94, 95, 96, 97, 103–104, 111–113, 114, 116, 118, 119, 120, 121, 122, 123, 124, 126, 127, 128, 129, 132, 135, 137, 138, 139, 140, 142, 143, 144, 145, 148, 149, 150, 153, 155, 156, 157, 158, 159, 160, 162, 163, 164, 165, 166, 167, 169, 170, 171, 173, 174, 175, 179, 180, 181, 182, 188, 190, 191, 193, 196, 197, 199, 201, 202, 204, 205, 206, 209, 210, 211, 213, 214, 215, 216, 217, 218, 219, 226, 227, 228, 229, 230, 232, 233, 234, 237, 238, 241, 242, 245, 246, 247, 249, 251, 254, 260, 261, 267, 268, 269, 272, 273, 280, 292, 294, 295, 298, 305, 309, 310, 312, 315, 317, 319, 320, 321, 324, 326, 327, 333, 336, 337, 341, 342
House of Lords 10–11, 21, 31, 37, 41, 44–45, 46, 68, 94, 95, 96, 111–112, 115, 117, 143, 144, 150, 156, 160, 165, 170, 174, 187, 196, 210, 227, 267, 317, 319, 322, 326, 327; rejection of the budget of 1909 10, 45
Housing Act (1914) 168
Housing Bill (1914) 162, 163, 166, 167
Housing Bill (1919) 305
Housing of the Working Classes Bill (1912) 114

Howard, Ebenezer 76, 77, 79, 102–103, 109, 115, 116, 146, 147, 151, 186, 264
Howard, Sir E. Stafford 14, 141, 152
Howard-Smith, Charles 314, 315
Howe, Robert 300, 301
Hudson, Sir Robert 73
Hughes, Spencer Leigh 41
Hughes, William, Australian PM 212, 323
Hull 184
Hungary Peace Treaty Bill (1921) 321
Huntingdon 314
Huntley & Palmer 181
Hyde, Clarendon 38
Hyde Park Hotel 36–37
Hymans, Paul 329, 330
Hyslop, Robert Murray 98

Ideal Homes Exhibition 120
Ilbert, Sir Courtenay 74
Illingworth, Albert Holden 244
Illingworth, Percy Holden 124, 127, 140, 177
Impey, Henry 287
India 81, 170, 173, 323
India Office 122
Inge, William Ralph 324
Inter-Allied Conference (1922) 329
International Commission for Air Navigation (1922) 341
International Garden Cities & Town Planning Association 147
Inwards, Harry 84, 155
Ireland 4, 9, 18, 22, 35, 39, 42, 96–101, 105, 114, 140, 156, 158, 171, 218, 220, 222, 223, 224, 225, 226, 227, 228, 229, 230, 231, 242, 251, 256, 258, 259, 263, 264, 265, 266, 268, 269, 273, 275, 277, 316, 322, 324, 325, 326; Dublin Castle 4, 98, 216, 223, 224, 225, 228; Easter Rising 5, 22, 216; Lord Lieutenant of 228; Irish crisis 156; Local Government Board in Ireland 105–106; Irish Senate 145; proposal for Irish Parliament 130; Irish struggle for independence 216, 219, 220, 221, 222, 223, 224, 322; military executions in 217, 219; War Bonus for elementary school teachers 231–232
Irish Agricultural Organisation Society 105
Irish Convention 252, 256, 258, 259, 260, 263, 264, 265, 266, 268
The Irish Independent 260
Irish Industries Sale 114
Irish Land Bill (1909) 41

INDEX

Irish Nationalists 7, 9–10, 42, 74, 88, 91, 106, 140, 163, 188, 189, 216, 219, 223, 228, 230, 231, 232, 242, 259, 263, 264
Irish Unionists 232, 259, 263
The Irish question 223, 226
Irish Republican Army (IRA) 322
Irish Textile Operatives' Society (ITOS) 97
Ishii, Viscount 330
Islington 198
Isaacs, Sir Rufus (Lord Reading) 90, 189, 191, 195, 196, 229, 232, 275
Italy 258, 279, 293, 301

Jacobs (Biscuits) 181
Japan 323, 330, 332
Jaspar, Henri 299
Jellicoe, Admiral Sir John 235, 240
Johnson Club 201
Johnson, Esther (Swift's 'Stella') 67
Jones, Sir David Brynmor 31
Jones, Thomas Artemus, KC 100

Kamenev, Lev Borisovich 312
Keens, Thomas 297
Kellaway, Frederick 85, 96, 150, 311
Kelmscott House 136
Kent 297
Kenworthy, J.M. 1
Kerr, Phillip 246, 251, 254, 265, 267, 276, 287
Keynes, John Maynard 293
King, Geraldine Adelaide Hamilton (Dot, diarist's sister) 3, 31, 40, 145, 221
King, Lucas Henry St Aubyn (Luke) 22, 183
King, Sir Lucas White 31, 145, 221, 222, 225
Kingston, Richard 100
Kildare Street Club 106
Kipling, Rudyard 160
Kitchener, Horatio Herbert 15, 165, 172, 183, 187, 196, 199, 204, 240
Klishko, Nicolas 311, 312
Knebworth Garden Village 23, 119, 120
Knight, E.A. 9
Krasin, Leonid Borisovich 311, 312
Kristallnacht 21

La Dragonnière, Cap Martin 142, 143
Labour Exchange 211
Labour Party 9, 10, 20, 42, 47, 70, 75, 88, 89, 91, 92, 95, 96, 123, 132, 141, 163, 165, 166, 186, 192, 200, 209, 235, 237, 238, 239, 251, 261, 277, 278, 280, 284, 285, 287, 305, 306, 310, 339, 343
Labourers Cottage Act in Ireland (1912) 106
Labourers (Ireland) Act (1906) 106, 108
Laking, Sir Guy 199
Lancashire 174, 214
Lane, D.H. 141
Lane, Ralph (Norman Angell) 60
Lansbury, George 123
Lascelles, Lord Henry 335
Lansdowne, Henry Petty-Fitzmaurice, Lord 36, 44, 162, 226, 227
Laszlo, Philip Alexius de 80
Latvia 324, 331
Laws, Hugh 132
Lawrence, Sir Walter 63
Le Bas, Sir Hedley 239, 240
Lea, Sir Sydney 120
League of Nations 18, 312, 320, 327, 329, 330
League of Young Liberals 116
Lee, Arthur (Lord Lee of Fareham) 89, 108
Lee, Grosvenor 51
Leese, Sir Joseph 80
Leighton Buzzard 12, 84, 96, 110, 134
Leinster Regiment 172
Lemieux, Rodolphe 42
Leon, Quinones de 330
Letchworth 23, 79, 102, 117, 144, 146, 151–152
Lever, Lady 137
Levy-Lawson, Henry, Baron Burnham 90
Lewis, Ellen 75
Lewisohn, Julia 68n
Liberal Imperialists 6–7
Liberal Insurance Committee 112–113, 140
Liberal League 37
Liberal Club, Bedford 96
Liberal Club, Luton 82, 88, 96, 111, 128, 130
Liberal Party 6, 10, 13, 15–16, 18, 20, 22, 46, 85, 88, 91–93, 96, 114, 120, 126, 127, 147, 149, 155, 163, 165, 184, 185, 188, 237, 238, 245, 246, 270, 285, 291, 319, 339, 340, 342; Coalition Liberal 311, 331, 332
Liberal Unionists 6–9
Liberalism 11, 22, 188
Liège 165, 166
The Life of William Morris, J.W. Mackail (1899) 136n

354 INDEX

Lincolnshire, Charles Wynn-Carrington, Marquess of 156
Lindley, Francis 337
Lindsay, David (Lord Crawford) 21, 298
Lindsay, Ronald 342
Lipton, Sir Thomas 63, 68
Lister, Grace 78
Lister, Thomas, Lord Ribblesdale ('The Ancestor') 38
Lithuania 324, 330, 331
Litvinoff, Maxim 306, 309
Liverpool 182, 317
Lloyd George Coalition 237, 238, 239, 246, 255, 265, 286; War Cabinet 247, 249, 253, 255, 260, 263, 264, 266, 269, 270, 271, 278, 294; 'Government Record' 255, 258, 265, 266
Lloyd George, David 1, 7, 10, 16–19, 22, 32, 33–35, 54, 57–58, 68–69, 74, 88, 94, 103, 110, 116, 129, 140, 141, 143, 146, 149–150, 153, 161, 162, 170, 181, 190, 196, 197, 214, 215, 222, 223, 225, 226, 228, 230, 231, 235, 236, 237, 238, 239, 241, 242, 244, 245, 246, 247, 248, 249, 251, 252, 253, 254, 255, 256, 257, 258, 259, 260, 261, 263, 264, 265, 266, 267, 268, 269, 270, 271, 272, 273, 274, 275, 276, 277, 278, 279, 280, 283, 286, 287, 289, 290, 291, 292, 293, 294, 298, 301, 304, 309, 310, 311, 315, 316, 319, 322, 323, 331, 332, 333, 334, 337, 338, 339, 340, 341; appointed PM 237; forms Coalition government in 1916 16, 237; 'Harmsworth Amendment' 110; land campaign 149, 152, 159; offers resignation 184–185; resignation as PM 341; speeches 110, 140, 150, 242, 254, 274, 293, 319, 332, 337–338
Lloyd George, Margaret, née Owen 68, 150, 225, 248, 272, 291
Lloyd George, Richard 150n, 248
Lloyd George, Roberta, née McAlpine 248
Lloyd George, Olwen 150n
Lloyd George, Gwilym 150n
Lloyd George, Megan 150n, 247, 291, 292, 315, 316
Lloyd George Liberals 19
Local Government Board (LGB) 105–106, 168
Locke, Arthur 180
Logue, Michael 98
London 2, 9, 38, 61, 67, 79, 126, 136, 156, 169, 173, 176, 186, 187, 201, 222, 225, 233, 238, 252, 255, 258, 260, 273, 286, 289, 292, 300, 312, 315, 326, 331; East End 171–172, 252, 255, 326
London Stock Exchange 164
London County Council (L.C.C) 34n, 75, 181n, 186n
Londonderry City, also called Derry 162
Londonderry House 114
Long, Walter 166, 167, 199, 226, 319
Lord Northcliffe: A Memoir, Max Pemberton (1922) 275
Lord's Cricket Ground 172, 173
Loreburn, Robert Reid, Earl 47
Loucheur, Louis 299
Lough, Thomas 218
Lovat, Lord 172
Lower Hagley 48, 56
Lowther, James 47, 93
Lucas, Auberon Thomas Herbert, Lord 114, 115, 125, 165, 179
Luton 12–13, 82, 84–88, 96, 110, 114, 116, 125, 126, 128, 144, 148, 151,173, 198, 200, 211, 276, 277, 282, 283, 284, 285, 295, 297, 315, 320, 326, 330, 339, 343; Diamond Foundry 84n; Luton Corporation 147; Poor Law Union House (workhouse) 151; Vauxhall Motors 12, 85, 284, 326
Luton Chamber of Commerce 155
Luton Conservative Club 282
Luton Liberal Association 285, 287
Luton News 13, 91
Luton Reporter 133
Lumsden, Lt Col. Dugald 104
Luxembourg 164
Lyell, Charles 118
Lyons, Sir Joseph 130
Lyttelton, Alfred 80, 141
Lyttelton, John 11–12, 54, 74, 119
Lytton, Victor Bulwer-Lytton, 2nd Earl of 119, 120

McCheane, Ethel 109
McCormick, Vance Criswell 292
McCurdy, Charles 298, 311, 323
MacDonagh, Thomas Stanislaus 217
MacDonald, Ramsay 89, 111
MacDonnell, Anthony 47, 222
McFadyean, John 129
Macfarlane, Lang 181
Mackail, J.W., *The Life of William Morris* (1899) 136

INDEX

McKenna, Reginald 13, 15–16, 120, 171, 175, 178, 179, 180, 182, 184, 185, 186, 189, 190, 191, 192, 194, 195, 196, 197, 199, 202, 203, 205, 207, 213, 214, 215, 217, 220, 228, 229, 231, 232, 235, 239, 240, 256
Maclay, Sir Joseph 276
Maclean, Donald, MP 68
Maclean, Gwendolen, née Devitt 68
Macnamara, Dr Thomas 150, 278, 311
MacNeill, Eoin 257
[for Swift MacNeill, see Swift]
Macquisten, Frederick, KC 304
MacSwiney, Terence, Lord Mayor of Cork 316
McVeagh, Jeremiah 89, 114
McVitie Price 181
Madresfield, Malvern Link 147
Maffett, Charles Hamilton 83n,
Maffett, Cuthbert William 82–83
Maffett, Dora Harriett, née Fenwick 83n, 296
Maffett, Henry Telford (Larry) 23, 75, 172, 174
Maffett, Oswald Bayly 109, 111
Maffett, Reginald 77
Maffett, William Hamilton 4
Mahaffy, John Pentland 145, 221, 252, 256
Mallaby-Deeley, Harry 153
Malvern 59
Mance, Harry 304
Manchester 193, 276, 277
Manchester Guardian 6, 236
Market Gardeners Bill (1912) 135
Markham, Violet 241
Marlow 147
Marlowe, Thomas 80
Martin, Albert 326
Martin, Richard Biddulph 6, 8–9
Mary, Princess 326, 335
Mary, Queen 111, 124, 144, 155, 160, 174, 296, 301, 319, 326
Marylebone Liberal Club 76
Massey, William Ferguson 323
Masterman, Charles Frederick Gurney 150, 179, 309
Maude, Frederick 75
Maurice, General Frederick 269
Maurice, Henry 111n, 115, 335
Maurice, Ruth, née Spencer, see Spencer
Maxwell, General John 217
May, Dr Gould 62, 65
May, Lt Col. Henry 172, 173

Meighen, Arthur, Canadian PM 322
Mental Treatment Bill (1914) 181, 182, 183
Mid-Worcestershire constituency 8, 65, 71, 73, 119
Mid-Worcestershire Liberal Association 68
Midleton, William Brodrick, 9th Viscount 257, 260, 263, 265
Middleton, Thomas Hudson 115, 125, 126
Midland Liberal Federation 55
Mildmay, Francis Bingham 321
Military Service Act (January 1916) 209n
Military Service Act (May 1916) 217
Military Service Bill (May 1916) 219
Milk & Dairies Bill (1914) 161
Milner, Alfred, Viscount 250, 251, 253, 255, 274, 278
Miners' Strike (1920) 313, 314, 315
Minimum Wage (Amendment) 111
Minimum Wage Bill for Coal Miners (1912) 115
Ministry for Air Service 210, 259, 269
Ministry of Food 250, 259, 265, 274
Ministry of Labour 17
Ministry of Munitions 17
Ministry of National Service 241, 270
Ministry of Shipping 253, 254, 271, 276, 312
Mocatta, Florence de (Lady Brynmor Jones) 31
Moltino, Percy 90
Mond, Sir Alfred 21, 218
Mond, Emile 81
Money, Leo 86
Monro, General Sir Charles 261
Mons 169, 170
Montagu, Edwin 40, 189, 192, 235, 290
Montagu Square 36–37, 42, 43, 48, 52, 53, 59, 61–62, 65, 73, 77–78, 79, 107, 125, 129, 132, 143, 147, 210, 277, 290, 300, 324
Montagu-Douglas-Scott, John 239
Monte Carlo 142, 251
Montgomery, Charles 342
Montgomery, Robert 195
Moore-Brabazon, J.T.C., aviator 42
Morane, Léon, aviator 64
'Moratorium' Bill 165
Morgan, John 36, 66
Morgan, John Hartman, KC 98, 114
Morgan, George Hay 175
Morley, John, Viscount 165
Morning Post 314
Morocco 311

356 INDEX

Morris, William 136
Mosley, Oswald 20–21
Moss Side Hospital, Maghull, Liverpool 182
Motor Committee 242
motor manufacturing 197–198
Moulton, John Fletcher 75
Mullaly, J.M. 104
Munich Crisis 21
Murphy, Henry 98
Murphy, William Martin 223, 260
Murray, Alexander, *see* Elibank
Murray, Lt Col. Arthur 127, 146, 148, 162
Murray, Douglas 45n
Murray, John 342
My Journey Round the World, 16 July 1921–26 Feb. 1922 (Lord Northcliffe, 1923) 20, 342n
Myers, Arthur 154

Namur 169, 170
Nansen, Fridtjof 312, 333
Nash, Vaughan 74, 220
Nathan, Matthew 216
The Nation 236
National Club of Ireland 97
National Farmers Union (NFU) 142, 153
National Government 339
National Insurance 11, 13
National Insurance Act (1911) 110–111, 114, 116–117, 128, 137
National Insurance Bill (1911) 13, 86, 94, 103–104
National Insurance Committee 108–109, 112
National Liberal Club 103, 140, 153, 159
National Service Bill (1917) 242, 248
National Sporting Club 155
National Review 35
Naval Review 30–31
Neild, Herbert, KC 186
Nelson, Admiral Lord Horatio 122
The New Irish Constitution: An Exposition and Some Arguments, ed. J.H. Morgan (1912) 114
'New Liberal' 9
New Liberal Review 7, 60
New Zealand 323
Newfoundland 22, 127–128, 247
Newnham 175
Newport 175, 305
Newspaper Press Fund 250
Neville, Ralph, KC 109

Nice 143
Nicholas II, Tsar of Russia 242
Nicholson, Arthur Pole 77
Nicholson, Charles 36, 127, 164
Nicholson, G.C.N., 70
Nitti, Francesco Saverio Vincenzo de Paola 301
Nixon, Sir Christopher 107
Nord Deutscher Lloyd 167
Norfolk 297, 314
North Fermanagh 162
Northcliffe, Alfred Charles William Harmsworth, Viscount 1–3, 5–6, 15–16, 18–19, 20, 22–23, 32, 73, 75,76, 78, 80–81, 88, 103, 108, 112, 119, 122, 124, 127, 128, 130, 142, 144, 145, 152, 155, 156, 175, 183,184, 187, 191, 199, 200, 203, 206, 207, 210, 211, 212, 214, 222, 223, 225, 230, 231, 235, 236, 237, 238, 240, 247–248, 250, 254, 256, 258, 258, 266, 267,268, 269, 271, 275, 276, 278, 279, 283, 286, 291, 293, 294, 295, 298, 311, 321, 322, 323, 324, 332, 334, 336, 337, 338; discussions with Lloyd George about the budget of 1909 32–33; declines appointment as Minister of the Air 258; *At the War* (1916) 238; *My Journey Round the World, 16 July 1921–26 Feb. 1922* (1923) 20, 342n; world tour 323, 332, 334; 342
Northcliffe Sports Association 155
Northern Junction Railway Bill (1913) 153
Norway 244
Nugent, Sir Walter 145

O'Brien, William 106n; O'Brienites 106, 269
O'Connor, John ('Long' John O'Connor) 135
O'Connor, T.P. 88, 135, 143, 145, 188
O'Donnell, Patrick Joseph, Bishop of Raphoe 264, 266
O'Grady, James 306, 307, 309
Oakley, Albert 111n, 126, 144
Oakley, Edwin 111, 125, 128, 277
old age pensions 41, 53
Old Age Pensions Bill (1908) 52–53
Old Boy Volunteer Training Corps 176, 177, 188, 194, 233
Oldswinford 56
'One of the Absentees' 133
Ongar camp 194
Orpen, Sir William, painter 20, 311

INDEX

Our Miss Gibbs, 'Cryptos' and James T. Tanner, 1909 43
Oxford 287, 324

Pacific Islands 239
Palestine 247
Palmerston, Lord 52
Pankhurst, Sylvia 171, 172
Paravicini, Charles 327
Pares, Bernard 225, 226
Paris 38, 60, 61, 143, 171, 176, 212, 278, 279, 283, 289, 290, 291, 292, 294, 300, 301, 302, 303, 304, 338
Parkes, Elizabeth 65, 77
Parliament Act (1912) 114, 157
Parliament Bill (1911) 88, 91, 93–96, 111
Parliamentary Air Committee (1916) 233
Parliamentary Recruiting Committee (1915) 192, 200
Parliamentary War Savings Committee (1915) 198
Parsons, Alan 236
Parsons, Frank 285, 339
Partington, Lillie 65n
Partington, Oswald 65
Pasha, Gabriel Haddad 300, 304
Paulhan, Louis, aviator 42
Peace Celebration Day 296–297
Pearsall, Howard 102, 103
Pearse, Patrick Henry 217
Pease, J. Beaumont 141
Pease, Hubert Pike 89, 146
Peek, Frean & Co. Ltd. 181
Peile, Dr William 131
Pelham, T.H.W. 141, 152
Pemberton, Max 275
Pentland, John Sinclair, Lord 47
Pepler, George 110
Pepler, Harry 136
Percy, Lord Eustace 291
Perks, Sir Robert 75
Perley, Sir George 303
Pershing, General John Joseph 296
Peters, Arthur 192, 312
Phoney War 21
Pirrie, William James Pirrie, Lord 220, 276
Pius X, Pope 106n
Plait Hall 144
'Pleasure and Problem in South Africa', Cecil Harmsworth (1908) 11n, 9–10
Plunkett, Horace 4, 229, 230, 256, 257, 258, 259, 260, 263, 264, 265, 266, 269, 277, 302

Plural Voting Bill (1912) 113, 146
Plymouth 135
Poë, William Hutcheson 229, 230, 232
Poincaré, Henri 338
Poland 239, 298, 313, 330, 331
Pollard, George 175
Pollock, Ernest 301
Polk, Frank Lyon 303
Ponsonby, Arthur 90
Poole 310
post-war coalition 19, 289, 298, 304, 320, 323, 326, 334, 339, 340, 342
post-war reconstruction 264, 283
Price, Dr Henry Gilbert 61
Printers' Pension Corporation 294, 325
Primett, Walter 151
Primrose, Neil 16, 75, 180, 242, 245, 246, 247
Prisoners (Temporary Discharge for Ill Health) Act (1913), 'Cat and Mouse Act' 316n
Proportional Representation 103, 130, 151
Proportional Representation Committee 152
Proportional Representation Society 107
Prothero, Rowland 253, 277
Prudential 130
Pryse, Gerald Spencer, artist 134, 136

Queen's University Belfast 137
Quai d'Orsay 300

railway strike 95
Railways (No. 2) Bill (1912) 143
Ramsay-Steel-Maitland (known as Steel-Maitland), Albert 192
Ranelagh 75
Raphael, Herbert Henry 62
Rattigan, William 6–7
Raw Materials Committee 299
Rawlinson, Alfred, aviator 64
Reade, Charles 154, 156
Readers' Pensions Committee 120
Reading, Daisy 78
Redmond, John 7, 22, 39, 88, 96, 137, 145, 161, 162, 211, 216, 217, 224, 229, 230, 231, 242, 256, 260, 265, 266; Redmondites 260
Redmond, William 88, 242
Rees, John David 40
Reeve, Lt Col. William 174
Reform Club 16, 237

Reid, George 71, 219
Remembrance Day (1921) 325
Report Development Bill (1909) 39
Report on the Decrepit Horse Trade 148–149
Report of Inshore Fisheries Committee 152, 158
Representation of the People Bill (1917) 260
Retrenchment Committee (1915) 195, 196
Revenue Bill (1913) 146
Review of Reviews 7
Reynolds, Stephen 14, 130–131, 132, 135, 136, 138, 139, 149
Rhondda, David Alfred Thomas, Viscount 253
Ribblesdale, Lord, (Thomas Lister, 'The Ancestor') 38
Richardson, Albion 128, 134
Richmond, Arthur 151
Richmond, Amelia, née Goodall 151
Richter, Hans 135
Riddell, Lord 24
Ridgeway, Col. Sir West 62, 75
Ritz Hotel 299
Roberts, Field Marshal Lord 160
Roberts, George Henry 209n
Robertson, Sir Henry 105
Robertson, John Mackinnon 218
Robertson, General Sir William 231, 235, 258
Robinson, George 4
Rolls, Charles Stewart 23, 64
Rolls-Royce 326
Romania 193, 234, 290
Rome, Kathleen 45n
Roper, E.W. 71, 286n
Rose, Sir Charles Day 75
Rosebery, Archibald Primrose, 5th Earl 6, 32, 37, 44, 197, 220, 245, 272
Ross, Sir John 223
Rotherhithe 70
Rothermere, Harold Sidney Harmsworth, Viscount 1–3, 5, 18, 20–21, 29, 33, 34, 61, 69, 78, 79, 81, 82, 107, 116, 121, 122, 142, 143, 148, 151, 153, 156, 160, 161, 175, 187, 190, 195, 197, 203, 205, 211, 226, 230, 234, 236, 237, 240, 254, 255, 256, 259, 265, 266, 269, 289, 298, 309, 319; cr. Baron Rothermere 156
Rowlands, James 280
Rowntree, Arnold 24, 166
Rowntree, Benjamin Seebohm 66
Rowntree, Frederick 136

Royal Army Medical Corps (RAMC) 213
Royal Automobile Club (RAC) 108–109, 127, 129, 211
Royal Commission on the Rebellion in Ireland 223
Royal Commissions House 116
Royal Horticultural Society 130
Royal Navy 11, 114,115, 124–125, 211, 240, 245, 254, 278; Navy estimates 211
Royal Society for the Prevention of Cruelty to Animals (RSPCA) 148
Runciman, Hilda 220n
Runciman, James 210n
Runciman, Walter 12–15, 104, 105, 112, 115–116, 123, 125, 126, 127, 130, 136, 138, 140, 141, 145, 148, 152, 153, 160, 161, 162, 165, 167, 168, 169, 170, 171, 172, 175, 178, 179, 184, 185, 189, 190, 199, 207, 210, 214, 215, 220, 237, 242, 245; appointed President of the Board of Agriculture and Fisheries 13, 104; appointed President of the Board of Trade 15, 165
Russell, George William, 'Æ' 256
Russell, Lord J. 52
Russell, Thomas 97, 106, 162, 217
Russell, Herbrand, 11th Duke of Bedford 121
Russia 163–164, 196, 199, 226, 234, 242, 244, 258, 312, 313, 324, 329, 333; overthrow of Nicholas II 242; Bolshevik revolution 258; Soviet Russia 306, 311, 312, 312, 313, 333; Russian civil war 306

St Aldwyn, Michael, Earl 199
St Helena, Finglas, County Dublin 105, 106–107
St Ives 139
St Moritz 60
St Paul's Cathedral 134
Salford 276
Salisbury, Lord 3rd Marquess of Salisbury, PM 6; 4th Marquess of Salisbury 327; *see also* Gascoyne-Cecil
Samuel, Herbert 167, 192, 224, 235, 236
Sanderson, A.D. 159
Sandown Park 42
Sargent, John Singer 38, 135
Sastri, Valangiman Sankaranarayana Srinivasa 323
Savage Club 71
Savoy Hotel 103, 269, 295

INDEX 359

Scotland Yard 297
Scott, Alexander MacCallum 12
Scott, Sir Edward H. 334n
Scott, Emilie 334n
Scott, Kathleen, née Bruce, sculptor 77, 142, 203
Scott, Capt. Robert Falcon, RN 77, 142, 203
Scott, William 108
Scottish Small-Holders Bill (1911) 104
Scottish Office 203
Scottish Temperance Bill (1912) 143
Seely, Col. John 62, 134, 157
Second Boer War 6, 9, 69, 271
Second World War 22
Selby-Bigge, Sir Lewis 202
Select Committee on Estimates 119
Selss, Albert Maximilian 4
Serbia 15, 163, 230, 279, 290
Seydoux, Jacques 292
Shaw, Robert Gould 304n
Shaw, Capt. Richard 264, 266
Sheppard, G. 119, 120
Sherwell, Arthur 90
Shillington 13, 126, 173
shipping and shipbuilding 17, 181, 205, 248, 252, 254, 256, 257
Shops Recruiting Committee (1915) 180, 181, 182, 184
Shortt, Edward 243, 273, 275, 323, 326
Shrewsbury 142
Sidmouth 131, 132
Simon, Sir John 15, 90, 112, 137, 186, 188, 190, 199, 204, 207, 219–220, 256
Simpson, Canon James 134
Sims, Admiral William Sowden, US Navy 273
Sinclair, Sir Archibald 342
Sinn Féin 216, 217, 220, 222, 224, 252, 256–259, 269, 316, 317, 322, 323, 324, 325, 326, 336
Slavonia 279
Small Holding Colonies Bill (1916) 227
Smartt, Sir Thomas 323
Smillie, Robert 7
Smith, F. E., KC, Lord Birkenhead 16, 41, 78, 88–89, 93, 112, 185, 220, 227, 230, 323, 325, 327, 335, 339
Smith, Sir Hubert Llewellyn 293
Smith, W.H., probably clerk to Leighton Buzzard Board of Guardians 110, 129
Smuts, General Jan Christiaan 273, 274

Snowden-Smith, Richard Talbot, aviator 81
Sonnino, Sidney Costantino 283
South Africa 9–10, 323
South Bedfordshire constituency 12, 82, 93, 117, 118, 153, 155, 159, 285, 326
South Bedfordshire Liberal Association 119, 212
Southampton 124–125
Spain 311, 330
Spencer, Charles, Viscount Althorp 47
Spencer, Frederick 107, 109, 111n
Spencer, Gertrude Mary 29
Spencer, Ruth 111, 112, 119, 120
Spender, Alfred 191, 215
Spitzbergen 294
Spokes, A.H. 70
Spottiswoode, Hugh 63
Stafford 70, 125
Stamboliyski, Aleksandar 303
Stanier, Beville 112, 280
Stanley, Albert 47
Sthamer, Gustav 327
Starkie, Professor William 221
The Statist 191
Steed, Henry Wickham 300
Steel-Maitland (Ramsay-Steel-Maitland), Albert 192
Stern, Herbert 291n
Stewart, George 223
Stewart-Smith, Dudley 108
Stoke Heath 52
Stoke Newington 188
Stoke Works 43, 59
Stone, Sir Benjamin 42
Stourbridge 36, 40, 47, 48, 51, 52, 56, 58, 71
Stourport 54
Strachey, John St Loe 80
Strachey, Henrietta, née Simpson 80
Strauss, Edward 70
Stuart, Sir Campbell 278
Stuart-Wortley, Charles, QC 219
Suffragettes and suffragists 113, 123, 125, 129, 159
Suffolk 314
Summer Fields 205
Sumner, Kate 78
Sunderland 70
Sunningdale 117
Supreme Economic Council 292–293, 299, 300, 312
Supreme War Council 293
Sutherland, Sir William 293

360 INDEX

Sutton, George 142
Sutton Place 80, 103
Swift, Jonathan 67
Swift MacNeill, John, QC 67, 88, 106
Swindon 120
Switzerland 329, 331
Sylvan Debating Club 78, 108, 152, 214

Tanner, James T. 43n
Tariffs 11, 197, 198
Tariff Reform 197, 198
Tasmania 307
Tennant, Sir Edward 62
Thatcher and Son, Messrs G. 129
Thomas, James Henry 261, 298
Thomas-Stanford, Charles 280
Thomson, William 72
Thurston, Frederick 86
Tilley, John 298
The Times 2, 7, 32, 68, 73, 77, 81, 117, 145, 162, 189, 191, 200, 235, 236, 238, 275, 278, 300, 323
The Times Literary Supplement 10
Todd, George 240
Totland 338–339
Totteridge 76, 110, 119, 206, 207, 311; Poynters Hall, Totteridge, Hertfordshire 62, 127, 144, 160, 175, 179, 199, 200, 205, 206, 322, 337
Toynbee Hall 136
trade unionists 95
Tramecourt 280
The Treasury 15, 29n, 36, 40, 47, 69, 118, 119, 181, 189, 190, 191, 192, 194, 195, 196, 198, 199, 200, 202, 207, 215, 217, 224, 228, 231, 232, 236
Treasury Bench 91, 92, 188, 229, 293, 336
Treaties Bill (1920) 310
Treaty of Neuilly 302, 303
Trevelyan, Charles 62, 150
Trevor, John 334
Trieste 239
Trippel, Major Sir Henry 63
Trinity College Dublin (TCD) 4, 22, 62, 67, 78, 121, 129, 136, 137, 189, 221, 252, 260, 324, 325
Troup, Sir Edward 180, 199
Tsai-Fou, Tang 330
Turkey 193, 279, 337
Turnball, Lt Arthur, RAMC 213
Turner, Ernest 43
Turnor, Christopher 117, 129, 152

Twisleton-Wykeham-Fiennes, Eustace 89
Tyrell, Sir William 291, 342

Ulster 117, 157, 161, 162, 216, 217, 263, 310
Ulster Liberal Association 97
United States of America 198, 229, 239, 256, 259, 274, 285, 298, 303
Unwin, Raymond 117, 152
Upper Hagley 54
Ure, Alexander 41, 91, 144
United Irish League of Great Britain 7, 101
US (American) army 253, 277

Valera, Eamon de 257, 258, 323, 324, 336
Vansittart, Sir Robert 337
Verney, Sir Harry 167
Vertroost, Ophelie 174
Versailles Peace Treaty 295, 303
Veterinary Surgeon's Act Amendment Bill 129
Victory Loan 295
Vote of Censure 158, 159
Vote of Credit (1917) 242

Wales 101; Neath 101
Walsh, John 67
War Council 234–235
War Loan Committee (1915) 205
War Office 17, 107, 168, 169, 170, 174, 182, 188, 195, 204, 244, 267, 270, 276, 278, 297
War Savings Certificate 205
War Savings Committee (1915) 192
War Savings Movement 198, 214
Ward, Sir Edward 107
Ward, Lt Col. John 209
Ward, Sir Joseph 275
Ward, Robert 65
Wargrave 159
Warren, George 85, 126, 283
Warren, Thomas, President of Magdalen College 110
Warsaw 194
Washington DC 294, 334, 335
Waugh, Robert 264
Weaver, Laurence 152
Webb, Beatrice 23
Webb, Henry 119, 175
Webheath 51
Wedgwood, Sir Josiah 261
Weir, Andrew 276
Welfare of the Blind Committee 339

Welsh Disestablishment 101, 108, 112, 120, 121–122, 135, 140, 171, 182
Welsh Disestablishment Bill (1911) 101, 120, 121–122, 137, 140, 256; guillotine resolution 135
Westminster Abbey 82–83, 207, 316, 335, 338
Westminster Cathedral 266
Westminster Gazette 191, 215
Wheat Executive 271
Wheler, Granville 304
White, Arnold 63
White, James Dundas 61
White, William Augustus 160
Whitehouse, John 146, 213
Whitelegge, Maurice 193, 202
Whitley, John 260, 321, 334
Williams, Aneurin 102, 103
Wilhelm II, Kaiser 38, 301
Willingdon, Freeman Freeman-Thomas, Lord 75
Wilson, Field Marshall Sir Henry 336
Wilson, John 53
Wilson, Philip 100
Wilson, Leslie 278
Wilson, President Woodrow 239, 278, 286
Windle, Dr Bertram, President of University College, Cork 101
Windsor 125
Wise, Edward 311

Withers, Hartley 189, 190, 191, 192, 194, 195
Wollaston 55
Wollescote 55, 57, 59
Women's Employment Committee (1916) 210, 211, 227
women's franchise 140, 172; woman's suffrage debate 141
Women's Liberal Association 53, 112
Women's Occupations Committee (1915) 207, 209
Women's Royal Air Force 279
Women's War Work Committee (1916) 237
Worcestershire 8, 43, 147
Wood, Fred 112
Wood, Thomas Mackinnon 181, 185, 215, 228, 232
woods and forests 123
Woolley, Harry 131
Woolley, Robert 132
Woolley, Samuel 131
Woolley, Tom 131
Wrangel, General Pyotr Nikolayevich 313
Wribbenhall 54, 58
Wright, Frank 48
Wychbold 52

Yeats, W.B. 20
Young, Edward Hilton 77n
York 66–67
Ypres 281